Steck-Vaughn

GED

LANGUAGE ARTS, READING

PROGRAM CONSULTANTS

Liz Anderson, Director of Adult Education/Skills Training
Northwest Shoals Community College
Muscle Shoals, Alabama

Mary Ann Corley, Ph.D., Director
Lindy Boggs National Center for Community Literacy
Loyola University New Orleans
New Orleans, Louisiana

Nancy Dunlap, Adult Education Coordinator
Northside Independent School District
San Antonio, Texas

Roger M. Hansard, Director of Adult Education
CCARE Learning Center
Tazewell, Tennessee

Nancy Lawrence, M.A.
Education and Curriculum Consultant
Butler, Pennsylvania

Pat L. Taylor, STARS Consultant for GEDTS
Adult Education/GED Programs
Mesa, Arizona

STECK-VAUGHN
ELEMENTARY · SECONDARY · ADULT · LIBRARY

A Harcourt Company

www.steck-vaughn.com

Acknowledgments

Executive Editor: Ellen Northcutt

Supervising Editor: Julie Higgins

Associate Editor: Sarah Combs

Associate Director of Design: Cynthia Ellis

Designers: Rusty Kaim
Katie Nott

Media Researcher: Sarah Fraser

Editorial Development: Learning Unlimited, Oak Park, Illinois

Production Development: LaurelTech

Photography: Cover: (old books) ©Strauss/Curtis/The Stock Market; (open books) ©Telegraph Colour Library/FPG International; (masks) ©Rick Gayle/The Stock Market; p.i ©Telegraph Colour Library/FPG International; p.32 ©Bob Daryll/Retna Limited, USA; p.98 ©Renato Rotolo/CORBIS; p.168 ©Archive Photos; p.208 ©Bettmann/CORBIS.

ISBN 0-7398-2836-3

Contents

What Are the GED Tests?

You have taken a big step in your life by deciding to take the GED Tests. By the time that you have opened this book, you have made a second important decision: to put in the time and effort to prepare for the tests. You may feel nervous about what is ahead, which is only natural. Relax and read the following pages to find out more about the GED Tests in general and the Language Arts, Reading Test in particular.

The GED Tests are the five tests of General Educational Development. The GED Testing Service of the American Council on Education makes them available to adults who did not graduate from high school. When you pass the GED Tests, you will receive a certificate that is regarded as equivalent to a high school diploma. Employers in private industry and government, as well as admissions officers in colleges and universities, accept the GED certificate as they would a high school diploma.

The GED Tests cover the same subjects that people study in high school. The five subject areas include: Language Arts, Writing and Language Arts, Reading (which, together, are equivalent to high school English), Social Studies, Science, and Mathematics. You will not be required to know all the information that is usually taught in high school. However, across the five tests you will be tested on your ability to read and process information, solve problems, and communicate effectively. Some of the states in the U.S. also require a test on the U.S. Constitution or on state government. Check with your local adult education center to see if your state requires such a test.

Each year more than 800,000 people take the GED Tests. Of those completing the test battery, 70 percent earn their GED certificates. The *Steck-Vaughn GED Series* will help you pass the GED Tests by providing instruction and practice in the skill areas needed to pass, practice with test items like those found on the GED Test, test-taking tips, timed-test practice, and evaluation charts to help track your progress.

There are five separate GED Tests. The chart on page 2 gives you information on the content, number of items, and time limit for each test. Because states have different requirements for how many tests you take in a day or testing period, you need to check with your local adult education center for the requirements in your state, province, or territory.

The Tests of General Educational Development

Test	Content Areas	Items	Time Limit
Language Arts, Writing, Part I	Organization 15% Sentence Structure 30% Usage 30% Mechanics 25%	50 questions	75 minutes
Language Arts, Writing, Part II	Essay		45 minutes
Social Studies	U.S. History 25% World History 15% Civics and Government 25% Geography 15% Economics 20%	50 questions	70 minutes
Science	Life Science 45% Earth and Space Science 20% Physical Science 35%	50 questions	80 minutes
Language Arts, Reading	Nonfiction Texts 25% Literary Texts 75% • Prose Fiction • Poetry • Drama	40 questions	65 minutes
Mathematics	Number Operations and Number Sense 25% Measurement and Geometry 25% Data Analysis, Statistics, and Probability 25% Algebra 25%	Part I: 25 questions with a calculator Part II: 25 questions	90 minutes

In addition to these content areas, you will be asked to answer items based on work- and consumer-related texts across all five tests. These do not require any specialized knowledge, but will ask you to draw upon your own observations and life experiences.

The Language Arts, Reading, Social Studies, and Science Tests will ask you to answer questions by interpreting reading passages, diagrams, charts and graphs, maps, cartoons, and practical and historical documents.

The Language Arts, Writing Test will ask you to detect and correct common errors in edited American English as well as decide on the most effective organization of text. The Essay portion of the Writing Test will ask you to write an essay offering your opinion or an explanation on a single topic of general knowledge.

The Mathematics Test will ask you to solve a variety of word problems, many with graphics, using basic computation, analytical, and reasoning skills.

GED Scores

After you complete each GED Test, you will receive a score for that test. Once you have completed all five GED Tests, you will receive a total score. The total score is an average of all the other scores. The highest score possible on a single test is 800. The scores needed to pass the GED vary depending on where you live. Contact your local adult education center for the minimum passing scores for your state, province, or territory.

Where Can You Go to Take the GED Tests?

The GED Tests are offered year-round throughout the United States and its possessions, on U.S. military bases worldwide, and in Canada. To find out when and where tests are held near you, contact the GED Hot Line at 1-800-62-MY-GED (1-800-626-9433) or one of these institutions in your area:

- An adult education center
- A continuing education center
- A local community college
- A public library
- A private business school or technical school
- The public board of education

In addition, the GED Hot Line and the institutions can give you information regarding necessary identification, testing fees, writing implements, and on the scientific calculator to be used on the GED Mathematics Test. Also, check on the testing schedule at each institution; some testing centers are open several days a week, and others are open only on weekends.

Other GED Resources

- www.acenet.edu This is the official site for the GED Testing Service. Just follow the GED links throughout the site for information on the test.

- www.steckvaughn.com Follow the Adult Learners link to learn more about available GED preparation materials and www.gedpractice.com. This site also provides other resources for adult learners.

- www.nifl.gov/nifl/ The National Institute for Literacy's site provides information on instruction, federal policies, and national initiatives that affect adult education.

- www.doleta.gov U.S. Department of Labor's Employment and Training Administration site offers information on adult training programs.

Why Should You Take the GED Tests?

A GED certificate is widely recognized as the equivalent of a high school diploma and can help you in the following ways:

Employment

People with GED certificates have proven their determination to succeed by following through with their education. They generally have less difficulty changing jobs or moving up in their present companies. In many cases, employers will not hire someone who does not have a high school diploma or the equivalent.

Education

Many technical schools, vocational schools, or other training programs may require a high school diploma or the equivalent in order to enroll in their programs. However, to enter a college or university, you must have a high school diploma or the equivalent.

Personal Development

The most important thing is how you feel about yourself. You now have the unique opportunity to accomplish an important goal. With some effort, you can attain a GED certificate that will help you in the future and make you feel proud of yourself now.

How to Prepare for the GED Tests

Classes for GED preparation are available to anyone who wants to prepare to take the GED Tests. Most GED preparation programs offer individualized instruction and tutors who can help you identify areas in which you may need help. Many adult education centers offer free day or night classes. The classes are usually informal and allow you to work at your own pace and with other adults who also are studying for the GED Tests.

If you prefer to study by yourself, the *Steck-Vaughn GED Series* has been developed to guide your study through skill instruction and practice exercises. *Steck-Vaughn GED Exercise* books and www.gedpractice.com are also available to provide you with additional practice for each test. In addition to working on specific skills, you will be able to take practice GED Tests (like those in this book) in order to check your progress. For information about classes available near you, contact one of the resources in the list on page 3.

What You Need to Know to Pass the Language Arts, Reading Test

The GED Language Arts, Reading Test focuses on applying reading and critical thinking skills to different types of texts. In other words, you will be tested on how well you understand and analyze what you read. You will not be tested on your knowledge of literature. You will have 65 minutes to read seven selections from the areas of nonfiction, prose fiction, poetry, and drama and answer 40 questions based on them. Each selection will be preceded by a "purpose question" which helps to direct your reading of the text.

Nonfiction Texts

The test includes two nonfiction selections of 200–400 words. These selections are drawn from the following areas: informational or persuasive texts (biography and autobiography, newspaper and magazine articles, editorials, speeches, reports, etc.), reviews of visual representation, and business documents (memos, letters, training handbooks, etc.).

Literary Text

Prose Fiction

The test includes three prose fiction selections of 200–400 words. These selections are generally excerpts from novels or short stories. There will be one selection written before 1920, one selection written between 1920 and 1960, and one selection written after 1960.

Poetry

There will be one selection of 8 to 25 lines on the test. This may be a complete poem or an excerpt from a longer poem.

Drama

There will be one selection of 200–400 words.

Thinking Skills

Questions on the GED Language Arts, Reading Test are based on four different types of thinking skills.

Comprehension

Comprehension questions require a basic understanding of the selection or a portion of a selection. They measure the ability to recognize a restatement, paraphrasing, or summary or to identify what is implied in the text.

Application

Application questions require the ability to use information from a text in a new context.

Analysis

Analysis questions require the ability to break down information in order to draw a conclusion, make an inference, identify elements of style and structure, identify cause-and-effect relationships, and recognize unstated assumptions.

Synthesis

Synthesis questions require the ability to put elements together to form a whole. They require an analysis of the overall structure of a text (for example: posing a problem and giving the solution or comparing and contrasting), interpreting the overall tone, point of view, or purpose of a text, or integrate provided information with the information in the text.

Sample Passages and Items

The following is a sample fiction reading passage and test items. The questions are similar to those found on the actual GED Test and illustrate the four types of thinking skills evaluated on the test. This sample passage is shorter than those on the test, which are about 200–400 words in length. The "purpose question" **(WHAT IS THIS BOY THINKING ABOUT?)** above the passage helps to focus your reading. The passages in this book and on the GED Language Arts Reading Test are preceded by a purpose question.

Following each question below is an explanation of the thinking skill and a discussion of the correct answer. To help you develop your reading and thinking skills, the answer for each item in this book has an explanation of why the correct answer is right and why the incorrect choices are wrong. By studying these explanations, you will learn strategies for understanding and thinking about reading skills.

Questions 1 through 4 refer to the following excerpt from a short story.

WHAT IS THIS BOY THINKING ABOUT?

All this time, of course (while he lay in bed), he had kept his eyes closed, listening to the nearer progress of the postman, the muffled footsteps thumping and slipping on
(5) the snow-sheathed cobbles; and all the other sounds—the double knocks, a frosty far-off voice or two, a bell ringing thinly and softly as if under a sheet of ice—had the same slightly abstracted quality, as if
(10) removed by one degree from actuality— as if everything in the world had been insulated by snow. But when at last, pleased, he opened his eyes, and turned them towards the window, to see himself
(15) this long-desired and now so clearly imagined miracle—what he saw instead was brilliant sunlight on a roof; and when, astonished, he jumped out of bed and stared down into the street, expecting to
(20) see the cobbles obliterated by the snow, he saw nothing but the bare, bright cobbles themselves.

Conrad Aiken, "Silent Snow, Secret Snow," *The Collected Short Stories of Conrad Aiken.*

1. Which one of the following phrases best describes what this boy is doing through most of the excerpt?

   (1) lying in bed awake
   (2) looking out the window
   (3) sleeping soundly
   (4) watching the snow fall
   (5) having a nightmare

Answer: **(1) lying in bed awake**

Explanation: This is an example of a comprehension question. It summarizes what you read about the boy. The first sentence of the excerpt states "while he lay in bed," and in the last sentence it refers to him jumping out of bed.

2. Based on the information in this excerpt, which one of the following phrases best describes what this boy would enjoy most?

   (1) staying in bed until noon
   (2) playing in the snow
   (3) having a vacation at the beach
   (4) being a postman
   (5) seeing the streets clean

Answer: **(2) playing in the snow**

Explanation: This is an example of an application item. From the selection, you understand that the boy is wishing for snow. You can apply this understanding to each of the possible answer choices. Even though it is not mentioned in the excerpt, option (2) is the best answer because it relates to his obvious interest in snow. You need to read and think carefully about all of the possible answers. Some answer choices, such as options (4) and (5), do refer to something mentioned in the excerpt and could be attractive choices if you fail to read the excerpt and question carefully.

3. Which of the following groups of words does the author use to help you picture what the boy is hoping for?

   (1) "kept his eyes closed" (line 2) and "jumped out of bed" (line 18)
   (2) "muffled footsteps" (line 4) and "bell ringing thinly and softly" (lines 7 and 8)
   (3) "long-desired and now so clearly imagined miracle" (lines 15–16)
   (4) "brilliant sunlight on a roof" (line 17)
   (5) "cobbles obliterated by the snow" (line 20)

Answer: **(5) "cobbles obliterated by the snow" (line 20)**

Explanation: This is an analysis question because it requires you to analyze how the writer's choice of words helps to portray the key inference of this piece—that the boy wants it to snow. He imagines that every sound is proof that it is snowing, and when he jumped up, he was expecting to see the "cobbles obliterated by the snow," option (5). The other answer choices are in the selection, but they do not help you to picture what the boy is hoping for.

4. Which one of the following words best describes the overall mood of this piece?

   (1) anticipation
   (2) loneliness
   (3) anxiety
   (4) giddiness
   (5) hesitation

Answer: **(1) anticipation**

Explanation: This is an example of a synthesis item because it requires that you put elements together to form a general impression about the mood of the work. Option (1) is correct because various elements portray an overall mood of anticipation, as the boy is looking forward to seeing that it has snowed.

The following is a sample of a nonfiction reading passage and test items. The questions are similar to those found on the actual GED Test and illustrate the four types of thinking skills evaluated on the test. Some of the passages on the test will be about the same length as this sample passage. Notice that nonfiction passages also have purpose questions to help you to focus your reading.

Following each question is an explanation of the thinking skill and a discussion of the correct answer.

Questions 1 through 4 refer to the following excerpt from an employee handbook.

WHAT TYPES OF INTERNET MESSAGES DOES THE COMPANY REGULATE?

Our company encourages the use of the Internet because the Internet makes communications more efficient and effective, and because it is a valuable
(5) source of information about our customers and business partners. However, the Internet must be used responsibly, and therefore, the following guidelines apply to all Internet use that:

(10) • takes place on company property;

• takes place using company equipment, including home computers connected to the company network;

(15) • identifies the company.

Appropriate Use
The Internet is intended for company business use only. Although use of the Internet for personal business may be
(20) understandable and acceptable at times, this is a privilege that the company reserves the right to control, similar to personal phone calls.
Acceptable business use of the Internet
(25) includes but is not limited to:

• research of other companies and their products;

• access to our company's information, products, and services;

(30) • communication with business partners and customers.

Any electronic communications sent by means of the Internet must responsibly represent our company just like any other
(35) official company communication.

Inappropriate Use
The Internet may not be used for any illegal or unethical purpose. It also may not be used for transmitting, retrieving,
(40) or storing any communications of an offensive or discriminatory nature, or in any other way that violates company policy.

• Employees may not use the company's resources to read or
(45) "hack" into other systems or to violate any computer security measures.

• Employees may not send communications over the Internet that attempt to conceal or misrepresent
(50) the sender's identity.

Privacy
Our company routinely monitors Internet usage and periodically reviews individual employee use. Therefore,
(55) employees should not assume that electronic communications are private and confidential, and should transmit personal information in other ways. Electronic communications should not
(60) contain sensitive information or company-protected information.

1. What is meant by the statement that "Any electronic communications sent by means of the Internet must responsibly represent our company" (lines 32–34)?

   Internet communications must

   (1) receive the approval of a supervisor
   (2) include the company's name and logo
   (3) avoid referring to competitors' products
   (4) describe the company's products and services
   (5) avoid portraying the company in a negative way

Answer: (5) avoid portraying the company in a negative way

Explanation: This is an example of a comprehension question. You must choose the best restatement of information in the excerpt. The words "responsibly represent" mean to represent in a way that is loyal to the company, or in a way that is not negative.

2. On the basis of the excerpt, which of the following Internet uses would be <u>least likely</u> to violate the company's policies?

   (1) using a home computer to publicly criticize a company practice
   (2) using a home computer to send a message to a business client
   (3) using a company computer to open confidential employee records
   (4) using a company computer to send an anonymous letter of complaint
   (5) using a company computer to transmit a classified company business plan

Answer: (2) using a home computer to send a message to a business client

Explanation: This is an example of an application item. You must first understand the company's Internet policies. Then you can apply this knowledge to decide which use would be least likely to violate these policies. Option (2) is the best answer because it does not break any of the company's rules.

3. Based on the excerpt, what is the company's <u>most likely</u> relationship to the Internet?

   (1) It conducts the vast majority of its business over the Internet.
   (2) It has only recently begun using the Internet as a business tool.
   (3) It has suffered financial difficulties as a result of its Internet usage.
   (4) It relies on the Internet as one of several communication methods.
   (5) It employs only a small number of workers who use the Internet regularly.

Answer: (4) It relies on the Internet as one of several communication methods.

Explanation: This is an example of an analysis question. You must determine the answer by using information that is implied or suggested in the excerpt. Option (4) is correct both because the excerpt mentions other types of company communication and because there is no direct evidence to support the other options.

4. In an earlier section of the handbook, employees are told to change their voice mail passwords every 120 days. Based on this information and on the information in this excerpt, what is most likely the <u>main</u> reason that communication systems (such as the Internet and voice mail) are discussed in the handbook?

   (1) to improve customer service
   (2) to increase the number of sales
   (3) to explain workers' right to privacy
   (4) to teach workers about new technology
   (5) to ensure the security of company data

Answer: (5) to ensure the security of company data

Explanation: This is an example of a synthesis item. It gives you extra information and requires you to connect it to information within the excerpt. Option (5) is correct because voice mail passwords as well as many of the company's Internet policies relate to the security of data.

Test-Taking Skills

The GED Language Arts, Reading Test will test your ability to apply reading and critical thinking skills to text. This book will help you prepare for this test. In addition, there are some specific ways that you can improve your performance on the test.

Answering the Test Items

- Never skim the directions. Read them carefully so that you know exactly what to do. If you are unsure, ask the test-giver if the directions can be explained.

- Read each question carefully to make sure that you know what it is asking.

- Read all of the answer options carefully, even if you think you know the right answer. Some of the answers may not seem wrong at first glance, but only one answer will be the correct one.

- Before you answer a question, be sure that there is evidence in the passage to support your choice. Don't rely on what you know outside the context of the passage.

- Answer all the items. If you cannot find the correct answer, reduce the number of possible answers by eliminating all the answers you know are wrong. Then go back to the passage to figure out the correct answer. If you still cannot decide, make your best guess.

- Fill in your answer sheet carefully. To record your answers, mark one numbered space on the answer sheet beside the number that corresponds to the item. Mark only one answer space for each item; multiple answers will be scored as incorrect.

- Remember that the GED is a timed test. When the test begins, write down the time you have to finish. Then keep an eye on the time. Do not take a long time on any one item. Answer each item as best you can and go on. If you are spending a lot of time on one item, skip it, making a very light mark next to the item number on the sheet. If you finish before time is up, go back to the items you skipped or were unsure of and give them more thought. (Be sure to erase any extraneous marks you have made.)

- Don't change an answer unless you are certain your answer was wrong. Usually the first answer you choose is the correct one.

- If you feel that you are getting nervous, stop working for a moment. Take a few deep breaths and relax. Then begin working again.

Tips for Passing the Language Arts, Reading Test

- **Passage** Always read the "purpose question" above each selection. It will help to focus your reading. Read the selection all the way through before you answer the questions.

- **Main Idea** If you do not find a directly stated main idea, it is probably implied by the details and examples. To find the details that add up to the main idea, ask yourself the following questions: *Who is doing something? What is happening? Why is it being done?*

- **Supporting Details** Each time that an author restates a main idea, he or she adds another detail or example to clarify the central idea of the passage. The details help to bring the idea to life, much as adding color to a black and white cartoon makes it more interesting.

- **Drawing Conclusions** When you draw a conclusion you go beyond what is stated in the text and think about what is implied and what could be a possible outcome.

- **Style and Structure** A writer's choice of words and development of the writing depends on the subject being presented and his or her attitude toward the subject. As you read, ask yourself why the writer chose to use certain words and why the ideas were organized into a certain pattern (i.e. cause and effect, comparison/contrast, etc.).

- **Mood** When you try to determine the mood of a passage, try to imagine yourself in the scene or situation. How would you feel? Imagine yourself as several of the characters. Would you feel the same as the characters feel? Which character's feelings do you understand the best?

- **Poems** When you read a poem, pay attention to the details as you would with a passage from a novel or short story. Pay particular attention to the images that the poet creates and the use of rhyme, rhythm, and figurative language to create an overall impression of the poet's feelings toward the subject.

- **Plays** When you read a passage from a play, pay attention to the stage directions, even if the questions do not ask about them. The stage directions can help you to picture the action in the scene and the tone of voice and attitude of the characters.

Study Skills

Study Regularly

- If you can, set aside an hour to study every day. If you do not have time every day, set up a schedule of the days you can study. Be sure to pick times when you will be the most relaxed and least likely to be bothered by outside distractions.

- Let others know your study time. Ask them to leave you alone for that period. It helps if you explain to others why this is important.

- You should be relaxed when you study, so find an area that is comfortable for you. If you cannot study at home, go to the library. Most public libraries have areas for reading and studying. If there is a college or university near you, find out if you can use its library. All libraries have dictionaries, encyclopedias, and other resources you can use if you need more information while you are studying.

Organize Your Study Materials

- Be sure to have pens, sharp pencils, and paper for any notes you might want to take.

- Keep all of your books together. If you are taking an adult education class, you probably will be able to borrow some books or other study material.

- Make a notebook or folder for each subject you are studying. Folders with pockets are useful for storing loose papers.

- Keep all of your materials in one place so you do not waste time looking for them each time you study.

Read Regularly

- Read the newspaper, read magazines, read books. Read whatever appeals to you—but read! Regular, daily reading is the best way to improve your reading skills.

- Use the library to find material you like to read. Check the magazine section for publications of interest to you. Most libraries subscribe to hundreds of magazines ranging in interest from news to cars to music to sewing to sports. If you are not familiar with the library, ask a librarian for help. Get a library card so that you can check out material to use at home.

Take Notes

- Take notes on things that interest you or things that you think might be useful.

- When you take notes, do not copy the words directly from the book. Restate the information in your own words.

- Take notes any way you want. You do not have to write in full sentences as long as you can understand your notes later.

- Use outlines, charts, or diagrams to help you organize information and make it easier to learn.

- You may want to take notes in a question-and-answer form, such as: *What is the main idea? The main idea is . . .*

Improve Your Vocabulary

- As you read, do not skip a word you do not know. Instead, try to figure out what the word means. First, omit it from the sentence. Read the sentence without the word and try to put another word in its place. Is the meaning of the sentence the same?

- Make a list of unfamiliar words, look them up in the dictionary, and write down the meanings.

- Since a word may have several meanings, it is best to look up the word while you have the passage with you. Then you can try out the different meanings in the context.

- When you read the definition of a word, restate it in your own words. Use the word in a sentence or two.

- Use the Glossary at the end of this book to review the meanings of the key terms. All of the words you see in **boldface** type are defined in the Glossary. In addition, definitions of other important words are included. Use this list to review important vocabulary for the content areas you are studying.

Make a List of Subject Areas that Give You Trouble

As you go through this book, make a note whenever you do not understand something. Then ask your instructor or another person for help. Later, go back and review the topic.

Taking the Test

Before the Test

- If you have never been to the test center, go there the day before you take the test. If you drive, find out where to park. This way you won't lose time or get lost the day of the test.

- Prepare the things you need for the test: your admission ticket (if necessary), acceptable identification, some sharpened No. 2 pencils with erasers, a watch, glasses, a jacket or sweater (in case the room is cold), and a snack to eat during breaks.

- You will do your best work if you are rested and alert. So do not cram before the test. In fact, if you prepared for the test, cramming should be unnecessary. Instead, eat a meal and get a good night's sleep. If the test is early in the morning, set the alarm.

The Day of the Test

- Eat a good breakfast. Wear comfortable clothing. Make sure that you have all of the materials you need.

- Try to arrive at the test center about twenty minutes early. This allows time if, for example, there is a last-minute change of room.

- If you are going to be at the test center all day, you might pack a lunch. If you have to find a restaurant or if you wait a long time to be served, you may be late for the rest of the test.

Using this Book

- Start with the Pretest. It is identical to the real test in format and length. It will give you an idea of what the GED Language Arts, Reading Test is like. Then use the Pretest Performance Analysis Chart at the end of the test to figure out your areas of strength and the areas you need to review. The chart will refer you to units and page numbers to study. You also can use the Study Planner on page 31 to plan your work after you take the Pretest and again, after the Posttest.

- As you study, use the Cumulative Review and the Performance Analysis chart at the end of each unit to find out if you need to review any lessons before continuing.

- After you complete your review, use the Posttest to decide if you are ready for the real GED test. The Performance Analysis Chart will tell you if you need additional review. Then use the Simulated Test and its Performance Analysis Chart as a final check of your test-readiness.

LANGUAGE ARTS, READING
Directions

The Language Arts, Reading Pretest consists of excerpts from fiction, nonfiction, poetry, and drama. Each excerpt is followed by multiple-choice questions about the reading material.

Read each excerpt first and then answer the questions that follow. Refer to the reading material as often as necessary in answering the questions.

Each excerpt is preceded by a "purpose question." The purpose question gives a reason for reading the material. Use these purpose questions to help focus your reading. You are not required to answer these purpose questions. They are given only to help you concentrate on the ideas presented in the reading material.

You should spend no more than 65 minutes answering the 40 questions on this pretest. Work carefully, but do not spend too much time on any one question. Do not skip any items. Make a reasonable guess when you are not sure of an answer. You will not be penalized for incorrect answers.

When time is up, mark the last item you finished. This will tell you whether you can finish the real GED Test in the time allowed. Then complete the test.

Record your answers to the questions on a copy of the answer sheet on page 348. Be sure that all required information is properly recorded on the answer sheet.

To record your answers, mark the numbered space on the answer sheet that corresponds to the answer you choose for each question on the test.

Example:

It was Susan's dream machine. The metallic blue paint gleamed, and the sporty wheels were highly polished. Under the hood, the engine was no less carefully cleaned. Inside, flashy lights illuminated the instruments on the dashboard, and the seats were covered by rich leather upholstery.

What does "It" most likely refer to in this excerpt?

(1) an airplane
(2) a stereo system
(3) an automobile
(4) a boat
(5) a motorcycle

The correct answer is "an automobile"; therefore, answer space 3 would be marked on the answer sheet.

Do not rest the point of your pencil on the answer sheet while you are considering your answer. Make no stray or unnecessary marks. If you change an answer, erase your first mark completely. Mark only one answer space for each question; multiple answers will be scored as incorrect. Do not fold or crease your answer sheet.

When you finish the test, use the Performance Analysis Chart on page 30 to determine whether you are ready to take the real GED Test, and, if not, which skill areas need additional review.

Directions: Choose the <u>one best answer</u> to each question.

<u>Questions 1 through 5</u> refer to the following excerpt from a novel.

WHAT DO YOU THINK OF WHEN YOU HEAR A FAVORITE OLD SONG?

"On second thought," said Helen, "I want to sing one for Francis for buying me that flower. Does your friend know 'He's Me Pal,' or 'My Man'?"

(5) "You hear that, Joe?"

"I hear," said Joe the piano man, and he played a few bars of the chorus of "He's Me Pal," as Helen smiled and stood and walked to the stage with an aplomb and

(10) grace befitting her reentry into the world of music, the world she should never have left, oh why did you leave it, Helen? She climbed the three steps to the platform, drawn upward by familiar chords that now

(15) seemed to her to have always evoked joy, chords not from this one song but from an era of songs, thirty, forty years of song that celebrated the splendors of love, and loyalty, and friendship, and family, and

(20) country, and the natural world. Frivolous Sal was a wild sort of devil, but wasn't she dead on the level too? Mary was a great pal, heaven-sent on Christmas morning, and love lingers on for her. The new-mown

(25) hay, the silvery moon, the home fires burning, these were sanctuaries of Helen's spirit, songs whose like she had sung from her earliest days, songs that endured for her as long as the classics she had

(30) committed to memory . . . in her youth, for they spoke to her, not abstractly of the aesthetic peaks of the art she had once hoped to master, but directly, simply, about the everyday currency of the heart and

(35) soul. The pale moon will shine on the twining of our hearts. My heart is stolen, lover dear, so please don't let us part. Oh love, sweet love, oh burning love—the songs told her—you are mine, I am yours,

(40) forever and a day.

You spoiled the girl I used to be, my hope has gone away. Send me away with a smile, but remember: you're turning off the sunshine of my life.

(45) Love.

A flood tide of pity rose in Helen's breast. Francis, oh sad man, was her last great love, but he wasn't her only one. Helen has had a lifetime of sadnesses with

(50) her lovers. Her first true love kept her in his fierce embrace for years, but then he loosened that embrace and let her slide down and down until the hope within her died. Hopeless Helen, that's who she

(55) was when she met Francis. And as she stepped up to the microphone on the stage of The Gilded Cage, hearing the piano behind her, Helen was a living explosion of unbearable memory and indomitable joy.

William Kennedy, *Ironweed*.

1. What does the author most likely mean by "the everyday currency of the heart and soul" (lines 34–35)?

    (1) the payment Helen earns for singing
    (2) the feelings that pass between people
    (3) the cost of Helen's musical education
    (4) the level of Helen's standard of living
    (5) the money Francis spent on flowers

2. Based on the information in the excerpt, which of the following statements best expresses the narrator's opinion of Helen and her music?

    (1) Helen should not have abandoned music.
    (2) Helen's life is better than the lives she sings about.
    (3) Helen may be the best singer of her time.
    (4) Helen should sing a wider variety of songs.
    (5) Helen is too serious about her singing.

3. Why does the author use the phrase "unbearable memory and indomitable joy" (line 59)?

    to emphasize that Helen

    (1) has not sung before
    (2) feels emotions deeply
    (3) is fooling herself
    (4) is overly romantic
    (5) is happy because of Francis

4. Based on the information in the excerpt, what would Helen most likely do if a handsome stranger tried to win her away from Francis?

    (1) consult her friends for advice
    (2) ask Francis for permission to leave
    (3) reluctantly go with the stranger
    (4) attempt to make Francis jealous
    (5) happily stay with Francis

5. Which of the following words best describes the overall mood of this piece?

    (1) melancholy
    (2) cautious
    (3) joyous
    (4) nostalgic
    (5) pleasant

WHY DOES LEE CHONG MAKE A DEAL WITH MACK?

Lee Chong stiffened ever so slightly when Mack came in and his eyes glanced quickly about the store to make sure that Eddie or Hazel or Hughes or Jones had
(5) not come in too and drifted away among the groceries.

Mack laid out his cards with a winning honesty. "Lee," he said, "I and Eddie and the rest heard you own the Abbeville
(10) place."

Lee Chong nodded and waited.

"I and my friends thought we'd ast you if we could move in there. We'll keep up the property," he added quickly. "Wouldn't let
(15) anybody break in or hurt anything. Kids might knock out the windows, you know—" Mack suggested. "Place might burn down if somebody don't keep an eye on it."

Lee tilted his head back and looked into
(20) Mack's eyes through the half-glasses and Lee's tapping finger slowed its tempo as he thought deeply. In Mack's eyes there was good will and good fellowship and a desire to make everyone happy. Why then
(25) did Lee Chong feel slightly surrounded? Why did his mind pick its way as delicately as a cat through cactus? It had been sweetly done, almost in a spirit of philanthropy. Lee's mind leaped ahead
(30) at the possibilities—no, they were probabilities, and his finger tapping slowed still further. He saw himself refusing Mack's request and he saw the broken glass from the windows. Then Mack would offer a
(35) second time to watch over and preserve Lee's property—and at the second refusal, Lee could smell the smoke, could see the little flames creeping up the walls. Mack and his friends would try to help to put it
(40) out. Lee's finger came to a gentle rest on the change mat. He was beaten. He knew that. There was left to him only the possibility of saving face and Mack was likely to be very generous about that. Lee
(45) said, "You like pay lent my place? You like live there same hotel?"

Mack smiled broadly and he was generous. "Say—" he cried. "That's an idear. Sure. How much?"
(50) Lee considered. He knew it didn't matter what he charged. He wasn't going to get it anyway. He might just as well make it a really sturdy face-saving sum. "Fi' dolla' week," said Lee.
(55) Mack played it through to the end. "I'll have to talk to the boys about it," he said dubiously. "Couldn't you make that four dollars a week?"

"Fi' dolla'," said Lee firmly.
(60) "Well, I'll see what the boys say," said Mack.

And that was the way it was. Everyone was happy about it. And if it be thought that Lee Chong suffered a total loss, at
(65) least his mind did not work that way. The windows were not broken. Fire did not break out, and while no rent was ever paid, if the tenants ever had any money, and quite often they did have, it never occurred
(70) to them to spend it any place except at Lee Chong's grocery.

John Steinbeck, *Cannery Row.*

6. What is Mack's most likely motivation in offering to "keep up the property" (lines 13–14) and "keep an eye on it" (line 18)?

   (1) He is trying to strike up a friendship.
   *(2) He is trying to improve the community.
   (3) He is asking Lee Chong for a job.
   (4) He is threatening Lee Chong.
   (5) He is trying to cheat his friends.

7. What would Mack and his friends most likely do if someone were to set fire to the Abbeville place?

   (1) move out
   (2) add fuel to the flames
   x(3) try to help put out the fire
   (4) run away
   (5) steal the groceries before they burn

8. Which of the following words best describes the deal between Lee Chong and Mack?

   (1) useful
   (2) immoral
   (3) dangerous
   x(4) pathetic
   (5) kind

9. If Lee Chong owned a car dealership, how would he most likely run his business?

   He would offer

   (1) discounted prices to his friends and family
   x(2) fair prices to ensure many repeat customers
   (3) low prices to keep his inventory small
   (4) inflated prices by using pressure tactics
   (5) higher prices to customers who are difficult

10. Which of the following ideas are most clearly contrasted in this excerpt?

    (1) wealth and poverty
    (2) innovation and tradition
    x(3) giving and receiving
    (4) power and practicality
    (5) anger and sympathy

11. Which of the following best states the theme of the excerpt?

    (1) Saving face is a weak approach.
    (2) True friends are helpful in times of trouble.
    x(3) Weighing risks helps in making good decisions.
    (4) Good negotiating skills cannot always solve problems.
    (5) Being unfair to a neighbor brings no reward.

12. What is the overall tone of the excerpt?

    (1) casual
    (2) humorous
    (3) tense
    (4) angry
    x(5) friendly

WHAT DID THESE MEN TAKE TO WAR?

Only a handful of novels and short stories have managed to clarify, in any lasting way, the meaning of the war in Vietnam for America and for the soldiers
(5) who served there. With *The Things They Carried,* Tim O'Brien adds his second title to the short list of essential fiction about Vietnam. As he did in his novel *Going After Cacciato* (1978), which won a National
(10) Book Award, he captures the war's pulsating rhythms and nerve-racking dangers. But he goes much further. By moving beyond the horror of the fighting to examine with sensitivity and insight the
(15) nature of courage and fear, by questioning the role that imagination plays in helping to form our memories and our own versions of truth, he places *The Things They Carried* high up on the list of best fiction
(20) about any war.

The Things They Carried is a collection of interrelated stories. . . .

In the title story, Mr. O'Brien juxtaposes the mundane and the deadly items that
(25) soldiers carry into battle. Can openers, pocketknives, wristwatches, mosquito repellent, chewing gum, candy, cigarettes, salt tablets, packets of Kool-Aid, matches, sewing kits, C rations are "humped" by the
(30) G.I.'s along with M-16 assault rifles, M-60 machine guns, M-79 grenade launchers. But the story is really about the other things the soldiers "carry": "grief, terror, love, longing . . . shameful memories" and,
(35) what unifies all the stories, "the common secret of cowardice." These young men, Mr. O'Brien tells us, "carried the soldier's greatest fear, which was the fear of blushing. Men killed, and died, because
(40) they were embarrassed not to."

Embarrassment, the author reveals in "On the Rainy River," is why he, or rather the fictional version of himself, went to Vietnam. He almost went to Canada
(45) instead. What stopped him, ironically, was fear. "All those eyes on me," he writes, "and I couldn't risk the embarrassment. . . . I couldn't endure the mockery, or the disgrace, or the patriotic ridicule. . . . I was
(50) a coward. I went to the war." . . .

Mr. O'Brien strives to get beyond literal descriptions of what these men went through and what they felt. He makes sense of the unreality of the war—makes
(55) sense of why he has distorted that unreality even further in his fiction—by turning back to explore the workings of the imagination, by probing his memory of the terror and fearlessly confronting the way
(60) he has dealt with it as both soldier and fiction writer. In doing all this, he not only crystallizes the Vietnam experience for us, he exposes the nature of all war stories.

Robert R. Harris, "Too Embarrassed Not to Kill," *New York Times Book Review.*

13. Why does the reviewer most likely discuss two stories from the book in detail?

   (1) to show off his extensive knowledge of the war
   (2) to show what the stories have in common
   (3) to give examples of the characters in the book
   (4) to relate those stories to his own experience
   (5) to demonstrate why the author disliked the war

14. Based on the information in the excerpt, what is the most important reason the reviewer thinks *The Things They Carried* is worth reading?

   (1) It describes the routines of men in war.
   (2) It is a collection of short stories.
   (3) It examines the soldiers' feelings.
   (4) It is not about just one person.
   (5) It describes battles in detail.

15. What does the author of *The Things They Carried* mean when he says that he "couldn't endure . . . the patriotic ridicule" (lines 48–49)?

   He did not want to

   (1) explain publicly his reasons for not going to war
   (2) be criticized for not going to war
   (3) be condemned for deciding to fight
   (4) feel embarrassed while wearing his uniform
   (5) receive a call from the president of the United States

16. How does the reviewer feel about the author's previous novel, *Going After Cacciato*?

   The reviewer thinks

   (1) it is better than *The Things They Carried*
   (2) it does not go far enough in examining the terror of war
   (3) it should be read in addition to *The Things They Carried*
   (4) it fails because it does not depict the typical war experience
   (5) it does not have enough exciting scenes

17. What is the overall tone of this article?

   (1) harsh
   (2) frustrated
   (3) indifferent
   (4) pleased
   (5) admiring

18. Based on the excerpt, what is *The Things They Carried* most likely to help the reader understand?

   (1) the author's life
   (2) the experience of war
   (3) certain battles in Vietnam
   (4) politics during the Vietnam war
   (5) the interrelation of stories

WHY IS THE MOVIE ALWAYS DIFFERENT FROM THE BOOK?

Because of the rather severe limitations imposed on the length of a film and on the amount of material it can successfully treat, a film is forced to suggest pictorially a

(5) great many things that a novel can explore in more depth. Novelist/screenwriter William Goldman sums up the problem this way:

When people say, "Is it like the

(10) book?" the answer is, "There has never in the history of the world been a movie that's really been like the book." Everybody says how faithful *Gone with the Wind* was.

(15) Well, *Gone with the Wind* was a three-and-a-half-hour movie, which means you are talking about maybe a two-hundred-page screenplay of a nine-hundred-page novel in which

(20) the novel has, say, five hundred words per page; and the screenplay has maybe forty, maybe sixty, depending on what's on the screen, maybe one hundred and fifty words

(25) per page. But you're talking a little, teeny slice; you're just extracting little, teeny *essences* of scenes. All you can ever be in an adaptation is faithful in spirit.

(30) At best, the film version can capture a small fraction of the novel's depth. It is doubtful that it can ever capture much of what lies beneath the surface. The filmmaker, nevertheless, must attempt

(35) to suggest the hidden material. The filmmaker's task is eased a bit if he or she can assume that viewers have read the novel. But we still must accept the fact that some dimensions of the novel are

(40) inaccessible to film.

A long novel creates an interesting dilemma: Should the filmmaker be satisfied with doing only part of the novel, dramatizing a single action that can be

(45) thoroughly treated within cinematic limits? Or should the filmmaker attempt to capture a sense of the whole novel by hitting the high points and leaving the gaps unfilled? If the latter strategy is attempted, complex

(50) time and character relationships may wind up being implied rather than clearly stated. Usually the filmmaker must limit not only the depth to which a character can be explored but also the actual number of

(55) characters treated. This limitation may give rise to the creation of composite characters, embodying the plot functions of two or more characters from the novel in one film character. Furthermore, in

(60) adapting a long novel to film, complex and important subplots might have to be eliminated.

Joseph M. Boggs, *The Art of Watching Films.*

19. What does William Goldman mean when he says, "All you can ever be in an adaptation is faithful in spirit" (lines 27–29)?

    (1) Filmmakers' attempts to be true to novels are rarely successful.
    (2) Authors seldom have filmmakers in mind when they write novels.
    (3) Filmmakers tend to reduce both the length and complexity of novels.
    (4) Filmmakers are limited to depicting a novel's basic meaning and mood.
    (5) The author's influence is readily apparent in most filmed versions of novels.

20. Based on the excerpt, what does the author most likely think about the use of composite characters in movies?

    He thinks the use of such characters

    (1) prevents filmmakers from exploring the less visual aspects of a novel
    (2) allows filmmakers to remain truer to the novel than if they altered the plot
    (3) shows that the filmmaker has succeeded in capturing the essence of a novel
    (4) represents a practical option for filmmakers attempting to cover entire novels
    (5) indicates that the filmmaker has chosen a novel that is too complex to be filmed well

21. What advice would the author most likely give to a beginning filmmaker?

    When choosing a novel to film, look for one that

    (1) contains detailed descriptions
    (2) has a large cast of characters
    (3) takes place over several years
    (4) will be unfamiliar to the audience
    (5) has a rather simple plot structure

22. In what way does the quotation from William Goldman differ from the rest of the excerpt?

    The quotation

    (1) uses language more figuratively than the rest of the excerpt does
    (2) offers opinions that are contrary to those in the rest of the excerpt
    (3) has a style that is less academic than that of the rest of the excerpt
    (4) uses a specific example to support its argument, but the rest of the excerpt relies on statistics
    (5) assumes that readers are familiar with the movie industry, but the rest of the excerpt does not

23. What is the main purpose of this excerpt?

    (1) to predict the types of novels that can be filmed most successfully
    (2) to explain some of the difficulties involved in basing a film on a novel
    (3) to convince readers that novels generally make poor sources for films
    (4) to discuss how characters in films tend to differ from characters in novels
    (5) to describe several ways in which a film can compress the events of a novel

HOW DOES THIS WOMAN FEEL ABOUT HER NEW HOME?

MOVING IN

The telephone-installer was interested
In the students helping me.
He said he had a father of 93, plus a mother 77
And his wife kept running her heart out.
(5) Students could help, what a good idea! Let me know
If at any time this telephone needs adjusting.

As he left, the upstairs apartment entered
With some slices of chocolate angel food cake
To make herself acquainted.
(10) She was a retired librarian and it turned out
The one librarian I knew in the town I came from
Was an old friend of hers, they both came
From South Dakota mining country.

The telephone-installer returned to ask
(15) If students were dependable? They can be.
Even more than a good chocolate cake, even more
Than a good telephone.
This could mean a new life for my wife and me, he said,
I think I'll bring you a longer cord for that phone.
(20) Don't let this last piece of cake go begging, begged the upstairs apartment.

Josephine Miles, "Moving In," *Collected Poems 1930–83.*

24. Which of the following sentences best describes what the speaker and her new neighbor have in common?

   (1) Both are friends with the installer.
   (2) Both are from South Dakota.
   (3) Both have a librarian friend.
   (4) Both have just moved into the building.
   (5) Both enjoy talking with neighbors.

25. Which of the following best describes what the speaker means by "And his wife kept running her heart out" (line 4)?

   (1) The installer's wife likes to exercise.
   (2) The installer's wife is very busy.
   (3) The students like the installer's wife.
   (4) The installer cannot keep up with his wife.
   (5) The installer's wife has a medical condition.

26. What does the author mean by the phrase "the upstairs apartment" (line 7)?

   (1) the rental unit above the speaker's
   (2) the installer's elderly parents
   (3) the speaker's neighbor
   (4) the telephone installer
   (5) the students working nearby

27. What is the most likely reason the speaker states that students can be more dependable than cakes and telephones?

   (1) She has faith in humanity.
   (2) Cake disappears too quickly.
   (3) Her telephone is not working properly.
   (4) She has known the students for years.
   (5) She does not trust the installer.

28. In what way are the installer, the students, and the neighbor similar?

They are

   (1) incompetent
   (2) unwanted
   (3) pushy
   (4) helpful
   (5) lonely

29. What is the tone of the poem?

   (1) conversational
   (2) celebratory
   (3) disapproving
   (4) forgiving
   (5) cautious

WHAT DOES ETHAN REQUEST FROM HIS EMPLOYER?

Ethan set about unloading the logs and when he had finished his job he pushed open the glazed door of the shed which the builder used as his office. Hale sat
(5) with his feet up on the stove, his back propped against a battered desk strewn with papers: the place, like the man, was warm, genial and untidy.

"Sit right down and thaw out," he
(10) greeted Ethan.

The latter did not know how to begin, but at length he managed to bring out his request for an advance of fifty dollars. The blood rushed to his thin skin under the
(15) sting of Hale's astonishment. It was the builder's custom to pay at the end of three months, and there was no precedent between the two men for a cash settlement.

Ethan felt that if he had pleaded an
(20) urgent need Hale might have made shift to pay him; but pride, and an instinctive prudence, kept him from resorting to this argument. After his father's death it had taken time to get his head above water,
(25) and he did not want Andrew Hale, or any one else in Starkfield, to think he was going under again. Besides, he hated lying; if he wanted the money he wanted it, and it was nobody's business to ask why.
(30) He therefore made his demand with the awkwardness of a proud man who will not admit to himself that he is stooping; and he was not much surprised at Hale's refusal.

The builder refused genially, as he did
(35) everything else: he treated the matter as something in the nature of a practical joke, and wanted to know if Ethan meditated buying a grand piano or adding a "cupolo" to his house; offering, in the latter case, to
(40) give his services free of cost.

Ethan's arts were soon exhausted, and after an embarrassed pause he wished Hale good day and opened the door of the office. As he passed out the
(45) builder suddenly called after him: "See here—you ain't in a tight place, are you?"

"Not a bit," Ethan's pride retorted before his reason had time to intervene.

"Well, that's good! Because I *am*, a
(50) shade. Fact is, I was going to ask you to give me a little extra time on that payment. Business is pretty slack, to begin with, and then I'm fixing up a little house for Ned and Ruth when they're married. I'm glad to do it
(55) for 'em, but it costs." His look appealed to Ethan for sympathy. "The young people like things nice. You know how it is yourself: it's not so long ago since you fixed up your own place for Zeena."

Edith Wharton, *Ethan Frome.*

30. What does the author mean when she says, "Ethan's arts were soon exhausted" (line 41)?

    (1) He had run out of ideas.
    (2) He could no longer remain calm.
    (3) He would have to get a new job.
    (4) He confessed to being untruthful.
    (5) He had no more respect for his boss.

31. Which of the following best describes the relationship between Ethan and Hale?

    (1) They do not like each other very much.
    (2) They are connected through business.
    (3) They have been friends for several years.
    (4) They are members of the same family.
    (5) They have just recently become acquainted.

32. Which of the following words best describes Ethan?

    (1) argumentative
    (2) intimidating
    (3) independent
    (4) charming
    (5) jealous

33. Which of the following ideas are most clearly contrasted in the excerpt?

    (1) generosity and rejection
    (2) friendship and deception
    (3) confidence and insecurity
    (4) pride and honesty
    (5) wealth and poverty

34. Earlier in the story, Hale is described as wearing a "clean shirt . . . always fastened by a small diamond stud." Based on this information and on the excerpt, which of the following best describes how Hale handles money?

    He is

    (1) uninterested
    (2) miserly
    (3) skilled
    (4) impractical
    (5) selfish

WHAT KIND OF FRIEND IS MRS. X?

MRS. X.: Now you must see what I have bought for my little chicks. *(Takes out a doll.)* Look at this. That's for Lisa. Do you see how she can roll her eyes and

(5) turn her head. Isn't she lovely? And here's a toy pistol for Maja.

(She loads the pistol and shoots it at MISS Y. who appears frightened.)

MRS. X.: Were you scared? Did you think I

(10) was going to shoot you? Really, I didn't think you'd believe that of me. Now if *you* were to shoot me it wouldn't be so surprising, for after all I did get in your way, and I know you never forget it—

(15) although I was entirely innocent. You still think I intrigued to get you out of the Grand Theatre, but I didn't. I didn't, however much you think I did. Well, it's no good talking, you will believe

(20) it was me . . . *(Takes out a pair of embroidered slippers.)* And these are for my old man, with tulips on them that I embroidered myself. As a matter of fact I hate tulips, but he has to have

(25) tulips on everything.

(MISS Y. looks up, irony and curiosity in her face.)

MRS. X: *(putting one hand in each slipper)* Look what small feet Bob has, hasn't

(30) he? And you ought to see the charming way he walks—you've never seen him in slippers, have you?

(MISS Y. laughs.)

MRS. X.: Look, I'll show you.

(35) *(She makes the slippers walk across the table, and MISS Y. laughs again.)*

MRS. X.: But when he gets angry, look, he stamps his foot like this. "Those damn girls who can never learn how to make

(40) coffee! Blast! That silly idiot hasn't trimmed the lamp properly!" Then there's a draught under the door and his feet get cold. "Hell, it's freezing, and the damn fools can't even keep

(45) the stove going!"

(She rubs the sole of one slipper against the instep of the other. MISS Y. roars with laughter.)

MRS. X.: And then he comes home and

(50) has to hunt for his slippers, which Mary has pushed under the bureau . . . Well, perhaps it's not right to make fun of one's husband like this. He's sweet anyhow, and a good, dear husband.

(55) You ought to have had a husband like him, Amelia. What are you laughing at? What is it? Eh? And, you see, I know he is faithful to me. Yes, I know it. He told me himself—what *are* you

(60) giggling at?—that while I was on tour in Norway that horrible Frederica came and tried to seduce him. Can you imagine anything more abominable?

August Strindberg, *The Stronger.*

35. Based on the information in the excerpt, how does Mrs. X. <u>most likely</u> feel about her husband?

    (1) She is angry that he is flirtatious.
    (2) She wishes he were less angry.
    (3) She thinks he is a silly old man.
    (4) She is thinking about a divorce.
    (5) She is glad that she married him.

36. Which of the following words <u>best</u> describes Mrs. X.?

    (1) friendly
    (2) grateful
    (3) vindictive
    (4) sinister
    (5) manipulative

37. Why does Mrs. X. say to Miss Y., "if *you* were to shoot me it wouldn't be so surprising" (lines 11–13)?

    (1) Miss Y. hates Mrs. X.
    (2) Miss Y. cannot be trusted.
    (3) Mrs. X. thinks Miss Y. resents her.
    (4) Mrs. X. and Miss Y. have long been enemies.
    (5) Miss Y. is emotionally unstable.

38. Which of the following words <u>best</u> describes the relationship between the two women?

    (1) warm
    (2) competitive
    (3) guarded
    (4) hostile
    (5) honest

39. If Miss Y. decided to speak her true feelings to Mrs. X., which of the following statements would she <u>most likely</u> make?

    (1) I never cared about the Grand Theatre.
    (2) That is a terrible imitation of your husband.
    (3) I know more about you than you think I do.
    (4) You are the funniest person I know.
    (5) Your husband is a lucky man.

40. Later in the play, Mrs. X. says, " You just sit there without moving—like a cat at a mouse-hole. You can't drag your prey out, you can't chase it, but you can out-stay it." Based on this information and the excerpt, which of the following <u>best</u> describes Miss Y.?

    (1) cunning
    (2) unintelligent
    (3) indifferent
    (4) mean
    (5) lazy

Answers start on page 275.

This chart can help you determine your strengths and weaknesses on the content and skill areas of the GED Language Arts, Reading Pretest. Use the Answers and Explanations starting on page 275 to check your answers to the test. Then circle on the chart the numbers of the test items you answered correctly. Put the total number correct for each content area and skill area in each row and column. Look at the total items correct in each column and row and decide which areas are difficult for you. Use the page references to study those areas. Use a copy of the Study Planner on page 31 to guide your studying.

Thinking Skill ⟍ Content Area	Comprehension	Application	Analysis	Synthesis	Total Correct
Nonfiction (Pages 32–97)	14, 15, 16, 19	21	13, 20	17, 18, 22, 23	____/11
Fiction (Pages 98–167)	30	4, 7, 9	1, 2, 6, 8, 31, 32	3, 5, 10, 11, 12, 33, 34	____/17
Poetry (Pages 168–207)	24, 26		25, 27	28, 29	____/6
Drama (Pages 208–241)	35, 37	39	36, 38	40	____/6
Total Correct	____/9	____/5	____/12	____/14	____/40

1–32 → Use the Study Planner on page 31 to organize your work in this book.
33–40 → Use the tests in this book to practice for the GED.

For additional help, see the *Steck-Vaughn GED Language Arts, Reading Exercise Book.*

Language Arts, Reading Study Planner

These charts will help you to organize your study after you take the Language Arts, Reading Pretest and Posttest. After each test, use your results from the Total Correct column in the corresponding Performance Analysis Chart to complete the study planner. Place a check mark next to the areas in which you need more practice. Copy the page numbers from the Performance Analysis Chart. Review your study habits by keeping track of the start and finish dates for each practice. These charts will help you to see your progress as you practice to improve your skills and prepare for the GED Test.

Pretest (pages 15–29): Use results from your **Performance Analysis Chart** (page 30).

Content Area	Correct/Total	✓	Page Numbers	Date Started	Date Finished
Nonfiction	____/11				
Fiction	____/17				
Poetry	____/6				
Drama	____/6				

Posttest (pages 243–257): Use results from your **Performance Analysis Chart** (page 258).

Content Area	Correct/Total	✓	Page Numbers	Date Started	Date Finished
Nonfiction	____/10				
Fiction	____/19				
Poetry	____/6				
Drama	____/5				

Interpreting Nonfiction

You probably read several types of nonfiction materials on a regular basis. Nonfiction materials include newspapers, magazines, textbooks, biographies, TV and movie reviews, manuals, and business documents. Their purpose is to convey information. Writing that explains how to do something or gives information is one of the most common types of reading material. In the workplace, for instance, you may have to refer to an employee manual to help you understand a policy relating to your job. At home, you may have to read directions to use your new compact disc player.

The GED Language Arts, Reading Test will include several nonfiction passages to determine how well you understand these forms of writing. Overall, nonfiction materials are the basis for 25 percent of the questions on the GED Reading Test.

Roger Ebert writes movie reviews in his regular series for the Chicago Sun-Times *newspaper.*

The lessons in this unit include:

Lesson 1: Finding the Main Idea and Supporting Details
Finding the main idea and supporting details will help you understand the main point a writer is making.

Lesson 2: Summarizing Major Ideas
Focusing on key words or phrases will help you translate what you read into information that you can use.

Lesson 3: Restating Information
By putting the information into your own words, you will show that you understand written materials.

Lesson 4: Applying Ideas
Applying ideas is a way to extend ideas from a reading passage to a new and related situation.

Lesson 5: Making Inferences
Making inferences involves figuring out unstated information based on what is stated or suggested in a passage.

Lesson 6: Identifying Style and Tone
Style and tone will help you understand how writers use language and sentence structure to express themselves.

Lesson 7: Drawing Conclusions
When you draw a conclusion, you interpret information to make a single, logical decision.

Lesson 8: Comparing and Contrasting Ideas
Identifying similarities and differences between ideas or things can show how they are related.

Lesson 9: Recognizing Author's Viewpoint
A writer's personal interests and background may influence his or her opinion toward a subject.

SELECTED READINGS

○ Newspaper and magazine articles

○ Workplace handbooks and manuals

○ Biographies and autobiographies

○ Warranty statements and insurance policies

○ Orientation booklets and other workplace training materials

GED SKILL Finding the Main Idea and Supporting Details

When you understand the **main idea** of a piece of writing, you understand the most important point a writer makes. The main idea can be stated at the beginning, middle, or end of a paragraph or passage.

In many paragraphs, the main idea is stated in a single sentence, the **topic sentence.** The topic sentence is often located at the beginning or at the end of a paragraph. If it is at the beginning, the rest of the sentences in the paragraph add details that support or explain the main idea. If the topic sentence is at the end, the **supporting details** are given first and then summed up in the topic sentence.

In some forms of nonfiction, the main idea is not stated at all. The reader must **infer,** or figure out the meaning by putting together the details the author provides.

main idea
the most important idea or point in a piece of writing

topic sentence
the sentence that contains the main idea

supporting details
information that supports or explains the main idea

infer
to figure out the meaning by using clues

Pay attention to headlines or titles; they usually contain key ideas.

Read the following excerpt from an article and complete the exercise on the following page.

Only in the Far West have windmills remained indispensable. On the open range, windmills serve as guideposts and landmarks, as familiar as neighbors. A windmill tower has pointed the way home to many a lost cowboy.

The windmill is usually what a cowboy sees first in the distance when riding in from a cattle drive. He begins thinking about a cool drink and a hot meal while the cattle mother-up[1] in the corrals.

For the ranch woman, the windmill is often used as a lookout tower which she can climb and look off to spot the return of her cowboy. When she sees a tide of red dust where the trails come together, she knows he's safe and it's time to put the biscuits in the oven.

The purr of the windmill is often the ranch woman's only company all day. She knows its pitch and tone, like the voice of a beloved friend, and will likely remember it until the day she dies.

Windmills speak to those who listen. Spring is seldom silent. The blades thrash and churn and chatter as the southwest wind batters the winter-worn plains. As spring storms violate the land, an old windmill turns its cheek to the anger of the storm and stands firm.

[1] protect themselves

Vera Schurer, "Windmills," *Country.*

1. Put a check mark next to the best description of the main idea of this excerpt.

    _____ a. Windmills pump water for use by people and cattle in the West.

    _____ b. Windmills are not needed in the eastern part of the country.

    __✓__ c. Windmills play an important role in the life of the West.

2. Put a check mark next to the phrase that tells where the main idea appears in this excerpt.

    _____ a. at the beginning

    _____ b. in the middle

    _____ c. at the end

3. Write the sentence from the excerpt that best states the main idea.

    _____

4. From the first paragraph, list two details about windmills that explain, describe, or support the main idea.

    _____

5. From the third paragraph, list one detail that supports the main idea.

    _____

    _____

6. The last paragraph describes how the windmills "speak." How does this detail support the main idea? Look at the fourth paragraph for clues.

    _____

    _____

Since all the paragraphs contain examples of ways in which windmills are important in the West, you were correct if you chose *option c* for question 1. For question 2, *option a* is the correct answer. For question 3, the correct answer is in the first paragraph: *Only in the Far West have windmills remained indispensable.* Details that you could have written for question 4 are *windmills are guideposts and landmarks* and *pointed the way home to many a lost cowboy.* For question 5, the answer is *the windmill is often used as a lookout tower.* For question 6, a correct answer would be similar to: *The sound of the windmill is compared to the voice of a friend that helps keep the ranch woman company. This function supports the main idea that windmills are indispensable.*

Read the following excerpt from an article and complete the exercise below.

Television remains a stepchild of the movie business. Movie stars and top directors often refuse to work in it, and they rarely admit to watching it. Movie agents advise clients that it's the last resort for careers in distress. Writers and intellectuals patronize[1] it.

(5)   But for a while now, the movie business has been confronted with an uncomfortable fact of life: In terms of dramatic value, relevance and humor, prime-time television—much of it, anyway—is far better than what's on at the movies.

Admissions of this come grudgingly for the most part, but they do come, especially this past week, when the film industry struggled to find five films to

(10)   nominate for the Academy Awards. . . .

No such difficulties face television.

Once or twice a night there are TV shows that are vivid or powerful or funny—sometimes all three—and that do not insult the intelligence of viewers beyond the age of consent. . . .

(15)   Perhaps the most significant reason television has surpassed movies, many people in Hollywood say, is that it is a writer's medium, while films are dominated by directors.

---

[1] look down on

Bernard Weinraub, "Pssst . . . TV Nudging Movies Aside as High Art. Pass It On," *The New York Times*.

1. Put a check mark next to the main idea of the first paragraph.

    _____ a. Television ought to be more respected.

    _____ b. Television is not as respected as the movie business.

2. List the four details that support the main idea of the first paragraph.

    a. _____

    b. _____

    c. _____

    d. _____

3. Is the main idea of the first paragraph the same as the main idea of the entire excerpt?

    _____ a. yes

    _____ b. no

4. Which of the following statements expresses the main idea of the entire excerpt?

_____ a. Television is not as entertaining as movies are.

_____ b. Television insults the intelligence of viewers.

_____ c. Television is often far better than the movies.

_____ d. Television does not live up to its potential.

5. Is the main idea of the entire excerpt stated directly, or do you have to infer it?

_____ a. It is stated directly.

_____ b. You must infer it.

6. Using a diagram can help you organize information. You can use the diagram below to show the main idea of the excerpt and details that support the main idea. One of the supporting details has been filled in for you. Complete the diagram by filling in the main idea and other supporting details.

SD:

SD:

SD:

Main Idea:

SD:

SD:
Some TV shows do not insult the intelligence of viewers.

7. How does the statement "No such difficulties face television" (line 11) support the main idea of the excerpt?

_____

_____

Answers start on page 279.

GED Practice • Lesson 1

Directions: Choose the <u>one best answer</u> to each question.

Questions 1 through 4 refer to the following excerpt from an article.

HOW DOES THIS FAMILY COMMUNICATE?

I was an extremely happy child at home. I remember many nights when my father would come back from work, and I'd hear him call out to my mother in Spanish,

(5) sounding relieved. In Spanish, he'd sound light and free notes he never could manage in English. Some nights I'd jump up just at hearing his voice. With *mis hermanos*[1] I would come running into the room where

(10) he was with my mother. Our laughing (so deep was the pleasure!) became screaming. Like others who know the pain of public alienation, we transformed the knowledge of our public separateness

(15) and made it consoling—the reminder of intimacy. Excited, we joined our voices in a celebration of sounds. *We are speaking now the way we never speak out in public. We are alone—together,* voices sounded,

(20) surrounded to tell me. Some nights, no one seemed willing to loosen the hold sounds had on us. At dinner, we invented new words. (Ours sounded Spanish, but made sense only to us.) We pieced together new

(25) words by taking, say, an English verb and giving it Spanish endings. My mother's instructions at bedtime would be lacquered with mock-urgent tones. Or a word like *sí* would become, in several notes, able

(30) to convey added measures of feeling. Tongues explored the edges of words, especially the fat vowels. And we happily sounded that military drum roll, the twirling roar of the Spanish *r.* Family language: my

(35) family's sounds. The voices of my parents and sisters and brother. Their voices insisting: *You belong here.*

---
[1] my siblings

Richard Rodriguez, *Hunger of Memory.*

1. The main idea of this excerpt chiefly concerns which of the following?

   (1) the family traditions of the author's culture
   (2) the way words united the author's family
   (3) the effort the author put into learning English
   (4) the author's preference of Spanish to English
   (5) the reason the author's family created words

2. Which of the following <u>best</u> describes the tone of the excerpt?

   (1) celebratory
   (2) detached
   (3) fanciful
   (4) regretful
   (5) urgent

3. What does the author reveal about his attitude toward Spanish with the statement, "Tongues explored the edges of words, especially the fat vowels" (lines 31–32)?

   He thinks

   (1) it is a constantly evolving language
   (2) it is a difficult language to speak well
   (3) its sounds are too often exaggerated
   (4) its sounds are related to its meaning
   (5) it has close ties to the sense of touch

4. Later in the book, the author states that "it is not possible for a child—any child—to use his family's language in school." Based on the excerpt, what does the author mean by "family language"?

   (1) language that reminds one of the past
   (2) the language that a person first learned
   (3) language that conveys private emotions
   (4) language that ignores the rules of grammar
   (5) a language spoken by a minority population

WHAT'S SO SPECIAL ABOUT NEWS MAGAZINES?

Beyond the bottom line, Wall Street doesn't much care about editorial quality; journalists do and others should. Not because journalism is perfect, but because
(5) it isn't.
News magazines come at the end of the food chain of journalism. First radio reports the news hourly, then the evening television news repeats it and adds
(10) pictures. Newspapers fill out the story in greater detail. Finally the news magazine comes along to summarize and analyze it. By that time the reader may be suffering an acute case of information glut. It takes
(15) wit, reflection, a gift for compression, some fresh reporting or consultation with experts, and an original turn of mind to add something new. The real job of the news magazine is to help the reader to make
(20) sense out of his times. Those who can do this, the best of them, form a shaggy group of contentious minds.

Thomas Griffith, "What's So Special About News Magazines?" *Newsweek.*

5. Which of the following is the best restatement of the phrase "Not because journalism is perfect, but because it isn't" (lines 3–5)?

   (1) Most journalists do not care about editorial quality.
   (2) Attention to editorial quality may help improve earnings.
   (3) Good journalists do not waste time trying to be perfect.
   (4) Attention to editorial quality may help improve journalism.
   (5) Good journalists pay attention to how many people buy magazines.

6. What is the main idea of the second paragraph of the excerpt (lines 6–22)?

   (1) It takes hard work to make a good news magazine.
   (2) Other media report stories before news magazines do.
   (3) News magazines are a collection of news reports.
   (4) News magazines often contain opposing points of view.
   (5) News magazines summarize and analyze the news.

7. Why is the statement "suffering an acute case of information glut" (lines 13–14) an effective use of figurative language?

   (1) It describes how the reader makes sense of the world.
   (2) It suggests that there is too much news on TV.
   (3) It reminds the reader of having an upset stomach from overeating.
   (4) It suggests that readers need to find new sources of information.
   (5) It implies that magazine readers should stop watching television news programs.

8. Which organizational pattern does the author use to describe the four news media that make up journalism (lines 6–12)?

   (1) time order—explaining the order in which the media cover the news
   (2) classification—grouping similar ideas together
   (3) comparison and contrast—finding similarities and differences among media
   (4) cause and effect—finding the connections between events and their causes
   (5) hierarchy—ranking media in terms of which is more important

Answers start on page 279.

Directions: This is a ten-minute practice test. After ten minutes, mark the last question you finished. Then complete the test and check your answers. If most of your answers were correct, but you didn't finish, try to work faster next time. Choose the one best answer to each question.

Questions 1 through 4 refer to the following excerpt from an article.

WHAT GOES ON AT THE COUNTY FAIR?

The crafts judges form a sorority of expert peers, most from out of county. Several have been to the judging school at the Augusta Presbyterian Church, with
(5) cards to prove it. Unwary novice judges are assigned to cookies, jellies, and jams. Hundreds of sweet things are entered: platters of brownies, cakes, jams, and jellies. You'd think it would be fun tasting
(10) them, until you thought twice. The jelly judges did stay for lunch afterwards (thanks to the Highland Girl Scouts), but they hardly ate a thing.

Sewing judges sit at a table while
(15) assistants bring them garments to inspect for fabric grain lines, stitching, suitable thread, smooth darts, pleats, tucks, gathers, and facings. One lady holds up a black-and-white checked child's jumper.
(20) "Oh, look, she's covered the buttons."

The second judge turns a sundress pocket inside out to inspect the stitching. "What do you do when they're both nice?" The senior judge says, "You get to
(25) nitpicking," and she awards first prize to the jumper. "I don't know how it is other places, but in Highland County, covered buttons are it.". . .

The canned vegetable judges look for a
(30) perfect seal and a nice-looking ring and label. The liquid should be free of sediment and bubbles. The color should be natural, pieces must be uniform and of good quality. Mildred Detamore holds a jar of
(35) stewed tomatoes up to the light and sighs, "The tomatoes are so much seedier this year. It's because of the drought."

Donald McCaig, "The Best Four Days in Highland County," *An American Homeplace.*

1. The author uses the quote "You get to nitpicking" (lines 24–25) to suggest which of the following?

   (1) The senior judge is a picky person.
   (2) Covered buttons are an important feature of all garments.
   (3) A judge may award a prize based upon some small point.
   (4) The sewing judges often like two garments equally well.
   (5) Small details are not the most important aspect of a garment.

2. What was most likely the deciding factor in awarding the first prize to the black-and-white child's jumper?

   (1) its fine stitches
   (2) its smooth darts
   (3) its covered buttons
   (4) its overall appearance
   (5) the grain lines on its fabric

3. What does the author's use of the word "sighs" (line 35) suggest?

   (1) The judge is tired of tasting samples.
   (2) Judging is hard work and often boring.
   (3) The judge thinks that the jar is defective.
   (4) The judge is dissatisfied with this year's crop.
   (5) The judge will not get paid for all her work.

4. Which of the following is the best description of the style in which this article is written?

   (1) dry and scholarly
   (2) informal and casual
   (3) complex and technical
   (4) formal and scientific
   (5) lighthearted and comical

Questions 5 through 7 refer to the following excerpt from an article.

WHY DID SUCCESS SPOIL ERNEST HEMINGWAY?

In 1928 Hemingway's mother mailed him a chocolate cake. Along with it she sent the .32-cal. Smith & Wesson revolver with which Hemingway's father had just
(5) killed himself. Hemingway dropped the pistol into a deep lake in Wyoming "and saw it go down making bubbles until it was just as big as a watch charm in that clear water, and then it was out of sight."
(10) The story is minutely savage in its details and haunting in its outcome: perfect Hemingway. And of course, there is the water. . . .—lake water and trout stream and Gulf Stream and the rains after
(15) Caporetto and the endless washes of alcohol refracting in his brain. His style was a stream with the stones of nouns in it and a surface of prepositional ripples. . . .
. . . Ernest Hemingway's books are
(20) easier to know, and love, than his life. He wrote, at his early best, a prose of powerful and brilliant simplicity. But his character was not simple. In one of his stories, he wrote: "The most complicated subject that I
(25) know, since I am a man, is a man's life." The most complicated subject that he knew was Ernest Hemingway.
. . . His life belonged as much to the history of publicity as to the history of
(30) literature. He was a splendid writer who became his own worst creation, a hoax and a bore. He ended by being one of the most famous men in the world, white-bearded Mr. Papa. He stopped observing
(35) and started performing. . . .
Still, a long mythic fiesta between two explosions may not be a bad way to have a life. The first explosion came in Fossalta di Piave in northeastern Italy at midnight on
(40) July 8, 1918. A shell from an Austrian trench mortar punctured Hemingway with 200-odd pieces of shrapnel. . . . The second explosion came 25 years ago this summer. Early one morning in Ketchum,
(45) Idaho, Hemingway (suffering from diabetes, nephritis, alcoholism, severe depression, hepatitis, hypertension, impotence and paranoid delusions, his memory all but ruined by electroshock
(50) treatments) slid two shells into his double-barreled Boss shotgun . . . the last creature Hemingway brought down was himself.
Hemingway was mourned mostly as a great celebrity, his worst side, and not as a
(55) great writer, which he was.

"A Quarter-Century Later, the Myth Endures," *Time Magazine.*

5. On the basis of the excerpt, how did the public most likely think of Hemingway in his later years?

   (1) as the most distinguished writer of his time
   (2) as an expert on big-game hunting
   (3) as a war correspondent
   (4) as an expert on bullfighting
   (5) as an international star

6. Which of the following would the writer of this article most likely enjoy?

   (1) a play about Hemingway's life
   (2) a biography about Hemingway's later years
   (3) an early Hemingway story
   (4) a newspaper article about Hemingway's fame
   (5) a picture of Hemingway performing

7. What is the purpose of the details in the first paragraph?

   (1) to explain why Hemingway's father killed himself
   (2) to criticize Hemingway's behavior
   (3) to introduce a discussion of Hemingway's life and style of writing
   (4) to explain Hemingway's relationship with his mother
   (5) to explain why Hemingway became a celebrity

Answers start on page 280.

Lesson 2

GED SKILL Summarizing Major Ideas

summarize
to express the main points of a piece of writing in your own words

You read workplace documents and other types of nonfiction materials to find information that you need. When you **summarize** the important ideas in what you read, you are actively translating these ideas into information you can use. Summarizing is often called an "active reading strategy."

You have probably summarized the important ideas in informational material quite often without realizing it. Imagine, for example, that you receive a memo at work about new safety regulations. One of your co-workers asks you what the memo says. You might reply, "It says that we are now required to wear ear plugs whenever we are on the shop floor." You have effectively summarized the main points of the memo without giving all the details.

Read the following excerpt from a memo and complete the exercise below.

Effective June 30th, Soft Touch Software Design will offer all regular full-time employees group health insurance coverage. "Full time" constitutes a 37.5-hour work week. Coverage takes effect on the first day of the month following the employee's starting date. Currently, two health insurance options are available: an HMO (health maintenance organization) or a PPO (preferred provider organization). Both plans require an annual deductible per covered individual of $250, with a family maximum of $750, but there are other important differences in the coverage. Read the attached material and contact Human Resources with any questions.

Headings are often used to summarize the main points in informational materials. Put a check mark by the heading that would better summarize the major ideas of this memo.

_____ a. Two New Healthcare Plans Are Available for Full-Time Employees

_____ b. Annual Deductibles for Healthcare Plans for Individuals and Families

You were correct if you chose *option a.* This heading summarizes the main points of the memo. *Option b* contains details, but not the most important information.

TIP

When you summarize what you read, try to answer these questions about the major points that were made: *Who? What? Where? When? Why?* or *How?*

Read the following excerpt from an employee handbook and complete the exercise below.

Peerless Laminating Service's electronic mail (e-mail) system is a business tool and is to be used only for communications with clients and employees. It is not to be used for personal correspondence. Nor is it to be used to create, send, or copy offensive or inappropriate messages of any kind.

(5)   Among those references that are considered to be offensive are any that contain sexual language or references, racial slurs, gender-specific comments, or any other writing that refers offensively to someone's age, sexual orientation, religious or political beliefs, national origin, or disability. Abuse of the company's e-mail system can lead to disciplinary action.

1. To whom is this excerpt directed?

_____ a. the owners of Peerless Laminating

_____ b. the employees of Peerless Laminating

2. Put a check mark next to the main point of the excerpt.

_____ a. The electronic mail system at Peerless Laminating Service is a business tool.

_____ b. Inappropriate messages include references to someone's age or disability.

3. In a sentence or two, explain why you think Peerless Laminating has the policy described in the excerpt.

_____

_____

_____

4. Put a check mark next to possible headings for this handbook excerpt. You should choose more than one.

_____ a. Why E-mail Is an Effective Form of Business Communication

_____ b. Grounds for Employee Dismissal from the Company

_____ c. Use and Misuse of the Company's E-mail System

_____ d. Rules for Sending Personal E-mails on the Job

_____ e. Guidelines for Appropriate Use of the E-mail System

_____ f. Illegal Uses of E-mail on the Job

Answers start on page 280.

Directions: Choose the <u>one best answer</u> to each question.

<u>Questions 1 through 4</u> refer to the following excerpt from an article.

WHY IS THE "WORLD WIDE WEB" A GOOD NAME FOR THE INTERNET?

The World Wide Web represents the greatest resource of information that the world has ever known. But without some preparation, Web searching can be a little
(5) like wandering in a library during a power outage—you know your answers are nearby, but you can't find them.

In order to fully utilize the search capacities of the Web, you've got to be
(10) familiar with the tools that are available, and you must have a solid understanding of how to prepare a search. Spending a few wise moments before you hit that "Submit" key can make all the difference.

(15) **The Search Engine**

Unlike your friendly neighborhood library, there's no Dewey Decimal System awaiting you on-line—just a collection of documents that experts say will soon
(20) reach 1 billion in number. The Web isn't indexed in any standard manner, either, so finding information can seem a daunting task. That's what makes the search engine such an essential tool. Search engines are
(25) the tools that find documents in response to a submitted query. Each engine maintains its own database created by computer programs or "robots." Also called "spiders," these programs travel along the
(30) Web (hence the nickname) locating new sites, updating old ones and removing obsolete ones from the database. In performing your search, they use both a title and a location technique: Pages
(35) containing your search-words (or keywords) in the title are considered most relevant.

Art Daudelin, "Keys to Effective Web Searching," *Physicians Financial News.*

1. Which of the following summarizes the main idea of this excerpt?

   (1) how the Web got its name
   (2) how to get a computer job
   (3) how to search the Web
   (4) how to create a search engine
   (5) how the Web is replacing the library

2. If you wanted information about jobs in cooking, which keywords would be the <u>most</u> helpful in getting results?

   (1) cooking techniques
   (2) job opportunities
   (3) food service opportunities
   (4) French cooking schools
   (5) catering services

3. Based on the information in this excerpt, which of the following inferences can you make about searching the Web?

   (1) The Web is a huge search engine.
   (2) No two search engines are alike.
   (3) The Web is an electronic library.
   (4) Updating Web sites is nearly impossible.
   (5) Word frequency is not an important searching technique.

4. Based on the information in the article, which of the following types of titles would attract the greatest number of interested searchers to a particular Web page?

   (1) a humorous title that makes readers laugh
   (2) a title consisting of a one-word summary of the page
   (3) a title containing a few important words from the page
   (4) a title with vivid, poetic words
   (5) a general, non-specific title

Questions 5 through 7 refer to the following excerpt from a company notice.

WHY IS THIS LAW IMPORTANT?

All employees must be informed of the law regarding health benefits for ex-employees.

(5) As an employer of more than 20 people, Jetstream Airways is required by law to let "qualified beneficiaries" keep their health insurance after separation from the company due to certain "qualifying events."

(10) A qualified beneficiary is a current or former employee covered under a group health plan, his or her spouse, dependent child, or a child born to or adopted by the employee when covered. For a covered employee, a "qualifying event" is voluntary

(15) or involuntary termination (except if fired for gross misconduct), reduction in hours of employment, or filing of bankruptcy by the employer. For a spouse or dependent child, it means the employee's loss of

(20) employment, the covered employee's death, a spouse's divorce or legal separation from the covered employee, a covered employee's eligibility for Medicare, a dependent's loss of dependent status, or

(25) the employer's filing of a bankruptcy proceeding.

Covered employees must be told of their rights when hired and upon leaving Jetstream Airways. Coverage can last up

(30) to 18 months for a termination or reduction in working hours, up to 29 months for certain disabled qualified beneficiaries, and up to 36 months for divorce or separation.

(35) Once coverage is elected, qualified beneficiaries are required to pay a premium, which includes a nominal administration fee, on the first day of the month for which coverage applies.

5. Which of the following reasons would most likely disqualify an employee for coverage under this policy?

   (1) bankruptcy of the company
   (2) job loss due to downsizing
   (3) adoption of a child
   (4) quitting one's job
   (5) theft of a computer

6. Which statement best summarizes this excerpt?

   (1) The company has clear policies dealing with ex-employees.
   (2) Ex-employees can often retain their health insurance after leaving.
   (3) Qualified ex-employees and their dependents can retain their health insurance.
   (4) Employees have rights, including the right to health insurance.
   (5) The government is concerned about the rising cost of medical care.

7. Which of the following inferences about health insurance laws is supported by the excerpt?

   (1) Dependents under age 21 who are not in school lose coverage.
   (2) Companies with fewer than 20 employees are exempt.
   (3) Covered employees cannot keep their insurance when they take a new job.
   (4) Ex-employees must pay enormous premiums to retain their coverage.
   (5) Illnesses occurring after an employee leaves a company are not covered.

 When summarizing a piece of writing, ask yourself, "What is the most important idea?" Then look at the details to see if they support your answer. If they do not, revise your idea.

Answers start on page 280.

Directions: This is a ten-minute practice test. After ten minutes, mark the last question you finished. Then complete the test and check your answers. If most of your answers were correct, but you didn't finish, try to work faster next time. Choose the one best answer to each question.

Questions 1 through 9 refer to the following excerpt from an employee handbook.

WHAT IS THE VALUE OF THIS PROGRAM?

Most personal problems do not disappear between the hours of 9 and 5. When employees experience difficulties at home, the problems usually follow them to
(5) work. In some instances, employees face additional problems at the workplace, such as deadline pressures and conflicts with co-workers. Situations like these can impede an employee's ability to perform
(10) well at work or in other activities.

Several types of problems can affect an employee's job performance. These problems can be emotional, marital, family related, occupational, financial, or
(15) substance abuse related. How can an employee address problems such as these? Often, short-term counseling is all that is necessary to help him or her resolve the problem before it begins to affect job
(20) performance seriously. That's where Employees' Advisory and Referral Service (EARS) comes in. EARS can help employees resolve many types of personal problems.

(25) EARS is staffed by highly trained counselors and is offered through the current medical insurance program. There is no cost for this benefit to the employee and his or her family members. However,
(30) employees are responsible for costs incurred if they are referred to a professional outside the EARS program. Under this circumstance, the group medical insurance will pay the same
(35) reasonable and customary charges that would be paid if an employee were being treated by a medical professional.

EARS counselors maintain strict confidentiality. No one, including the
(40) employer, will be informed of an employee's participation in the program unless he or she reveals it. Nor will participation in the program jeopardize an employee's job.

(45) The EARS program is based on self-referral, meaning that the employee refers himself or herself. He or she will discuss the problem with an EARS counselor, who will help determine what kind of help is
(50) needed. EARS is staffed 24 hours a day. If the problem cannot be resolved by one of the staff's counselors, the employee will be referred to a qualified professional outside the program.

(55) During the course of participation, the employee's EARS counselor will maintain support and follow-up. In the event that an outside referral becomes necessary, the employee's financial circumstances and
(60) geographical location will be taken into consideration.

At EARS we strive to offer you the best service that we can. We listen. We care. After all, we're all EARS.

1. Which of the following best summarizes the excerpt?

   (1) Domestic problems can affect the work environment.
   (2) All that troubled employees need is a sympathetic ear.
   (3) An employer-sponsored program is available to help troubled employees.
   (4) Healthcare includes mental health as well as physical health.
   (5) Employers have a vested interest in their employees' well being.

2. What is the main idea of the second paragraph?

The EARS program

(1) supplements the medical insurance program
(2) can help with many types of problems
(3) uses a confidential process for participation
(4) can be of great value to the average employee
(5) has helped many employees in the past

3. Which of the following best restates the phrase "Situations like these can impede an employee's ability to perform well" (lines 8–10)?

Situations like these can

(1) make it impossible to do a good job
(2) make medical intervention necessary
(3) make the employee not care about job performance
(4) make it difficult to excel at work
(5) make it necessary to fire an employee

4. Which of the following problems could be helped through the EARS program?

(1) a problem with repetitive motion injury
(2) a shortage of adequate child care
(3) having too much work
(4) feeling overwhelmed by a project
(5) a desire to retire early

5. Based on the excerpt, which of the following can be inferred about the directors of the company that offers EARS to employees?

(1) They place little value on employee benefits.
(2) They think this benefit will help to attract high-quality employees.
(3) They want their employees to function well.
(4) They require their employees to leave their problems at home.
(5) They want to refer employees with problems to outside professionals.

6. What does the reference to payment of "reasonable and customary charges" (line 35) imply?

It implies that the group medical insurance

(1) charges standard fees to employees
(2) does not ordinarily charge its customers
(3) will not cover costs it considers to be too high
(4) will cover only those types of treatments that physicians provide
(5) will pay the same amount as the employee's regular doctor charges

7. On the basis of the excerpt, why would an employer want a counseling program such as EARS to be confidential?

(1) Employers do not want to know about employees' problems.
(2) Employees might not seek help if the program were not confidential.
(3) Employees should keep their personal problems to themselves.
(4) Counseling programs such as this one are independent organizations.
(5) The counselors refuse to break confidentiality.

8. Which of the following best describes the style in which this excerpt is written?

(1) straightforward and matter-of-fact
(2) dry and scholarly
(3) technical and challenging
(4) lighthearted and amusing
(5) detailed and clinical

9. Which of the following best describes the way in which the excerpt is organized?

(1) by giving a sequence of events
(2) by comparing and contrasting information
(3) by listing information in order of importance
(4) by introducing a problem and offering a solution
(5) by discussing familiar items first, then moving to unfamiliar items

Answers start on page 281.

GED SKILL Restating Information

You can show you understand something you read by **restating** it in your own words. This is an active reading strategy that you can use to deepen and reinforce your understanding of written materials. You use this skill often in daily life. For example, imagine that you are helping a friend assemble his new desk. You read "Insert dowel A into hole A." Your friend asks you to explain the directions more clearly, so you say, "Put the long peg in the hole that connects the desk top to the desk side." You have just restated information.

restating
showing that you understand something by putting it into your own words

Read the following excerpt from an article and complete the exercise below.

Despite the flashiness of the Web, e-mail is and has always been the primary reason most people go online, followed by research, according to a survey by Louis Harris & Associates. More than 1.6 billion noncommercial e-mail messages are sent each day in the United States, which is nearly three times the number of first-class postal mailings, according to an analysis by eMarketer, an Internet market research firm in New York City.

It's easy to see why. E-mail is cheaper and faster than a letter, less intrusive than a phone call, and more flexible than a fax. You can e-mail at work, school, and home, 24 hours a day, exchanging not only text but also photos, voice messages, and even video.

Reid Goldsborough, "We've All Got E-Mail," *The Editorial Eye.*

1. Put a check mark next to one of the following statements that <u>better</u> restates the main idea of this excerpt?

   _____ a. E-mail is not being used to its fullest potential.

   _____ b. E-mail is superior to many other communication methods.

2. The second sentence of the second paragraph lists three reasons for the popularity of e-mail. Write each of the reasons next to its correct two-word restatement below.

   a. more efficient: _____

   b. more welcome: _____

   c. more adaptable: _____

   You were correct if you chose *option b* for question 1. For question 2 the correct answers are: a. *cheaper and faster than a letter,* b. *less intrusive than a phone call,* and c. *more flexible than a fax.*

TIP

To restate ideas, find the main idea of a piece of writing and then put it in words that make the most sense to you.

Read the following excerpt from a textbook and complete the exercise below.

The most critical stage of writing business letters is the planning stage. Planning begins even *before* you write. How soundly a house is built depends largely on the thought that goes into an architect's plans. The same principle applies when you write business letters. The effectiveness of your letter depends
(5) on the quality of your preparation. There are logical steps for writers of business letters to follow in the planning stage. Following these steps makes it easier to create good letters consistently. These steps are: follow established policy, identify your objective, identify your reader's needs, visualize your reader, choose an appropriate type of letter, and organize your ideas.

In Plain Words: A Guide to Financial Services Writing.

1. Titles sometimes restate the most important information in a piece of writing. Which of the following would be the <u>best</u> title for the excerpt?

   _____ a. The Importance of Business Letters

   _____ b. How E-Mail Is Replacing the Business Letter

   _____ c. The Business of Writing Effective Letters

   _____ d. Six Logical Steps to Plan a Business Letter

2. The phrase "decide on your goal" is a restatement of which step mentioned in the excerpt?

   _____

3. What does it mean to "visualize your reader" (line 8)?

   _____

4. Choose the sentence from the excerpt that is closest to the following restatement, and write it on the line below: Thorough planning results in a letter that meets its objective.

   _____

5. On the line below, restate the first sentence of this excerpt.

   _____

Answers start on page 282.

Directions: Choose the one best answer to each question.

Questions 1 through 4 refer to the following excerpt from an article.

WHAT IS A BILL GATES BILL?

Consider that Bill Gates, whose personal net worth has recently soared to over $40 billion, made this money in the twenty-two years or so since he founded
(5)   Microsoft. If we presume that he has worked fourteen hours a day on every business day since then, that means he's been making money at a staggering $500,000 per hour, or about $150 per
(10) second. This, in turn, means that if Bill Gates saw or dropped a $500 bill on the ground, it wouldn't be worth his time to take the four seconds required to bend over and pick it up.
(15)   The "Too-small-a-bill-for-Bill" index has risen dramatically over the years. When Microsoft went public in 1986, the new multimillionaire would have lost out by leaving behind anything but $5 bills. And I
(20) can remember speaking to him at a conference in 1993, thinking, "$31 per second, $31 per second" as we talked.
       Another way to examine this staggering net worth is to compare it with that of an
(25) average American of reasonable but modest wealth. Perhaps she has a net worth of $100,000. Mr. Gates's net worth is 400,000 times larger. Which means that to Bill, $100,000 (her entire net worth) is
(30) like 25 cents. You can work out the right multiplier for your own net worth. So, a new Lamborghini Diablo, which we think of as costing $250,000, would be 63 cents in Bill Gates dollars. And that fully loaded,
(35) multimedia, active-matrix 233-MHz laptop with the 1024 x 768 screen? A penny. A nice home in a rich town like Palo Alto, California? $2. You might be able to buy a plane ticket on a Boeing 747 for $1,200,
(40) full-fare coach. In Bill bills, Mr. Gates could buy three 747s: one for him, one for his wife, Melinda, and one for young Jennifer Katharine.

Brad Templeton, "It's Net Worth It," "Bill Gates Wealth Index."

1. What does the author mean by the statement, "The 'Too-small-a-bill-for-Bill' index has risen dramatically over the years" (lines 15–16)?

   (1) Gates is worth more, so his time is more valuable.
   (2) Gates has to work more to earn more.
   (3) Gates has become more generous with his money.
   (4) Gates will probably earn less in the future.
   (5) Gates earns much more than the average American earns.

2. What is the tone of this article?

   (1) congratulatory
   (2) envious
   (3) critical
   (4) disgusted
   (5) humorous

3. What does the author mean by the statement "(her entire net worth) is like 25 cents" (lines 29–30)?

   (1) Gates treats others as if they are not worth very much.
   (2) The average American cannot afford luxury items.
   (3) Gates spends fortunes without a second thought.
   (4) Modest wealth seems like pocket change to Gates.
   (5) Most Americans do not save enough money.

4. Based on the excerpt, which approach would the author most likely use to describe the distance from Earth to the moon?

   (1) He would use highly technical language.
   (2) He would make comparisons.
   (3) He would use exaggeration for emphasis.
   (4) He would describe different viewpoints.
   (5) He would state the information matter-of-factly.

Questions 5 through 8 refer to the following product warranty statement.

WHAT DOES THIS WARRANTY DO?

CYBERTECH COMPUTER TECHNOLOGIES, INC. warrants that this product is free from defective materials or defects in factory workmanship and will
(5) replace or repair this unit or any part thereof, if it proves to be defective in normal use or service within one year from the date of original purchase. Our obligation under this warranty is the repair
(10) or replacement of the defective instrument or any part thereof. This warranty will be considered void if the unit is tampered with, improperly serviced, or subjected to misuse, negligence, or accidental damage.
(15) There are no other express warranties other than those stated herein.

EXCLUSIONS: This limited warranty does not apply to repairs or replacement necessitated by any cause beyond
(20) the control of Cybertech Computer Technologies including, but not limited to, any malfunction, defects, or failures which in the opinion of the Company are caused by or resulting from unauthorized service
(25) or parts, improper maintenance, operation contrary to furnished instructions, shipping or transit accidents, modification or repair by the user, abuse, misuse, neglect, accident, fire, flood or other acts of God,
(30) incorrect line voltage, cosmetic damages, defaced or removed parts, and normal wear and tear.

The limited warranty does not apply to damage that occurs during unpacking,
(35) setup, or installation; removal of the Product for repair; or reinstallation of the Product after repair.

At the Company's discretion, a labor charge may be assessed on Products
(40) returned for Limited Warranty repairs in which no fault is found.

This warranty gives you specific legal rights, and you may also have other rights, which vary from state to state.

5. Which of the following best expresses the main idea of the second paragraph?

   (1) Any customer who breaks a computer must purchase it.
   (2) The warranty applies only to manufacturing defects.
   (3) The warranty is no good if the purchaser breaks the computer.
   (4) The warranty applies only to repairs beyond the control of Cybertech.
   (5) Purchasers must treat the computer with great care.

6. What is the purpose of this warranty statement?

   (1) to describe the conditions under which the company will replace or repair the product
   (2) to exempt the company from responsibility for replacing or repairing the product
   (3) to guarantee that purchasers will be completely satisfied
   (4) to serve as proof that the product passed a careful inspection before it was sold
   (5) to explain that the manufacturer will provide no refunds or exchanges

7. For the manufacturer to honor the warranty, which of the following criteria is the purchaser most likely to have to meet?

   (1) be a resident of the United States
   (2) furnish proof of the date of purchase
   (3) show that the product was defective
   (4) return the product to the place of purchase
   (5) complete a questionnaire about buying habits

8. Which words best describe the style of this document?

   (1) informal and conversational
   (2) vague and misleading
   (3) harsh and threatening
   (4) boring and repetitive
   (5) formal and legal

Answers start on page 282.

Directions: This is a ten-minute practice test. After ten minutes, mark the last question you finished. Then complete the test and check your answers. If most of your answers were correct, but you didn't finish, try to work faster next time. Choose the one best answer to each question.

Questions 1 through 9 refer to the following excerpt from an insurance policy.

WHAT DOES YOUR AUTO POLICY COVER?

Even the most basic auto insurance policies contain a number of key provisions. These include liability coverage, limits and declarations,
(5) medical payments coverage, underinsured/uninsured motorists coverage, collision coverage, and comprehensive coverage.

Liability coverage protects you from
(10) damage your car does to others—damage for which you are legally responsible. If an accident occurs in which someone is injured or killed, it covers you and family members or relatives who live with you
(15) under these circumstances:
• You are driving your own car.
• You are driving another car with that vehicle owner's permission.
• A family member or relative is driving
(20) your car with your permission.

Liability coverage pays the insured for legal defense costs, bail bond costs, and emergency first aid to the injured. It pays other people whom you've injured for
(25) property damage, loss of services, bodily injury, sickness, medical services, disease, and death.

The limits tell you the maximum amounts for which you are covered. The
(30) declarations indicate the limits you've chosen, the vehicles you are insuring, amendments to the base contracts, and other information that you declare as factual on the application. For instance, the
(35) policy limits of 100/300/100 indicate the maximum amount to be paid per person for bodily injury, the total paid per accident for bodily injury, and the limit paid for property damage you caused.

(40) Medical payments coverage pays for the emergency medical treatment required after an accident. It is paid regardless of who was at fault in the accident. It covers the insured, covered passengers, and
(45) covered family members. It pays for the following services: X-rays, surgery, ambulance, physicians, hospital, and funeral expenses.

Underinsured/uninsured motorists
(50) coverage pays for damage to you and your property caused by another driver who doesn't have adequate insurance to pay you for all of the injury inflicted, or who doesn't have insurance at all. It covers you,
(55) passengers covered under the contract, and covered family members for bodily injury, disease, sickness, and death. Property damage coverage is not available in all states.

(60) Collision coverage pays for damage to your car resulting from an accident with another car or object. It pays for repair of the car up to its actual cash value, taking into account its age, use, and wear
(65) and tear.

Comprehensive coverage applies to most other damage to your car. You can choose limits of these coverages as well as the amount of your deductible—the
(70) loss amount you agree to pay out of pocket before the insurance company reimburses you.

1. Which of the following best restates the key point of this excerpt?

   (1) Every car owner should be insured.
   (2) Car insurance is a necessary evil.
   (3) All auto insurance contracts have certain basic features.
   (4) Liability insurance coverage is more important to have than collision coverage.
   (5) Those covered by insurance have a menu of choices from which to pick.

2. Imagine that you have liability coverage for your car. Which of the following drivers would it protect based on this excerpt?

(1) your son, who lives with you and is driving his own car
(2) your son, who borrowed your car without permission
(3) you, while driving a car borrowed from your neighbor
(4) a friend to whom you lent the car
(5) a friend who crashed into your car

3. Based on the information in the excerpt, which of the following would be considered a "declaration" (line 30) in an insurance policy?

(1) the amount you will be paying for car insurance
(2) the type of insurance you are choosing and the provisions it contains
(3) the greatest amount the insurance company will pay if you injure someone
(4) factual information about the insurance company
(5) a statement that defines violations of the contract

4. Based on the description in the excerpt of the phrase "liability coverage" (lines 9–27), which of the following has the same meaning?

Coverage when the insured

(1) is guilty of causing an accident
(2) is responsible for damage
(3) is seriously injured
(4) does not have adequate coverage
(5) has permission to drive the car

5. You ran off the road into a tree, which toppled over and broke a pedestrian's arm. What type of coverage would pay for the pedestrian's hospital visit?

(1) liability
(2) medical payment
(3) underinsured/uninsured
(4) collision
(5) comprehensive

6. Imagine that you own an older car that is not worth very much. Which two coverages would probably be of least benefit to you?

(1) liability and medical
(2) uninsured and liability
(3) collision and medical
(4) comprehensive and medical
(5) collision and comprehensive

7. Imagine that you borrowed money to buy a new car. Which two coverages would the loan company probably require?

(1) liability and underinsured
(2) medical and underinsured
(3) comprehensive and collision
(4) uninsured and underinsured
(5) liability and medical

8. The "deductible" (line 69) is the amount of money you agree to pay yourself before the insurance company starts to pay. How might a high deductible benefit you?

(1) It might give you more coverage.
(2) It might lower your insurance payment.
(3) It might improve your cash flow.
(4) It might reduce small claims that can drive up the cost of insurance.
(5) It might lower your risk to the insurance company.

9. Which of the following patterns is used in this excerpt to introduce the basic features of an automobile insurance policy?

(1) arranging features in sequence, or time order
(2) comparing and contrasting different features
(3) explaining features in order of their importance
(4) describing a problem and offering a solution
(5) showing cause-and-effect relationships

Answers start on page 283.

GED SKILL Applying Ideas

Applying ideas means taking information that you read and using it. For example, when you follow the steps of a recipe to make a certain dish, you are taking the words and putting them into action— in other words, you are applying ideas. A number of reading materials that you encounter in daily life require you to use this skill.

applying ideas
the ability to take information you read and transfer it to a new situation

Read the following excerpt from an employee orientation manual and complete the exercise below.

One of the major benefit changes that takes effect on the first day of January is the Company's match of employees' contributions to their 401(k) account. The reason for this benefit is to encourage employees to contribute to their own retirement accounts beyond what the Company contributes. Employees can do so by making elective deferrals from their paychecks to their 401(k) accounts. For every dollar invested up to 1 percent of your base salary over the next year, the Company will match it with a dollar. This represents an immediate 100 percent return on your investment. For every dollar that you invest up to the next 1 percent of your base salary the Company will match it with 50 cents—a 50 percent return on your investment. All contributions are made on a pre-tax basis.

TIP

Applying ideas is a two-step process. Step 1: Make sure you understand the main idea or supporting details. Step 2: Apply that information to the new situation you are given.

1. Fill in the blanks with the correct word from the list below.

    bank   money   401(k)   paycheck

    On the basis of this excerpt, an elective deferral is
    _____ that is taken out of your
    _____ each pay period and deposited
    in your _____ account.

2. Which of the following activities is similar to an elective deferral?

    _____ a. regular withdrawals from a savings account

    _____ b. regular meetings with an investment counselor

    _____ c. regular deposits to a savings account

3. What other account would have the same purpose as a 401(k)?

    _____ a. savings account

    _____ b. checking account

    _____ c. government bonds

    _____ d. individual retirement account

    _____ e. stocks

You were correct if you wrote *money, paycheck,* and *401(k)* for question 1. The answer to question 2 is *option c* because both involve saving money regularly. The answer to question 3 is *option d;* both individual retirement accounts and 401(k) accounts involve saving money for retirement.

Read the following excerpt from a plant care manual and complete the exercise below.

Fungus infection diseases are passed from one plant to another by air circulation, hands (yours), dirty pots, planters, and baskets.

Fungus infections, as a rule, get a start because you get lax in your everyday care and plant comfort conditions. You let the temperatures run above 75° or

(5) below 50° for long periods of time and allow the humidity to get above 60%. Other causes are overwatering, not enough light, pots too close together, and poor air circulation.

If house plant care becomes as much a part of your everyday routine as your daily chores, odds are you won't have these problems.

(10) As a rule, damage caused by these fungus diseases turns the plant tissue soft and mushy, rots leaves and turns foliage gray or brown, fuzzy, and powdered white. With some of the fungus diseases, spots, dents, and depressions appear. If you don't treat these diseases right away, they will end up killing your plants.

Jerry Baker, *Jerry Baker's Happy, Healthy House Plants.*

1. Put a check mark by a conclusion that can be drawn from this article.

_____ a. Plants in hanging baskets are less likely to have fungus infections.

_____ b. Plants in tropical areas are at greater risk of having fungus infections.

_____ c. Plants can die from fungus infections.

2. Explain your answer for question 1.

_____

3. The excerpt states that a person's hands can cause plants to catch fungus infections. Why does this occur?

_____

4. Put a check mark next to the meaning of one of the following sayings that is most like that of the sentence in the third paragraph (lines 8–9).

_____ a. An ounce of prevention is worth a pound of cure.

_____ b. You cannot bake a cake without breaking some eggs.

_____ c. Waste not; want not.

_____ d. A watched pot never boils.

5. Explain your answer for question 4.

_____

_____

Answers start on page 284.

Directions: Choose the <u>one best answer</u> to each question.

<u>Questions 1 through 3</u> refer to the following excerpt from an employee benefits guide.

WHAT ARE THE FEATURES OF THIS PLAN?

  The Company is pleased and proud to announce the addition of vision benefits to our already exceptional benefits package. We pride ourselves on being one of the
(5) most progressive and employee-friendly companies to work for in the United States. Our motto is "We take care of our employees, and they take care of us!" With this in mind, we have added the following
(10) benefits. Please review these benefits carefully. If you have any questions, contact the Human Resources Department.
  The Company will enroll in the EyeCare
(15) Vision Plan, one of the largest networks in the metropolitan area. All employees who are current enrollees in the Company's medical plan will automatically be covered. In order to accomplish this, the Company
(20) will be increasing each employee's health insurance premium by $10 per month, or $120 per year. The plan requires the payment of a $50 yearly deductible per family, after which the network pays
(25) 90 percent of the covered charges.
  In order to receive the 90 percent coinsurance provision, employees must use the ophthalmologists, optometrists, or opticians who participate in the EyeCare
(30) network. Employees who elect to use nonparticipating eyecare professionals will be reimbursed at a 75 percent rate.
  Under the plan, lens replacement (eyeglasses or contact lens) is allowed
(35) every 12 months, but only if necessary due to a change in prescription or damage to the lenses. Frames may be replaced every 24 months. Laser surgery for purely cosmetic purposes is not covered under
(40) the plan. Please contact Human Resources for an enrollment form, description of benefits, and list of participating vision professionals.

1. Based on the excerpt, which of the following defines a "coinsurance provision" (line 27)?

 It is the amount that

 (1) the insurance plan pays
 (2) the employee's company pays
 (3) a second insurer must pay
 (4) the employee pays
 (5) the optometrist must pay

2. Based on the description of the company in the first paragraph, which of the following is the <u>most likely</u> description of the company's policy on paternity leave (time off from work given to new fathers)?

 (1) No paternity leave is granted other than taking accrued sick or personal days.
 (2) Up to 6 months' leave is granted if the father is to be the primary caretaker.
 (3) Paternity leave may be granted for an unlimited period of time.
 (4) Paternity leave is granted for biological children only.
 (5) Paternity leave is not granted other than as a leave of absence.

3. You can infer that the use of approved eyecare professionals is encouraged by the company for which of the following reasons?

 (1) They are more qualified than out-of-network professionals.
 (2) The company receives a fee from them for every employee referral.
 (3) Their use helps to control insurance costs.
 (4) They do not overcharge their patients.
 (5) They have received high professional ratings by healthcare authorities.

WHAT IS THE ADVANTAGE OF VOICE MAIL?

Used correctly, voice mail is a tool to enhance your personal effectiveness and your company's productivity. When it comes to leaving voice mail messages,

(5) your motto should be "Be Prepared." We have already seen that a good number of business telephone calls won't reach their intended parties. You may have also suspected that a detailed message is more than a busy receptionist can handle. That

(10) is where voice mail comes in.

Most voice mail systems let you record a message of any length. Even the ones that put a limit on the length of the

(15) message often give you a minute or more. That is long enough for even the most detailed message. Take advantage of it.

Some people, even those who are comfortable with home answering

(20) machines, still get steamed when they encounter voice mail. After a few bad experiences with people hiding behind their voice mail, anyone can sour on the concept. People who hide behind voice

(25) mail let the machine answer their calls even if they are in the office and not busy. Then they don't return the calls.

The thing to remember about voice mail is that it is not the machine that is keeping

(30) you from the person you want to speak to—not if the company is using the system correctly. What voice mail *is* keeping you from is a harried secretary or receptionist who keeps putting you on hold after taking

(35) your name and phone number and who hangs up on you before you can leave a message.

Madeline Bodin, "Using Voice Mail: A Help or a Hindrance to Your Telephone Effectiveness?" from *Using the Telephone More Effectively.*

4. Based on this excerpt, what is the main purpose of voice mail?

   (1) to take the place of a secretary or receptionist
   (2) to relieve a busy telephone system
   (3) to receive information
   (4) to increase efficiency and productivity
   (5) to eliminate callers being put on hold indefinitely

5. Which of the following is most like voice mail as it is described in this excerpt?

   (1) a cash (ATM) machine
   (2) a home computer
   (3) a calculator
   (4) a digital thermostat
   (5) an office alarm system

6. On the basis of the excerpt, which of the following would the author most likely consider to be a misuse of voice mail?

   (1) choosing to leave a voice mail message rather than speaking to a person directly
   (2) allowing salespeople to call in sales figures to a mail box at the end of the day
   (3) leaving an after-hours message to a client who lives in a different time zone
   (4) leaving a long, detailed message
   (5) using voice mail instead of leaving a message with a receptionist

7. Which of the following best describes the style in which the excerpt is written?

   (1) humorous
   (2) direct
   (3) elaborate
   (4) technical
   (5) dry

TIP When applying ideas, look for similarities between the information you read and the situation to which you must apply it.

Answers start on page 284.

Directions: This is a ten-minute practice test. After ten minutes, mark the last question you finished. Then complete the test and check your answers. If most of your answers were correct, but you didn't finish, try to work faster next time. Choose the one best answer to each question.

Questions 1 through 9 refer to the following excerpt from a writing guide.

WHAT IS SO PAINFUL ABOUT REVISING?

Count on it: the last five minutes you spend on your letter or memo are infinitely more valuable than the first five minutes you spend on it.

(5) Unfortunately, many business writers skip that last five minutes. You know the result. Letters and memos go out filled with errors in fact, logic, spelling, grammar, and punctuation. Just as serious are unrevised

(10) errors in tone—those snarling or petty messages that, with a moment's review, would have been (and should have been) reconsidered.

Like revision? That's a tall order,
(15) especially when business writing itself may not be high on your list of cuddly things.

Writers sometimes have the mistaken notion that revision itself is a form of assassination—killing inch by inch the

(20) gorgeous flow of the first draft. They associate revision with a Mr. or Ms. Gradgrind, English instructor, at some time in their education. Picky, picky, picky.

But contrast that negative mindset with
(25) the attitudes of other creators toward their works. A painter looks at the final touchups of a painting as perfecting it, not fretting it. A musician looks forward to checking out the notes for the final score; without such

(30) checking, the performance may sound like fingernails on a blackboard. Writers, too, should learn to revise with pleasure.

The final check-out and revision of letters and memos may be more palatable
(35) if it happens in five quick steps.

Step One: Does your main message stand out?

Reread your letter or memo from the point of view of your reader. Can you
(40) quickly locate the clear, concise statement

of your main message? Or is it found here and there all over the page, half-buried in long paragraphs? Solutions: Use short, direct sentences to state your main
(45) message. Put your main message in a short paragraph by itself. Tell your reader when you reach your main idea.

Step Two: Will your language appeal to your reader?
(50) Think about the words you've used in your letter or memo. How will your reader interpret those words? Will your message sound too bureaucratic? Too academic? Too chatty? Solutions: Trust common,
(55) simple words to carry your meaning. Use jargon and "intellectual" verbiage only when such words communicate better than any others. Read your message aloud.

Step Three: Do your ideas hang
(60) together logically and persuasively . . . ? Solution: As you reread your message, mentally paraphrase the gist of your idea in each paragraph. . . .

Step Four: Is your letter or memo free
(65) of surface errors? Solutions: Use a spell-checker but don't depend on it to correct incorrect word forms ("bare" when you intended "bear," "it" where you intended "is"). Read your document aloud to
(70) discover omitted words. Scan your letter or memo from back to front to pick up spelling mistakes.

Step Five: How does your letter or memo look on the page? The final "look" of
(75) your document matters as much as all the hard work you've poured into its language and content. . . . Solutions: Ask a co-worker or friend to look over your final draft and make suggestions for improvement. Set
(80) the document aside for a few hours,

then review it at your leisure. In the heat of composition, what looks "good enough" may cry out for revision a few hours later.

Arthur H. Bell and Cherie Kester, "Changing and Rearranging," *Writing Effective Letters and Memos.*

1. According to the authors, what is the most important stage of writing a business letter or memo?

   (1) planning
   (2) writing
   (3) reviewing
   (4) revising
   (5) rewriting

2. Which of the following types of attitudes do the authors think that writers should develop towards revision?

   The attitude of

   (1) a teacher
   (2) a lawyer
   (3) an artist
   (4) an assassin
   (5) a scientist

3. On the basis of the excerpt, which of the following words best describes the process of revising?

   (1) nitpicking
   (2) criticizing
   (3) perfecting
   (4) paraphrasing
   (5) assassinating

4. Which of the following would be the best title for this excerpt?

   (1) Revision in Five Easy Steps
   (2) Writing Is Revising
   (3) Writing Is Rewriting
   (4) Why Writers Hate to Revise
   (5) Revision: The First Step in Rewriting

5. Mark Twain once said that "the difference between the right word and the almost right word is the difference between lightning and the lightning bug." To which step would this saying most apply?

   (1) Step 1
   (2) Step 2
   (3) Step 3
   (4) Step 4
   (5) Step 5

6. According to the excerpt, why is the spell-check mechanism not foolproof?

   (1) Most writers don't know how to use it.
   (2) It sometimes overlooks misspelled words.
   (3) It will not detect context errors.
   (4) It is no substitute for careful proofreading.
   (5) Most writers forget to use it.

7. Step 5 in the revision process is most like which of the following sayings?

   (1) If the shoe fits, wear it.
   (2) It takes a confident person to ask for help.
   (3) When in Rome, do as the Romans.
   (4) Dress for success.
   (5) Pretty is as pretty does.

8. Which of the following best describes the style in which this excerpt is written?

   (1) friendly and informal
   (2) dry and academic
   (3) technical and difficult
   (4) concise and to the point
   (5) humorous and wordy

9. In which of the following patterns is the excerpt primarily organized?

   (1) arranging events by cause and effect
   (2) comparing and contrasting information
   (3) posing a problem and giving a solution
   (4) listing items in order of importance
   (5) discussing familiar items before unfamiliar items

Answers start on page 284.

Lesson 5

GED SKILL Making Inferences

Sometimes when you read nonfiction, facts are only implied or suggested. In such cases you must figure out what the author is saying by using both stated and suggested information. This skill is called **making an inference.**

In Lesson 1, you learned that in some forms of nonfiction writing, the main idea is not directly stated. When the author does not directly state the main idea, you must make an inference to figure it out.

making an inference using stated and suggested information to figure out an unstated idea

To infer the main idea of a paragraph, identify the topic and the details that support it. By seeing how the topic and details are related, you will be able to determine the main idea.

Read the following excerpt from an article and complete the exercise below.

It was the early 1980s. . . . An expert interviewed for the news piece said that in 20 years, thanks to computers, the average workweek was going to be reduced to 20 hours. The United States was going to become a country of leisure and culture. We were going to have more time on our hands to fulfill our dreams. Computers were going to revolutionize medicine, business, communication, government, education, make our existence easier than we could imagine and rid us of the anxieties that plague us. . . .

Jump to the present, the year 2000. The personal computer has proliferated. PCs are saturating larger and larger chunks of U.S. households, and Internet companies are dominating the stock market. Computers have paved the way for extraordinary research in genetics and quantum physics and space exploration. And we work more hours, are more harried and more anxious than ever before.

So much for the 20-hour workweek. . . .

Víctor Landa, "My 20-Hour Workweek Never Arrived," © 2000 Hispanic Link News Service.

1. Put a check mark next to the implied main idea of this excerpt.

    ____ a. Computers have revolutionized many areas of modern life.

    ____ b. Despite predictions to the contrary, computers have made life busier than ever.

2. Put a check mark next to each detail that helped you answer question 1. You should check more than one.

    ____ a. An expert predicted that computers would reduce the average workweek to 20 hours.

    ____ b. Internet companies play an important role in the stock market.

    ____ c. Today we work more hours than ever before.

You were correct if you chose *option b* for question 1. For question 2, the details that support the main idea are *options a* and *c*.

Read the following excerpt from an article and complete the exercise below.

Twyla Tharp is working these days without a company of her own and, until tax structures change, without a permanent base of support. When she gives a performance, as she is now doing at the Brooklyn Academy, the stage is bare, the dancers wear practice clothes and dance to taped music, and the ticket

(5) prices are scaled down. A "poverty" format becomes Twyla Tharp as it does few choreographers. But the economic picture that dancers face today is not pretty. At lunch in a downtown coffee shop recently, Tharp refused to discuss it. "Everybody knows how bad it is and how bad it's going to get. It's boring. I'll have the chicken soup, please. And, by the way, when was it ever good?"

Arlene Croce, "Twyla Tharp Looks Ahead and Thinks Back," *The New Yorker.*

1. Put a check mark by the topic of this paragraph.

   _____ a. dance

   _____ b. the arts

   _____ c. business

   _____ d. theater

2. Based on the information in the paragraph, you can infer that the phrase "'poverty' format" (line 5) means which of the following?

   _____ a. Tharp's performers use musicians and costumes only for performances.

   _____ b. Tharp's pieces deal with the topic of economic struggle.

   _____ c. Tharp has little money to spend to put on performances.

   _____ d. Tharp and her performers are fairly poor.

3. Put a check mark next to the statement that <u>best</u> expresses the main idea of this paragraph.

   _____ a. Tharp's art is thriving because of a very strong economy.

   _____ b. The economy is forcing Tharp's performers to give up their art.

   _____ c. The tax laws penalize those who support the arts.

   _____ d. Due to the economy, the future of Tharp's art is bleak.

4. List four details that show how Tharp's performances have been affected.

   a. _____

   b. _____

   c. _____

   d. _____

Answers start on page 285.

Directions: Choose the one best answer to each question.

Questions 1 through 4 refer to the following excerpt from a biography.

HOW MANY SIDES ARE THERE TO A MAN?

Whiteside was right. All the characteristics of Majority Leader and President Lyndon Baines Johnson that were so unique and vivid when unveiled on
(5) a national stage—the lapel-grabbing, the embracing, the manipulating of men, the "wheeling and dealing"—all these were characteristics that the students at San Marcos had seen. And the similarity
(10) extended to aspects of the man less public. The methods Lyndon Johnson used to attain power on Capitol Hill were the same ones he had used on College Hill, and the similarity went far beyond the
(15) stealing of an election. At San Marcos, the power resided in the hands of a single older man. Johnson had begged that man for the opportunity to run his errands, had searched for more errands to run, had
(20) offered that man an audience when he felt talkative, companionship when he was lonely. And he had flattered him—flattered with a flattery so extravagant and shameless (and skillful) that his peers had
(25) marveled at it. And the friendship of that one older man had armored him against the enmity of hosts of his peers, had given him enough power of his own so that it no longer mattered to him what others thought
(30) of him. In Washington, the names of his patrons—of older men who bestowed power on Lyndon Johnson—would be more famous: Rayburn, Russell, Roosevelt. But the technique would be
(35) the same.

Robert A. Caro, *The Years of Lyndon Johnson: The Path to Power.*

1. On the basis of the excerpt, what is the author's opinion of Lyndon Johnson?

    The author

    (1) admires his skill at campaigning
    (2) believes that he was self-serving
    (3) ranks him as one of the best U.S. presidents
    (4) thinks that he was unqualified to serve
    (5) hates what he stood for

2. Based on the excerpt, which of the following characteristics best explains how Lyndon Johnson attained power?

    (1) He was forceful.
    (2) He had a vivid presence.
    (3) He was extravagant.
    (4) He was a flatterer.
    (5) He was a lapel-grabber.

3. Based on the excerpt, which of the following inferences can you make about Lyndon Johnson's friendships?

    (1) He had more in common with older men than he did with men his own age.
    (2) He tried to become friends with men who could help him.
    (3) He had little respect for men his own age.
    (4) He disliked older men but befriended them anyway.
    (5) He befriended only powerful men.

4. President Johnson got more civil rights legislation passed through Congress than any other U.S. president. Which key idea from the excerpt is supported by this fact?

    (1) Johnson did not care about others' opinions.
    (2) Johnson could wheel and deal.
    (3) Johnson was shameless.
    (4) Johnson wanted to please.
    (5) Johnson was a great man.

Questions 5 through 7 refer to the following excerpt from an editorial.

WHY ARE THESE BUILDINGS THREATENED?

The buildings in the Washington Square Park area provide a unique glimpse into our city's past.

(5) The tourist-drawing character of this and other downtown neighborhoods is under an increasing threat. Residential construction is booming in the South Loop, West Loop, and Near North Side. In general this is a great thing for our city.

(10) But what if a potential construction site is already occupied by beautiful buildings?

Sadly, this question is sometimes answered by the sound of a wrecking ball. Never mind that a piece of land may

(15) already be occupied by Victorian mansions or an attractive row of Italianate, three-story buildings from the 1870s. In response to such concerns, the new buildings often are made very enticing.

(20) "We'll even make it Art Deco," a developer might say. Or, "How about a Beaux Arts design?"

Given these options, we should keep the 1870s buildings every time. In such

(25) cases, no new building—no matter how elegant the design—can improve on what is already there.

This principle applies to a potential new project at the corner of Dearborn and

(30) Elm Streets in the Washington Square Park area.

One of the development-inducing buzzwords is "underutilized." You might hear this word in reference to a piece of

(35) land that has not achieved its highest tax-generating potential.

Sure, a new high-rise structure will generate more real estate tax revenue. But when there is demand in the marketplace

(40) for such buildings, they should *first* be placed on *non-historic* sites.

. . . The rights of property owners should be balanced against the wider public good. This good includes preserving

(45) beauty and history, as well as achieving the related (though sometimes intangible) economic benefits of preservation.

Michael C. Moran, "Saving downtown's gems,"
Chicago Tribune.

5. Which of the following is the <u>best</u> restatement of the last sentence of the excerpt?

  (1) Preserving historic properties brings in sizable tourist dollars.
  (2) Historic preservation is directly related to a city's economic growth.
  (3) The public interest should come before private interests.
  (4) The benefits of preservation can't always be measured in dollars and cents.
  (5) There is no comparison between tax dollars realized and tourist dollars spent.

6. Based on the information in the excerpt, what is <u>most likely</u> the chief concern of real estate developers?

  (1) increasing the city's property tax rolls
  (2) increasing the office space available
  (3) making profits from new building projects
  (4) maintaining the character of the neighborhoods
  (5) relieving the shortage in affordable housing

7. Which of the following is the overall purpose of this editorial?

  (1) to raise awareness about the importance of preserving historic buildings
  (2) to stimulate tourism by promoting the city's past
  (3) to criticize the city's zoning officials
  (4) to put a stop to all downtown construction
  (5) to impress readers with the author's knowledge of architectural styles

 TIP To figure out an implied main idea, read the entire excerpt. What does the author's attitude seem to be toward his or her topic? What is the author hinting at? Asking these questions may give you clues that help you determine the main idea.

Answers start on page 285.

Directions: This is a ten-minute practice test. After ten minutes, mark the last question you finished. Then complete the test and check your answers. If most of your answers were correct, but you didn't finish, try to work faster next time. Choose the <u>one best answer</u> to each question.

Questions 1 through 9 refer to the following excerpt from a biography.

WHERE WILL ISHI GO?

The black face of the white man's Demon rushed toward the platform, pouring out clouds of sparks and smoke, and filling the ears with its hollow, moaning
(5) voice. Mill Creek and Deer Creek were within range of the sound of that voice; twice a day Ishi had heard it ever since he could remember, and he had watched the train hundreds of times as it snaked along
(10) below him, bellowing and belching. His mother had reassured him as a small boy when he was afraid of it, telling him that it was a Demon who followed white men wherever they went, but that Indians need
(15) have no fear of it; it never bothered them.
        Today, Ishi wondered. He had not been so near it before; it was larger and noisier and speedier than he had realized. Would the Demon know that he was Indian? He
(20) was wearing white men's clothes, and his hair was short like theirs. It might be as well to watch from a little distance, from the shelter of a tree or bush, as he was accustomed to, at least until he made sure
(25) that his friend was correct in his assurance that the Demon always stayed in its own old tracks, and that it carried people safely from place to place. He stepped behind a cottonwood tree alongside the platform.
(30) The Demon drew up beside the station and came to a halt. Ishi saw that it was as his friend had said—it did not leave its tracks. The white men who should have the most reason to be afraid, showed no
(35) signs of uneasiness, rather they climbed in and out of it, and one of them sat in its head waving to those below. Ishi came back onto the platform, and made no

objection to going aboard with Waterman.
(40) He had committed himself too far to turn back, nor did he wish to do so; where his new friend led he would follow.
        During the trip, Ishi sat very quiet. He found the speed of the train exciting; also
(45) the view through the window of hills and fields and houses racing in and out of sight. He averted his eyes from the strangers in the car, blotting out their nearness by not looking directly at them.
(50) The Demon carried them rapidly down its old tracks and after some hours onto a ferry boat which took them, engine, cars, and passengers, across Carquinez Straits. Waterman pointed out to him that this was
(55) where the Sacramento and San Joaquin rivers join, flow into the bay, and out the Golden Gate to the ocean. Like all inland Indians, Ishi knew that such was the destination of the creeks and rivers of his
(60) home, but, again like other inlanders, he was vague about how the river journey was actually accomplished, for his informants had known of it only traditionally and at many removes from any one who
(65) had seen either river mouth or ocean. He was sorry to leave the train at the Oakland Mole, but ahead lay further wonders— another ferry trip, this time across the bay to San Francisco; and after that, a long
(70) ride in a trolley car to the Museum of Anthropology.

Theodora Kroeber, *Ishi in Two Worlds: A Biography of the Last Wild Indian in North America.*

1. Who or what is the "Demon" according to this excerpt?

    (1) Ishi
    (2) a train
    (3) Waterman
    (4) a trolley car
    (5) a boat

2. Which of the following writing techniques is used in this excerpt?

It is written

(1) as if the author knows what Ishi is thinking
(2) as if Ishi himself were telling the story to an audience
(3) as if Ishi had written the story in the form of a diary
(4) as if the author does not understand the way Ishi feels
(5) as if it were a newspaper report

3. Based on the information in the excerpt, which of the following best describes how the author feels about the subject?

(1) fearful
(2) confused
(3) sympathetic
(4) bored
(5) angry

4. The description of the train in the excerpt accomplishes which of the following?

(1) It explains why white men like trains.
(2) It emphasizes that the train seemed alive.
(3) It proves that trains are evil.
(4) It shows the beauty and power of technology.
(5) It suggests the reason for the failure of the railroad.

5. Which of the following best describes Ishi?

(1) He often misses his mother.
(2) He tries to avoid unfamiliar situations.
(3) He has many close friends.
(4) He had never expected to ride a train.
(5) He believes whatever others tell him.

6. To which of the following does the phrase "hollow, moaning voice" (lines 4–5) most likely refer?

(1) the noise of the passengers getting on and off the train
(2) the clank of the train's wheels
(3) a noise Ishi made as a child to imitate the sound of the train
(4) the hooting of the train's whistle
(5) the clouds of smoke and sparks that pour out of the train

7. Based on the excerpt, Ishi would most likely have which of the following reactions to a ride in a taxi cab?

(1) resistance to experiencing another white man's invention
(2) excitement at another new experience
(3) disappointment that the taxi cab does not move as fast as the train
(4) disgust at the replacement of older forms of transportation
(5) a desire to get a job as a taxi cab driver

8. Based on the excerpt, which of the following is the best explanation of why the train route is important to Ishi?

(1) It will be the only time he ever experiences a train ride.
(2) It gives him time to get to know Waterman.
(3) It lets him experience the journey of rivers and creeks.
(4) It allows him to experience technology.
(5) It is the means to his reaching San Francisco.

9. Based on the information in the excerpt, why does Ishi ask himself if the Demon would know he was Indian (lines 18–19)?

(1) Ishi believed the Demon hated Indians.
(2) Ishi wanted the Demon to notice him.
(3) Ishi wanted the Demon to think he was a white man.
(4) Ishi did not want the Demon to follow him.
(5) Ishi did not want the Demon to become angry.

Answers start on page 286.

GED SKILL **Identifying Style and Tone**

Style and tone are two important aspects of writing. **Style** is the way a writer writes—the kinds of words he or she chooses and the way they are arranged to form sentences and paragraphs. Writers choose a style of writing that best fits the subject they are writing about. A writer's style sometimes indicates how he or she feels about the subject. **Tone** results from style. It is the feeling that a writer wants you to get from a piece of writing. It is revealed through word choice and it reflects the author's attitudes and feelings about a subject.

style
the way a writer writes—the words and sentence structure used to convey ideas

tone
the writer's attitude as revealed by the words he or she chooses

Read the following excerpt from a personal essay and complete the exercise below.

Until I moved to western South Dakota, I did not know about rain, that it could come too hard, too soft, too hot, too cold, too early, too late. That there could be too little at the right time, too much at the wrong time, and vice versa.

I did not know that a light rain coming at the end of a hot afternoon, with the temperature at 100 degrees or more, can literally burn wheat, steaming it on the stalk so it's not worth harvesting.

I had not seen a long, slow rain come at harvest, making grain lying in the swath begin to sprout again, ruining it as a cash crop.

Kathleen Norris, "Rain," from *Dakota*.

1. Which of the following characteristics describe the style of the first paragraph? Put a check mark next to all that apply.

 _____ a. repetition of a key word

 _____ b. short, simple sentences

 _____ c. use of the first-person pronoun "I"

 _____ d. use of a string of opposites

2. Put a check mark next to the two words that describe the style of this excerpt.

 _____ a. technical

 _____ b. simple

 _____ c. informal

3. Which word best describes the tone of the excerpt?

 _____ a. serious

 _____ b. sarcastic

 _____ c. sentimental

TIP

Listen to the way the words "sound" in your ear. What emotion do they communicate?

You were correct if you checked *options a, c,* and *d* for question 1. The correct answers to question 2 are *options b* and *c;* the correct answer for question 3 is *option a.*

Read the following excerpt from a speech and complete the exercise below.

Sure, I'm lucky. Who wouldn't consider it an honor to have known Jacob Ruppert; also the builder of baseball's greatest empire, Ed Barow; to have spent six years with that wonderful little fellow Miller Huggins; then to have spent the next nine years with that outstanding leader, that smart student of psychology—the

(5) best manager in baseball today—Joe McCarthy!

Sure, I'm lucky. When the New York Giants, a team you would give your right arm to beat, and vice versa, sends you a gift, that's something. When everybody down to the groundskeepers and those boys in white coats remember you with trophies, that's something.

(10) When you have a wonderful mother-in-law who takes sides with you in squabbles against her own daughter, that's something. When you have a father and mother who work all their lives so you can have an education and build your body, it's a blessing. When you have a wife who has been a tower of strength and shown more courage than you dreamed existed, that's the finest I know.

(15) So I close in saying that I might have had a tough break, but I have an awful lot to live for!

"Baseball Great Lou Gehrig, Suffering from a Fatal Disease, Thanks His Fans and Considers Himself the 'Luckiest Man on the Face of the Earth,'" *In Our Own Words: Extraordinary Speeches of the American Century.*

1. Put a check mark next to the word that best describes the language in the excerpt.

_____ a. exaggerated

_____ b. conversational

_____ c. intellectual

2. Put a check mark next to the word that best describes the tone conveyed by this excerpt.

_____ a. sad

_____ b. ironic

_____ c. sincere

3. List two phrases that are repeated for emphasis in this excerpt.

_____

_____

4. Put a check mark next to the word that best describes the style of this excerpt.

_____ a. formal

_____ b. informal

_____ c. complex

Answers start on page 287.

Directions: Choose the one best answer to each question.

Questions 1 through 4 refer to the following excerpt from an essay.

HOW DOES A TEACHER AND POET GRADE HIS STUDENTS?

There are two ways of coming close to poetry. One is by writing poetry. And some people think I want people to write poetry, but I don't; that is, I don't necessarily. I only
(5) want people to write poetry if they want to write poetry. I have never encouraged anybody to write poetry that did not want to write it, and I have not always encouraged those who did want to write it. That ought
(10) to be one's own funeral. It is a hard, hard life, as they say. . . .
There is another way to come close to poetry, fortunately, and that is in the reading of it, not as linguistics, not as
(15) history, not as anything but poetry. It is one of the hard things for a teacher to know how close a man has come in reading poetry. How do I know whether a man has come close to Keats in reading Keats? It is
(20) hard for me to know. I have lived with some boys a whole year over some of the poets and I have not felt sure whether they have come near what it was all about. One remark sometimes told me.
(25) One remark was their mark for the year; had to be—it was all I got that told me what I wanted to know. And that is enough, if it is the right remark, if it came close enough. I think a man might make twenty
(30) fool remarks if he made one good one some time in the year. His mark would depend on that good remark.

Robert Frost, "Education by Poetry," *The Selected Prose of Robert Frost.*

1. What does Frost mean when he talks about "coming close to poetry" (lines 1–2)?

   (1) being near great poets
   (2) leading a poetic life
   (3) being able to recite poetry
   (4) understanding poetry
   (5) translating poetry

2. On the basis of the excerpt, which of the following best describes what Frost thinks about teaching and understanding poetry?

   (1) Both are inexact and unscientific.
   (2) Both require historical knowledge.
   (3) Both benefit from religious faith.
   (4) Both are a waste of time.
   (5) Both are subjects for linguists.

3. Which of the following statements best sums up Frost's ideas about grading?

   (1) A student who doesn't wish to write poetry will not receive a good mark.
   (2) A student must be exact in his or her understanding of a poem.
   (3) Grading a student's understanding of poetry is difficult and circumstantial.
   (4) A student who makes more than 20 foolish remarks will fail.
   (5) Grading a student's understanding of poetry can sometimes take a whole year.

4. Which of the following phrases best describes the style in which the essay is written?

   (1) formal and informative
   (2) dry and complex
   (3) technical and scientific
   (4) emotional and artistic
   (5) serious and conversational

Questions 5 through 8 refer to the following excerpt from a speech.

WHAT IS THIS LEADER'S GOAL FOR HIS COUNTRY?

We have waited too long for our freedom! We can no longer wait. Now is the time to intensify the struggle on all fronts. To relax our efforts now would be a
(5) mistake which generations to come will not be able to forgive. The sight of freedom looming on the horizon should encourage us to redouble our efforts. It is only through disciplined mass action that our victory can
(10) be assured.

We call on our white compatriots to join us in the shaping of a new South Africa. The freedom movement is a political home for you, too. We call on the international
(15) community to continue the campaign to isolate the apartheid regime. To lift sanctions now would be to run the risk of aborting the process towards the complete eradication of apartheid.
(20) Our march to freedom is irreversible. We must not allow fear to stand in our way. Universal suffrage on a common voters' roll in a united, democratic and non-racial South Africa is the only way to peace and
(25) racial harmony.

In conclusion, I wish to go to my own words during my trial in 1964. They are as true today as they were then. I quote:
'I have fought against white domination
(30) and I have fought against black domination. I have cherished the ideal of a democratic and free society in which all persons live together in harmony and with equal opportunity. It is an ideal which I
(35) hope to live for and to achieve. But if needs be, it is an ideal for which I am prepared to die. *Amandla* (power)!'

Nelson Mandela, Cape Town, 11 February 1990, "Our March to Freedom Is Irreversible," *The Penguin Book of Twentieth-Century Speeches.*

5. What is the speaker in this excerpt appealing to South Africans to do?

   (1) go to the polls and vote
   (2) step up their efforts to end apartheid
   (3) give up the fight for equal rights
   (4) be patient with the apartheid regime
   (5) petition the international community for help

6. Which of the following phrases is closest in meaning to that of the phrase "freedom looming on the horizon" (lines 6–7)?

Freedom is

   (1) just out of reach
   (2) like the dawn of a new day
   (3) waiting nearby
   (4) inevitable
   (5) in view

7. What is the main effect of the speaker's repeated use of the word "we"?

   (1) It puts him on the level of the common people.
   (2) It emphasizes the need to work together.
   (3) It takes the focus off the speaker himself.
   (4) It sets up a contrast with the use of "I" in the last two paragraphs.
   (5) It demonstrates the selflessness of the speaker.

8. Which of the following **best** describes the tone of this speech?

   (1) apologetic
   (2) snobby
   (3) defiant
   (4) impassioned
   (5) hostile

 TIP Look at the types of sentences in an excerpt. Short sentences with strong verbs often indicate an urgent tone.

Answers start on page 287.

Directions: This is a ten-minute practice test. After ten minutes, mark the last question you finished. Then complete the test and check your answers. If most of your answers were correct, but you didn't finish, try to work faster next time. Choose the <u>one best answer</u> to each question.

<u>Questions 1 through 8</u> refer to the following excerpt from an essay.

IS IT POSSIBLE TO RECAPTURE THE PLEASURES OF THE PAST?

One summer, along about 1904, my father rented a camp on a lake in Maine and took us all there for the month of August. We all got ringworm from some

(5) kittens and had to rub Pond's Extract on our arms and legs night and morning, and my father rolled over in a canoe with all his clothes on; but outside of that the vacation was a success and from then on none of

(10) us ever thought there was any place in the world like that lake in Maine. We returned summer after summer—always on August 1 for one month. I have since become a salt-water man, but sometimes in summer

(15) there are days when the restlessness of the tides and the fearful cold of the sea water and the incessant wind which blows across the afternoon and into the evening make me wish for the placidity of a lake in

(20) the woods. A few weeks ago this feeling got so strong I bought myself a couple of bass hooks and a spinner and returned to the lake where we used to go, for a week's fishing and to revisit old haunts.

(25) I took along my son, who had never had any fresh water up his nose and who had seen lily pads only from train windows. On the journey over to the lake I began to wonder what it would be like. I wondered

(30) how time would have marred this unique, this holy spot—the coves and streams, the hills that the sun set behind, the camps and paths behind the camps. I was sure the tarred road would have found it out and

(35) I wondered in what other ways it would be desolated. It is strange how much you can remember about places like that once you allow your mind to return into the grooves which lead back. You remember one thing,

(40) and that suddenly reminds you of another thing. I guess I remembered clearest of all the early mornings, when the lake was cool and motionless, remembered how the bedroom smelled of the lumber it was

(45) made of and of the wet woods whose scent entered through the screen. The partitions in the camp were thin and did not extend clear to the top of the rooms, and as I was always the first up I would

(50) dress softly so as not to wake the others, and sneak out into the sweet outdoors and start out in the canoe, keeping close along the shore in the long shadows of the pines. I remembered being very careful never to

(55) rub my paddle against the gunwale for fear of disturbing the stillness of the cathedral.

The lake had not been what you would call a wild lake. There were cottages

(60) sprinkled around the shores, and it was in farming country although the shores of the lake were quite heavily wooded. Some of the cottages were owned by nearby farmers, and you would live at the shore

(65) and eat your meals at the farmhouse. That's what our family did. But although it wasn't wild, it was a fairly large and undisturbed lake and there were places in it that, to a child at least, seemed infinitely

(70) remote and primeval.

I was right about the tar: it led to within half a mile of the shore. But when I got back there, with my boy, and we settled into a camp near a farmhouse and into the

(75) kind of summertime I had known, I could tell that it was going to be pretty much the same as it had been before—I knew it, lying in bed the first morning, smelling the bedroom and hearing the boy sneak

(80) quietly out and go off along the shore in a boat. I began to sustain the illusion that he was I, and therefore, by simple transposition, that I was my father. This sensation persisted, kept cropping up all

(85) the time we were there. It was not an
entirely new feeling, but in this setting it
grew much stronger. I seemed to be living
a dual existence. I would be in the middle
of some simple act, I would be picking up
(90) a bait box or laying down a table fork, or I
would be saying something, and suddenly
it would be not I but my father who was
saying the words or making the gesture. It
gave me a creepy sensation.

E.B. White, "Once More to the Lake," *One Man's Meat.*

1. Which of the following characterizes this
   excerpt as informal writing?

   (1) It is very serious and dignified.
   (2) It reads like a scientific report.
   (3) It has an urgent, emotional tone.
   (4) It has an easygoing, chatty tone.
   (5) It has a cool, impersonal tone.

2. What does the author mean when he says he
   was afraid "the tarred road would have found
   it out" (line 34)?

   (1) The road would no longer be there.
   (2) Civilization would have come to the lake.
   (3) A tar factory would have been built there.
   (4) Little change would have occurred there.
   (5) No one would have paved the road yet.

3. What does the author mean when he says
   that his son "never had any fresh water up his
   nose" (lines 25–26)?

   (1) His son was very good at swimming.
   (2) His son hated the water.
   (3) His son had never been in the water.
   (4) His son had never swum in a lake.
   (5) His son was used to swimming pools.

4. Which of the following expressions <u>best</u> states
   the main idea of this excerpt?

   (1) He's a chip off the old block.
   (2) There is nothing new under the sun.
   (3) The more things change, the more they
       stay the same.
   (4) The child is father of the man.
   (5) A wise son maketh a glad father.

5. Which of the following does the excerpt <u>most</u>
   strongly imply about the author's feelings?

   (1) He is happy only when spending time
       outdoors.
   (2) He disapproves of all signs of progress.
   (3) He longs to recapture the joys of his
       youth.
   (4) He is bored with vacations by the sea.
   (5) He has a passion for freshwater fishing.

6. Which of the following statements <u>best</u>
   explains what the author means by "dual
   existence" (line 88)?

   (1) He was developing two personalities.
   (2) He was experiencing the lake from both
       his own and his father's perspectives.
   (3) He was becoming both a saltwater and a
       freshwater man.
   (4) He and his son were living together.
   (5) His son was becoming more like him
       while at the lake.

7. Which of the following sentences <u>best</u>
   explains the author's statement "It gave me a
   creepy sensation" (lines 93–94)?

   (1) He found it strange that nothing about the
       lake had changed.
   (2) He felt his father's spirit during the
       vacation.
   (3) He realized how much children take on
       the habits of their parents.
   (4) He had a premonition that he would die
       soon.
   (5) He felt himself turning into the man his
       father once was.

8. What is the main purpose of the first
   paragraph?

   (1) to introduce the basic situation that the
       essay will address
   (2) to put the reader in the mood to
       experience the author's recollections
   (3) to describe the author's relationship with
       his father
   (4) to establish the theme of the essay
   (5) to describe the author's relationship with
       his son

Answers start on page 287.

GED SKILL **Drawing Conclusions**

When you **draw conclusions,** you consider the facts presented in a given situation and then think of reasonable explanations for those facts. Consider the following situation: You put a slice of bread in the toaster and push down the lever to toast it. After a minute you come back to find your toaster cold and your bread unbrowned. You unplug the toaster and plug it into a different outlet. This time the toaster works perfectly. Based on the fact that the toaster worked in the second outlet, you conclude that there is a problem with the original outlet.

drawing conclusions making decisions based on all the facts provided in a given situation

TIP

To draw a correct conclusion, list all of the available facts and then think of reasonable explanations for them.

Read the following excerpt from an article and answer the questions below.

Perhaps we should give a hand to Linda Hamilton's arms. After the "Terminator 2" actress unveiled her buff biceps eight years ago, more and more women ventured where none dared go before, embracing weight lifting, boxing, rock climbing, martial arts and almost every other form of vigorous exercise once known only to man. "There is no gender difference in working out anymore," says Radu, a New York City trainer whose clients include Cindy Crawford. It's not just about vanity—although the possibility of banishing cellulite forever is certainly part of the lure of extreme exercise. Intense workouts also head off osteoporosis and depression and build self-esteem, says Dr. Miriam Nelson, author of "Strong Women Stay Young": "The whole mind-body connection is really there." And there's the lift that comes from knowing that whatever he can do, you can probably do better.

"Living Well," *Newsweek.*

1. Which of the following conclusions does this excerpt support?

    _____ a. Intense exercise is the most popular form of exercise among women today.

    _____ b. Intense exercise is good for everyone.

    _____ c. Intense exercise has several benefits for women.

2. Which two details from the excerpt support your choice for question 1?

    _____

    _____

You were correct if you chose *option c* for question 1. Details that you may have written for question 2 include *the possibility of banishing cellulite forever,* and *head off osteoporosis and depression and build self-esteem.*

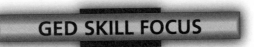

Read the following excerpt from a biography and complete the exercise below.

Here was this man, Louis Armstrong, just before the show was due to start, waiting silently. He was smartly dressed, in dinner jacket, and holding his Selmer trumpet. The band was ready—there had been no rehearsal—and he was about to perform. Then Collins suddenly said, "Where's the dough? If I don't get the

(5) dough, Louis don't play." The promoter had a huge crowd and there was no problem. He offered a cheque but Collins was adamant—no cash, no Louis. It must have been humiliating for Louis, though he showed no sign of it. He just looked at the floor and went on swinging his trumpet in his hand until such time as matters were settled. He seemed utterly detached as this pasty-faced man with

(10) the cigar in his mouth demanded the money there and then, or no show. I estimate they had some two thousand people in there, and the promoter went to his box office and came back with several bags of half-crowns, of silver anyway, and put them down in front of Collins. "There's your money," he told Collins, and I remember thinking: he doesn't know how to count it.

Max Jones and John Chilton, *Louis, The Louis Armstrong Story 1900–1971.*

1. Which of the following is a conclusion that can be drawn from this excerpt?

_____ a. Collins is the promoter of Armstrong's show.

_____ b. Armstrong and Collins often argue publicly.

_____ c. Collins handles Armstrong's money.

_____ d. Collins is one of Armstrong's biggest fans.

2. Put a check mark next to each fact that supports this conclusion.

_____ a. Collins demands payment from the promoter.

_____ b. Armstrong waited for the matter to be settled.

_____ c. A huge crowd came to hear Armstrong play.

_____ d. The promoter went to his office to get the money.

3. For which of the following reasons can you conclude that this scene did not occur in the United States? Put a check mark next to all that apply.

_____ a. The word "cheque" is a spelling of "check" not used in the United States.

_____ b. Collins refused to accept a cheque, demanding cash.

_____ c. The promoter came back with several bags of half-crowns of silver.

_____ d. The band had not rehearsed.

_____ e. The speaker thought that Collins did not know how to count the money.

Answers start on page 288.

Directions: Choose the <u>one best answer</u> to each question.

<u>Questions 1 through 3</u> refer to the following excerpt from an article.

HOW IS THIS SHOW KEPT RUNNING?

Any visitor to the Burbank production offices of "E.R.," the NBC medical drama series, could quickly discern who is the guiding force behind the biggest network
(5) hit in several years.

It is not Michael Crichton, the novelist and screenwriter, who created the show, wrote its pilot episode—and departed almost immediately to write new novels.
(10) It is not Steven Spielberg, whose Amblin Television company took the project to a big studio, Warner Brothers. It is not Leslie Moonves, the president of Warner Brothers Television, which produces the
(15) show for NBC.

It is a man named John Wells, a veteran television scriptwriter, most notably for "China Beach."

At any one moment, Mr. Wells is
(20) supervising the content and execution of at least four one-hour episodes in various stages of development—from script to filming to editing to post-production. Future story lines of the series are also his
(25) responsibility. . . . In the terms of the trade, Mr. Wells is "E.R." 's show runner.

For the last 10 years at least, the person with that unofficial title has been the true auteur [creator] of series
(30) television. Day to day, a show runner makes all important decisions about the series' scripts, tone, attitude, look and direction. He or she oversees casting, production design and budget. This person
(35) chooses directors and guest stars, defends the show against meddling by the network or production company and, when necessary, changes its course.

Even in this notoriously collaborative
(40) medium, show runners are responsible for what viewers see on the screen. Yet the show runner's true position and influence are unknown to nearly everyone on the other side of the picture tube.

Andy Meisler, "The Man Who Keeps *E.R.'s* Heart Beating," *The New York Times.*

1. Based on this excerpt, which of the following conclusions can be made about producing a television series?

   (1) Show runners and screenwriters share responsibility for a show's success.
   (2) Production companies often interfere with a show's management.
   (3) Show runners are among the most important people in television.
   (4) The creation of a hit show is often a matter of luck.
   (5) Veteran scriptwriters are responsible for television shows.

2. Which of the following responsibilities might a show runner delegate to someone else?

   (1) writing the pilot for a related new show
   (2) hiring actors
   (3) approving the story line for an episode
   (4) reducing actors' salaries
   (5) changing the location of the set

3. Irony can be defined as the difference between what you expect to be true and what actually is true. Which of the following is <u>most</u> ironic in this excerpt?

   (1) The most important person on the set of a TV series is the director.
   (2) The guiding force behind *E.R.* is largely unknown to viewers.
   (3) Show runners do not like to collaborate.
   (4) The show runner supervises more than one show at a time.
   (5) *E.R.* remains one of the most highly watched shows on TV.

Questions 4 through 7 refer to the following excerpt from an article.

WHAT IS HAPPENING AT THE ROOSEVELT HOTEL?

By seven o-clock I was dead tired and soaked with rain and perspiration. I walked to the Roosevelt, hoping to get a room for a brief rest. Instead of taking guests,

(5) however, the hotel was busy evacuating them. There were no lights, and the threat of explosion from escaping gas had increased throughout the demolished area. Another warning of the possibility of a

(10) second tornado had been issued. Fearful persons jammed the lobby in silent wait for the next blow.

The Roosevelt switchboard had one telephone circuit in operation. The operator

(15) called the Raleigh Hotel up the street and reserved rooms for Roy Miller and me, although I did not know Roy's whereabouts at the time. Next time I saw him he said he had driven to Hillsboro, about thirty-five

(20) miles away, to telephone his wife and reassure her of his safety. He was fuming.

"I drive seventy miles to call my wife," he said; "I says, 'Honey, I'm all right. I'm safe. You don't need to worry any longer.' And

(25) what do I get? She says, 'Who's worried? You always have been all right. Why do you have to call me long distance to tell me so? Roy Miller,' she says, 'what have you been up to?'" Mrs. Miller had not heard of

(30) the storm.

Ira A. J. Baden as told to Robert H. Parham, "Forty-five Seconds Inside a Tornado," *Man Against Nature.*

 TIP

When drawing conclusions, eliminate explanations that the facts do not support.

4. Which of the following conclusions most accurately sums up the general situation described in the excerpt?

   (1) Men worry about what their wives will think.
   (2) The Raleigh Hotel had a great deal of business during the storm.
   (3) People were reacting to the tornado's effects.
   (4) The tornado had shut down phone service near the town.
   (5) Tornadoes can cause gas leaks.

5. Why did Mrs. Miller respond to her husband's phone call the way that she did?

   (1) She was not afraid of tornadoes.
   (2) She was too worried about the tornadoes near her to think about her husband.
   (3) She did not care about her husband.
   (4) She had slept through the tornado.
   (5) She did not understand why her husband had contacted her.

6. Which of the following best describes the tone of this excerpt?

   (1) suspenseful
   (2) comical
   (3) tragic
   (4) mournful
   (5) playful

7. Which of the following describes the style in which this excerpt is written?

   It is written in the style of

   (1) an urban legend
   (2) a newspaper article
   (3) an eyewitness account
   (4) a television interview
   (5) a police report

 TIP

You can use your own knowledge and experience combined with the facts from an excerpt to help you draw conclusions.

Answers start on page 288.

GED Mini-Test • Lesson 7

Directions: This is a ten-minute practice test. After ten minutes, mark the last question you finished. Then complete the test and check your answers. If most of your answers were cor~~~~ but you didn't finish, try to work faster next time. Choose the one best answer to each qu~~~~

Questions 1 through 4 refer to the following excerpt from a nonfiction book.

WHERE IS THE EDGE OF NOWHERE?

My mother was Athabascan, born around 1875 in a little village at the mouth of the Hogatza River, a long day's walk north of the Arctic Circle. The country
(5)   was wild enough—blizzards and sixty-below cold all the winter months, and floods when the ice tore loose in spring, swamping the tundra with spongy muskegs[1] so that a man might travel down
(10)   the rivers, but could never make a summer portage[2] of more than a mile or so between them.
And the people matched the land. From the earliest time in Alaska, there had been
(15)   bad feeling between Indian and Eskimo, and here the two lived close together, forever stirring each other to anger and violence. If an Indian lost his bearings and tracked the caribou past the divide that
(20)   separated the two hunting grounds, his people would soon be preparing a potlatch in his memory, for he was almost sure to be shot or ground-sluiced, and his broken body left for the buzzards. Naturally this
(25)   worked both ways. Then, in the 1890's, prospectors found gold to the west, on the Seward Peninsula, and the white man came tearing through. Mostly he was mean as a wounded grizzly. He never
(30)   thought twice about cheating or stealing from the native people, or even killing a whole family if he needed their dog team— anything to get to Nome and the gold on those beaches.

---
[1] swamps or bogs
[2] carrying a boat between waterways

James Huntington and Lawrence Elliott, *On the Edge of Nowhere.*

1. Which of the following conclusions c~~~~ drawn from the authors' statement, ~~~~ people matched the land" (line 13)?

    (1) The white man cheated and s~~~~
    (2) The people looked rugged ar~~~~gy.
    (3) A man killed by an enemy was n~~~~uried.
    (4) The people were as violent as the weather.
    (5) The people endured cold winters.

2. Based on context clues, what is the most likely meaning of the phrase "preparing a potlatch in his memory" (lines 21–22)?

    (1) preparing a dance of celebration
    (2) preparing a special ceremony
    (3) preparing a ceremonial bowl
    (4) preparing a welcome-home dinner
    (5) preparing an annual party

3. Based on the excerpt, what happened when gold was discovered on Seward Peninsula?

    (1) Both Indians and Eskimos made fortunes.
    (2) The white man invaded native lands.
    (3) Violence between Indians and Eskimos decreased.
    (4) The country was tamed.
    (5) The white man began to work with the Indians and Eskimos.

4. Which of the following is the most likely reason that the authors titled this book *On the Edge of Nowhere*?

    The land the authors describe

    (1) is not located on any map
    (2) is easy to become lost in
    (3) is located in a very remote region
    (4) exists only in the authors' imagination
    (5) is unpopulated today

Questions 5 through 8 refer to the following excerpt from a review.

WHAT IS ONE OF THE MOST OVERESTIMATED PAINTINGS?

Unquestionably the most glittering personality of the high renaissance in Italy and the pioneer in its new and magnificent form of expression was Leonardo da Vinci.
(5) Even as a youth he displayed an aptitude for all manner of achievement, a winning charm, and a personal strength and beauty which have become almost legendary. In time this brilliant boy would
(10) become not only one of the leading artists of the sixteenth century, but its greatest contributor to the advancement of modern ideas as well. Leonardo possessed a variety of artistic talents—he was
(15) architect, sculptor, musician. He also mastered and did original work in the fields of mathematics, geology, engineering, anatomy, and every other science known in his day. More than anyone else he had
(20) "taken all knowledge as his sphere." Leonardo spent the early part of his life in Florence and then stayed in Milan for a number of years working on many important projects, including the *Madonna*
(25) *of the Rocks* and the *Last Supper*. The latter (perhaps the best known painting in the world) offers one of the finest instances of a rigid geometric enclosure. Everything turns inward toward the head of Christ,
(30) even the expressive gestures of His own hands. In spite of the great excitement within the work, complete formal control is maintained. . . .
In the *Mona Lisa*, one of the most
(35) overdiscussed and overrated pictures of all time (through no fault of its own), the same balance of monumental form and lyrical feeling is evident. This poetic sense, here as in many other works, is a definite
(40) Leonardo quality. It has little to do with portraiture, that is, with analysis of the sitter. If it is considered part of the painter's own personality, and not that of the somewhat smug[1] lady, the picture takes
(45) on a different meaning. Certainly it is mysterious, but so are Leonardo's other paintings. To this artist, all things, human and divine, were fit subjects for the searching analysis of his extraordinary
(50) mind.

---

[1] self-satisfied

Bernard Myers, *Fifty Great Artists*.

5. What does it mean that da Vinci took "all knowledge as his sphere" (line 20)?

   (1) He was a brilliant man.
   (2) He was confused by career possibilities.
   (3) He had varied interests.
   (4) He felt unhappy being a painter.
   (5) He could not concentrate on one subject.

6. Based on this excerpt, which of the following describes why the *Mona Lisa* is mysterious?

   (1) Dark and gloomy colors were used.
   (2) Everything turns inward towards the lady's head.
   (3) This quality is common to da Vinci's style.
   (4) The lady in the painting is somewhat smug.
   (5) Da Vinci analyzed the sitter before painting.

7. Which of the following is most likely true of the author based on the excerpt?

   (1) He is an artist himself.
   (2) He is a knowledgeable art critic.
   (3) He is an authority on the Renaissance.
   (4) He collects da Vinci's works.
   (5) He owns an art gallery.

8. Which statement accurately contrasts the *Last Supper* and the *Mona Lisa* based on the opinions expressed in the excerpt?

   (1) Both paintings remain relatively unknown.
   (2) Critics have overrated the *Mona Lisa*.
   (3) The *Mona Lisa* is a bad painting; the *Last Supper* is a great one.
   (4) The *Mona Lisa* is a good painting; the *Last Supper* is a great one.
   (5) The *Mona Lisa* was painted much earlier than the *Last Supper*.

Answers start on page 289.

GED SKILL Comparing and Contrasting Ideas

compare
to show how
things are similar

contrast
to show how
things are different

When you **compare** ideas, you look for ways in which they are alike. When you **contrast** ideas, you look for ways in which they are different. Writers often use comparison and contrast as a way to organize ideas based on similarities and differences. Certain words often signal when two things are being compared or contrasted.

Read the following paragraphs and complete the exercise below.

Commercial TV, once the undisputed king of entertainment and information, is facing a serious threat from cable television, and it appears to be losing the battle. With its seemingly endless number of channels, cable TV offers the viewing public an extensive menu of programming, while commercial TV is limited to the warmed over fare served up by the "big four" networks.

In its effort to capture the interest of the American public, cable TV has excelled at televising programs that are more imaginative, risk-taking, and thoughtful than the insipid, predictable, and insulting shows that commercial TV calls "entertainment." In a feeble effort to compete with a medium that clearly has found its audience, commercial TV has chosen to push the envelope further and further, resulting in shows that have reached new lows in good taste.

TIP

These clue words indicate similarities: *and, also, likewise, in addition to, similarly.* These clue words indicate differences: *although, however, yet, but, on the other hand, on the contrary, while, versus, in contrast to, either . . . or.*

1. This passage contrasts _____ with

   _____ .

2. What word in the last sentence of the first paragraph signals that a

   contrast is being made? _____

3. List the three words in the second paragraph that describe cable TV and the three words that describe commercial TV.

cable TV	commercial TV
_____	_____
_____	_____
_____	_____

You were correct if you wrote the phrases *commercial TV* and *cable TV* for question 1. For question 2, the word that signals a contrast is *while*. For question 3, you were correct if you listed the words *imaginative, risk-taking,* and *thoughtful* under cable TV and the words *insipid, predictable,* and *insulting* under commercial TV.

Read the following excerpt from a nonfiction book and complete the exercise below.

"Now," said Applebaum, "have you ever said to a taxi driver, 'Follow that car and don't lose him'?"

"Not really."

"Well, if you had, the driver would have told you to blow it out your ear. No taxi
(5) driver is in a mood to follow another car because that means he's going to get involved. But on TV every cabdriver looks as if he'd like nothing better to do than to drive 90 miles an hour through a rain-swept street trying to keep up with a carful of hoods. And the worst thing is that the kids believe it."

"What else have you discovered?"

(10) "Kids have a perverted sense of what emergency wards of hospitals are really like. On TV shows they take a kid to an emergency ward and four doctors come rushing down to bandage his leg. In a real life situation the kid would be sitting on the bench for two hours before he even saw an intern. On TV there always happens to be a hospital bed available when a kid needs it. What the kids in this country
(15) don't know is that sometimes you have to wait three days to get a hospital bed and then you have to put a cash deposit of $500 down before they give it to you."

Art Buchwald, "Unreality of TV," *The Buchwald Stops Here.*

1. Based on this excerpt, with what is TV being contrasted?

    _____ a. movies

    _____ b. the real world

    _____ c. fantasy

2. In the third paragraph (lines 4–8), what two subjects are being compared and contrasted?

    a. _____

    b. _____

3. What word in the third paragraph is a clue that two things are being contrasted?

    _____

4. Based on the excerpt, which statement accurately compares real life and television?

    _____ a. Television and real life are often indistinguishable.

    _____ b. Television does not show the way things are in real life.

    _____ c. Television and real life contain many of the same places and things.

Answers start on page 290.

Directions: Choose the <u>one best answer</u> for each question.

Questions 1 through 3 refer to the following excerpt from a book review.

WHY WAS THIS DUEL FAMOUS?

    In "Duel," Thomas Fleming fills a gap in many Americans' knowledge of our early history. . . .

(5)   Fleming uses the occasion of the famous duel between [Aaron] Burr and [Alexander] Hamilton to make a sweeping examination of the nation's affairs from about 1795 until Burr's death in 1836. . . .

(10)   Both Burr and Hamilton were flawed, both were excessively ambitious, both posed significant threats to the new nation's equilibrium. It is to Fleming's credit that he portrays them for what they were and still manages to make them strangely

(15) likeable.

    Hamilton was well past his wartime heroics when Fleming introduces him. He had returned to his private law practice in New York without achieving either of his

(20) two most cherished goals: formation of a strong central government and a lasting place at its head. He was debt-ridden and barely clinging to leadership of the Federalist Party. . . .

(25)   Burr, on the other hand, had come close to the presidency in 1800, when he and Thomas Jefferson each received 73 electoral votes. Burr had only to persuade a few people to change their positions and

(30) the office would have been his. However, for complex private reasons, he chose not to make the effort, and Jefferson was declared president.

    In 1804, Burr was in New York, making

(35) a last effort to win control of the state in the gubernatorial election. But Burr's longtime nemesis, George Clinton, routed him again. Hamilton contributed significantly to the result and precipitated vengeful plotting

(40) by Burr. . . .

With one bullet, Burr sealed his fate, ever to be a pariah. Hamilton, aging but game, was denied his last best wish to care for his family.

Lowe Bibby, "'Duel' comes to terms with our nation's early history," The Associated Press.

1. What was the outcome of the famous duel between Hamilton and Burr?

   (1) Hamilton wounded the unpopular Burr.
   (2) Hamilton and Burr were both seriously injured.
   (3) Burr killed Clinton, his longtime rival.
   (4) Hamilton killed Burr and was put in prison.
   (5) Burr killed the aging Hamilton.

2. Based on the excerpt, which sentence accurately compares Burr and Hamilton?

   (1) Neither man came close to winning the presidency.
   (2) Both men became outcasts.
   (3) Burr was more dangerous to the nation.
   (4) Both men sought power.
   (5) Both men were Federalists.

3. Which of the following <u>most likely</u> represents Fleming's attitude toward his subjects?

   (1) He thinks that Hamilton was the more likable of the two men.
   (2) He admires Burr's strong ambition.
   (3) He feels that the country was hurt by Hamilton's failure to be elected president.
   (4) He is sympathetic toward both men.
   (5) He believes that Burr deserved to become a pariah.

TIP

To contrast two subjects, list adjectives used to describe them that are different or opposite.

Questions 4 through 7 refer to the following excerpt from a nonfiction book.

WHAT IS THE DEFINITION OF A BEAUTIFUL PHOTOGRAPH?

In photography's early decades, photographs were expected to be idealized images. This is still the aim of most amateur photographers, for whom a
(5) beautiful photograph is a photograph of something beautiful, like a woman, a sunset. In 1915 Edward Steichen photographed a milk bottle on a tenement fire escape, an early example of a quite
(10) different idea of the beautiful photograph. And since the 1920s, ambitious professionals, those whose work gets into museums, have steadily drifted away from lyrical subjects, conscientiously exploring
(15) plain, tawdry, or even vapid material. In recent decades, photography has succeeded in somewhat revising, for everybody, the definitions of what is beautiful and ugly—along the lines that
(20) Whitman had proposed. If (in Whitman's words) "each precise object or condition or combination or process exhibits a beauty," it becomes superficial to single out some things as beautiful and others as not.
(25) If "all that a person does or thinks is of consequence," it becomes arbitrary to treat some moments in life as important and most as trivial.
To photograph is to confer importance.
(30) There is probably no subject that cannot be beautified; moreover, there is no way to suppress the tendency inherent in all photographs to accord value to their subjects. But the meaning of value itself
(35) can be altered—as it has been in the contemporary culture of the photographic image which is a parody of Whitman's evangel. In the mansions of pre-democratic culture, someone who gets photographed
(40) is a celebrity. In the open fields of American experience, as catalogued with passion by Whitman and as sized up with a shrug by Warhol, everybody is a celebrity. No moment is more important than any other
(45) moment; no person is more interesting than any other person.

Susan Sontag, *On Photography.*

4. What is the tone of this excerpt?

   (1) argumentative
   (2) persuasive
   (3) descriptive
   (4) explanatory
   (5) analytical

5. According to this excerpt, what is the aim of many recent professional photographers?

   (1) to make beautiful and lyrical photographs
   (2) to photograph precise images of places
   (3) to photograph everyday subjects
   (4) to make ordinary and tasteless photographs
   (5) to make photographs that will get into museums

6. Based on the information given in lines 41–43 about Whitman and Warhol, which of the following comparisons is most accurate?

   Whitman is to Warhol as

   (1) a photograph is to a subject
   (2) a celebrity is to a non-celebrity
   (3) beauty is to ugliness
   (4) special is to ordinary
   (5) feeling is to indifference

7. Based on the information in the excerpt, with which of the following statements would Whitman most likely agree?

   (1) Every being has dignity and worth.
   (2) The best photographs are not in museums.
   (3) The ugliest subjects are frequently the most beautiful.
   (4) Art should be based on feeling rather than thought.
   (5) Many people are superficial.

Answers start on page 290.

Directions: This is a ten-minute practice test. After ten minutes, mark the last question you finished. Then complete the test and check your answers. If most of your answers were correct, but you didn't finish, try to work faster next time. Choose the one best answer to each question.

Questions 1 through 8 refer to the following excerpt from a newspaper column.

WHAT SETS THESE TWO MEN APART?

You really had to search for clues to the dynamic of the Democratic presidential race in the first televised question-and-answer session with Vice President Al
(5) Gore and former Sen. Bill Bradley. . . .

What viewers who passed up the final game of the World Series saw was two tall men, one (Gore) well-tailored and the other (Bradley) in an ill-fitting suit, giving
(10) thoughtful answers to serious policy questions from a roomful of New Hampshire voters.

. . . It was not Outsider Bradley vs. Insider Gore. The former U.S. senator from
(15) New Jersey talked at least as much about his legislative initiatives in 18 years on Capitol Hill as Gore did about his work in more than two decades in Washington.

Nor was it New Democrat Gore vs. Old
(20) Democrat Bradley. Gore did argue that Bradley's healthcare plan would use up all the projected budget surplus and then some. But the vice president proposed enough new programs of his own that New
(25) Hampshire Republican Chairman Steve Duprey greeted reporters leaving the debate with a press release plausibly claiming that both men "spent the entire $1 trillion surplus in 60 minutes on national
(30) television."

. . . In personal style, the differences were clearer. Bradley was, as usual, quiet almost to the point of diffidence,[1] treating questioners with respect but seeking no
(35) intimacy. Gore worked much harder to make an impression. He came on stage with a head of steam, and for 15 minutes before the telecast began he invited questions from the audience, dragging a

(40) reluctant-looking Bradley into the unscheduled warm-up exercise.

But Gore never seems to know when to leave well enough alone. His efforts at humor fell flat, his inquiries about the
(45) questioners' families seemed contrived. . . . At the end, when he thanked the voters of New Hampshire for the "great learning experience" of campaigning for their votes, he was almost a caricature of the
(50) pandering[2] politician.

The most revealing moment drew almost no notice. Asked about leaders and leadership, Gore and Bradley each cited three role models. Gore's were utterly safe
(55) and predictable choices: Lincoln for his values, FDR for his powers of persuasion, Lyndon Johnson for the scope of his domestic agenda. No risk of offending with those names; and no originality.

(60) Bradley chose differently: Jimmy Carter for his veracity;[3] Woodrow Wilson for his farsightedness; Mikhail Gorbachev for his courage.

Those three men were certainly
(65) visionaries. . . .

But that is an odd pantheon.[4] It may not have occurred to Bradley—who identifies himself as a "big ideas" leader—that each of his role models overreached so badly
(70) that he very quickly lost the support of public opinion and his hold on power. All three were highly intelligent men, whose ideas still resonate. But their failures dwarfed their accomplishments. Is there a
(75) cautionary message there?

---

[1] shyness   [2] catering to the wishes of
[3] truthfulness   [4] hall of heroes

David Broder, "Holding the applause," *The Washington Post Writers Group.*

1. According to the author, what do the two candidates have in common?

   (1) Both are tall men and shallow thinkers.
   (2) Both are well-tailored and professional.
   (3) Both are relative newcomers to Washington.
   (4) Both portray themselves as New Democrats.
   (5) Both came across as big spenders.

2. On the basis of the excerpt, which of the following most effectively contrasts the personal styles of the two men?

   (1) Bradley is an outsider; Gore is an insider.
   (2) Bradley is reserved; Gore is friendly.
   (3) Gore worked to impress the audience; Bradley did not.
   (4) Gore has a sense of humor; Bradley does not.
   (5) Bradley is serious; Gore lacks substance.

3. According to the author, which of the following provided the clearest insight into each candidate's character?

   (1) their choice of political role models
   (2) their position on the economy
   (3) their plans for the budget surplus
   (4) their vision for national healthcare
   (5) their behavior toward the audience

4. On the basis of the excerpt, which of the following is the most likely reason Gore started an impromptu question-and answer-session before the telecast?

   (1) Gore wanted to embarrass Bradley.
   (2) Gore had more information to convey than he had time for in the debate.
   (3) Gore wanted to appear accessible to the public.
   (4) Gore was making a genuine display of enthusiasm.
   (5) Gore could not wait to begin talking to the public.

5. What does the author most likely mean when he says that "Gore never seems to know when to leave well enough alone" (lines 42–43)?

   (1) Gore tends to worry too much.
   (2) Gore was bothering Bradley.
   (3) Gore offended people.
   (4) Gore often goes too far.
   (5) Gore appeared insincere.

6. According to the author, which of the following words best describes the role models for leadership that Gore selected?

   (1) inspiring
   (2) original
   (3) unacceptable
   (4) unexpected
   (5) inoffensive

7. Which two paragraphs focus mainly on the similarities between the candidates?

   (1) paragraphs 1 and 2
   (2) paragraphs 3 and 4
   (3) paragraphs 4 and 5
   (4) paragraphs 6 and 7
   (5) paragraphs 8 and 9

8. Which of the following points of view is supported by the writer's statement that "you really had to search for clues to the dynamic of the Democratic presidential race in the first televised question-and-answer session" (lines 1–4)?

   (1) The debate was not worth watching.
   (2) The contrast between the candidates was not as sharp as expected.
   (3) The candidates held back more than they gave to the audience.
   (4) The candidates did a good job of evading the key issues of the campaign.
   (5) The Republicans offer a clearer choice of candidates than the Democrats.

Answers start on page 290.

GED SKILL Recognizing Author's Viewpoint

viewpoint
a writer's attitude or opinion about a subject

TIP

Look for positively- or negatively- charged words that indicate how a writer feels about a subject.

A writer's attitude, or **viewpoint,** toward a subject often influences how he or she treats it. For example, a movie critic might dislike comedies but love dramas. Such a critic might be likely to say more positive things about a dramatic movie than about a humorous one. Readers can identify an author's viewpoint based on clues about the writer's background or interests, the vocabulary used, and details that point toward the writer's likes and dislikes.

Read the following excerpt from an article and complete the exercise below.

As an improviser, Hines's choices are *always* surprising and wild. He takes you in unpredictable directions, cutting into phrases in unexpected places, alternating rest periods with full-blown movement as he skitters over the surface of his soundstage. A tough, get-down tapper who hunches over his feet, Hines keeps his head low like a fighter, listening, focusing himself and us on the sound of his feet. Neither graceful nor light (although he makes his feet whisper sweet nothings when he wants to) Hines is something better and rarer in the tap dance world, a sexy and compelling performer. Of all the tappers I know, Hines is perhaps the most inventive because he is fearless. Almost single-handedly he is pushing tap's technology and is a true modernist in how he uses rhythms. Frequently, he'll wrench phrases out of rhythm to create tension. On the feet of a lesser performer it could be chaotic. On Hines, it is exhilarating.

Sally R. Sommer, "Superfeet," *The Village Voice.*

1. What is this critic's attitude toward Hines's tap dancing?

    _____ a. indifferent

    _____ b. unfavorable

    _____ c. admiring

2. List the words and phrases from the excerpt that are clues to the critic's point of view.

    _____

    _____

    _____

You were correct if you chose *option c* for question 1. For question 2, the clues include *surprising, wild, better, rarer, sexy, compelling, inventive, fearless, true modernist,* and *exhilarating.* Each of these says something very positive about Hines's dancing.

Read the following excerpt from a magazine article and complete the exercise below.

There's a paradox at the heart of the weather report today: people watch weather on TV because it seems real, in a way that political scandals and stock-market gyrations sometimes do not. But the more weather we watch on TV the less time we spend in it. One becomes attuned to the movement of energy around the
(5) globe—the jet stream, the flow of high pressure down from the North Pole, the path of the storm—while at the same time becoming detached from the weather outside.

I remember standing on the battery in Charleston, South Carolina, waiting for Floyd: Wednesday, September 15, 1999. The old town was eerily deserted, the windows of the great Georgian houses protected by plywood cut into neoclassical
(10) shapes. TV crews were lined up all along the stone promenade: weather paparazzi straining before the velvet rope of the ocean, waiting for the celebrity to arrive. A Weather Channel producer, Dwight Woods, tried the shot: Charleston Bay, with Fort Sumter in the background. He didn't like it, and decided to see whether a marina that Bruce Fauzer, the satellite-truck operator, had scouted out
(15) earlier offered better pictures. As Jeff Morrow, the meteorologist, was climbing into the truck, he pointed at the sky and said, "By the way, there's the hurricane."

I looked up, and there it was. You could see the cloud, a huge dark plume that went up at least fifty thousand feet into the atmosphere. It was astounding, almost Biblical in size, especially in contrast to the televised satellite picture I had been
(20) seeing for so long. Television simply can't convey the immensity of the weather— that feeling you get just from looking up at the sky.

John Seabrook, "Selling the Weather," *The New Yorker.*

1. What does the author imply about his background in this excerpt?

   a. He lives in an area frequented by hurricanes.

   b. He is a frequent watcher of weather reports.

   c. He once worked as a television journalist.

2. Put a check mark next to the words that best describe the author's attitude toward weather (as opposed to television coverage of weather).

   _____ a. fascinated and awed

   _____ b. obsessed and uneasy

   _____ c. excited and overeager

3. Which of the following best describes the author's viewpoint toward television weather broadcasts?

   a. He finds them informative, yet slightly boring.

   b. He finds them deeply flawed, yet entertaining.

   c. He finds them interesting, yet a bit artificial.

4. List two details from the excerpt that support your answer for question 3.

   a. _____

   b. _____

Answers start on page 291.

Directions: Choose the one best answer to each question.

Questions 1 through 3 refer to the following excerpt from a movie review.

IS *HENRY V* A SUCCESS?

Shakespeare's plays rarely translate into great cinema, because they're either made on low budgets or look like filmed stage plays. So it's quite a surprise that
(5) *Henry V,* not Shakespeare's best, is one of the few movies in which Shakespeare seems not only a great playwright, but a seasoned screenwriter.

A lot of it has to do with Kenneth
(10) Branagh, a little-known English actor whose identification with Henry V is like Laurence Olivier's with Hamlet. He plays the title role, directs and adapts this play dealing with his psychological transition
(15) from Prince Hal to King Henry during the ruler's heroic campaigns into France. Branagh is young enough that his face has a boyish fleshiness, but old enough to project the charisma of a king. Even if you
(20) gasp to keep up with the Elizabethan language, his natural, eloquent inflections and the details of his direction clearly convey what he—and the large cast—is talking about.

(25) The film is full of beautifully photographed images, but they're never just decorative. In fact, it has a rough, primitive medieval look in keeping with its 15th-century setting. Though the battle
(30) sequences are sweeping, their details show the suffering, sorrow, and pettiness of Henry's men. The film even inspires us with their battle heroism. After all, their wars were more a sport than a means of
(35) annihilation.

Henry V emerges a first-class epic film, so entertaining that it needs no apologies for being based on a 400-year-old play. The only disappointments: Paul Scofield, whose
(40) portrayal of the French king is surprisingly dour, and the last 10 minutes, which turn

needlessly cute as Henry courts his future wife, Katherine. But that's as much Shakespeare's fault as Branagh's.

David Patrick Stearns, "Majestic *Henry V* does justice to the bard," *USA Today.*

1. Which statement best expresses the reviewer's opinion of the movie *Henry V*?

   (1) It contains realistic action sequences.
   (2) It is as good as other movies based on Shakespeare's plays.
   (3) It is an entertaining film.
   (4) It is a poor translation of the original play.
   (5) It has a large cast.

2. Which of the following most accurately states the main idea of the second paragraph?

   (1) Branagh is as good an actor as Olivier.
   (2) Branagh is perfect for the role of Henry V.
   (3) Branagh will become a better-known actor as a result of the film.
   (4) Branagh is a director as well as an actor.
   (5) Branagh really looks the part of Henry V.

3. In which of the following ways are the first and last paragraphs of this review similar?

   (1) Shakespeare's play *Henry V* is criticized.
   (2) Scenes from the movie are summarized.
   (3) Branagh is credited with rescuing the movie.
   (4) Shakespeare's reputation is attacked.
   (5) The critic says his expectations were not fulfilled.

 TIP To identify the author's viewpoint, try to separate the facts in a piece of writing from the opinions. The relationship between facts and opinions can give you a good idea of the author's point of view.

Questions 4 through 6 refer to the following excerpt from a review.

IS THIS FILM A SLAM DUNK?

There are quite a few strong players in Love and Basketball, but for the most part they have to stay on the bench. Four talented actors (Alfre Woodard, Dennis
(5) Haysbert, Debbi Morgan and Harry J. Lennix) play the stars' parents, and every one of them turns out to be more interesting than the young lovers who are the focus of the movie.
(10) This is not to say that stars Sanaa Lathan and Omar Epps are less than adequate as hoopsters who take a long, long time to realize they love each other as much as they love the game. Lathan and
(15) Epps are appealing (though they seem rather short for the roles) as suburban kids who grow up so close that one can hear the other whispering through a bedroom window. The actors do what they can to
(20) give life to these glossy characters, but they have no rough edges and their struggles turn out to be far more predictable than the average basketball game.
Though writer/director Gina Prince-
(25) Bythewood's direction is smooth and slick (especially so considering that this is her first feature), her plot is awkwardly structured. The movie is divided into four periods, like a basketball game, but this
(30) attempt to impose structure on a meandering tale feels arbitrary. Childhood conflicts we were never told about suddenly become plot complications midway through the movie—then are
(35) resolved just as abruptly a few scenes later. A basketball game played strip poker-style looks exciting in the coming attractions trailer, but it lacks snap in the actual movie because the competitors are
(40) already lovers when they play the scene.
By the very nature of its subject, Love and Basketball holds some interest, and anyone curious about what basketball players go through in the college and pro
(45) years will learn a thing or two (though not a lot). But a love story with a basketball backdrop is by its very nature so unusual, so there's no excuse for this one to feel so pat and predictable. One wishes producer
(50) Spike Lee had stepped in to give the dialogue some sass. . . .

Andy Seiler, " 'Love and Basketball' misses the net," *USA Today.*

4. Which of the following statements expresses the reviewer's overall opinion of the movie?

   (1) It is an appealing, though flawed, love story.
   (2) It is based upon a clichéd combination of sports and romance that does not work.
   (3) It fails miserably in its attempt to portray first love.
   (4) It successfully tells the story of the coming-of-age of a basketball player.
   (5) It is a believable, true-to-life story of young love.

5. What is the effect of the author's repetition of the word "long" in the phrase "hoopsters who take a long, long time to realize they love each other" (lines 12–13)?

   (1) It expresses the reviewer's enthusiasm for his subject.
   (2) It suggests that there is a slow, plodding pace to the movie.
   (3) It shows that the reviewer is very patient.
   (4) It implies that the movie is actually too short.
   (5) It suggests that the main characters are cautious about love.

6. Which of the following changes most likely would have caused the reviewer to react more favorably to the film?

   (1) if the lead actors were different
   (2) if the director were more experienced
   (3) if the subject matter did not involve basketball
   (4) if the setting were the inner city rather than the suburbs
   (5) if the plot were structured differently

Answers start on page 291.

Directions: This is a ten-minute practice test. After ten minutes, mark the last question you finished. Then complete the test and check your answers. If most of your answers were correct, but you didn't finish, try to work faster next time. Choose the <u>one best answer</u> to each question.

<u>Questions 1 through 9</u> refer to the following excerpt from a review.

HOW DOES THIS AUTHOR READ *TV GUIDE*?

The first thing I do upon picking up *TV Guide* at the supermarket is to tear out the superabundance of commercial inserts. It's not the advertisements I mind but that

(5) they're printed on heavy stock which makes locating desired pages annoyingly difficult. After removing the obstacles, I settle down to scanning the schedule and noting which programs are to be viewed

(10) and/or video taped for subsequent retrieval. Owing to the numbers of channels chronicled, this too can prove frustrating especially when attempting to compile a list of movies other than those

(15) offered exclusively on premium cable channels. It would be far more advantageous for discerning film and, indeed, sport fans if *TV Guide* provided separate and complete schedules catering

(20) to both interests. Considering the diversity of special interest programs, they might adopt a similar scheme for listing children's, news and special events.

Through no fault of its own, *TV Guide*

(25) lists little else but the title of programs broadcast by the A&E Network, The Discovery Channel, The Disney Channel and absolutely nothing for C-Span. With the exception of The Disney Channel, each

(30) sells its own monthly program guide for anywhere between $15.00 and $30.00 annually (The Disney Channel Magazine is included with the monthly cable fee). . . .

Programs on The Discovery Channel

(35) are continually interesting. Notable among them is Gus MacDonald's engrossing series on the archaeology and evolution of

still photography and his very stimulating history on early cinema both here and

(40) abroad; in addition to a variety of foreign documentaries including those exploring all aspects of the life and times of the British Empire. Yet they hardly warrant the extra expenditure for a program guide as so

(45) many are repeats. The same is true of A&E but even more so. Repeats, for example, far exceed new programs. While the occasional foreign language film is a bonus to be sure, what isn't welcomed is the

(50) frequency of movies shown where scenes have been deleted for time's sake. . . .

Some of the most significant programming on television is supplied by the combined C-Span channels and as

(55) such ought to be listed in *TV Guide* and all daily newspapers, but it is not. Hence, C-Span's monthly guide is invaluable save only for inevitable late hour changes in the schedule.

(60) What is needed is a comprehensive weekly teleguide encompassing, in depth, programs on all the channels in any given area; one whose information is arranged for the viewer to gain access to it with a

(65) minimum of difficulty.

Chris Buchman, "The Television Scene," *Films in Review.*

1. Based on the excerpt, which of the following channels is <u>most likely</u> the author's favorite?

   (1) A&E
   (2) The Disney Channel
   (3) The Discovery Channel
   (4) sports channels
   (5) news channels

2. Where in this excerpt does the author state his most important idea?

   (1) in the first paragraph
   (2) in the last paragraph
   (3) in the middle paragraphs
   (4) in the middle and the last paragraphs
   (5) in the first and last paragraphs

3. Which of the following is the main idea of the excerpt?

   The author

   (1) thinks that the programming on C-Span is very significant
   (2) would like more interest-focused, detailed program guides
   (3) doesn't like the programming choices or the number of repeats on A&E
   (4) wants people to buy TV Guide
   (5) wishes more people shared his reading and viewing habits

4. Which of the following best expresses the author's opinion of A&E?

   (1) Its programming is much better than what is offered on C-Span.
   (2) It is necessary to have a special program guide for its broadcasts.
   (3) Its program guide is a waste of money.
   (4) It shows some of the best programs on television.
   (5) It should never be watched.

5. Which of the following best describes the tone of this excerpt?

   (1) informative
   (2) angry
   (3) humorous
   (4) overwhelmed
   (5) pleased

6. Which of the following is the best explanation for the author's discussion of commercial inserts in TV Guide?

   (1) They are the only bad aspects of TV Guide.
   (2) They are the best part of TV Guide.
   (3) They prove his point about the waste of paper by national magazines.
   (4) They introduce his discussion of the virtues and limitations of TV Guide.
   (5) They give TV Guide the edge over the competition.

7. Which of the following best describes the style in which this review is written?

   (1) technical
   (2) casual
   (3) methodical
   (4) ornate
   (5) economical

8. Based on the information in the excerpt, what is the most likely reason that TV Guide does not contain complete listings?

   (1) TV Guide lists only commercial channels and cable channels that have paid a fee.
   (2) TV Guide devotes a great deal of space to premium movie channels.
   (3) TV Guide does not have room to describe every show on every channel.
   (4) TV Guide contains many advertisements on heavy stock that take up space.
   (5) TV Guide must compete with cable channel program guides.

9. According to the author, which of the following words best describes TV Guide?

   (1) thoughtful
   (2) detailed
   (3) superficial
   (4) confusing
   (5) biased

Answers start on page 292.

Unit 1 Cumulative Review Interpreting Nonfiction

Directions: Choose the <u>one best answer</u> to each question.

Questions 1 through 4 refer to the following excerpt from an article.

WHAT CAN WILLIE DO WITH A POOL CUE?

The old man with the custom cue knocks the balls off the table as if he were a schoolboy with a slingshot and the stripes and solids were so many crows
(5) perched on a telephone wire. *Click click click.* When the pool table has been cleared, 74-year-old Willie Mosconi shrugs and says, "Nothin' to this game." He's playing in front of the Sears store at the
(10) Northridge shopping mall in Milwaukee; the pool legend is making another exhibition appearance.

"I could arrange it so she doesn't make a ball," Mosconi tells the audience while
(15) setting up a trick shot for a young woman he has selected from the crowd. Almost 200 people are watching, if you count shopping-weary passersby and ascending escalator riders. It turns out the woman
(20) *can't* make a ball, even though Mosconi has arranged it so that a simple shot should pocket six at once. After three failed attempts and as many tedious setups, the Showman grows impatient and the Shark
(25) in Mosconi surfaces.

"Ever play this game before?" he asks her. (By his tone he is clearly saying, "You *have* played this game before, *haven't* you?")
(30) "No," the woman says.

The Shark takes—yanks, really—the cue from her hand and the woman slinks back into the crowd, disappearing behind a potted palm. Then Mosconi the Salesman
(35) catches himself and remembers that he's here to pitch pool tables and make friends for Sears.

"Thank you," he says to the potted palm. "Uh, let's hear it for the young lady."

Steve Rushin, "In Pool, the Shark Still Leaves a Wide Wake," *Sports Illustrated*.

1. What two things are being compared in the phrase "the stripes and solids were so many crows perched on a telephone wire" (lines 3–5)?

   (1) the cue stick and balls
   (2) the pattern on the pool table and the pattern of telephone wires
   (3) the birds Willie hit with a slingshot and the balls Willie hits in pool
   (4) the balls on the pool table and birds about to be hit
   (5) the balls on the table and the bystanders watching the exhibition

2. Which of the following <u>best</u> explains why Mosconi is nicknamed The Shark?

   (1) He is kind and patient.
   (2) He has steel-gray hair and moves quickly.
   (3) He is ferocious toward his prey.
   (4) He likes to harm his opponents physically.
   (5) He is an excellent salesperson.

3. What is <u>most likely</u> meant by comparing Mosconi to "a schoolboy with a slingshot" (line 3)?

   (1) Playing pool is easy.
   (2) Mosconi is having fun.
   (3) Mosconi had good aim as a child.
   (4) Pool players can be careless.
   (5) Crows can be hit with pool balls.

4. Based on the description of Mosconi's behavior in this excerpt, which of the following generalizations is valid?

   (1) Celebrity appearances are certain to bring out a crowd.
   (2) Celebrity endorsements are a guaranteed way to sell a product.
   (3) Celebrity status does not automatically qualify someone to sell a product.
   (4) Celebrities are comfortable playing more than one role.
   (5) Celebrities are better at selling themselves than selling a product.

Questions 5 through 7 refer to the following excerpt from a handbook.

WHY IS TEMPING GAINING POPULARITY?

The temporary help field is quite unlike any other in the scope of its complexity. It is actually an industry consisting of many industries. Temporary help can be
(5) classified in any one of four categories: office, industrial, medical, and technical/professional. Under these four banner heads are numerous job titles and occupations. The temporary help industry
(10) is the only one where construction workers, chemists, X-ray technicians, and switchboard operators can all fall under the management of a single employer—a temporary help service.
(15) In simplest terms, temping is work for a temporary help firm that pays you an hourly wage and all the costs associated with employment insurance: FICA, disability, worker's compensation, fringe
(20) benefits, and so on. The temporary service sends you out on short- or long-term assignments at one of their client organizations, and the client is billed an hourly charge for your services. A
(25) temporary employee is *never* the employee of the organization, individual, or business where he or she is fulfilling an assignment. A temporary employee is *always* the employee of the temporary help firm which
(30) sends the temp out.
Let's take a look at the breakdown of personnel within the four categories of temporary help. Not surprisingly, the leader is office personnel, where you'll find
(35) 63 percent of the total annual temporary payroll. Following office is industrial/labor, with a 15.8 percent share of the population; health care, with 10.8 percent; and technical/professional, not far behind
(40) with 10.4 percent. . . .
A temporary help service is unique in structure because it is both a private-sector business and a labor intermediary. As a private-sector business, it has its own
(45) market and sells its product to a variety of customers. As a labor intermediary, a

temporary help service can have considerable influence on the supply and demand of the customers it serves.

William Lewis and Nancy Schuman, "Temping: Who, What, and Why," *The Temp Worker's Handbook.*

5. What is the main idea of the first paragraph?

The temporary help industry

(1) is another name for the employment industry
(2) is an umbrella for a number of other industries
(3) is the largest employer in the world
(4) has grown enormously within the last 10 years
(5) is the "employer of last resort" for many people

6. If a temporary worker were being harrassed by his supervisor at his temporary job, to whom would he likely bring a complaint?

(1) the person who is harrassing him
(2) the boss of the person harrassing him
(3) the human resources department at his job site
(4) the supervisor to whom he reports at the client company
(5) the temporary service for which he works

7. Based on the excerpt, which of the following conclusions can you make about the temporary help industry?

(1) It suffers from negative perceptions.
(2) It is unable to compete favorably with the full-time, permanent workforce.
(3) Its workers will soon be back on the unemployment rolls.
(4) It offers excellent wages.
(5) It offers opportunities for almost any profession.

WHAT DOES RENTERS INSURANCE COVER?

Renters insurance is an important commodity that too many renters overlook. Two key terms that are used in discussing renters insurance are *peril* and *risk*. Perils

(5) are the potential causes of a loss, such as a fire, windstorm, hail, theft, and vandalism. Risk is the chance of experiencing a loss.

Two other key terms that pertain to

(10) renters insurance are *actual cash value* and *replacement cost coverage*. Both have to do with ways in which a claim to a property loss can be settled.

Actual cash value means, in many

(15) states, that if a loss occurs, you will be paid the current replacement cost minus depreciation (wear and tear due to age and use). The total amount to be paid is subject to the terms of your policy.

(20) *Replacement cost coverage* means that in case of loss, you will be repaid for the cost you incur to replace the damaged property with comparable new property, subject to the terms of your policy.

(25) Other key terms in a renters insurance policy are *deductible,* the portion of the loss the insured is willing to pay out of pocket, and coverage *limits,* the maximum amounts the insurer will pay a policyholder

(30) for a covered loss. Keeping the coverage limits low correspondingly keeps the cost of the insurance low.

Renters insurance offers the following coverage options: personal property

(35) protection, family liability protection, and guest medical protection. Personal property protection is protection against loss to *movable* property. Family liability protection is protection against certain

(40) liability claims brought against you because of property damage or bodily injury you may have accidentally caused. Guest medical protection is reimbursement for expenses incurred if visitors to your

(45) home are injured, regardless of who was at fault.

8. Which statement best summarizes this excerpt?

(1) Renters insurance and homeowners insurance differ in many key areas.
(2) It is prudent for all renters to have renters insurance.
(3) Renters insurance policies can protect renters in a number of ways.
(4) There is a renters insurance plan to fit any pocketbook.
(5) Next to auto insurance, renters insurance is the most popular type of coverage.

9. According to the information in this excerpt, which of the following types of insurance should a person with a large collection of valuable dolls buy?

(1) replacement cost coverage renters insurance
(2) actual cash value renters insurance
(3) a policy with a high deductible
(4) a family liability policy
(5) fire insurance

10. What is the author's viewpoint toward renters insurance?

(1) Family liability protection is costly.
(2) Many people later wish that they had purchased renters insurance.
(3) People should choose coverage limits that keep the premium low.
(4) All renters should consider buying renters insurance.
(5) Renters have more risk than homeowners.

11. Which of the following best describes the style in which this excerpt is written?

(1) legal and technical
(2) informative and direct
(3) scholarly and dull
(4) casual and conversational
(5) light and breezy

Questions 12 through 15 refer to the following excerpt from a business guide.

WHY ARE TELEPHONE SKILLS SO IMPORTANT?

The secret to using the telephone effectively is *planning.* However, planning a telephone call seems unnatural to many of us. We are used to picking up the phone to
(5) chat with family and friends whenever the mood strikes. Planning a telephone call is unnatural in a social situation. For most of us, using the telephone is a social skill, not a business skill.
(10) The rules differ for business telephone calls. Making a business call requires the same skills as participating in a meeting, sending a memo, or writing a business letter. It requires thought and planning.
(15) You can easily understand how to plan your calls to other people, but you may not think it is possible to plan for other people's calls to you. It is possible, and necessary, to plan for these incoming calls. The first
(20) thing to plan is how you will answer your telephone.

Answering Your Phone

Many telephone effectiveness experts feel that the first ten to fifteen seconds of a
(25) telephone call set the tone of the entire conversation. It is therefore easy to see why the way you answer your telephone is important. "You should answer your telephone with a couple of key words that
(30) let your callers know they have reached the right place," says Gail Cohen, president of the Telemarketing Learning Center and a telephone consultant.

Answering your phone with a brusque
(35) "What do you want?" will set a negative tone for the conversation that follows. You must answer your phone with a phrase that is both pleasant and professional.

Nancy Friedman, a St. Louis-based
(40) communications consultant who dubs herself "the Telephone Doctor" says this key phrase should contain three things:
• a greeting
• the name of your company or
(45) department
• your name.

Madeline Bodin, "Basic Telephone Skills," *Using the Telephone More Effectively.*

12. According to the author, what is the main reason people fail to plan their business telephone calls?

   (1) They like to be spontaneous.
   (2) They think of telephone calls as social.
   (3) They believe it is a waste of time.
   (4) They are too busy to take the time.
   (5) They rely on voice mail.

13. According to the author, why are the first ten to fifteen seconds of a phone call important?

   (1) They let the caller know he or she has reached the right number.
   (2) They give the receiver time to plan what to say.
   (3) They let the caller know what mood the receiver is in.
   (4) They give the caller time to state his or her business.
   (5) They determine how successful the exchange will be.

14. Which of the following would be the best title for this excerpt?

   (1) How Poor Telephone Skills Hurt Business
   (2) Proper Telephone Etiquette
   (3) Planning a Phone Call Is Like Planning a Letter
   (4) Tips for Answering the Telephone Effectively
   (5) How to Differentiate Social Phone Calls from Business Phone Calls

15. Which of the following best describes the style in which this excerpt is written?

   (1) formal
   (2) academic
   (3) conversational
   (4) humorous
   (5) technical

Questions 16 through 18 refer to the following excerpt from a review.

DID THIS TELEVISION ADAPTATION SUCCEED?

"She is," said Katherine Anne Porter of the great American writer Willa Cather, "a curiously immovable shape, monumental, virtue itself in her art and symbol of
(5) virtue—like certain churches, in fact, or exemplary women, revered and neglected."
Neglected no more. While Willa Cather's magnificent novels have long been a staple of American literature
(10) courses, her stories have rarely been filmed. Indeed, in her lifetime, Miss Cather was adamantly opposed to dramatizations of her work. Perhaps even she understood the difficulties inherent in transferring her
(15) almost perfect prose onto stage or screen. Recently, however, the oversight has been remedied. . . . the USA network will present an adaptation of perhaps the most popular of Miss Cather's novels, "My Antonia." . . .
(20) Any dramatization of "My Antonia" will be hobbled by the inability to reproduce the lyrical, dreamy prose of Willa Cather. To compensate, there are a few voice-overs lifted almost directly from the text. . . .
(25) This excellent adaptation also presents magnificent prairie vistas—brilliantly green grasses, tall corn, golden wheat, open skies—that almost make up for the missing prose. The Nebraska prairie, much like the
(30) English countryside in Thomas Hardy's novels, is almost a character in itself. And the Shimerda's dire poverty is also more obvious on screen than in the novel. . . .
Overall, it is a wonderful introduction for
(35) those unfamiliar with Willa Cather, and for those already fans, encountering this little television movie is like running into a long-lost friend.

James Martin, "O Pioneers," *America.*

16. According to the excerpt, which of the following statements best explains the difficulty in adapting Cather's novels to television?

   (1) Cather was opposed to all dramatizations of her novels.
   (2) It is hard to capture the beauty of Cather's writing on televison.
   (3) The filmmakers had difficulty finding a place to film in Nebraska.
   (4) No one in the television industry had heard of "My Antonia."
   (5) Cather's novels had been neglected.

17. What is the author suggesting by saying that watching "My Antonia" is like "running into a long-lost friend" (lines 37–38)?

   (1) Some viewers will feel comfortable and familiar with the story.
   (2) Viewers who need an introduction to Cather will feel welcomed.
   (3) The program is an excellent introduction to Cather's work.
   (4) The television adaptation is a warm and friendly program.
   (5) Willa Cather and Katherine Anne Porter were friends.

18. What does Katherine Anne Porter's description of Willa Cather suggest about Cather?

   (1) She was a self-righteous woman.
   (2) Her work concerns only religious subjects.
   (3) Her work is experiencing a rebirth in colleges across the country.
   (4) She is a towering figure in American literature.
   (5) She symbolizes the neglected American female writer.

Questions 19 through 23 refer to the following excerpt from an essay.

WOULD YOU HIRE THIS MAN?

As for my own business, even that kind of surveying which I could do with most satisfaction my employers do not want. They would prefer that I should do my work
(5) coarsely and not too well, ay, not well enough. When I observe that there are different ways of surveying, my employer commonly asks which will give him the most land, not which is most correct. I
(10) once invented a rule for measuring cordwood, and tried to introduce it in Boston; but the measurer there told me that the sellers did not wish to have their wood measured correctly—that he was
(15) already too accurate for them, and therefore they commonly got their wood measured in Charlestown before crossing the bridge.
      The aim of the laborer should be, not to
(20) get his living, to get "a good job," but to perform well a certain work; and, even in a pecuniary sense, it would be economy for a town to pay its laborers so well that they would not feel that they were working for
(25) low ends, as for a livelihood merely, but for scientific, or even moral ends. Do not hire a man who does your work for money, but him who does it for love of it.

Henry David Thoreau, "Life Without Principle," from *Major Writers of America.*

19. Why does the author sometimes feels unsatisfied with his work?

    (1) He is not paid well enough.
    (2) He does not need the money.
    (3) His clients do not always want his best effort.
    (4) His customers often go to other surveyors.
    (5) He has not been able to invent a new measuring rule.

20. Based on the excerpt, which of the following opinions does the author most likely hold about some of his clients?

    (1) They criticize his work too much.
    (2) They like Charlestown better than Boston.
    (3) They don't pay him enough.
    (4) They are a little dishonest.
    (5) They are very lazy.

21. Based on the excerpt, what would the author most likely do if he were offered a job doing something that he did not like?

    (1) accept the job for the money
    (2) turn down the job
    (3) accept it but do a bad job
    (4) demand more money
    (5) hire someone else to do the job

22. Based on the excerpt, which statement correctly contrasts Thoreau (the author) and his employers?

    (1) Thoreau is hardworking, and his employers are not.
    (2) Thoreau and his employers are both surveyors.
    (3) Thoreau loves his work, and his employers do not.
    (4) Thoreau prefers accuracy, and his employers prefer money.
    (5) Thoreau invents new rules, and his employers steal his ideas.

23. What is the main idea of the last paragraph?

    (1) Workers should not care about money or other material things.
    (2) Towns should pay workers very well.
    (3) Workers should do what they love and be paid well for it.
    (4) Workers who are paid well will love their jobs.
    (5) Towns should hire people with high morals.

Questions 24 through 27 refer to the following excerpt from an autobiography.

WHAT WAS IT LIKE TO BE A SLAVE DURING THE WAR?

I had no schooling whatever while I was a slave, though I remember on several occasions I went as far as the schoolhouse door with one of my young mistresses to
(5) carry her books. The picture of several dozen boys and girls in a schoolroom engaged in study made a deep impression upon me, and I had the feeling that to get into a schoolhouse and study in this way
(10) would be about the same as getting into paradise.

So far as I can now recall, the first knowledge that I got of the fact that we were slaves, and that freedom of the
(15) slaves was being discussed, was early one morning before day, when I was awakened by my mother kneeling over her children and fervently praying that Lincoln and his armies might be successful, and that one
(20) day she and her children might be free. In this connection I have never been able to understand how the slaves throughout the South, completely ignorant as were the masses so far as books or newspapers
(25) were concerned, were able to keep themselves so accurately and completely informed about the great National questions that were agitating the country. From the time that Garrison, Lovejoy, and
(30) others began to agitate for freedom, the slaves throughout the South kept in close touch with the progress of the movement. Though I was a mere child during the preparation for the Civil War and during the
(35) war itself, I now recall the many late-at-night whispered discussions that I heard my mother and the other slaves on the plantation indulge in. These discussions showed that they understood the situation,
(40) and that they kept themselves informed of events by what was termed the "grape-vine" telegraph.

Booker T. Washington, *Up from Slavery.*

24. Who were Garrison and Lovejoy, based on the information in the excerpt?

(1) friends of the author
(2) members of Lincoln's cabinet
(3) well-known slavery opponents
(4) wealthy slaveholders
(5) troublemakers

25. Based on the excerpt, what is the author's attitude toward the slaves' understanding of the Civil War?

He is

(1) doubtful of it
(2) impressed with it
(3) disappointed in it
(4) irritated by it
(5) overjoyed by it

26. Based on the context in which it is used, what is "the 'grape-vine' telegraph" (lines 41–42)?

(1) telegraph messages sent from the North to the South
(2) telegraph wires that looked like grapevines
(3) a person-to-person means of transmitting information
(4) a direct pipeline from the Union forces' command posts
(5) a means of communication using secret codes

27. The author of this excerpt, Booker T. Washington, built Tuskegee Institute into a respected and important college. What quality exhibited in this excerpt does this accomplishment reflect?

(1) the author's fervent desire for freedom
(2) the author's desire for fame
(3) the author's lack of schooling
(4) the author's deep interest in education
(5) the author's exposure to knowledgeable slaves

Answers start on page 292.

Cumulative Review Performance Analysis
Unit 1 ● Interpreting Nonfiction

Use the Answers and Explanations starting on page 292 to check your answers to the Unit 1 Cumulative Review. Then use the chart to figure out the skill areas in which you need more practice.

On the chart, circle the questions that you answered correctly. Write the number correct for each skill area. Add the number of questions that you got correct on the Cumulative Review. If you feel that you need more practice, go back and review the lessons for the skill areas that were difficult for you.

Questions	Number Correct	Skill Area	Lessons for Review
5, 8, 12, 13, 14, 16, 19, 23, 24	____/9	Comprehension	1, 2, 3, 5, 7, 8
6, 9, 21	____/3	Application	4
1, 2, 3, 7, 10, 17, 20, 25, 26	____/9	Analysis	3, 7, 8, 9
4, 11, 15, 18, 22, 27	____/6	Synthesis	5, 6, 7, 8
TOTAL CORRECT	____/27		

UNIT 2

Understanding Fiction

Fiction is a form of writing that tells a story. A fiction writer creates a world from imagination. The most common works of fiction are novels and short stories. Fiction can be about any subject: adventure, romance, sports, mystery, or a combination of these.

The selections in this book and the questions that follow them are very similar to the ones on the GED Test. When you take the GED, you will not be required to know who wrote a particular work, or to remember special terms. You will be reading selections from different kinds of literature and answering questions to show that you understand what you have read. Remember to rely on your own common sense and what you have learned from experience.

Understanding fiction is an important part of passing the GED Language Arts, Reading Test. Questions about fiction passages make up approximately 75% of the test questions.

Alice Walker's stories have won her great acclaim, including the Pulitzer Prize for her novel The Color Purple.

The lessons in this unit include:

Lesson 10: **Getting Meaning from Context**
You can use clues to help you figure out the meaning of unfamiliar words or phrases.

Lesson 11: **Identifying Plot Elements**
Identifying plot elements helps you understand which events in a story are the most important and how the events tie together.

Lesson 12: **Applying Ideas**
One way to demonstrate your understanding of a character or an idea in a story is to apply what you have learned to a related situation.

Lesson 13: **Identifying Cause and Effect**
Part of understanding a story is being able to identify the causes of events and the effects that result.

Lesson 14: **Analyzing Character**
To analyze characters in a story, examine what the characters say, do, and think, as well as what other characters say about them.

Lesson 15: **Analyzing Tone**
Analyzing tone involves understanding an author's attitude toward the characters and events.

Lesson 16: **Identifying Figurative Language**
Identifying figurative language helps you appreciate the ways that fiction writers use words to create vivid images.

Lesson 17: **Making Inferences**
Getting the full meaning of a story often involves making inferences, or "reading between the lines" of what the writer says directly.

Lesson 18: **Comparing and Contrasting**
Using comparison and contrast to determine how characters and situations are alike or different is an important skill in understanding a work of fiction.

Lesson 19: **Interpreting Theme**
Interpreting the theme, the central idea of a short story or novel, requires making multiple inferences about the writer's views and perspective.

> **SELECTED FICTION WRITERS**
> - Julia Alvarez
> - Rudolfo Anaya
> - Jane Austen
> - Toni Cade Bambara
> - Charles Dickens
> - William Faulkner
> - Ernest Hemingway
> - Langston Hughes
> - John Steinbeck
> - Amy Tan
> - Mark Twain

WASHINGTON IRVING EDUCATIONAL CENTER
ADULT AND CONTINUING EDUCATION
422 MUMFORD STREET
SCHENECTADY, NEW YORK 12307

GED SKILL Getting Meaning from Context

When writers present words or situations that are unfamiliar, you can rely on surrounding words and phrases, or **context,** to help find meaning. These words and phrases may be in the same sentence or in a group of nearby sentences. Study these words for clues to understand what you are reading.

Even if you cannot figure out the exact meaning of a word or phrase, clues from the context will help you to make a good guess. For example, if you saw an unfamiliar item in a store, you would probably look around at the other items on the shelf for clues. Then, you can make a reasonable guess as to what the unfamiliar item is.

context
the words or sentences that surround words

TIP

To figure out unfamiliar words in an excerpt, substitute words you know in their place. If the substituted words make sense within the context, you have made a good guess at the definition.

Read the following excerpt from a novel and complete the exercise below.

Mark went over the engine room slowly, double-checking everything. He washed the dishes in the galley, placing them carefully behind the little racks that held them tight in a gale. He checked the log, put away the charts, made up the berths, cleaned the refrigerator, and closed the portholes. When he was done, the sun was high in the sky, and he went out on deck to await the canoes.

Margaret Craven, *I Heard the Owl Call My Name.*

1. Where is Mark when he is doing these things?

_____

Underline each context clue in the excerpt that helped you answer the question.

The context clues tell you that Mark is on a boat or ship. The words *engine room, galley, gale, log, berths, portholes, deck,* and *canoes* all relate to boating.

2. Based on the context clues in the excerpt, what is a *gale?*
   _____ a. a gentle breeze
   _____ b. a strong wind

You were correct if you chose *option b, a strong wind.* Dishes need to be held in place to keep them from breaking when a boat is rocked by strong winds.

Read the following excerpt from a novel and complete the exercise below.

Glancing down the interminable Brooklyn street you thought of those joined brownstones as one house reflected through a train of mirrors, with no walls between the houses but only vast rooms yawning endlessly one into the other. Yet, looking close, you saw that under the thick ivy each house had something

(5) distinctively its own. Some touch that was Gothic, Romanesque, baroque or Greek triumphed amid the Victorian clutter. Here, Ionic columns framed the windows while next door gargoyles scowled up at the sun. There, the cornices were hung with carved foliage while Gorgon heads decorated others. Many houses had bay windows or Gothic stonework; a few boasted turrets raised high above the other

(10) roofs. Yet they all shared the same brown monotony. All seemed doomed by the confusion in their design.

Paule Marshall, *Brown Girl, Brownstones.*

1. a. Put a check mark by the meaning of the word *interminable* in line 1.

   _____ unsafe

   _____ unfamiliar

   _____ unending

   b. Put a check mark by the other word from the first sentence that is the best clue to the meaning of *interminable*.

   _____ glancing

   _____ mirrors

   _____ endlessly

2. Put a check mark next to what the terms *Gothic, Romanesque, baroque,* and *Greek* refer to in lines 5–10.

   _____ types of gargoyles

   _____ styles of design

   _____ kinds of roofs

3. a. Put a check mark by the meaning of *turrets* as used in "a few boasted turrets" (line 9).

   _____ flower gardens

   _____ little towers

   b. Explain the context clues you used to choose your answer to 3a. _____

   _____

4. Look at the word *monotony* (line 10). Write two clues that help you determine its meaning.

   _____

   _____

Answers start on page 295.

Directions: Choose the <u>one best answer</u> to each question.

<u>Questions 1 through 5</u> refer to the following excerpt from a novel.

WHAT WERE THE EARLIEST POLITICAL PARTIES IN THE UNITED STATES?

During the last session of the Third Congress I led the battle in the Senate against ratification of Jay's treaty with England. The treaty was clumsily drawn
(5) and to our disadvantage. It actually contained a clause forbidding us to export cotton in *American* ships. In effect, the treaty made us a colony again. It also revealed for the first time the deep and
(10) irreconcilable division between the Republican and Federalist parties—and they were now actual political parties, no longer simply factions. One was pro-French; the other pro-British. One wanted
(15) a loose confederation of states, the other a strong central administration; one was made up of independent farmers in alliance with city workers; the other was devoted to trade and manufacturing. One
(20) was Jefferson; the other was Hamilton.

Gore Vidal, *Burr: A Novel.*

1. What does the word *drawn* mean in the phrase "clumsily drawn" (line 4)?

   (1) pulled
   (2) drafted
   (3) illustrated
   (4) removed
   (5) deduced

2. What is the "battle in the Senate" mentioned in line 2?

   (1) the narrator's campaign to be elected
   (2) the rebellion against England
   (3) the disagreement between parties over a treaty
   (4) the argument between the narrator and Jefferson
   (5) the dispute over whether political parties will be allowed

3. Which one of the following narrative techniques is used in this excerpt?

   (1) describing a conflict between a character and nature
   (2) telling the story through one character
   (3) having the characters speak in dialect
   (4) using dialogue to reveal personalities
   (5) using a flashback to give background information

4. Which of the following <u>best</u> describes the narrator?

   (1) modest
   (2) opinionated
   (3) impassioned
   (4) uninformed
   (5) heroic

5. According to the excerpt, which one of the following was a key difference between the Republican and Federalist parties?

   (1) support for exporting cotton in American ships
   (2) the personalities of their leaders
   (3) positions on the relationship between the states and the central government
   (4) the decisions of their members to become political parties
   (5) positions on becoming a colony again

Questions 6 through 10 refer to the following excerpt from a novel.

WHAT IS THIS MAN'S JOB?

It was a pleasure to burn.

It was a special pleasure to see things eaten, to see things blackened and *changed.* With the brass nozzle in his fists,
(5) with this great python spitting its venomous kerosene upon the world, the blood pounded in his head, and his hands were the hands of some amazing conductor playing all the symphonies of blazing and
(10) burning to bring down the tatters and charcoal ruins of history. With his symbolic helmet numbered 451 on his stolid head, and his eyes all orange flame with the thought of what came next, he flicked the
(15) igniter and the house jumped up in a gorging fire that burned the evening sky red and yellow and black. He strode in a swarm of fireflies. He wanted above all, like the old joke, to shove a marshmallow on a
(20) stick in the furnace, while the flapping pigeon-winged books died on the porch and lawn of the house. While the books went up in sparkling whirls and blew away on a wind turned dark with burning.

Ray Bradbury, *Fahrenheit 451.*

6. Based on the information in the excerpt, what is the character doing?

(1) fighting a huge house fire
(2) conducting a training session for firefighters
(3) burning a pile of trash at the local dump
(4) burning a house filled with books
(5) supervising a display of fireworks

7. Which of the following jobs would the character in this excerpt most likely enjoy?

(1) conductor
(2) construction worker
(3) demolition worker
(4) librarian
(5) chef

8. Which of the following techniques does the author use to bring the excerpt to life?

(1) detailed imagery
(2) realistic dialogue
(3) first-person narration
(4) conflict between characters
(5) a sense of humor

9. What is the meaning of the statement "the house jumped up in a gorging fire" (lines 15–16)?

(1) The flames descended from the top of the house.
(2) The flames immediately engulfed the house.
(3) The flames on the lawn suddenly illuminated the house.
(4) The house collapsed as the fire turned it to ashes.
(5) The house glowed in the weakening flames.

10. To what does the phrase "this great python spitting its venomous kerosene" (lines 5–6) refer?

(1) the character, who feels like a poisonous snake getting ready to strike
(2) a poisonous snake that will be let loose upon the world
(3) a hose that is suggestive of a snake
(4) the flames that curve upward like a snake about to strike
(5) the stream of water being sprayed on the fire like a spitting snake

 TIP To figure out what is happening in a complex excerpt, try to ignore the descriptive words and phrases and focus on the action words (verbs) instead. These words can point to what a character is actually doing.

Answers start on page 295.

Directions: This is a ten-minute practice test. After ten minutes, mark the last question you finished. Then complete the test and check your answers. If most of your answers were correct, but you didn't finish, try to work faster next time. Choose the one best answer to each question.

Questions 1 through 7 refer to the following excerpt from a novel.

HOW DOES THIS MAN FIGHT COMMERCIAL TV?

Years before, he had invented a module that, when a television commercial appeared, automatically muted the sound. It wasn't at first a context-recognition

(5) device. Instead, it simply monitored the amplitude of the carrier wave. TV advertisers had taken to running their ads louder and with less audio clutter than the programs that were their nominal vehicles.

(10) News of Hadden's module spread by word of mouth. People reported a sense of relief, the lifting of a great burden, even a feeling of joy at being freed from the advertising barrage for the six to eight

(15) hours out of every day that the average American spent in front of the television set. Before there could be any coordinated response from the television advertising industry, Adnix had become wildly popular.

(20) It forced advertisers and networks into new choices of carrier-wave strategy, each of which Hadden countered with a new invention. Sometimes he invented circuits to defeat strategies which the agencies

(25) and the networks had not yet hit upon. He would say that he was saving them the trouble of making inventions, at great cost to their shareholders, which were at any rate doomed to failure. As his sales volume

(30) increased, he kept cutting prices. It was a kind of electronic warfare. And he was winning.

They tried to sue him—something about a conspiracy in restraint of trade.

(35) They had sufficient political muscle that his motion for summary dismissal was denied, but insufficient influence to actually win the case. The trial had forced Hadden to investigate the relevant legal codes. Soon

(40) after, he applied, through a well-known

Madison Avenue agency in which he was now a major silent partner, to advertise his own product on commercial television. After a few weeks of controversy his

(45) commercials were refused. He sued all three networks and in *this* trial was able to prove conspiracy in restraint of trade. He received a huge settlement, that was, at the time, a record for cases of this sort,

(50) and which contributed in its modest way to the demise of the original networks.

There had always been people who enjoyed the commercials, of course, and they had no need for Adnix. But they were

(55) a dwindling minority. Hadden made a great fortune by eviscerating[1] broadcast advertising. He also made many enemies. . . .

As he further developed context-

(60) recognition chips, it became obvious to him that they had much wider application—from education, science, and medicine, to military intelligence and industrial espionage. It was on this issue

(65) that lines were drawn for the famous suit *United States v. Hadden Cybernetics.* One of Hadden's chips was considered too good for civilian life, and on recommendation of the National Security

(70) Agency, the facilities and key personnel for the most advanced context-recognition chip production were taken over by the government. It was simply too important to read the Russian mail. God knows,

(75) they told him, what would happen if the Russians could read our mail.

---

[1] depriving of vital force or power

Carl Sagan, *Contact.*

1. What is suggested about Hadden's personality by the detail in lines 21–23 "each of which Hadden countered with a new invention"?

   (1) He likes to annoy people.
   (2) He is persistent.
   (3) He is devious.
   (4) He is lazy.
   (5) He is not trustworthy.

2. To what does the phrase "nominal vehicles" (line 9) refer?

   (1) television commercials
   (2) a type of car popular with TV advertisers
   (3) TV ads featuring cars and other vehicles
   (4) television programs
   (5) ads with less audio clutter

3. Based on this excerpt, what is "Adnix"?

   (1) a device that silences TV commercials
   (2) a machine that recognizes voices
   (3) a computer chip used to spy on enemies
   (4) a device to add audio clutter to commercials
   (5) a computer chip that causes commercials to short circuit

4. Based on this excerpt, which of these statements most likely describes Hadden's attitude toward television?

   (1) The quality of commercials needs to be improved.
   (2) Television networks should produce more educational programming.
   (3) Television networks do not have viewers' best interests at heart.
   (4) People are very careful about what they watch on television.
   (5) Viewers must tolerate commercials as a necessary evil.

5. Based on the details in this excerpt, what is its theme, or message?

   (1) the dangers of watching too much television
   (2) the undesirable nature of commercials
   (3) the superiority of public television over commercial television
   (4) the workings of the mind of an inventor
   (5) the benefits of commercial TV

6. Which of the following developments in commercial television might Hadden disapprove of most?

   (1) the increasing use of profanity during prime time
   (2) the scarcity of minorities in the prime-time lineup
   (3) the unnecessary sex and violence
   (4) the acceptance of "infomercials" to promote products
   (5) the blurring of the lines between news and entertainment

7. Based on the excerpt, what was the central issue of the suit *United States v. Hadden Cybernetics?*

   (1) Television networks refused to air Hadden's commercials.
   (2) Hadden wanted to use his chip to spy on his competitors.
   (3) The U.S. government wanted to prevent Hadden from using his chip to gather military information.
   (4) The U.S. government wanted to take over production and use of Hadden's chip.
   (5) The United States wanted Hadden to stop producing chips that blocked commercials.

Answers start on page 295.

Lesson 11

GED SKILL Identifying Plot Elements

plot
the order of events in a story and the relationships between these events

When identifying plot elements, look for the important characters and any conflicts that may influence the outcome of events.

Plot refers to what happens to characters in a story, and the order in which those events take place. Through the plot, writers arrange events to create a believable and interesting story.

A plot has a beginning, middle, and end. The beginning, or **exposition,** introduces the characters, setting, and other details and hints at an unstable situation. The middle introduces **complications** that create **conflict** and increase the story's tension. Complications reach their highest intensity at the **climax,** after which the conflict is resolved and the end, or **resolution,** is reached.

Read the following plot summary and complete the exercise below.

A young man crashes a party and is attracted to a beautiful woman. Despite a feud between their families, they fall in love and are secretly married. The woman's cousin kills the young man's friend over an insult. Avenging his friend's death, the man kills his wife's cousin and flees. Meanwhile, the woman's family attempts to force her to marry another man. On her wedding day, she takes a drug that makes her appear to be dead. She is taken to the family tomb, where she is to meet her lover when she awakes. He arrives, thinks she is dead, and commits suicide by drinking poison. The woman awakens to find her lover dead and kills herself with his dagger. After discovering the lovers' fate, the grieving families end their feud.

Identify each plot element by writing *E* for exposition, *C* for complication, *Con* for conflict, *Cl* for climax, and *R* for resolution.

_____ a. The young man and woman fall in love.

_____ b. The woman's cousin kills her lover's friend.

_____ c. The families agree to end their feud.

_____ d. The woman commits suicide with a dagger.

_____ e. The lovers' families hate each other.

You were correct if you chose *E* for *option a* because this is important information about the characters introduced in the beginning. The answer is *C* for *option b* because it is a complication that creates or heightens the conflict. *R* is the answer for *option c* because it is the outcome of the story. *Cl* is the answer for *option d* because it is the point where complications reach their highest intensity, and *Con* is the answer to *option e* because it is the underlying conflict that creates the tension in the story.

Read the following excerpt from a short story and complete the exercise below.

Young Goodman Brown came forth at sunset into the street at Salem village, but put his head back, after crossing the threshold, to exchange a parting kiss with his young wife. And Faith, as the wife was aptly named, thrust her own pretty head into the street, letting the wind play with the pink ribbons of her cap while she

(5) called to Goodman Brown.

"Dearest heart," whispered she, softly and rather sadly, when her lips were close to his ear, "prithee[1] put off your journey until sunrise and sleep in your own bed to-night. A lone woman is troubled with such dreams and such thoughts that she's afeard of herself sometimes. Pray tarry[2] with me this night, dear husband, of

(10) all nights in the year."

---

[1] a word used to express a request   [2] stay

Nathaniel Hawthorne, "Young Goodman Brown."

1. Where does the conversation take place?

_____

2. When does it take place?

_____

3. List three details about the character Faith.

a. _____

b. _____

c. _____

4. Put a check mark by the details from the excerpt that hint at an unstable situation that may lead to conflict.

_____ a. The wife is afraid to be left alone.

_____ b. The wife begs her husband to stay.

_____ c. The husband leaves as darkness falls.

_____ d. The wife wears pink ribbons in her cap.

_____ e. The husband is described as young.

 TIP
To identify important plot information, look at how events are ordered. Ask yourself whether tensions among characters increase or decrease after a certain event. This will help you to locate the climax of the plot.

Answers start on page 296.

Directions: Choose the one best answer to each question.

Questions 1 through 4 refer to the following excerpt from a short story.

WHERE WILL THEY VACATION?

The grandmother didn't want to go to Florida. She wanted to visit some of her connections in east Tennessee and she was seizing at every chance to change
(5) Bailey's mind. Bailey was the son she lived with, her only boy. He was sitting on the edge of his chair at the table, bent over the orange sports section of the *Journal.* "Now look here, Bailey," she said, "see
(10) here, read this," and she stood with one hand on her thin hip and the other rattling the newspaper at his bald head. "Here this fellow that calls himself The Misfit is aloose from the Federal Pen and headed toward
(15) Florida and you read here what it says he did to these people. Just you read it. I wouldn't take my children in any direction with a criminal like that aloose in it. I couldn't answer to my conscience if I did."
(20) Bailey didn't look up from his reading so she wheeled around then and faced the children's mother, a young woman in slacks, whose face was as broad and innocent as a cabbage and was tied
(25) around with a green head-kerchief that had two points on the top like a rabbit's ears. She was sitting on the sofa, feeding the baby his apricots out of a jar. "The children have been to Florida before," the
(30) old lady said. "You all ought to take them somewhere else for a change so they would see different parts of the world and be broad. They never have been to east Tennessee."
(35) The children's mother didn't seem to hear her but the eight-year-old boy, John Wesley, a stocky child with glasses, said, "If you don't want to go to Florida, why dontcha stay at home?" He and the little
(40) girl, June Star, were reading the funny papers on the floor.

Flannery O'Connor, "A Good Man Is Hard to Find,"
A Good Man Is Hard to Find and Other Stories.

1. Based on this excerpt, which of the following words best describes the grandmother?

   (1) selfish
   (2) worried
   (3) innocent
   (4) timid
   (5) devoted

2. How do the other family members respond to the grandmother's behavior?

   (1) They poke fun at her.
   (2) They ignore her for the most part.
   (3) They exclude her from their activities.
   (4) They let her have her way.
   (5) They openly defy her.

3. Which of the following situations is most similar to the situation in the excerpt?

   (1) a conference in which teachers discuss the best way to educate children
   (2) a meeting in which a boss tries to change his staff's mind about an issue
   (3) a gathering in which neighbors vote on how to curb crime in their community
   (4) a family reunion in which relatives express their love for one another
   (5) a classroom in which students share their views about current events

4. What is the main way in which the grandmother's character is revealed in this excerpt?

   (1) description of what she looks like
   (2) background about her Tennessee heritage
   (3) details about what she likes to read
   (4) explanations of what the other characters think of her
   (5) dialogue in which her manner of speaking is shown

Questions 5 through 7 refer to the following excerpt from a short story.

WHY IS THIS BOY IN TROUBLE?

She was a large woman with a large purse that had everything in it but a hammer and nails. It had a long strap, and she carried it slung across her
(5) shoulder. It was about eleven o'clock at night, dark, and she was walking alone, when a boy ran up behind her and tried to snatch her purse. The strap broke with the sudden single tug the boy gave it from
(10) behind. But the boy's weight and the weight of the purse combined caused him to lose his balance. Instead of taking off full blast as he had hoped, the boy fell on his back on the sidewalk and his legs flew
(15) up. The large woman simply turned around and kicked him right square in his blue-jeaned sitter. Then she reached down, picked the boy up by his shirt front, and shook him until his teeth rattled.
(20) After that the woman said, "Pick up my pocketbook, boy, and give it here."

She still held him tightly. But she bent down enough to permit him to stoop and pick up her purse. Then she said, "Now
(25) ain't you ashamed of yourself?"

Firmly gripped by his shirt front, the boy said, "Yes'm."

The woman said, "What did you want to do it for?"
(30) The boy said, "I didn't aim to."

She said, "You a lie!"

By that time two or three people passed, stopped, turned to look, and some stood watching.
(35) "If I turn you loose, will you run?" asked the woman.

"Yes'm," said the boy.

"Then I won't turn you loose," said the woman. She did not release him.
(40) "Lady, I'm sorry," whispered the boy.

"Um-hum! Your face is dirty. I got a great mind to wash your face for you. Ain't you got nobody home to tell you to wash your face?"

(45) "No'm," said the boy.

"Then it will get washed this evening," said the large woman, starting up the street, dragging the frightened boy behind her.

Langston Hughes, "Thank You, M'am," *Short Stories.*

5. Which of the following best describes the woman in this excerpt?

   (1) mean
   (2) fearful
   (3) caring
   (4) careful
   (5) dishonest

6. Based on the excerpt, which of the following is the woman most likely to do to the boy?

   (1) take him to her house and feed him
   (2) escort him home and speak to his parents
   (3) turn him over to the police
   (4) offer to give him money and send him away
   (5) give him a warning and let him go

7. Based on its title ("Thank You, M'am") and the way the woman treats the boy in the excerpt, what is the most likely resolution for this story?

   (1) The boy later steals from the woman and ends up in jail.
   (2) The woman realizes she made a mistake in being nice to the boy.
   (3) The boy tries to be nice and helps the woman with her housework.
   (4) The woman hires the boy to help her in her store.
   (5) The woman helps the boy make something of himself.

Answers start on page 296.

Directions: This is a ten-minute practice test. After ten minutes, mark the last question you finished. Then complete the test and check your answers. If most of your answers were correct, but you didn't finish, try to work faster next time. Choose the <u>one best answer</u> to each question.

<u>Questions 1 through 6</u> refer to the following excerpt from a novel.

WHY DO THESE WOMEN DISAGREE?

Naomi let the cardboard fan from Gilchrist's Funeral Home fall into her lap and assessed her daughter, stretched out on the bed, wrapped in the too-neat
(5) tranquil repose that precedes upheaval. She wanted to ask simply and boldly, "Who is he?" but she could not bear the thought of hearing a lie and the sensation that had come upon her informed Naomi
(10) that Esther would interpret curiosity as trespass. Naomi picked up the fan and felt the warm air against her cheek as forlorn as a goodbye kiss.

The phone rang and Esther said, "If it's
(15) Bruce, tell him I'm not here."

"I'm not gonna lie for you, young lady. You're big enough to do that for yourself."

The phone rang several times with a persistence that Esther associated with
(20) Bruce. She had met him at Howard. He was a mannerly young junior from Newark, New Jersey, who wanted to be a lawyer and who bored Esther more than she'd imagined possible. The phone was finally
(25) silent after the twelfth ring.

"What's wrong with this Bruce anyway?" Naomi asked.

"He's so young."

"Young, well, *you're* young. What do
(30) you want? A man? You're not ready for that. A man right now wouldn't do you nothing but harm."

"You married at seventeen."

"Yeah and I wish I hadn't. And that don't
(35) mean I was ready for it. That was the only thing a girl could do, where I come from, to prove herself."

"I just can't stand Bruce. He's got no imagination."

(40) "Sometimes I'm sorry you're in college. You come home throwing around all those words like they've got something to do with life. Man don't need imagination to love a woman. He needs to look her in the eye
(45) and see her for everything she is when he finds her, forget about fantasies and dreams and what he thinks he got to have, man has to look at a woman like she is and love her anyway."

(50) "Imagination got you everything you have."

"Being hungry got me what I own. When you're hungry you'll do almost anything, when it's imagination that's
(55) driving you, you get picky."

Marita Golden, *Long Distance Life.*

1. Based on the excerpt, what can be inferred about Naomi and Esther's relationship?

   (1) They dislike each other.
   (2) They are close to one another.
   (3) They agree on most points.
   (4) They have shared similar experiences.
   (5) They have no respect for each other.

2. Which of the following <u>best</u> describes the underlying conflict between the two women?

   (1) They have different ideas about love.
   (2) Naomi seeks to control her daughter's future.
   (3) Esther thinks her mother is old-fashioned.
   (4) Naomi dislikes her daughter's new boyfriend.
   (5) Naomi and her daughter have nothing in common.

3. Based on Naomi and Esther's discussion, which of the following is the best conclusion that can be drawn about Naomi?

(1) She does not want Esther to be happy.
(2) She is afraid that Esther will make the same mistakes she made.
(3) She is angry that Esther no longer seems to listen to her.
(4) She is not supportive of Esther's pursuing a college education.
(5) She thinks Esther is too concerned with money.

4. If Bruce were to come for a visit, how would Naomi most likely react?

She would

(1) pretend that Esther was not at home
(2) try to persuade Esther to talk to him
(3) send him away
(4) ask him to marry Esther
(5) inquire about his studies

5. Which of the following events would best resolve the conflict in this excerpt?

(1) Esther decides to give Bruce one more chance.
(2) Naomi accepts her past mistakes.
(3) Esther and Naomi decide to respect their differences.
(4) Esther decides that she will never get married.
(5) Naomi enrolls in college to pursue her dreams.

6. Which of the following ideas are most clearly contrasted in this passage?

(1) knowledge and ignorance
(2) openness and secrecy
(3) truth and deception
(4) youth and experience
(5) trust and fear

Questions 7 and 8 refer to the following excerpt from a short story.

WHAT IS THIS MAN LOOKING FORWARD TO?

They had lasagna for Thanksgiving dinner that year. The meatless kind. From a can.
"Nothing like the smell of a good bird
(5) in the oven," Mike Senior announced, scraping his boots on the doormat, inhaling.
"Uh, Pop?" Janet whispered.
"Yes, ma'am?"
(10) "Never mind. Happy Thanksgiving, Pop. Let me help you with your coat. There are a few things in the kitchen I've got to see to yet. Mike should be back any minute. I'll leave you and Shawn to get reacquainted."
(15) He smelled it all morning. He smelled it when he woke up in the cramped, stuffy bedroom he rented near the school in South Boston where he worked as a custodian part-time—fresh, brought in
(20) from the woodshed where it had been kept during the night to keep it moist. He smelled it as the bus crossed the state line into Maine—skin turning brown, the first drippings running down the sides.

W. D. Wetherell, "If a Woodchuck Could Chuck Wood."

7. Based on the information in this excerpt, what relation is Janet to Mike Senior?

(1) daughter
(2) daughter-in-law
(3) stepdaughter
(4) granddaughter
(5) niece

8. What important fact about the family can you infer from the first two paragraphs?

(1) The family enjoys cooking together.
(2) The family does not celebrate holidays.
(3) The family has fallen on hard times.
(4) The family prefers Italian food.
(5) The family thinks Mike Senior is losing touch with reality.

Answers start on page 296.

GED SKILL **Applying Ideas**

One way to show an understanding of what you read is to take information and **apply** it to a related situation. In fiction, writers develop characters that usually act consistently. Based on characters' actions, what motivates them, and how they react to events in a story, you can often predict how they might react in new situations. Applying information to a new context can help you better understand the characters and the plot of a story.

apply
to take information and transfer it to a new situation

TIP

Questions that ask you to predict what a character would say or do are usually application questions.

Read the following excerpt from a short story and complete the exercise below.

. . . My own talent was I could always make money. I had a touch for it, unusual in a Chippewa. From the first I was different that way, and everyone recognized it. I was the only kid they let in the American Legion Hall to shine shoes, for example, and one Christmas I sold spiritual bouquets for the mission door to door. The nuns let me keep a percentage. Once I started, it seemed the more money I made the easier the money came. Everyone encouraged it. When I was fifteen I got a job washing dishes at the Joliet Café, and that was where my first big break happened.

Louise Erdrich, "The Red Convertible," *Love Medicine.*

1. Based on the excerpt, for which job would the character be most suited if he were to volunteer at a homeless shelter?

   ——— a. soup kitchen worker

   ——— b. fund-raiser

You were correct if you chose *option b, fund-raiser.* The excerpt states that the character's talent is making money; therefore, he would likely be most suited for fund-raising.

2. Based on this excerpt, which of the following phrases best describes the character's way with money?

   ——— a. Money burns a hole in his pocket.

   ——— b. Everything he touches turns to gold.

You were correct if you chose *option b, Everything he touches turns to gold.* The excerpt states that he could always make money—that he had a touch for it.

Read the following excerpt from a piece of fiction and complete the exercise below.

My mother believed you could be anything you wanted to be in America. You could open a restaurant. You could work for the government and get good retirement. You could buy a house with almost no money down. You could become rich. You could become instantly famous.

(5) "Of course you can be prodigy,[1] too," my mother told me when I was nine. "You can be best anything. What does Auntie Lindo know? Her daughter, she is only best tricky."

America was where all my mother's hopes lay. She had come here in 1949 after losing everything in China: her mother and father, her family home, her first
(10) husband, and two daughters, twin baby girls. But she never looked back with regret. There were so many ways for things to get better.

_____
[1] a highly talented child or youth

Amy Tan, "Two Kinds," *The Joy Luck Club.*

1. If the mother learned that her daughter bought several lottery tickets, how would she most likely react?

   _____ a. She would become angry with her daughter for wasting her money.

   _____ b. She would wish for the best and hope that her daughter wins.

2. Based on the excerpt, which of the following actions is most consistent with the mother's character?

   _____ a. denying her daughter the opportunity to take violin lessons

   _____ b. encouraging members of her household to register to vote

   _____ c. saving her money to go back to China to rebuild her life

   _____ d. becoming an active member of a political party

3. On the basis of this excerpt, put a check mark by the three statements with which the mother might agree.

   _____ People rarely get ahead in life.

   _____ Prosperity is just around the corner.

   _____ Things could be much worse than they are.

   _____ It is always darkest before dawn.

4. Write a sentence from the excerpt that supports your choices for question 3.

   _____

   _____

Answers start on page 297.

Directions: Choose the one best answer to each question.

Questions 1 through 3 refer to the following excerpt from a novel.

HOW WILL THEY CELEBRATE?

I raced down the block from where the number eight bus dropped me off, around the corner from our house. The fall was slowly settling into the trees on our block,
(5) some of them had already turned slightly brown.

I could barely contain my excitement as I walked up the steps to the house, sprinting across the living room to the
(10) kitchen.

Ma was leaning over the stove, the pots clanking as she hummed a song to herself.

"My passport should come in a month or so," I said, unfolding a photocopy of the
(15) application for her to see.

She looked at it as though it contained boundless possibilities.

"We can celebrate with some strong bone soup," she said. "I am making some
(20) right now."

In the pot on the stove were scraps of cow bones stewing in hot bubbling broth.

Ma believed that her bone soup could cure all kinds of ills. She even hoped that
(25) it would perform the miracle of detaching Caroline from Eric, her Bahamian fiancé. Since Caroline had announced that she was engaged, we'd had bone soup with our supper every single night.

(30) "Have you had some soup?" I asked, teasing Caroline when she came out of the bedroom.

"This soup is really getting on my nerves," Caroline whispered in my ear
(35) as she walked by the stove to get some water from the kitchen faucet.

Edwidge Danticat, *Krik? Krak!*

1. On the basis of this excerpt, which of the following would be the mother's most likely reaction if Caroline were to break her engagement with her fiancé?

She might

(1) think the bone soup was responsible
(2) go to the Bahamas to find a husband for Caroline
(3) ask her other daughter to postpone her trip
(4) cast a spell over the fiancé
(5) scold Caroline for making a mistake

2. Why does the narrator ask Caroline if she had some soup?

(1) She worries that Caroline does not eat enough.
(2) She hopes Caroline will break off her engagement.
(3) They like to poke fun at their mother's beliefs.
(4) She wants Caroline to celebrate.
(5) They enjoy their mother's cooking.

3. Which of the following can you infer about the mother based on the way she responds to her daughters' plans?

(1) She wants her daughters to stay at home.
(2) She hopes her daughters will become good cooks like she is.
(3) She supports her daughters' decisions.
(4) She cares about her daughters' futures.
(5) She wishes her daughters were more tolerant of other cultures.

To answer application questions, read each answer choice and look for details such as behaviors or beliefs. Eliminate choices that contain details that do not fit the character.

Questions 4 through 7 refer to the following excerpt from a novel.

WHAT HAPPENS BEFORE THIS BOY BEGINS SCHOOL?

"Today is Antonio's first day at school," she said.

"Huh! Another expense. In California, they say, the land flows with milk and
(5) honey—"

"Any land will flow with milk and honey if it is worked with honest hands!" my mother retorted. "Look at what my brothers have done with the bottomland of El Puerto—"

(10) "Ay, mujer, always your brothers! On this hill only rocks grow!"

"Ay! And whose fault is it that we bought a worthless hill! No, you couldn't buy fertile land along the river, you had to buy this
(15) piece of, of—"

"Of the llano[1]," my father finished.

"Yes!"

"It is beautiful," he said with satisfaction.

"It is worthless! Look how hard we
(20) worked on the garden all summer, and for what? Two baskets of chile and one of corn! Bah!"

"There is freedom here."

"Try putting that in the lunch pails of
(25) your children!"

"Tony goes to school today, huh?" he said.

"Yes. And you must talk to him."

"He will be all right."

(30) "He must know the value of his education," she insisted. "He must know what he can become."

"A priest."

"Yes."

(35) "For your brothers." His voice was cold.

"You leave my brothers out of this! They are honorable men. They have always treated you with respect. They were the first colonizers of the Llano Estacado. It
(40) was the Lunas who carried the charter from the Mexican government to settle the valley. That took courage—"

[1] an open grassy plain

Rudolfo Anaya, *Bless Me, Ultima.*

4. Based on the details in lines 31–39, what is the occupation of Antonio's uncles?

    (1) fishermen
    (2) farmhands
    (3) cattle ranchers
    (4) priests
    (5) government officials

5. On the basis of this excerpt, which of the following would make Antonio's mother the happiest?

    (1) getting a divorce from her husband and moving in with her brothers
    (2) having her son drop out of school and help with the farm
    (3) selling their land and moving near the river
    (4) renouncing her Mexican citizenship
    (5) having Antonio move in with her brothers in El Puerto

6. What does the mother's statement, "Try putting that in the lunch pails of your children" (lines 24–25), indicate about her opinion of her husband?

    She thinks he is

    (1) stubborn
    (2) lazy
    (3) sensible
    (4) impractical
    (5) disrespectful

7. Which of the following best characterizes the author's style in this excerpt?

    (1) long, complex sentences
    (2) formal, scholarly language
    (3) an emphasis on dialogue
    (4) detailed descriptive passages
    (5) frequent use of humor

Answers start on page 297.

Directions: This is a ten-minute practice test. After ten minutes, mark the last question you finished. Then complete the test and check your answers. If most of your answers were correct, but you didn't finish, try to work faster next time. Choose the <u>one best answer</u> to each question.

Questions 1 through 9 refer to the following excerpt from a novel.

HOW DOES THIS FAMILY GET ALONG?

"Hi, Daddy!" Feather screamed. She was so excited to see me after all those hours asleep that she ran right for me, banging her nose against my knee. She
(5) started to cry and I picked her up. Jesus slipped into the room as silent as mist. He was small for fifteen, slight and surefooted. He was the star long-distance runner at Hamilton High School. He smiled at me,
(10) not saying a word.

Jesus hadn't said a thing in the thirteen years I'd known him. He wrote me notes sometimes. Usually about money he needed and events at school that I should
(15) attend. The doctors said that he was healthy, that he could talk if he wanted to. All I could do was wait.

Jesus took over the breakfast while I cooed to Feather and held her close.
(20) "You hurt me," she whined.

"You want peanut butter or salami for lunch?" I answered.

Feather's skin was light brown and fleshy. Her stomach rumbled against my
(25) chest. I could see in her face that she didn't know whether to cry or run for the table.

"Lemme go! Lemme go!" she said, pushing at my arms to get down to her
(30) chair.

The moment she was on her stack of phone books, Jesus put a slice of bread covered with strawberry jam in front of her.

"I dreamed," Feather said, then she
(35) stared off into space lost for a moment. Her amber eyes and crinkled golden hair were both made almost transparent from the light through the kitchen window. "I dreamed, I dreamed," she continued.
(40) "There was a scary man in the house last night."

"What kind of man?"

"She held out her hands and opened her eyes wide to say she just didn't know.
(45) "I didn't see him. I just hearded him."

Walter Mosley, *Black Betty.*

1. What is the relationship between the narrator and Feather?

   The narrator is Feather's

   (1) mother
   (2) father
   (3) sister
   (4) brother
   (5) son

2. Which of the following is the <u>most likely</u> reason for Feather's first response to seeing the narrator?

   (1) She is happy to see him when she wakes up in the morning.
   (2) She is jealous of Jesus and his accomplishments.
   (3) She wants him to make her breakfast.
   (4) She is afraid of the strange man in the house.
   (5) She wants someone to talk to besides Jesus.

3. What is likely true of Jesus based on the description that he "slipped into the room as silent as mist" (line 6)?

   He is

   (1) sneaky
   (2) quiet
   (3) helpful
   (4) small
   (5) scared

4. Based on the excerpt, what can be inferred about Jesus?

   (1) His vocal cords are damaged, which makes it impossible for him to speak.
   (2) He is responsible for all of the cooking in the household.
   (3) He has chosen not to speak to other people.
   (4) He is in danger of dropping out of school.
   (5) He cannot budget his money well.

5. Based on the excerpt, which of the following best explains the relationship between Jesus and the narrator?

   (1) Jesus is the narrator's son.
   (2) The narrator has known Jesus since his birth.
   (3) Jesus is a neighbor's child.
   (4) The narrator provides a home for Jesus.
   (5) Jesus and the narrator are brothers.

6. Based on the excerpt, which of the following words best describes Jesus?

   (1) outspoken
   (2) unreliable
   (3) whiny
   (4) ambitious
   (5) responsible

7. What is worrying Feather?

   (1) She banged her nose against the narrator's knee.
   (2) She does not want peanut butter for lunch.
   (3) She is hungry.
   (4) She had a scary dream.
   (5) She dislikes Jesus.

8. Based on the excerpt, how would this family be described in today's terms?

   (1) a foster family
   (2) a single-parent family
   (3) a dysfunctional family
   (4) an extended family
   (5) an isolated family

9. What is the effect of the depiction of the narrator's relationship with Feather and Jesus?

   It

   (1) makes the reader wonder about the whereabouts of his wife
   (2) encourages the reader to worry about his family life
   (3) shows a softer, nurturing side to him
   (4) makes the reader dislike him
   (5) makes the reader question his job and lifestyle

Answers start on page 298.

Lesson 13

GED SKILL Identifying Cause and Effect

cause
an action that makes something else happen

effect
the result of an action

A **cause** is an initial action—a thought, word, or deed—that makes something else happen. An **effect** is the consequence, or result of that action. Often, a cause has more than one effect, or an effect may have more than one cause. Sometimes the link between a cause and effect is not obvious, and you need to think carefully about how the events are related.

A fiction writer uses causes and effects to create a story. Paying careful attention to the causes and effects in a story can give you a better understanding of its plot.

Read the following excerpt from a novel and complete the exercise below.

He was an old man who fished alone in a skiff in the Gulf Stream and he had gone eighty-four days now without taking a fish. In the first forty days a boy had been with him. But after forty days without a fish the boy's parents had told him that the old man was now definitely and finally *salao*, which is the worst form of unlucky, and the boy had gone at their orders in another boat which caught three good fish the first week. It made the boy sad to see the old man come in each day with his skiff empty and he always went down to help him carry either the coiled lines or the gaff and harpoon and the sail that was furled around the mast. The sail was patched with flour sacks and, furled, it looked like the flag of permanent defeat.

Ernest Hemingway, *The Old Man and the Sea*.

1. The boy's parents force him to go in another boat. What is the cause of this effect?

　　　 a. The first week the other boat caught three fish.

　　　 b. The old man goes forty days without catching a fish.

You were correct if you chose *option b*. The boy's parents feel the old man is unlucky, and they make the boy go to another boat.

2. The old man came in each day with his boat empty. What is the effect of this cause?

　　　 a. The old man was very unlucky.

　　　 b. The boy felt sad.

You were correct if you chose *option b*. The excerpt directly states that the boy is sad because the boat is empty.

TIP

You can identify a cause-and-effect relationship by asking why something happened and what its results were.

Read the following excerpt from a novel and complete the exercise below.

. . . For [her father's] seventieth birthday, the youngest daughter, Sofía, wanted the celebration at her house. Her son had been born that summer, and she did not want to be traveling in November with a four-month-old and her little girl. And yet, she, of all the daughters, did not want to be the absent one because for the first

(5) time since she'd run off with her husband six years ago, she and her father were on speaking terms. In fact, the old man had been out to see her—or really to see his grandson—twice. It was a big deal that Sofía had had a son. He was the first male born into the family in two generations. In fact, the baby was to be named for the grandfather—Carlos—and his middle name was to be Sofía's maiden name,

(10) and so, what the old man had never hoped for with his "harem of four girls," as he liked to joke, his own name was to be kept going in this new country!

Julia Alvarez, "The Kiss," How the García Girls Lost Their Accents.

1. Put a check mark by the two causes of Sofía's wanting to have her father's party at her house.

_____ a. She loves giving surprise parties.

_____ b. She does not want to travel in November with small children.

_____ c. She is naming the baby after her father.

_____ d. She does not want to miss the celebration.

2. Choose the most reasonable cause of Sofía's estrangement from her father.

_____ a. She ran off to get married.

_____ b. Her first child was a daughter.

3. Put check marks by all of the following that are probable causes of the grandfather's visits to his daughter.

_____ a. The baby is the first male born in the family in two generations.

_____ b. The baby was to be named after the grandfather.

_____ c. The grandfather wants to reconcile with Sofía.

_____ d. The grandfather is very close to his daughter.

_____ e. The grandfather enjoys traveling.

4. Write one effect of Sofía's naming her son after her father.

_____

_____

_____

Answers start on page 298.

GED Practice • Lesson 13

Directions: Choose the <u>one best answer</u> to each question.

Questions 1 through 4 refer to the following excerpt from a short story.

WHAT HAS INVADED THE FARM?

She went out to join the old man, stepping carefully among the insects. They stood and watched. Overhead the sky was blue, blue and clear.

(5)   "Pretty," said old Stephen with satisfaction.

Well, thought Margaret, we may be ruined, we may be bankrupt, but not everyone has seen an army of locusts
(10) fanning their wings at dawn.

Over the slopes, in the distance, a faint red smear showed in the sky, thickened and spread. "There they go," said old Stephen. "There goes the main army,
(15) off South."

And from the trees, from the earth all round them, the locusts were taking wing. They were like small aircraft, maneuvering for the take-off, trying their wings to see if
(20) they were dry enough. Off they went. A reddish brown stream was rising off the miles of bush, off the lands, the earth. Again the sunlight darkened.

And as the clotted branches lifted, the
(25) weight on them lightening, there was nothing but the black spines of branches, trees. No green left, nothing. All morning they watched, the three of them, as the brown crust thinned and broke and
(30) dissolved, flying up to mass with the main army, now a brownish-red smear in the Southern sky. The lands which had been filmed with green, the new tender mealie plants, were stark and bare. All the trees
(35) stripped. A devastated landscape. No green, no green anywhere.

Doris Lessing, "A Mild Attack of Locust," *The Habit of Loving.*

1. What effect did the locusts have on the land?

   (1) They left it bare of leaves.
   (2) They turned it brownish-red.
   (3) They stirred up clouds of dust.
   (4) They broke branches from the trees.
   (5) They littered it with their shells.

2. To what does the phrase "a faint red smear" (lines 11–12) refer?

   (1) the rosy color of dawn
   (2) the dust raised by a group of soldiers
   (3) the colors of sunset
   (4) the swarm of locusts
   (5) the pesticides spread by crop dusters

3. Which of the following conflicts is highlighted in this excerpt?

   (1) people versus themselves
   (2) people versus society
   (3) people versus fate
   (4) people versus nature
   (5) people versus machines

4. Which of the following details is used most frequently throughout this excerpt?

   (1) color
   (2) texture
   (3) size
   (4) shape
   (5) sound

 Ask yourself, "What happened?" The answer is an effect. Then ask yourself, "Why did it happen?" The answer is the cause.

Questions 5 through 9 refer to the following excerpt from a novel.

HOW HAVE THESE PEOPLE CHANGED?

On the morning of the thirteenth sleep of sickness in the Lone Eater camp, Fools Crow and his father, Rides-at-the-door, walked through the village. They went from
(5) lodge to lodge and called to the people within. There were still many sick and dying, but the number of new victims had gone down. The rage of the white-scabs was subsiding. It seemed impossible that
(10) it would last such a short time and leave so many dead or scarred for life by the draining sores. Others were out walking listlessly in the warm sun or just sitting outside their lodges. There was none of
(15) the bustle that usually occurred on a morning of winter camp. The people did not greet each other. If they met on the path to the river, they would move off the path and circle warily until they were well
(20) beyond. If a child was caught playing with the children from a family hard hit by the bad spirit, he would be called inside and scolded. But it was one old woman, the only survivor of her lodge, who sat and
(25) wailed and dug at the frozen ground until her fingers were raw and bloody—it was this old woman who made the people realize the extent of their loss. Gradually they emerged from the deep void of
(30) sickness and death and saw that they had become a different people.

James Welch, *Fools Crow.*

5. What has happened to the people in the village?

   (1) They are dying of starvation.
   (2) They are victims of a natural disaster.
   (3) They have contracted a contagious disease.
   (4) They are afraid to leave their lodges.
   (5) They are at war with another village.

6. A villager walking far around another villager to avoid coming into contact with the bad spirit is most similar to which of the following situations?

   (1) a person catching a horrible disease
   (2) a person taking a new route to avoid someone he dislikes
   (3) a person wearing a face mask in the hospital to avoid germs
   (4) a person leaving a path to walk through the woods
   (5) a person sneezing on another person and giving her a cold

7. What do the people believe is causing their problems?

   (1) the white man's invasion of their territory
   (2) the presence of a bad spirit
   (3) punishment from the gods
   (4) pollution from the river
   (5) being forced to live close together

8. Lines 30–31 state that "they had become a different people." Which of the following is the most probable change?

   (1) They were disheartened and sad.
   (2) Their faces were scarred for life.
   (3) They were happy to have survived.
   (4) They decided to join a new camp.
   (5) They no longer cared what happened to them.

9. What is the effect of telling the story mainly from the villagers' point of view?

   (1) It distances readers from the events of the story.
   (2) It helps readers understand how the characters feel.
   (3) It suggests that the people like to gossip about each other.
   (4) It biases readers against the white man.
   (5) It demonstrates the villagers' dislike of outsiders.

Answers start on page 298.

Directions: This is a ten-minute practice test. After ten minutes, mark the last question you finished. Then complete the test and check your answers. If most of your answers were correct, but you didn't finish, try to work faster next time. Choose the <u>one best answer</u> to each question.

<u>Questions 1 through 9</u> refer to the following excerpt from a novel.

ARE THESE TWO SISTERS HAVING THE SAME LUCK AT LOVE?

Yet the misery, for which years of happiness were to offer no compensation, received soon afterwards material relief, from observing how much the beauty of
(5)   her sister re-kindled the admiration of her former lover. When first he came in, he had spoken to her but little; but every five minutes seemed to be giving her more of his attention. He found her as
(10) handsome as she had been last year; as good natured, and as unaffected, though not quite so chatty. Jane was anxious that no difference should be perceived in her at all, and was really persuaded that she
(15) talked as much as ever. But her mind was so busily engaged, that she did not always know when she was silent.
     When the gentlemen rose to go away, Mrs. Bennet was mindful of her intended
(20) civility, and they were invited and engaged to dine at Longbourn in a few days time. . . .
     As soon as they were gone, Elizabeth walked out to recover her spirits; or in other words, to dwell without interruption
(25) on those subjects that must deaden them more. Mr. Darcy's behavior astonished and vexed her.
     "Why, if he came only to be silent, grave, and indifferent," said she, "did he
(30) come at all?"
     She could settle it in no way that gave her pleasure.

"He could be still amiable, still pleasing, to my uncle and aunt, when he was in
(35) town; and why not to me? If he fears me, why come hither? If he no longer cares for me, why silent? Teasing, teasing man! I will think no more about him."
     Her resolution was for a short time
(40) involuntarily kept by the approach of her sister who joined her with a cheerful look, which showed her better satisfied with their visitors, than Elizabeth.
     "Now," said she, "That this first meeting
(45) is over, I feel perfectly easy. I know my own strength, and I shall never be embarrassed again by his coming. I am glad he dines here on Tuesday. It will then be publicly seen, that on both sides, we meet only as
(50) common and indifferent acquaintance."
     "Yes, very indifferent indeed," said Elizabeth, laughingly. "Oh Jane, take care."
     "My dear Lizzy, you cannot think me so weak, as to be in danger now."
(55) "I think you are in very great danger of making him as much in love with you as ever."

Jane Austen, *Pride and Prejudice.*

1. Which of the following words <u>best</u> describes what Elizabeth feels toward <u>Mr. Darcy</u>?

   (1) attraction
   (2) envy
   (3) gratitude
   (4) respect
   (5) suspicion

2. How has Jane's visitor left her feeling?

   (1) unimpressed by him
   (2) superior to him
   (3) overwhelmed by emotion
   (4) shy and awkward
   (5) more sure of herself

3. Why is Elizabeth upset?

   (1) Her sister flirts with Mr. Darcy.
   (2) Mr. Darcy has ignored her.
   (3) Mr. Darcy fusses over her too much.
   (4) Her mother intrudes on the men's visit.
   (5) Mr. Darcy has been rude to her relatives.

4. Based on the men's visit, which of the following conclusions can be drawn?

   (1) Mr. Darcy is painfully shy.
   (2) Mr. Darcy had earlier shown interest in Elizabeth.
   (3) Mr. Darcy is in danger of falling in love with Jane.
   (4) The two sisters will both be disappointed in love.
   (5) Jane is more flirtatious than Elizabeth is.

5. Based on the excerpt, what is Elizabeth most likely to do in the future?

   (1) She will apologize to Mr. Darcy for her rude behavior.
   (2) She will be preoccupied with thoughts about Mr. Darcy.
   (3) She will try to convince Jane to drop her boyfriend.
   (4) She will stop speaking to her aunt and uncle.
   (5) She will give up all hope of romance.

6. Based on the excerpt, which description best characterizes the relationship between Elizabeth and Jane?

   (1) critical and competitive
   (2) distant but polite
   (3) close and affectionate
   (4) turbulent and troubled
   (5) fragile but deepening

7. Which of the following best describes what Elizabeth means when she says "very indifferent indeed" (line 51)?

   (1) She is commending Jane for her behavior.
   (2) She is describing Mr. Darcy's attitude.
   (3) She is questioning Jane's claims of indifference.
   (4) She is giving her opinion of the planned dinner.
   (5) She is sharing her observations about Mrs. Bennet.

8. Of the characters in this excerpt, whose inner thoughts are hidden from the reader?

   (1) Elizabeth's
   (2) Jane's
   (3) Jane's visitor's
   (4) Mr. Darcy's
   (5) Mrs. Bennet's

9. In which of the following ways are Jane and Mr. Darcy alike?

   (1) Neither is very talkative on the day of the visit.
   (2) Both question Elizabeth about her behavior.
   (3) Neither has any desire to go to Longbourn.
   (4) Both seem especially cheerful after the visit.
   (5) Both appear to enjoy teasing Elizabeth.

Answers start on page 299.

GED SKILL Analyzing Character

Fiction writers create people, or **characters,** to capture a reader's interest. There are several ways to find out about characters in literature. Writers develop characters by describing what the characters look like, how they behave, what they think and say, and what other characters say about them.

characters
the people in a work of fiction

Read the following excerpt from a novel and complete the exercise below.

Mr. Chadband is a large yellow man, with a fat smile and a general appearance of having a good deal of train-oil[1] in his system. . . . Mr. Chadband moves softly and cumbrously,[2] not unlike a bear who has been taught to walk upright. He is very much embarrassed about the arms, as if they were inconvenient to him, and he wanted to grovel; is very much in a perspiration about the head; and never speaks without first putting up his great hand, as delivering a token to his hearers that he is going to edify[3] them.

"My friends," says Mr. Chadband, "peace be on this house! On the master thereof, on the mistress thereof, on the young maidens, and on the young men! My friends, why do I wish for peace? What is peace? Is it war? No. Is it strife? No. Is it lovely, and gentle, and beautiful, and pleasant, and serene, and joyful? Oh yes! Therefore, my friends, I wish for peace upon you and upon yours."

TIP

Characters' actions do not always match their words. Just as in real life, you will have to judge whether characters are honest and reliable.

---

[1] oil from a marine animal, such as a whale   [2] moving with difficulty due to weight or size   [3] enlighten

Charles Dickens, *Bleak House.*

1. Put a check mark by all of the following that are true of Mr. Chadband.

    _____ a. He is a man of few words.

    _____ b. He is preachy.

    _____ c. He is self-important.

    _____ d. He frowns a lot.

2. Underline descriptive phrases in the excerpt that tell you something about Mr. Chadband's character.

You were correct if you chose *options b* and *c.* Mr. Chadband speaks as if he is giving a sermon and behaves as if he is going to enlighten his audience. Examples of phrases that you may have underlined are *a fat smile; a general appearance of having a good deal of train-oil in his system;* and *never speaks without first putting up his great hand.*

Read the following excerpt from a novel and complete the exercise below.

"It is a known truth that gray-eyed people are jealous."

"I told you I wasn't jealous," Frankie said, and she was walking fast around the room. "I couldn't be jealous of one of them without being jealous of them both. I sociate the two of them together."

(5)   "Well, I were jealous when my foster brother married," said Berenice. "I admit that when John married Clorina I sent a warning I would tear the ears off her head. But you see I didn't. Clorina got ears like anybody else. And now I love her."

"J A," said Frankie. "Janice and Jarvis. Isn't that the strangest thing?"

"What?"

(10)   "J A," she said. "Both their names begin with J A."

"And? What about it?"

Frankie walked round and round the kitchen table. "If only my name was Jane," she said. "Jane or Jasmine."

"I don't follow your frame of mind," said Berenice.

(15)   "Jarvis and Janice and Jasmine. See?"

"No," said Berenice.

Carson McCullers, *The Member of the Wedding.*

1. Put a check mark by what walking around the room suggests about Frankie's character.

    _____ a. She has pent-up nervous energy.

    _____ b. She is being rude to Berenice.

    _____ c. She wants to work off a few pounds.

2. Put a check mark by the statement that best describes Frankie's feelings.

    _____ a. Frankie feels left out because Jarvis and Janice are getting married.

    _____ b. Frankie feels that Janice is not good enough for her brother Jarvis.

3. Explain your answer to question 2.

_____

_____

_____

4. What does the dialogue in this excerpt accomplish?

    _____ a. It resolves the conflict between Frankie and Berenice.

    _____ b. It contrasts the emotions of Frankie and Berenice.

Answers start on page 300.

Directions: Choose the one best answer to each question.

Questions 1 through 4 refer to the following excerpt from a short story.

WHY DOES THIS WOMAN BUY POISON?

"I want some poison," she said to the druggist. She was over thirty then, still a slight woman, though thinner than usual, with cold, haughty black eyes in a face the
(5) flesh of which was strained across the temples and about the eyesockets as you imagine a lighthouse-keeper's face ought to look. "I want some poison," she said.
"Yes, Miss Emily. What kind? For rats
(10) and such? I'd recom—"
"I want the best you have. I don't care what kind."
The druggist named several. "They'll kill anything up to an elephant. But what you
(15) want is—"
"Arsenic," Miss Emily said. "Is that a good one?"
"Is . . . arsenic? Yes, ma'am. But what you want—"
(20) "I want arsenic."
The druggist looked down at her. She looked back at him, erect, her face like a strained flag. "Why, of course," the druggist said. "If that's what you want. But the law
(25) requires you to tell what you are going to use it for."
Miss Emily just stared at him, her head tilted back in order to look him eye for eye, until he looked away and went and got the
(30) arsenic and wrapped it up.

William Faulkner, "A Rose for Emily," *Collected Stories of William Faulkner.*

1. What is meant by the description of Miss Emily's face as being similar to a "strained flag" (line 23)?

   (1) She is about to cry.
   (2) She is very tense.
   (3) She appears lonely.
   (4) She seems quite fragile.
   (5) She is strangely pale.

2. Based on this excerpt, how would Miss Emily most likely walk across a crowded room?

   (1) carefully, trying not to bump into anyone
   (2) energetically stomping with heavy footsteps
   (3) shyly, with her head down and with small footsteps
   (4) confidently, with her head held high
   (5) clumsily, sometimes stumbling into people

3. Based on this excerpt, which of the following descriptions best characterizes Miss Emily?

   (1) She cannot make up her mind.
   (2) She is open about her life.
   (3) She is embarrassed that her house has rats.
   (4) She has a limited income.
   (5) She intimidates other people.

4. Based on the dialogue in this excerpt, how is Miss Emily's demeanor different from that of the druggist?

   (1) Miss Emily is grumpy, but the druggist is friendly.
   (2) Miss Emily is talkative, but the druggist is brief.
   (3) Miss Emily is forceful, but the druggist is accommodating.
   (4) Miss Emily is calm, but the druggist is impatient.
   (5) Miss Emily is rational, but the druggist is suspicious.

Questions 5 through 7 refer to the following excerpt from a short story.

WHAT KIND OF PERSON IS GRANNY WEATHERALL?

She flicked her wrist neatly out of Doctor Harry's pudgy careful fingers and pulled the sheet up to her chin. The brat ought to be in knee breeches. Doctoring
(5) around the country with spectacles on his nose! "Get along now, take your schoolbooks and go. There's nothing wrong with me."

Doctor Harry spread a warm paw like a
(10) cushion on her forehead where the forked green vein danced and made her eyelids twitch. "Now, now, be a good girl, and we'll have you up in no time."

"That's no way to speak to a woman
(15) nearly eighty years old just because she's down. I'd have you respect your elders, young man."

"Well, Missy, excuse me." Doctor Harry patted her cheek. "But I've got to warn you,
(20) haven't I? You're a marvel, but you must be careful or you're going to be good and sorry."

"Don't tell me what I'm going to be. I'm on my feet now, morally speaking.
(25) It's Cornelia. I had to go to bed to get rid of her."

Her bones felt loose, and floated around in her skin, and Doctor Harry floated like a balloon around the foot of
(30) the bed. He floated and pulled down his waistcoat and swung his glasses on a cord. "Well, stay where you are, it certainly can't hurt you."

"Get along and doctor your sick," said
(35) Granny Weatherall. "Leave a well woman alone. I'll call for you when I want you. . . . Where were you forty years ago when I pulled through milk-leg and double pneumonia? You weren't even born.
(40) Don't let Cornelia lead you on," she shouted, because Doctor Harry appeared to float up to the ceiling and out. "I pay my own bills, and I don't throw money away on nonsense!"

(45) She meant to wave good-by, but it was too much trouble. Her eyes closed of themselves, it was like a dark curtain drawn around the bed. The pillow rose and floated under her, pleasant as a
(50) hammock in a light wind. She listened to the leaves rustling outside the window. No, somebody was swishing newspapers: no, Cornelia and Doctor Harry were whispering together. She leaped broad
(55) awake, thinking they whispered in her ear.

"She was never like this, *never* like this!" "Well, what can we expect?" "Yes, eighty years old . . ."

Katherine Anne Porter, "The Jilting of Granny Weatherall," *Flowering Judas and Other Stories.*

5. Which of the following is probably true about Granny?

(1) She is healthier now than when she was younger.
(2) She is much sicker than she says she is.
(3) She believes that doctors are well worth the money.
(4) She is able to get around easily.
(5) She thinks Cornelia is a fine woman.

6. Which of the following best describes the doctor's tone?

(1) understanding but firm
(2) distant and scientific
(3) gentle but unsure
(4) serious and gloomy
(5) bright and cheery

7. Which of the following reveals the most about Granny Weatherall's character?

(1) what others say about her
(2) what she says
(3) what she thinks
(4) what others do in her presence
(5) what she feels

Answers start on page 300.

Directions: This is a ten-minute practice test. After ten minutes, mark the last question you finished. Then complete the test and check your answers. If most of your answers were correct, but you didn't finish, try to work faster next time. Choose the one best answer to each question.

Questions 1 through 11 refer to the following excerpt from a novel.

WHAT DID GRANDPA BLAKESLEE'S WILL SAY?

"Now I want my burying to remind folks that death aint always awful. God invented death. Its in God's plan for it to happen. So when my time comes I do not want no trip
(5) to Birdsong's Emporium or any other. Dressing somebody up to look alive don't make it so. . . .

"I don't want no casket. Its a waste of money. What I would really like is to be
(10) wrapped up in two or three feed sacks and laid right in the ground. But that would bother you all, so use the pine box upstairs at the store that Miss Mattie Lou's coffin come in. I been saving it. And tho I just as
(15) soon be planted in the vegetable patch as anywhere, I don't think anybody would ever eat what growed there, after. Anyhow, take me right from home to the cemetery.

"Aint no use paying Birdsong for that
(20) hearse. Get Loomis to use his wagon. Specially if it is hot weather, my advisement is dont waste no time."

Mama, scandalized, had both hands up to her mouth. Mary Toy had turned white
(25) as a sheet. I held her tight. Aunt Loma seemed excited, like when watching a spooky stage play. I felt excited myself. I wondered was this Grandpa's idea of a practical joke or was it a sermon.
(30) Maybe after he made his point, he'd put a postscript saying that when he was dead it really wouldn't matter to him what kind of funeral he had. But I doubted it. . . .

Papa read on. "I want Loomis and them
(35) to dig my grave right next to Miss Mattie Lou. I don't want no other preacher there but him, but don't let him give a sermon. It would go on for hours. Just let him pray for God to comfort my family. . . ."

(40) Papa read on. "I don't want nobody at the burial except you all and them at the store that want to come. Don't put *Not Dead But Sleeping* on my stone. Write it *Dead, Not Sleeping.* Being dead under six
(45) foot of dirt wont bother me a-tall, but I hate for it to sound like I been buried alive. . . ."

Olive Ann Burns, *Cold Sassy Tree.*

1. Based on the excerpt, what does Grandpa Blakeslee probably think about death?

   He thinks death is

   (1) the end of everything
   (2) the beginning of the afterlife
   (3) a waste of money
   (4) normal and natural
   (5) a little frightening

2. Based on the excerpt, what type of person is Grandpa Blakeslee?

   (1) conventional in his behavior
   (2) very vain about his appearance
   (3) mindful of others' expectations
   (4) unconcerned with what society thinks
   (5) negative in his outlook on life

3. Which of the following would Grandpa Blakeslee most likely enjoy?

   (1) attending a formal dinner
   (2) spending a quiet evening at home
   (3) having a large party thrown in his honor
   (4) shopping at a local department store
   (5) listening to a lengthy sermon

4. Which of the following best expresses the main idea of the excerpt?

   (1) Grandpa Blakeslee does not want a fuss made at his funeral.
   (2) Death eventually happens to everyone.
   (3) Birdsong's Emporium is too expensive.
   (4) Funerals should be simple and dignified.
   (5) The writer of the will does not want to be dressed up after he dies.

5. What is the main purpose of the second paragraph of the excerpt?

   (1) It provides a contrast to the first paragraph of the excerpt.
   (2) It explains why Grandpa Blakeslee believes dressing up a dead person is wrong.
   (3) It explains why Grandpa Blakeslee wants to go to the cemetery.
   (4) It provides specific details that support the main idea of the excerpt.
   (5) It explains the reason Grandpa Blakeslee has been saving a pine box.

6. Which of the following best expresses why the women were shocked at the will?

   (1) They thought Grandpa Blakeslee was playing a practical joke on them.
   (2) They thought Grandpa Blakeslee's comments and wishes were strange.
   (3) They were hurt that Grandpa Blakeslee wanted Loomis to give the sermon.
   (4) They expected to receive a lot of money.
   (5) They were upset about what Grandpa Blakeslee wanted on his stone.

7. Grandpa Blakeslee likely held which of the following jobs?

   (1) a general storekeeper
   (2) an undertaker
   (3) a farmer
   (4) a minister
   (5) a lawyer

8. Which of the following best describes the tone of this excerpt?

   (1) lighthearted
   (2) morbid
   (3) sad
   (4) solemn
   (5) plainspoken

9. The author establishes Grandpa Blakeslee's character primarily through which of the following methods?

   (1) reporting what his family says about him
   (2) having him "speak from the grave"
   (3) giving a detailed description of him
   (4) sharing his private thoughts
   (5) referring to his actions when he was alive

10. Which of the following is the best description of Grandpa Blakeslee's last will and testament?

    (1) a slap in the face to his heirs
    (2) an attack on organized religion
    (3) an endorsement of the back-to-nature movement
    (4) the last gasp of a practical joker
    (5) a humorous criticism of the funeral industry

11. What is the main effect of the author's use of phrases such as "Aint no use" (line 19) and "dont waste no time" (line 22)?

    (1) It shows that Grandpa Blakeslee was an unintelligent man.
    (2) It creates the impression that Grandpa Blakeslee likes to talk.
    (3) It creates the impression that Grandpa Blakeslee wrote his will in a hurry.
    (4) It makes it seem as though Grandpa Blakeslee is actually speaking.
    (5) It creates the impression that Grandpa Blakeslee is a practical man.

Answers start on page 300.

GED SKILL Analyzing Tone

When you talk, the **tone** of your voice reveals your attitude—how you feel about your subject and audience. A writer's tone also conveys how he or she feels about a subject. A writer's words may suggest emotions or attitudes such as seriousness, humor, anger, or sympathy. **Mood** is the emotional **atmosphere** of a piece of literature. Mood is the feeling the author wants the reader to experience. The mood can be the same as or different from the tone. A writer often uses description to help create these feelings. As you read, look for these clues: how an author uses descriptive words and how a story builds to its conclusion.

tone
the details present in a writer's work that suggest how he or she feels about a subject

mood
the emotional climate or atmosphere conveyed by the words a writer chooses

TIP

Word choice is a clue to determining the tone of a piece of fiction.

Read the following excerpt from a short story and complete the exercise below.

During the whole of a dull, dark, and soundless day in the autumn of the year, when the clouds hung oppressively low in the heavens, I had been passing alone, on horseback, through a singularly dreary tract of country; and at length found myself, as the shades of the evening drew on, within view of the melancholy House of Usher. I do not know how it was—but, with the first glimpse of the building, a sense of insufferable gloom pervaded my spirit . . . There was an iciness, a sinking, a sickness of the heart. . . .

Edgar Allan Poe, "The Fall of the House of Usher," *The Fall of the House of Usher and Other Writings.*

1. Put a check mark by one of the following words that describes the tone of this excerpt.

    _____ a. puzzled

    _____ b. angry

    _____ c. gloomy

2. Underline the words in the first line of the excerpt that suggest the author's tone.

3. The excerpt takes place in early evening. How do you think the time of day contributes to the mood?

    _____

    _____

You were correct if you chose *option c* for question 1 and underlined *dull, dark,* and *soundless* for question 2. The time of day contributes to the mood because many people associate darkening skies with fear or sadness.

Read the following excerpt from a short story and complete the exercise below.

I know what is being said about me and you can take my side or theirs, that's your own business. It's my word against Eunice's and Olivia-Ann's, and it should be plain enough to anyone with two good eyes which one of us has their wits about them. I just want the citizens of the U.S.A. to know the facts, that's all.

(5)   The facts: On Sunday, August 12, this year of our Lord, Eunice tried to kill me with her papa's Civil War sword and Olivia-Ann cut up all over the place with a fourteen-inch hog knife. This is not even to mention lots of other things.

It began six months ago when I married Marge. That was the first thing I did wrong. We were married in Mobile after an acquaintance of only four days. We

(10) were both sixteen and she was visiting my cousin Georgia. Now that I've had plenty of time to think it over, I can't for the life of me figure how I fell for the likes of her. She has no looks, no body, and no brains whatsoever. But Marge is a natural blonde and maybe that's the answer.

Truman Capote, "My Side of the Matter," *The Grass Harp and A Tree of Night and Other Stories.*

1. Put a check mark by the <u>best</u> description of the tone of this excerpt.

   _____ a. sorrowful

   _____ b. defensive

   _____ c. serious

2. Put a check mark by the two statements from the first paragraph that contribute <u>most</u> to the tone of the excerpt.

   _____ a. "I know what is being said about me"

   _____ b. "you can take my side or theirs"

   _____ c. "that's your own business"

   _____ d. "It's my word against Eunice's and Olivia-Ann's"

3. The author's attitude toward the narrator is an important part of the excerpt's tone. What feeling or impression does the author convey about the narrator?

   _____ a. He may not be completely reliable.

   _____ b. He should be taken very seriously.

   _____ c. He is an innocent victim.

4. List one or more details from the third paragraph to support your answer to question 3.

_____

_____

Answers start on page 301.

Directions: Choose the one best answer to each question.

Questions 1 through 4 refer to the following excerpt from a novel.

WHAT IS THE SIGNIFICANCE OF CARTER DRUSE'S DECISION?

The sleeping sentinel in the clump of laurel was a young Virginian named Carter Druse. He was the son of wealthy parents, an only child, and had known such ease
(5) and cultivation and high living as wealth and taste were able to command in the mountain country of western Virginia. His home was but a few miles from where he now lay. One morning he had risen from
(10) the breakfast-table and said, quietly but gravely: "Father, a Union regiment has arrived at Grafton. I am going to join it."
The father lifted his leonine head, looked at the son a moment in silence, and
(15) replied: "Well, go, sir, and whatever may occur do what you conceive to be your duty. Virginia, to which you are a traitor, must get on without you. Should we both live to the end of the war, we will speak
(20) further of the matter. Your mother, as the physician has informed you, is in a most critical condition; at the best she cannot be with us longer than a few weeks, but that time is precious. It would be better not to
(25) disturb her."
So Carter Druse, bowing reverently to his father, who returned the salute with a stately courtesy that masked a breaking heart, left the home of his childhood to go
(30) soldiering. By conscience and courage, by deeds of devotion and daring, he soon commended himself to his fellows and his officers; and it was to these qualities and to some knowledge of the country that he
(35) owed his selection for his present perilous duty at the extreme outpost.

Ambrose Bierce, *A Horseman in the Sky.*

1. Which of the following best describes Carter Druse's father?

   (1) a hard-hearted man who cares little for his wife and son
   (2) a demanding individual who wants his son to follow in his footsteps
   (3) a coward who wants to avoid his responsibilities
   (4) a man of honor who respects his son's beliefs
   (5) a poor man with simple tastes and limited education

2. Which of the following actions would be in keeping with Carter Druse's character as described in the excerpt?

   (1) running away from a battle
   (2) lying to one of his officers
   (3) keeping a difficult promise
   (4) deserting to the Confederate Army
   (5) stealing from his father

3. Which of the following best describes the tone of this excerpt?

   (1) threatening
   (2) formal
   (3) envious
   (4) comical
   (5) chatty

4. Carter Druse's decision brings into sharp focus which of the following realities about the Civil War?

   (1) The war led to western Virginia's secession from the state.
   (2) The war resulted in more deaths than any war before it.
   (3) The war divided even the closest families.
   (4) The war produced unlikely heroes.
   (5) The war was fought mainly in the South.

Questions 5 through 8 refer to the following excerpt from a short story.

WHY DID THIS WOMAN'S SISTER LEAVE HOME?

I was getting along fine with Mama, Papa-Daddy, and Uncle Rondo until my sister Stella-Rondo just separated from her husband and came back home again.

(5) Mr. Whitaker! Of course I went with Mr. Whitaker first, when he first appeared here in China Grove, taking "Pose Yourself" photos, and Stella-Rondo broke us up. Told him I was one-sided. Bigger on one

(10) side than the other, which is a deliberate, calculated falsehood: I'm the same. Stella-Rondo is exactly twelve months to the day younger than I am and for that reason she's spoiled.

(15) She's always had anything in the world she wanted and then she'd throw it away. Papa-Daddy gave her this gorgeous Add-a-Pearl necklace when she was eight years old and she threw it away playing baseball

(20) when she was nine, with only two pearls.

So as soon as she got married and moved away from home the first thing she did was separate! From Mr. Whitaker! This photographer with the popeyes she said

(25) she trusted. Came home from one of those towns up in Illinois and to our complete surprise brought this child of two.

Mama said she like to make her drop dead for a second. "Here you had this

(30) marvelous blonde child and never so much as wrote your mother a word about it," says Mama. "I'm thoroughly ashamed of you." But of course she wasn't.

Stella-Rondo just calmly takes off this

(35) *hat,* I wish you could see it. She says, "Why, Mama, Shirley T.'s adopted, I can prove it."

"How?" says Mama, but all I says was, "H'm!" There I was over the hot stove,

(40) trying to stretch two chickens over five people and a completely unexpected child into the bargain, without one moment's notice.

Eudora Welty, "Why I Live at the P.O.," *A Curtain of Green and Other Stories.*

5. What does the narrator mean when she says she was "trying to stretch two chickens over five people" (lines 40–41)?

She did not have enough

(1) recipes to suit everyone's taste
(2) food to feed everyone
(3) time to go grocery shopping
(4) feather blankets for all the beds
(5) room in the kitchen to cook dinner

6. What would the narrator most likely do if Mr. Whitaker were to drop in?

She would

(1) scold him for running off with her younger sister
(2) refuse to let him in
(3) tell him how disappointed she is in him
(4) make room for a sixth person at the table
(5) ask him if Stella-Rondo is telling the truth about the child

7. Which of the following best describes the tone of this excerpt?

(1) dramatic
(2) suspenseful
(3) lighthearted
(4) serious
(5) irritable

8. Which of the following words best describes the narrator's attitude toward Stella-Rondo?

(1) protective
(2) resentful
(3) supportive
(4) suspicious
(5) concerned

TIP To understand tone, try "hearing" how the characters in a story would speak their lines.

Answers start on page 301.

Directions: This is a ten-minute practice test. After ten minutes, mark the last question you finished. Then complete the test and check your answers. If most of your answers were correct, but you didn't finish, try to work faster next time. Choose the <u>one best answer</u> to each question.

Questions 1 through 10 refer to the following excerpt from a novel.

IS THIS FAMILY HAVING A SATISFYING MEAL?

"George is in town, Papa; and has gone to the Horse Guards, and will be back to dinner."

"Oh, he is, is he? I won't have the
(5) dinner kept waiting for *him,* Jane"; with which this worthy man lapsed into his particular chair, and then the utter silence in his genteel, well-furnished drawing-room was only interrupted by the alarmed ticking
(10) of the great French clock.

When [it. . .] tolled five in a heavy cathedral tone, Mr. Osborne pulled the bell at his right hand violently, and the butler rushed up.
(15) "Dinner!" roared Mr. Osborne.

"Mr. George isn't come in, sir," interposed the man.

"Damn Mr. George, sir. Am I master of the house? DINNER!" Mr. Osborne
(20) scowled. Amelia trembled. A telegraphic communication of eyes passed between the other three ladies. The obedient bell in the lower regions began ringing the announcement of the meal. The tolling
(25) over, the head of the family thrust his hands into the great tail-pockets of his great blue coat and brass buttons, and without waiting for a further announcement, strode downstairs
(30) alone, scowling over his shoulder at the four females.

"What's the matter now, my dear?" asked one of the other, as they rose and tripped gingerly behind the sire.
(35) "I suppose the funds are falling," whispered Miss Wirt; and so, trembling and in silence, this hushed female company followed their dark leader.

They took their places in silence. He
(40) growled out a blessing, which sounded as gruffly as a curse. The great silver dishcovers were removed. Amelia trembled in her place, for she was next to the awful Osborne, and alone on her side of the
(45) table—the gap being occasioned by the absence of George.

"Soup?" says Mr. Osborne, clutching the ladle, fixing his eyes on her, in a sepulchral[1] tone; and having helped her
(50) and the rest, did not speak for a while.

"Take Miss Sedley's plate away," at last he said. "She can't eat the soup—no more can I. It's beastly. Take away the soup, Hicks, and to-morrow turn the cook out of
(55) the house, Jane."

Having concluded his observations upon the soup, Mr. Osborne made a few curt remarks respecting the fish. . . .

---
[1] deathly

William Makepeace Thackeray, *Vanity Fair.*

1. Which of the following words <u>best</u> describes Mr. Osborne's daughters?

   (1) fearful
   (2) snobbish
   (3) considerate
   (4) friendly
   (5) obedient

2. To what does the phrase "tripped gingerly" in line 34 refer?

   (1) fell gracefully
   (2) whispered softly
   (3) stumbled clumsily
   (4) ran quickly
   (5) walked carefully

3. Based on the excerpt, which of the following is an explanation given by another character for Mr. Osborne's behavior?

    (1) He is angry with George for being late.
    (2) He is dissatisfied with the food served at dinner.
    (3) His position in the household is challenged.
    (4) He may be losing money on his investments.
    (5) He is angry that he must wait for his dinner.

4. Based on this excerpt, how would Osborne react if one of his daughters were late for an important appointment with him?

    (1) He would pace the floor nervously.
    (2) He would dismiss her without seeing her.
    (3) He would lecture her on the importance of being punctual.
    (4) He would forgive her without a second thought.
    (5) He would wait patiently for her arrival.

5. Which of the following words best describes the mood of this excerpt?

    (1) cheerful
    (2) melancholy
    (3) comical
    (4) tense
    (5) cool

6. Based on the context, to what does the phrase "Mr. Osborne made a few curt remarks respecting the fish" (lines 57–58) likely refer?

    (1) Mr. Osborne was ordering his daughters to taste the fish.
    (2) Mr. Osborne was impressed by the way the cook had prepared the fish.
    (3) Mr. Osborne did not seem satisfied with the fish.
    (4) Mr. Osborne did not have much to say about the fish.
    (5) Mr. Osborne was trying to make dinner conversation.

7. Which of the following best indicates Osborne's lack of warmth?

    (1) the reference to Mr. Osborne as the "head of the family" (line 25)
    (2) Mr. Osborne's referring to himself as the "master of the house" (lines 18–19)
    (3) the reference to Amelia's fear when she sits next to him
    (4) Jane's referring to her father as "Papa" (line 1)
    (5) Osborne's refusal to address any of his daughters by name

8. What is suggested about Mr. Osborne's character when he tells his daughter to fire the cook?

    (1) He is extremely intolerant.
    (2) He is a former gourmet cook.
    (3) He has poor taste in food.
    (4) He is very alarmed.
    (5) He has a weakness for teasing.

9. Who is George?

He is

    (1) a visiting family acquaintance
    (2) a general in the Horse Guards
    (3) the real master of the house
    (4) one of Jane's siblings
    (5) Mr. Osborne's business partner

10. Which of the following best describes the narrator's attitude toward Mr. Osborne?

Mr. Osborne is

    (1) a serious man
    (2) an admirable man
    (3) a patient man
    (4) a grumpy man
    (5) a terrible man

Answers start on page 302.

GED SKILL Identifying Figurative Language

figurative language
words used imaginatively to create vivid pictures

simile
a comparison between two different people, places, or things signaled by the words *like, than, similar to,* or *as*

metaphor
a comparison that states one thing is another

symbol
a person, place, or thing that stands for a larger idea

Fiction writers often use words to create vivid images. This technique is called **figurative language.** Most figurative language is based on comparisons that make a point. A **simile** makes a comparison using *than, as,* or *like*. For instance, the statement "His hair was <u>like</u> a bad dream" is a simile. A **metaphor,** on the other hand, makes a comparison by simply stating that one thing is another—for example, "His hair was a nightmare."

A third type of figurative language is a **symbol**—a person, place, or thing that stands for some other, larger idea. For example, a character's cunning may be suggested by a frequent reference to a fox.

Figurative language is different from literal language. Literal language is factual; it is not exaggerated for effect. The description "Maria is very tall" is a literal statement; however, "Maria towers over everyone like a skyscraper" is a figurative statement.

Read the following excerpt from a short story and complete the exercise below.

His mother didn't know how to paint her face; she just put on all the makeup and probably didn't even know she looked like an old, tired clown. She had red tomatoes for cheeks and red strawberries for lips. The lines of her eyebrows were drawn with a black pencil, and she looked horrible. I never understood why she wore so much paint on her face.

Enedina Cásarez Vásquez, "The House of Quilts," *Daughters of the Fifth Sun.*

1. Place a check mark by the type of figurative language used in the line "she looked like an old, tired clown."

   _____ a. simile

   _____ b. symbol

   _____ c. metaphor

2. What clue helped you to answer question 1? _____

3. Write two metaphors from the excerpt.

   _____

   _____

TIP

To identify figurative language, look for comparisons between two different things. In what ways does the writer suggest they are alike?

You were correct if you chose *simile* for question 1. The clue word is *like*. Two metaphors are *red tomatoes for cheeks* and *red strawberries for lips.*

Read the following excerpt from a novel and complete the exercise below.

The tractors came over the roads and into the fields, great crawlers moving like insects, having the incredible strength of insects. They crawled over the ground, laying the track and rolling on it and picking it up. Diesel tractors, puttering while they stood idle; they thundered when they moved, and then settled down to a

(5) droning roar. Snub-nosed monsters, raising the dust and sticking their snouts into it, straight down the country, across the country, through fences, through dooryards, in and out of gullies in straight lines. They did not run on the ground, but on their own roadbeds. They ignored hills and gulches, water courses, fences, houses.

John Steinbeck, *The Grapes of Wrath.*

1. Put a check mark by the two things that are compared in lines 1 and 2.

   _____ a. tractors and insects

   _____ b. tractors and strength

   _____ c. roads and fields

2. Put a check mark by the type of comparison that is made in lines 1 and 2.

   _____ a. metaphor

   _____ b. simile

3. Put a check mark by the verb that develops the comparison.

   _____ a. crawled

   _____ b. laying

   _____ c. rolling

4. Which word is used instead of *tractor* in line 5 to create a comparison (metaphor)?

   _____

5. Put a check mark by the most likely reason the writer uses the word *snouts.*

   _____ a. to make the story believable

   _____ b. to give the machines a human-like quality

   _____ c. to show how the machines resemble living creatures

6. Put a check mark by the way in which the author is using the tractor as a symbol.

   _____ a. as a symbol of destruction

   _____ b. as a symbol of progress

   _____ c. as a symbol of freedom

Answers start on page 303.

Directions: Choose the <u>one best answer</u> to each question.

Questions 1 through 4 refer to the following excerpt from a short story.

HOW ARE INSECTS LIKE MEN?

Dr. Nahum Fischelson paced back and forth in his garret room in Market Street, Warsaw.[1] Dr. Fischelson was a short, hunched man with a grayish beard, and
(5) was quite bald except for a few wisps of hair remaining at the nape of the neck. His nose was as crooked as a beak and his eyes were large, dark, and fluttering like those of some huge bird. It was a hot
(10) summer evening, but Dr. Fischelson wore a black coat which reached to his knees, and he had on a stiff collar and a bow tie. From the door he paced slowly to the dormer window set high in the slanting
(15) room and back again. One had to mount several steps to look out. A candle in a brass holder was burning on the table and a variety of insects buzzed around the flame. Now and again one of the creatures
(20) would fly too close to the fire and sear its wings, or one would ignite and glow on the wick for an instant. At such moments Dr. Fischelson grimaced. His wrinkled face would twitch and beneath his disheveled[2]
(25) mustache he would bite his lips. Finally he took a handkerchief from his pocket and waved it at the insects.

"Away from there, fools and imbeciles," he scolded. "You won't get warm here;
(30) you'll only burn yourself."

The insects scattered but a second later returned and once more circled the trembling flame. Dr. Fischelson wiped the sweat from his wrinkled forehead
(35) and sighed, "Like men they desire nothing but the pleasure of the moment."

---

[1] the largest city in Poland   [2] disorderly

Isaac Bashevis Singer, "The Spinoza of Market Street."

1. Based on the clues in this excerpt, what type of room is a garret?

   (1) a dining room
   (2) a basement
   (3) a room in a dormitory
   (4) a room in an attic
   (5) a penthouse suite

2. Based on this excerpt, how would Dr. Fischelson likely respond to a stray cat that appeared on his doorstep?

   (1) He would chase the cat away.
   (2) He would call the animal control center.
   (3) He would care for the cat.
   (4) He would scold the cat.
   (5) He would try to kick the cat.

3. Which of Dr. Fischelson's features are compared to a bird's?

   (1) nose and eyes
   (2) head and feet
   (3) eyes and neck
   (4) nose and feet
   (5) feet and eyes

4. What is the tone of the excerpt?

   (1) frightened
   (2) violent
   (3) ominous
   (4) silly
   (5) painful

TIP To create symbols, writers use words and images in original ways. Is an image or word repeated? If so, it usually has a larger meaning.

Questions 5 through 9 refer to the following excerpt from a short story.

WHAT HAPPENED TO THEIR LOVE?

. . . There was a letter lying on the table, it read:

"Dear, I send you this little bunch of flowers as my Easter token. . . . I laid the

(5) flowers away for awhile in our favorite book,—Byron[1]—just at the poem we loved best, and now I send them to you. Keep them always in remembrance of me, and if aught [anything] should occur to separate

(10) us, press these flowers to your lips, and I will be with you in spirit, permeating [filling] your heart with unutterable [indescribable] love and happiness."

. . . Far away in a distant city, a man,

(15) carelessly looking among some papers, turned over a faded bunch of flowers tied with a blue ribbon and a lock of hair. He paused meditatively awhile, then turning to the regal-looking woman lounging before

(20) the fire, he asked:

"Wife, did you ever send me these?"

She raised her great, black eyes to his with a gesture of ineffable [indescribable] disdain, and replied languidly [slowly]:

(25) "You know very well I can't bear flowers. How could I ever send such sentimental trash to any one? Throw them into the fire."

And the Easter bells chimed a solemn requiem as the flames slowly licked up

(30) the faded violets. Was it merely fancy on the wife's part, or did the husband really sigh,—a long, quivering breath of remembrance?

---

[1] an English Romantic poet

Alice Moore Dunbar Nelson, *Violets.*

5. According to the excerpt, why does the letter writer send the flowers?

(1) to declare her love of poetry
(2) to prove her feelings for Byron
(3) to express her disdain for the wife
(4) to urge the receiver to return to her
(5) to show the receiver she loves him

6. On the basis of the excerpt, what would the wife be most likely to do if her husband sent a dozen roses to her?

(1) stuff them in a garbage can
(2) yell at him for wasting money
(3) display them near the fireplace
(4) thank him for his thoughtfulness
(5) share them with the letter writer

7. What does this statement in lines 30–33 suggest about the husband's character?

"Was it merely fancy on the wife's part, or did the husband really sigh,—a long, quivering breath of remembrance?"

(1) He may be less forgetful than his wife.
(2) He may be less regretful than his wife.
(3) He may be less emotional than his wife.
(4) He may be more imaginative than his wife.
(5) He may be more sentimental than his wife.

8. Which statement best describes the difference between the letter writer and the wife?

(1) The letter writer is industrious, while the wife is lazy.
(2) The letter writer is religious, while the wife is worldly.
(3) The letter writer is attentive, while the wife is forgetful.
(4) The letter writer is shy, while the wife is outgoing.
(5) The letter writer is sentimental, while the wife is haughty.

9. The bunch of flowers best symbolizes which of the following?

(1) Easter
(2) the wife
(3) Byron's poetry
(4) the letter writer
(5) sentimental trash

Answers start on page 303.

Directions: This is a ten-minute practice test. After ten minutes, mark the last question you finished. Then complete the test and check your answers. If most of your answers were correct, but you didn't finish, try to work faster next time. Choose the one best answer to each question.

Questions 1 through 11 refer to the following excerpt from a short story.

DOES THIS WOMAN LIVE IN A DREAM WORLD?

The windows of the drawing-room opened on to a balcony overlooking the garden. At the far end, against the wall, there was a tall, slender pear tree in fullest,
(5) richest bloom; it stood perfect, as though becalmed against the jade-green sky. Bertha couldn't help feeling, even from this distance, that it had not a single bud or a faded petal. Down below, in the garden
(10) beds, the red and yellow tulips, heavy with flowers, seemed to lean upon the dusk. A grey cat, dragging its belly, crept across the lawn, and a black one, its shadow, trailed after. The sight of them, so intent
(15) and so quick, gave Bertha a curious shiver.

"What creepy things cats are!" she stammered, and she turned away from the window and began walking up and down. . . .
(20) How strong the jonquils smelled in the warm room. Too strong? Oh, no. And yet, as though overcome, she flung down on a couch and pressed her hands to her eyes.

"I'm too happy—too happy!" she
(25) murmured.

And she seemed to see on her eyelids the lovely pear tree with its wide open blossoms as a symbol of her own life.

Really—really—she had everything.
(30) She was young. Harry and she were as much in love as ever, and they got on together splendidly and were really good pals. She had an adorable baby. They didn't have to worry about money. They
(35) had this absolutely satisfactory house and garden. And friends—modern, thrilling friends, writers and painters and poets or

people keen on social questions—just the kind of friends they wanted. And then there
(40) were books, and there was music, and she had found a wonderful little dressmaker, and they were going abroad in the summer, and their new cook made the most superb omelettes. . . .
(45) "I'm absurd! Absurd!" She sat up; but she felt quite dizzy, quite drunk. It must have been the spring.

Yes, it was the spring. Now she was so tired she could not drag herself upstairs
(50) to dress.

A white dress, a string of jade beads, green shoes and stockings. It wasn't intentional. She had thought of this scheme hours before she stood at the
(55) drawing-room window.

Katherine Mansfield, "Bliss," *The Short Stories of Katherine Mansfield.*

1. When does the scene in this excerpt take place?

    (1) early morning
    (2) noontime
    (3) afternoon
    (4) early evening
    (5) night

2. Which of the following colors is most emphasized throughout this excerpt?

    (1) white
    (2) grey
    (3) green
    (4) black
    (5) yellow

3. Which of the following is the most likely reason that Bertha felt dizzy?

   (1) She has had too many cocktails.
   (2) She is overcome with emotion.
   (3) She is affected by the jonquils' odor.
   (4) She is feeling spring fever.
   (5) She is upset after seeing the cats.

4. Based on the information in this excerpt, Bertha would most likely participate in which of the following activities?

   (1) visiting art galleries
   (2) going on fox hunts
   (3) grooming cats
   (4) cleaning the house
   (5) cooking gourmet meals

5. Which of the following characterizes the writing in this excerpt?

   (1) rich dialogue
   (2) reliance on action verbs
   (3) carefully controlled emotion
   (4) sensory words
   (5) short economical sentences

6. Why does Bertha see the pear tree as a symbol of her life?

   (1) It seems perfect, just as her circumstances do.
   (2) It is tall and slender, just as she is.
   (3) It will soon be bearing fruit, and she is pregnant.
   (4) It is growing and changing, just as she is.
   (5) It projects a sense of calmness, and she is calm.

7. What effect is produced by the cats creeping across the garden?

   (1) playfulness
   (2) uneasiness
   (3) terror
   (4) sadness
   (5) tranquility

8. What is the most likely meaning of lines 52−55: "It wasn't intentional. She had thought of this scheme hours before she stood at the drawing-room window"?

   (1) The colors she planned to wear matched her surroundings.
   (2) The colors she planned to wear matched her mood.
   (3) Bertha did not believe in coincidences.
   (4) Bertha was rehearsing what she would tell those who commented on her attire.
   (5) Bertha was plotting to do something evil.

9. What effect is created by the repetition in line 29: "Really—really—she had everything"?

   (1) It shows how happy Bertha is.
   (2) It emphasizes how confident Bertha feels.
   (3) It indicates that Bertha is hiding something.
   (4) It hints that Bertha is not really in love with Harry.
   (5) It suggests that something is missing from Bertha's life.

10. What effect does the season in which it is set (spring) have on the mood of the story?

    (1) It contributes to a fresh, new feeling.
    (2) It contributes to the feeling of unreality.
    (3) It contributes to a joyous, playful feeling.
    (4) It enables the pear tree to be a more effective symbol.
    (5) It gives the feeling of a new beginning for Bertha.

11. Based on the excerpt, which of the following words would the narrator most likely use to describe Bertha?

    (1) intelligent
    (2) naïve
    (3) careless
    (4) sensible
    (5) hateful

Answers start on page 303.

GED SKILL **Making Inferences**

making an inference
putting together clues
or details to reach a
logical conclusion
when facts are not
stated directly

In everyday life, you often encounter situations in which you do not have all of the information you need. In such cases, you must make decisions based on the facts you do have, as well as your knowledge and experience. This skill is called **making an inference.** You can also make inferences when reading fiction. First, you find out what an author is suggesting, and then you make a decision based on your own understanding of what the writer said indirectly. Writers often imply information about characters, setting, atmosphere, and tone.

Read the following excerpt from a short story and complete the exercise below.

> The big kids call me Mercury cause I'm the swiftest thing in the neighborhood. Everybody knows that—except two people who know better, my father and me. He can beat me to Amsterdam Avenue with me having a two fire-hydrant headstart and him running with his hands in his pockets and whistling. But that's private information. Cause can you imagine some thirty-five-year-old man stuffing himself into PAL shorts to race little kids? So as far as everyone's concerned, I'm the fastest and that goes for Gretchen, too, who has put out the tale that she is going to win the first-place medal this year. Ridiculous.

Toni Cade Bambara, "Raymond's Run," *Gorilla, My Love.*

To make inferences, look for clue words in a passage and add to them what you already know from personal experience.

1. Write *F* by the statement that is a fact, and *I* by the statement that is an inference.

   ——— a. The narrator has a good sense of humor.

   ——— b. The narrator's father can run faster than she can.

2. Put a check mark by all of the statements that support the inference that the narrator has great confidence in her ability.

   ——— a. "He can beat me to Amsterdam Avenue"

   ——— b. "I'm the swiftest thing in the neighborhood"

   ——— c. "Ridiculous"

You were correct if you chose *inference* for *option a.* The excerpt does not state this directly, but the narrator makes two humorous comments about her father, so you can infer that she has a good sense of humor. *Option b* is a *fact* mentioned by the narrator. For question 2, you should have checked *b* and *c.* Only someone with confidence in her ability would state that she was the fastest in the neighborhood and that it was ridiculous that someone else thought she could be beaten.

Read the following excerpt from a short story and complete the exercise below.

      If Jimmie had been there he could have read those papers and explained to her what they said. Ayah would have known then, never to sign them. The doctors came back the next day and they brought a BIA [Bureau of Indian Affairs] policeman with them. They told Chato they had her signature and that was all they

(5) needed. Except for the kids. She listened to Chato sullenly; she hated him when he told her it was the old woman who died in the winter, spitting blood; it was her old grandma who had given the children this disease. "They don't spit blood" she said coldly. "The whites lie." She held Ella and Danny close to her, ready to run to the hills again. "I want a medicine man first," she said to Chato, not looking at him.

(10) He shook his head. "It's too late now. The policeman is with them. You signed the paper." His voice was gentle.

      Leslie Marmon Silko, "Lullaby," *Storyteller.*

1. Put a check mark by the most reasonable inference you can make from lines 1–3.

    ____ a. Jimmie is smarter than Ayah is.

    ____ b. Ayah did not bother to read the papers.

    ____ c. Ayah cannot read.

2. Put a check mark by one of the following inferences that can be reasonably made from the excerpt.

    ____ a. Ella and Danny are not very sick because they do not spit blood.

    ____ b The doctors are very understanding.

    ____ c. Ella and Danny have a dangerous disease.

    ____ d. Ayah is too sick to take care of Ella and Danny.

3. In one or two sentences, explain your choice for question 2.

  _____

  _____

4. Ayah does not trust the doctors. Find two statements from the excerpt that support this inference, and write them on the lines below.

  _____

  _____

  _____

  _____

Answers start on page 304.

Directions: Choose the <u>one best answer</u> to each question.

Questions 1 through 4 refer to the following excerpt from a novel.

**HOW DOES THE NARRATOR
FEEL ABOUT THIS WOMAN?**

. . . She put me in them new clothes again, and I couldn't do nothing but sweat and sweat, and feel all cramped up. Well, then the old thing commenced again.
(5) The widow rung a bell for supper, and you had to come to time. When you got to the table you couldn't go right to eating, but you had to wait for the widow to tuck down her head and grumble a little over the
(10) victuals, though there warn't really anything the matter with them—that is, nothing only everything was cooked by itself. In a barrel of odds and ends it is different; things get mixed up, and the juice
(15) kind of swaps around, and the things go better.

After supper she got out her book and learned me about Moses and the Bulrushers, and I was in a sweat to find out
(20) all about him; but by and by she let it out that Moses had been dead a considerable long time; so then I didn't care no more about him, because I don't take no stock in dead people.
(25) Pretty soon I wanted to smoke, and asked the widow to let me. But she wouldn't. She said it was a mean practice and wasn't clean, and I must try to not do it any more. That is just the way with some
(30) people. They get down on a thing when they don't know nothing about it. Here she was a-bothering about Moses, which was no kin to her, and no use to anybody, being gone, you see, yet finding a power of fault
(35) with me for doing a thing that had some good in it. And she took snuff, too; of course that was all right, because she done it herself.

Mark Twain, *The Adventures of Huckleberry Finn*.

1. What is the widow trying to do to the narrator?

   (1) adopt him
   (2) reform him
   (3) annoy him
   (4) poke fun at him
   (5) entertain him

2. Based on the information in this excerpt, the narrator would most enjoy eating which of the following?

   (1) a hotdog
   (2) mashed potatoes
   (3) a bowl of beef stew
   (4) cheese and crackers
   (5) a fresh green salad

3. Which of the following words <u>best</u> describes the tone of this excerpt?

   (1) suspenseful
   (2) formal
   (3) serious
   (4) cheerful
   (5) conversational

4. What is the main effect of the author's use of slang and nonstandard English?

   (1) It gives clues about the time and place.
   (2) It creates a contrast with the widow's speech.
   (3) It results in a likable character.
   (4) It creates a humorous situation.
   (5) It makes the excerpt easier to understand.

 TIP To check your skill in making inferences, ask yourself "Are there clues in this passage that support my inference? If so, what are they?"

Questions 5 through 8 refer to the following excerpt from a short story.

WHY IS UNCLE LUIS SO UPSET?

Just before I started the first grade we moved from Los Rafas into town. It created a family uproar that left hard feelings for a long time.

(5) "You think you're too good for us," Uncle Luis shouted at Papa in Spanish, "just because you finished high school and have a job in town! My God! We grew up in the country. Our parents and grandparents

(10) grew up in the country. If New Mexico country was good enough for them—"

Papa stood with his cup and saucer held tightly in his hands, his knuckles bleached by the vicious grip as if all the

(15) blood had been squeezed up to his bright red face. But even when angry, he was polite to his older brother.

"I'll be much closer to work, and Josie can have the car to shop once in a while.

(20) We'll still come out on weekends. It's only five miles."

Uncle Luis looked around in disbelief. My aunt tried not to look at either him or Papa, while Grandma sat on her rocking

(25) chair smoking a hand-rolled cigarette. She was blind and couldn't see the anger on the men's faces, but she wasn't deaf. Her chair started to rock faster, and I knew that in a moment she was going to scream at

(30) them both.

"It's much closer to work," Papa repeated.

Before Uncle Luis could shout again, Grandma blew out a puff of cigarette

(35) smoke in exasperation. "He's a grown man, Luis. With a wife and children. He can live anywhere he wants."

"But what about the—"

He was going to say orchard next to

(40) Grandma's house. It belonged to Papa and everyone expected him to build a house there someday. Grandma cut Uncle short: "Enough!"

Nash Candelaria, "The Day the Cisco Kid Shot John Wayne," *The Day the Cisco Kid Shot John Wayne.*

5. Based on the information in this excerpt, which of the following is most likely true of Uncle Luis?

   (1) He hopes to inherit Grandma's orchard.
   (2) He never finished high school.
   (3) He has a great job in town.
   (4) He considers his brother to be a role model.
   (5) He wishes Grandma would move into town.

6. Based on this excerpt, how would the father likely respond to someone who disagreed with him?

   (1) He would storm out of the room in anger.
   (2) He would stammer nervously while trying to explain.
   (3) He would calmly justify his position.
   (4) He would raise his voice and shake his fist.
   (5) He would refuse to discuss the matter.

7. Of the characters in this excerpt, whose reaction to the move is most surprising to the other family members?

   (1) the narrator's
   (2) the father's
   (3) the aunt's
   (4) the grandmother's
   (5) the uncle's

8. Which of the following ideas are most clearly contrasted in this passage?

   (1) tradition and self-determination
   (2) knowledge and ignorance
   (3) respect and disrespect
   (4) truth and deception
   (5) pride and shame

 TIP Use your inference skills to understand the meaning of what is left unsaid.

Answers start on page 304.

Directions: This is a ten-minute practice test. After ten minutes, mark the last question you finished. Then complete the test and check your answers. If most of your answers were correct, but you didn't finish, try to work faster next time. Choose the one best answer to each question.

Questions 1 through 9 refer to the following excerpt from a short story.

WHO IS THE NEW CHOIR SOLOIST?

In the centre row of women singers stood Alma Way. All the people stared at her, and turned their ears critically. She was the new leading soprano. Candace
(5) Whitcomb, the old one, who had sung in the choir for forty years, had lately been given her dismissal. The audience considered that her voice had grown too cracked and uncertain on the upper notes.
(10) There had been much complaint, and after long deliberation the church-officers had made known their decision as mildly as possible to the old singer. She had sung for the last time the Sunday before, and
(15) Alma Way had been engaged to take her place. With the exception of the organist, the leading soprano was the only paid musician in the large choir. The salary was very modest, still the village people
(20) considered it large for a young woman. Alma was from the adjoining village of East Derby; she had quite a local reputation as a singer.

Now she fixed her large solemn blue
(25) eyes; her long, delicate face, which had been pretty, turned paler; the blue flowers on her bonnet trembled; her little thin gloved hands, clutching the singing-book, shook perceptibly; but she sang out
(30) bravely. That most formidable mountain-height of the world, self-distrust and timidity, arose before her, but her nerves were braced for its ascent. In the midst of the hymn she had a solo; her voice rang
(35) out piercingly sweet; the people nodded admiringly at each other; but suddenly there was a stir; all the faces turned toward the windows on the south side of the church. Above the din of the wind

(40) and the birds, above Alma Way's sweetly straining tones, arose another female voice, singing another hymn to another tune.

"It's her," the women whispered to each
(45) other; they were half aghast, half smiling.

Candace Whitcomb's cottage stood close to the south side of the church. She was playing on her parlor organ, and singing, to drown out the voice of her rival.
(50) Alma caught her breath; she almost stopped; the hymn-book waved like a fan; then she went on. But the long husky drone of the parlor organ and the shrill clamor of the other voice seemed louder
(55) than anything else.

When the hymn was finished, Alma sat down. She felt faint; the woman next to her slipped a peppermint into her hand. "It ain't worth minding," she whispered, vigorously.
(60) Alma tried to smile; down in the audience a young man was watching her with a kind of fierce pity.

In the last hymn Alma had another solo. Again the parlor organ droned above
(65) the carefully delicate accompaniment of the church organ, and again Candace Whitcomb's voice clamored forth in another tune.

Mary Wilkins Freeman, "A Village Singer."

1. Why did Candace Whitcomb stay home to play the organ and sing?

(1) She did not feel well that day.
(2) She had the day off so a new soloist could be auditioned.
(3) She felt she needed the practice for the following Sunday.
(4) She was envious of the new soloist.
(5) She had decided to retire.

2. The sentence "That most formidable mountain-height of the world, self-distrust and timidity, arose before her, but her nerves were braced for its ascent" (lines 30–33) means which of the following?

(1) Alma had climbed mountains before.
(2) Alma was prepared to conquer her fear.
(3) Alma did not trust her voice to hit the high notes.
(4) Alma believed nervousness before a performance was normal.
(5) Alma felt the walk to the singer's podium was like climbing a mountain.

3. Which of the following best explains the meaning of the phrase "half aghast" in line 45?

(1) The women's mouths were half-open.
(2) Half of the women were opposed to Alma.
(3) The women were smiling weakly.
(4) The women were trying to be quiet.
(5) The women were partially horrified.

4. Why did Alma feel faint (line 57)?

(1) She was exhausted after her incredible performance.
(2) She was dizzy from the heat inside the church.
(3) She was nervous because a young man in the audience was watching her.
(4) She felt weak from the strain of having to compete with Candace's singing.
(5) She was scared that Candace's singing might be better than her own.

5. If Alma were to quit singing with the choir, what would Candace most likely do?

(1) try to convince Alma to return
(2) try to get reinstated as the choir's soloist
(3) ask Alma to sing duets with her
(4) apologize for making Alma feel bad
(5) continue to perform from her cottage

6. Which of the following details from the excerpt helps the reader to understand the emotional atmosphere in the church?

(1) "her voice had grown too cracked and uncertain" (lines 8–9)
(2) "the leading soprano was the only paid musician in the large choir" (lines 17–18)
(3) "All the people stared at her, and turned their ears critically." (lines 2–3)
(4) "she had quite a local reputation as a singer" (lines 22–23)
(5) "She was the new leading soprano." (lines 3–4)

7. Which of the following can be learned about Alma's personality from this excerpt?

(1) She is willing to face a challenge.
(2) She is vain about her looks.
(3) She resents competition.
(4) She does not value her talent.
(5) She is often pessimistic.

8. Which of the following descriptions best characterizes the style of writing in this excerpt?

(1) dry and scholarly
(2) flat and unemotional
(3) ironic and joking
(4) informal and serious
(5) complex and confusing

9. Based on the excerpt, which of the following pairs shows the same relationship as that between Candace's voice and Alma's voice?

(1) a crow's voice and an eagle's
(2) an eagle's voice and a hummingbird's
(3) a hummingbird's voice and a crow's
(4) an owl's voice and a songbird's
(5) a crow's voice and a canary's

Answers start on page 305.

GED SKILL Comparing and Contrasting

compare
show how things are alike

contrast
show how things are different

TIP

Identify comparisons by looking for clue words such as *like, likewise, also, compared to,* and *similarly*. To identify contrasts, look for clue words such as *unlike, however, but, on the other hand,* and *differently*.

When you **compare** things, you show how they are alike. When you **contrast** them, you show how they are different. One of the joys of reading fiction is in the development of the characters. Writers may compare and contrast the characters' personalities in a story to give the reader a vivid image. This character development can also provide insight into the conflict of the story.

When you read fiction, understanding the process of compare and contrast can help you better understand what you read.

Read the following excerpt from a novel and complete the exercise below.

Mr. Bennet was so odd a mixture of quick parts, sarcastic humour, reserve, and caprice,[1] that the experience of three and twenty years had been insufficient to make his wife understand his character. *Her* mind was less difficult to develop. She was a woman of mean[2] understanding, little information, and uncertain temper. When she was discontented she fancied herself nervous. The business of her life was to get her daughters married; its solace[3] was visiting and news.

_____
[1] impulsiveness   [2] limited   [3] comfort

Jane Austen, *Pride and Prejudice.*

1. Circle the correct underlined word in the sentence below.

   This paragraph <u>compares</u>/<u>contrasts</u> Mr. and Mrs. Bennet.

2. Put a check mark by the sentence that contrasts two things.

   _____ a. Mr. Bennet is more difficult to understand than his wife.

   _____ b. Mrs. Bennet thrives on gossip and visiting.

   _____ c. Mrs. Bennet is confused by her own feelings.

3. Underline the sentence in the excerpt that indicates that the characters will be contrasted.

You were correct if you circled *contrasts* for question 1. The excerpt shows how the characters are different. In question 2, *option a* is the correct response. For question 3, you should have underlined *Her mind was less difficult to develop.* The emphasis of the word *her* combined with the word *less* tells you that she is being contrasted with Mr. Bennet.

Read the following excerpt from a novel and complete the exercise below.

Ray Pearson and Hal Winters were farm hands employed on a farm three miles north of Winesburg. On Saturday afternoons they came into town and wandered about through the streets with other fellows from the country.

Ray was a quiet, rather nervous man of perhaps fifty with a brown beard and
(5) shoulders rounded by too much and too hard labor. In his nature he was as unlike Hal Winters as two men can be unlike.

Ray was an altogether serious man and had a little sharp-featured wife who had also a sharp voice. The two, with half a dozen thin-legged children, lived in a tumbledown frame house beside a creek at the back end of the Wills farm where
(10) Ray was employed.

Hal Winters, his fellow employee, was a young fellow. . . . Hal was a bad one. Everyone said that. There were three of the Winters boys in that family, John, Hal, and Edward, all broad-shouldered big fellows . . . and all fighters and woman-chasers and generally all-around bad ones.
(15) Hal was the worst of the lot and always up to some devilment.

Sherwood Anderson, *Winesburg, Ohio.*

1. Put a check mark by the way in which Ray and Hal are alike.

   _____ a. They are about the same age.

   _____ b. They work at the same place.

2. Write one more way in which the two men are alike.

   _____

3. Ray and Hal are also contrasted in this excerpt. Write the sentence that tells you that the two men will be contrasted.

   _____

4. List four ways in which Ray and Hal are different. (Hint: You may want to underline or list them as you reread the excerpt.)

   Ray   **Hal**

   a. _____   _____

   b. _____   _____

   c. _____   _____

   d. _____   _____

Answers start on page 306.

Directions: Choose the <u>one best answer</u> to each question.

<u>Questions 1 through 3</u> refer to the following excerpt from a novel.

WHERE ARE THESE TWO BOYS?

Ralph did a surface dive and swam under water with his eyes open; the sandy edge of the pool loomed up like a hillside. He turned over, holding his nose, and a
(5) golden light danced and shattered just over his face. Piggy was looking determined and began to take off his shorts. Presently he was palely and fatly naked. He tiptoed down the sandy side of the pool, and sat
(10) there up to his neck in water smiling proudly at Ralph.
"Aren't you going to swim?"
Piggy shook his head.
"I can't swim. I wasn't allowed. My
(15) asthma—"
"Sucks to your ass-mar!"
Piggy bore this with a sort of humble patience.
"You can't half swim well."
(20) Ralph paddled backwards down the slope, immersed his mouth and blew a jet of water into the air. Then he lifted his chin and spoke.
"I could swim when I was five. Daddy
(25) taught me. He's a commander in the Navy. When he gets leave he'll come and rescue us. What's your father?"
Piggy flushed suddenly.
"My dad's dead," he said quickly, "and
(30) my mum—"
He took off his glasses and looked vainly for something with which to clean them.
"I used to live with my auntie. She kept
(35) a candy store. I used to get ever so many candies. As many as I liked. When'll your dad rescue us?"
"Soon as he can."
Piggy rose dripping from the water and
(40) stood naked, cleaning his glasses with a sock. The only sound that reached them now through the heat of the morning was the long, grinding roar of the breakers on the reef.

William Golding, *Lord of the Flies.*

1. What has happened to the two boys in this excerpt?

   (1) They have been kidnapped.
   (2) They have run away from home.
   (3) They have been stranded.
   (4) They have gone to summer camp.
   (5) They have escaped from a reformatory.

2. Based on the details in this excerpt, what would Piggy likely do if he were teased for wearing glasses?

   (1) pick a fight with his tormentor
   (2) go and tell an adult
   (3) join in and laugh at himself
   (4) suffer in silence
   (5) walk away crying

3. How are Ralph and Piggy alike?

   (1) Both seem to envy each other.
   (2) Both have grown up without their mothers.
   (3) Both believe Ralph's father will rescue them.
   (4) Both learned to swim at a young age.
   (5) Both suffer from asthma.

 TIP To identify comparison and contrast patterns, underline the adjectives used to describe characters. Are the descriptive words about one character similar to or different from those used to describe another character? If they are similar, a comparison is being made; if dissimilar, a contrast is being made.

Questions 4 through 8 refer to the following excerpt from a novel.

HOW ARE THESE TWO ISLANDS DIFFERENT?

Twenty miles from the city a pair of enormous eggs, identical in contour and separated only by a courtesy bay, jut out into the most domesticated body of salt
(5) water in the Western hemisphere, the great wet barnyard of Long Island Sound. They are not perfect ovals—like the egg in the Columbus story, they are both crushed flat at the contact end—but their physical
(10) resemblance must be a source of perpetual confusion to the gulls that fly overhead. To the wingless a more arresting phenomenon is their dissimilarity in every particular except shape and size.
(15) I lived in West Egg, the—well, the less fashionable of the two, though this is a most superficial tag to express the bizarre and not a little sinister contrast between them. My house was at the very tip of the
(20) egg, only fifty yards from the Sound, and squeezed between two huge places that rented for twelve or fifteen thousand a season. The one on my right was a colossal affair by any standard—it was a
(25) factual imitation of some Hotel de Ville in Normandy, with a tower on one side, spanking new under a thin beard of raw ivy, and a marble swimming pool, and more than forty acres of lawn and garden.
(30) It was Gatsby's mansion. Or rather, as I didn't know Mr. Gatsby, it was a mansion, inhabited by a gentleman of that name. My own house was an eyesore, but it was a small eyesore, and it had been overlooked,
(35) so I had a view of the water, a partial view of my neighbor's lawn, and the consoling proximity of millionaires—all for eighty dollars a month.
Across the courtesy bay the white
(40) palaces of fashionable East Egg glittered along the water . . .

F. Scott Fitzgerald, *The Great Gatsby.*

4. What is the author referring to when he uses the word *wingless* (line 12)?

(1) seagulls
(2) airline pilots
(3) prisoners
(4) inhabitants
(5) servants

5. How are East Egg and West Egg alike?

(1) They are equally fashionable.
(2) They are the same shape and size.
(3) They are both bizarre and a little sinister.
(4) They both contain only mansions.
(5) They are both superficial.

6. East Egg and West Egg are most similar to which of the following places?

(1) two bordering countries in which people follow the same customs
(2) two sides of the same town, one side upper class, the other side middle class
(3) two neighboring nations that have declared war on each other
(4) two exclusive clubs that admit only wealthy people as members
(5) two rooms in the same mansion, one room for family, the other room for guests

7. What does the narrator imply about the mansions in West Egg?

(1) They are older than those in East Egg.
(2) They are rented only part of the year.
(3) They have been converted into hotels.
(4) They are designed like French castles.
(5) They are smaller than those in East Egg.

8. Which of the following characterizes the style of this excerpt?

(1) short, punchy sentences
(2) vividly descriptive detail
(3) rip-roaring action
(4) carefully controlled language
(5) frequent use of slang

Answers start on page 306.

Directions: This is a ten-minute practice test. After ten minutes, mark the last question you finished. Then complete the test and check your answers. If most of your answers were correct, but you didn't finish, try to work faster next time. Choose the <u>one best answer</u> to each question.

Questions 1 through 11 refer to the following excerpt from a novel.

HOW ARE THESE SISTERS DIFFERENT?

Miss Brooke had that kind of beauty which seems to be thrown into relief by poor dress. Her hand and wrist were so finely formed that she could wear sleeves
(5) not less bare of style than those in which the blessed Virgin appeared to Italian painters; and her profile as well as her stature and bearing seemed to gain the more dignity from her plain garments,
(10) which by the side of provincial fashion gave her the impressiveness of a fine quotation from the Bible—or from one of our elder poets—in a paragraph of today's newspaper. She was usually spoken of
(15) as being remarkably clever, but with the addition that her sister Celia had more common sense. Nevertheless, Celia wore scarcely more trimmings, and it was only to close observers that her dress differed
(20) from her sister's and had a shade of coquetry in its arrangements; for Miss Brooke's plain dressing was due to mixed conditions, in most of which her sister shared. The pride of being ladies had
(25) something to do with it: the Brooke connexions, though not exactly aristocratic, were unquestionably "good"; if you inquired backward for a generation or two, you would not find any yard-measuring or
(30) parcel-tying forefathers—anything lower than an admiral or a clergyman . . . Young women of such birth, living in a quiet country-house and attending a village church hardly larger than a parlour,
(35) naturally regarded frippery[1] as the ambition of a huckster's daughter. . . .
      The rural opinion about the new young ladies, even among the cottagers, was generally in favour of Celia as being so
(40) amiable and innocent looking, while Miss Brooke's large eyes seemed, like her religion, too unusual and striking. Poor Dorothea! Compared with her, the innocent-looking Celia was knowing and
(45) worldly wise, so much subtler is a human mind than the outside tissues which make a sort of blazonry[2] or clock-face for it. . . .
      She was open, ardent, and not in the least self-admiring; indeed, it was pretty to
(50) see how her imagination adorned her sister, Celia, with attractions altogether superior to her own, and if any gentleman appeared to come to the Grange from some other motive than that of seeing
(55) Mr. Brooke, she concluded that he must be in love with Celia: Sir James Chettam, for example, whom she constantly considered from Celia's point of view, inwardly debating whether it would be
(60) good for Celia to accept him.

---
[1] showy dress   [2] dazzling display

George Eliot, *Middlemarch.*

1. What is meant by the phrase "that kind of beauty which seems to be thrown into relief by poor dress" (lines 1–3)?

   (1) Miss Brooke gave little thought to her appearance.
   (2) Miss Brooke's poor dress detracted from her looks.
   (3) Miss Brooke's poor dress made her beauty all the more noticeable.
   (4) Miss Brooke was relieved that people found her beautiful.
   (5) Miss Brooke dressed poorly for one so beautiful.

2. What is another way to say "so much subtler is a human mind than the outside tissues" (lines 45–46)?

   (1) Pretty is as pretty does.
   (2) Be careful of innocent-looking people.
   (3) The intellect is more important than the body.
   (4) Appearances can be deceiving.
   (5) A person's true self is unchanging.

3. To which of the following is Miss Brooke compared in this excerpt?

   (1) a poet
   (2) a fine quotation
   (3) a paragraph
   (4) a French painter
   (5) a biblical figure

4. What is one reason given in the excerpt for the sisters' choosing to wear plain garments?

   (1) They are very poor.
   (2) They do not want to attract attention.
   (3) They try to dress like ladies.
   (4) They are not interested in clothes.
   (5) They live in a rural area.

5. Based on the excerpt, how would Dorothea most likely react to a marriage proposal?

   She would

   (1) be flattered
   (2) reject the offer
   (3) distrust her suitor's motives
   (4) think it was a mistake
   (5) be overjoyed

6. Which of the following words best describes Dorothea's character?

   (1) coquettish
   (2) vain
   (3) modest
   (4) temperamental
   (5) jealous

7. What is suggested by the statement that Celia has more common sense than Dorothea?

   Dorothea is

   (1) foolish
   (2) careless
   (3) down-to-earth
   (4) slow-witted
   (5) impractical

8. What is one difference between Celia and Dorothea?

   (1) Dorothea is more innocent than Celia.
   (2) Celia is shyer than Dorothea.
   (3) Celia is more beautiful than Dorothea.
   (4) Dorothea is more popular than Celia.
   (5) Dorothea is more fashionable than Celia.

9. Based on the excerpt, whom would the Brooke family consider a good husband for Celia?

   (1) a clever dressmaker
   (2) a kind shopkeeper
   (3) a wealthy baker
   (4) a distinguished minister
   (5) an educated watchmaker

10. Which of the following characterizes the style of this excerpt?

   (1) long, complex sentences
   (2) matter-of-fact description
   (3) lengthy, spirited dialogue
   (4) faithfulness to regional dialect
   (5) precise word pictures

11. Which of the following best describes the narrator's attitude toward Dorothea?

   (1) mocking
   (2) respectful
   (3) sympathetic
   (4) loathing
   (5) scornful

Answers start on page 306.

GED SKILL Interpreting Theme

The **theme** is the general idea about life or human nature that a short story or novel reveals. Theme is sometimes compared to the **moral** of a story, a lesson meant to teach right from wrong. Morals are often stated at the end of a fable. However, the theme is usually not stated directly; you must infer it. Nor does a theme necessarily tell the reader how to behave. It simply expresses the author's views about the way life is.

theme
the general idea about the way life is that you infer from a short story or novel

moral
a lesson that can be applied to your life

TIP

As you read, ask yourself "Is the author trying to give me advice or express a truth or insight?"

Read the following excerpt from a fable and complete the exercise below.

An Eagle swooped down upon a Serpent and seized it in his talons with the intention of carrying it off and devouring it. But the Serpent was too quick for him and had its coils round him in a moment; and then there ensued a life-and-death struggle between the two. A countryman, who was a witness of the encounter, came to the assistance of the eagle, and succeeded in freeing him from the Serpent and enabling him to escape. In revenge, the Serpent spat some of his poison into the man's drinking-horn. Heated with his exertions, the man was about to slake[1] his thirst with a draught[2] from the horn, when the Eagle knocked it out of his hand, and spilled its contents upon the ground.

_____
[1] quench   [2] drink

Aesop's Fables, "The Serpent and the Eagle."

1. Put a check mark by the reason that the eagle knocked the thirsty man's drink from his hand.

_____ a. The eagle was still angry after his fight with the serpent.

_____ b. The eagle was trying to protect the man.

2. Put a check mark by the statement that <u>best</u> expresses the moral of this fable.

_____ a. Birds of a feather flock together.

_____ b. One good turn deserves another.

_____ c. Little friends may prove great friends.

3. Explain briefly why you chose your answer to question 2.

_____

You were correct if you chose *option b* for question 1. The drink was poisoned. For question 2, the correct answer is *option b*. Your explanation in question 3 might say something such as *The countryman's helping the eagle resulted in the eagle's saving his life.*

GED SKILL FOCUS

Read the following excerpt from a short story and complete the exercise below.

When it occurs to a man that nature does not regard him as important, and that she feels she would not maim the universe by disposing of him, he at first wishes to throw bricks at the temple, and he hates deeply the fact that there are no bricks and no temples. Any visible expression of nature would surely be pelleted with
(5) his jeers.

Then, if there be no tangible thing to hoot, he feels, perhaps, the desire to confront a personification[1] and indulge in pleas, bowed to one knee, and with hands supplicant,[2] saying, "Yes, but I love myself."

A high cold star on a winter's night is the word he feels that she says to him.
(10) Thereafter he knows the pathos[3] of his situation.

The men in the dinghy had not discussed these matters, but each had, no doubt, reflected upon them in silence and according to his mind. There was seldom any expression upon their faces save the general one of complete weariness. Speech was devoted to the business of the boat.

---

[1] an object given human form   [2] begging   [3] tragic sorrow

Stephen Crane, "The Open Boat," *The Portable Stephen Crane.*

1. Put a check mark by how the man in this excerpt feels about nature.

_____ a. indifferent

_____ b. angry

2. Put a check mark by the best description of nature as it is portrayed in this excerpt.

_____ a. nurturing

_____ b. vengeful

_____ c. indifferent

3. Put a check mark by the phrase that best describes the relationship between mankind and nature as portrayed in this excerpt.

_____ a. an ongoing power struggle

_____ b a balance of power

_____ c. nature does not care about human beings

4. Put a check mark by the best expression of the theme of this excerpt.

_____ a. Human beings are like grains of sand on a beach.

_____ b. Human beings are the kings of the mountain.

_____ c. Human beings are brothers in spirit with nature.

5. Explain your choice for question 4 by writing the phrase from the first paragraph that helped you arrive at your answer.

_____

Directions: Choose the <u>one best answer</u> to each question.

Questions 1 through 4 refer to the following excerpt from a novel.

WHAT INFECTED RICHMOND?

A carnival of hope infected Richmond.
McClellan stayed at Harrison's Landing.
He plopped there like a frog full of
buckshot. He moved neither forward nor
(5) backward, but seemed imprisoned by
his own weight. Richmond was saved.
Churches offered up services, people
shouted, "Gloria in Excelsis," and Lee,
instead of being the goat, was now the
(10) hero.
While Lutie, like everyone around her,
offered up prayers of thanksgiving to
Almighty God, she thought of the weeks
of battles as the slaughterhouse of heroes.
(15) The death lists were appalling. The best
families of the South lost their husbands,
sons, and brothers. Hardly anyone was
untouched, especially since the upper
classes led the regiments, brigades, and
(20) divisions. The leaders, the wealthy and
the gifted, were cut down by the scythe
of war no less than the small farmer, the
shopkeeper, even the vagrant seeking to
redeem himself by military service. They
(25) died alike, and Death, as always,
impartially selected his victims. She used
to think of Death as a personal force, the
god of the underworld, Hades or Pluto.
Odd, too, that Pluto was the god of riches.
(30) Each day you bargained with this god, but
in the end he got the better of the deal.
She put aside that embroidered, mythical
notion. Death these days was a threshing
machine. Someone started the blades
(35) whirling, and it wouldn't cut off.

Rita Mae Brown, *High Hearts*.

1. Why did Lutie offer up prayers of thanksgiving (line 12)?

   (1) She was praying for the soldiers who had died in the war.
   (2) She was thankful that the war was over.
   (3) She was thankful that Richmond had not been attacked.
   (4) She was thankful that death had not touched Richmond.
   (5) She was praying for Lee to win the war.

2. If Lutie's final image of "Death" in lines 33 and 34 were to be modernized, which of the following images would carry a similar meaning?

   (1) a Wall Street success
   (2) a bulldozer
   (3) an electric fan
   (4) a computer game
   (5) a wealthy politician

3. What does the author imply when she compares McClellan to a "frog full of buckshot" (lines 3 and 4)?

   (1) McClellan's troops were about to attack Richmond.
   (2) McClellan had been wounded in battle.
   (3) McClellan had the sympathy of the people.
   (4) McClellan was not to be trusted.
   (5) McClellan seemed incapable of moving his forces.

4. Which of the following <u>best</u> states the theme of this excerpt?

   (1) War is an equal opportunity employer.
   (2) War is soon followed by peace.
   (3) War is an instrument of death.
   (4) Lutie was tired of the war.
   (5) The god of death is the god of riches.

WHAT IS BEHIND THE CHAIN AND THE CURTAIN?

When I got home that same evening, the fellow wasn't there. He'd gone. Not a word, not a note; nothing. Every time I heard the lift [elevator] rattling I thought,
(5) here he is. But he didn't come. When I was home on Saturday afternoon I couldn't stand it any longer and I went up to the Versfelds and asked the old lady if I couldn't sleep there a few days, I said my
(10) flat [apartment] was being painted and the smell turned my stomach. I thought, if he comes to the garage, there are people around, at least there are the boys. I was smoking nearly as much as *he* used to and
(15) I couldn't sleep. I had to ask Mr. Levine to give me something. The slightest sound and I was in a cold sweat. At the end of the week I had to go back to the flat, and I bought a chain for the door and made a
(20) heavy curtain so's you couldn't see anyone standing there. I didn't go out, once I'd got in from work—not even to the early flicks [movies]—so I wouldn't have to come back into the building at night. You know how it
(25) is when you're nervous, the funniest things comfort you: I'd just tell myself, well, if I shouldn't turn up to work in the morning, the boy'd send someone to see.
　　Then slowly I was beginning to forget
(30) about it. I kept the curtain and the chain and I stayed at home. . . .

Nadine Gordimer, "A Correspondence Course,"
Something Out There.

5. What is the main idea of this excerpt?

(1) The woman is highly allergic to paint.
(2) The woman does not like her apartment any longer.
(3) The woman is becoming ill.
(4) The woman is afraid of someone she knows.
(5) The woman is very careful to maintain a secure apartment.

6. Based on the information in the excerpt, which of the following would the woman most likely do if she were given the choice?

(1) give up smoking
(2) move out of the apartment
(3) hire someone to protect her
(4) quit her job
(5) install an alarm

7. What is suggested by the statement "well, if I shouldn't turn up to work in the morning, the boy'd send someone to see" (lines 26–28)?

The woman

(1) fears for her life
(2) will call in sick for work
(3) plans to take her own life
(4) intends to flee the city
(5) is suffering from paranoia

8. Which word best describes the tone of this excerpt?

(1) serious
(2) anxious
(3) playful
(4) sarcastic
(5) gleeful

9. Which word best describes the style of writing in this excerpt?

(1) elaborate
(2) formal
(3) descriptive
(4) conversational
(5) colorful

 The images and symbols that a writer uses can be clues to the underlying theme. Is there a symbol that is referred to repeatedly? If so, it could point to the story's theme.

Answers start on page 307.

Directions: This is a ten-minute practice test. After ten minutes, mark the last question you finished. Then complete the test and check your answers. If most of your answers were correct, but you didn't finish, try to work faster next time. Choose the <u>one best answer</u> to each question.

<u>Questions 1 through 10</u> refer to the following excerpt from a novel.

WHY DOES THE WAR STILL LIVE FOR THE NARRATOR?

Everyone has a moment in history which belongs particularly to him. It is the moment when his emotions achieve their most powerful sway over him, and
(5) afterward when you say to this person "the world today" or "life" or "reality" he will assume that you mean this moment, even if it is fifty years past. The world, through his unleashed emotions, imprinted itself
(10) upon him, and he carries the stamp of that passing moment forever.

For me, this moment—four years is a moment in history—was the war. The war was and is reality for me. I still instinctively
(15) live and think in its atmosphere. These are some of its characteristics: Franklin Delano Roosevelt is the President of the United States, and he always has been. The other two eternal world leaders are Winston
(20) Churchill and Josef Stalin. America is not, never has been, and never will be what the songs and poems call it, a land of plenty. Nylon, meat, gasoline, and steel are rare. There are too many jobs and not enough
(25) workers. Money is very easy to earn but rather hard to spend, because there isn't very much to buy. Trains are always late and always crowded with "servicemen." The war will always be fought very far from
(30) America, and it will never end. Nothing in America stands still for very long, including the people who are always either leaving or on leave. People in America cry often. Sixteen is the key and crucial and natural
(35) age for a human being to be, and people of all other ages are ranged in an orderly manner ahead of and behind you as a harmonious setting for the sixteen-year-

olds of the world. When you are sixteen,
(40) adults are slightly impressed and almost intimidated by you. This is a puzzle finally solved by the realization that they foresee your military future, fighting for them. You do not foresee it. To waste anything
(45) in America is immoral. String and tinfoil are treasures. Newspapers are always crowded with strange maps and names of towns, and every few months the earth seems to lurch from its path when you see
(50) something in the newspapers, such as the time Mussolini, who had almost seemed one of the eternal leaders, is photographed hanging upside down on a meathook. Everyone listens to news broadcasts five
(55) or six times every day. All pleasurable things, all travel and sports and entertainment and good food and fine clothes, are in the very shortest supply, always were and always will be. There are
(60) just tiny fragments of pleasure and luxury in the world, and there is something unpatriotic about enjoying them. All foreign lands are inaccessible except to servicemen; they are vague, distant, and
(65) sealed off as though behind a curtain of plastic. The prevailing color of life in America is a dull, dark green called olive drab. That color is always respectable and always important. Most other colors risk
(70) being unpatriotic.

John Knowles, *A Separate Peace.*

1. What is the main idea of the first paragraph?

   (1) Emotions may influence history.
   (2) People should not dwell on the past.
   (3) People should learn more about history.
   (4) Life in America is not all it is claimed to be.
   (5) A person's worldview is shaped by key events.

2. Which of the following best restates lines 48 and 49: "every few months the earth seems to lurch from its path"?

   (1) Every few months the earth is shaken by earthquakes.
   (2) Every few months there is a bomb attack.
   (3) Every few months America attacks another country.
   (4) Every few months something shocking occurs.
   (5) Every few months there is another shortage of supplies.

3. With which of the following statements would the narrator be most likely to agree?

   (1) Politics makes strange bedfellows.
   (2) There is no time like the present.
   (3) Time is something we will never understand.
   (4) The historical era affects the individual.
   (5) Time stands still for no one.

4. How does the narrator help the reader understand how he feels about the war?

   (1) by explaining that adults were intimidated by soldiers
   (2) by talking about the war as if it were happening now
   (3) by referring to well-known world leaders
   (4) by specifically stating his emotions in clear terms
   (5) by making the war years sound romantic and appealing

5. What is the main purpose of the narrator's discussion of World War II?

   (1) to recall events that took place during his adolescence
   (2) to describe realities of America that remain with us
   (3) to criticize the state of affairs in the world
   (4) to call for a return to the "good old days"
   (5) to speak out against the horrors of war

6. Based on the excerpt, why did the war years affect the narrator as they did?

   (1) He was young and impressionable.
   (2) He admired Roosevelt's policies.
   (3) Money was easy to get.
   (4) Everyone was very sad.
   (5) He feared becoming a soldier.

7. Which of the following best describes the tone of this excerpt?

   (1) critical
   (2) upbeat
   (3) sentimental
   (4) expectant
   (5) serious

8. Which of the following best describes the style of writing in this excerpt?

   (1) formal and scholarly
   (2) witty and sarcastic
   (3) engaging and colorful
   (4) matter-of-fact and repetitive
   (5) flowery and inspiring

9. Which of the following is the main effect of the author's style in this excerpt?

   It helps to

   (1) appeal to the reader's sense of patriotism
   (2) convey the horrors of war
   (3) make Americans count their blessings
   (4) indicate the monotony imposed by war
   (5) reveal how a sixteen-year-old thinks

10. Which of the following statements best expresses the narrator's point of view?

   (1) Everyone has fifteen minutes of fame.
   (2) Those who do not remember the past are doomed to repeat it.
   (3) The "good old days" were not always good.
   (4) The world is too much with us.
   (5) There will always be wars and rumors of war.

Answers start on page 308.

Unit 2 Cumulative Review **Understanding Fiction**

Directions: Choose the <u>one best answer</u> to each question.

Questions 1 through 5 refer to the following excerpt from a short story.

WHAT ARE THIS FATHER'S VIEWS?

     I am not unsympathetic, Jack, to your views on the war. I am not unsympathetic to your views on the state of the world in general. From the way you wear your hair
(5) and from the way you dress I do find it difficult to decide whether you or that young girl you say you are about to marry is going to play the male role in your marriage—or the female role. But even that I don't find
(10) offensive. And I am not trying to make crude jokes at your expense. You must pardon me, though, if my remarks seem too personal. I confess I don't know you as well as a father *ought* to know his son, and
(15) I may seem to take liberties. . . .
     I don't honestly know when I decided to go into college teaching, Jack. I considered doing other things—a career in the army or navy. Yes, I might have gone to Annapolis
(20) or West Point. Those appointments were much to be desired in the Depression years, and my family did still have a few political connections. One thing was certain, though. Business was just as much
(25) out of the question for me as politics had been for my father. An honest man, I was to understand, had too much to suffer there. Yes, considering our family history, an ivory tower didn't sound like a bad thing at all for
(30) an honest man and a serious man . . . .

    Peter Taylor, "Dean of Men," *The Collected Stories.*

1. What would the father likely feel if he were invited to Jack's wedding?

    (1) disappointment
    (2) resentment
    (3) amusement
    (4) gladness
    (5) fear

2. Which of the following is <u>most likely</u> true of the narrator's past?

    (1) He became a college teacher reluctantly.
    (2) He was extremely conventional.
    (3) He had a brief career in the army.
    (4) He did not follow in his father's footsteps.
    (5) His father was dishonest.

3. What is the main effect of the phrase "ivory tower" (lines 28–29)?

    (1) It emphasizes that the narrator wanted to escape into a safer world.
    (2) It shows how much the narrator reveres the college where he works.
    (3) It shows that the narrator realizes he has not been a good father.
    (4) It reflects the narrator's opinion that Jack is not facing real life.
    (5) It shows how much the narrator and his son have in common.

4. If Jack told his father that he was becoming a vegetarian, how would his father <u>most likely</u> react, based on the information in the excerpt?

    (1) He would tell Jack he was being illogical.
    (2) He would conclude that Jack was acting out of rebellion.
    (3) He would assume that Jack's wife was pushing him into it.
    (4) He would predict that Jack would soon change his mind.
    (5) He would do his best to accept Jack's views.

5. Which of the following words <u>best</u> describes the tone of this excerpt?

    (1) biting
    (2) serious
    (3) accusing
    (4) taunting
    (5) humorous

Questions 6 through 9 refer to the following excerpt from a short story.

WHAT HAS THIS NEWCOMER OVERLOOKED?

The man flung a look back along the way he had come. The Yukon lay a mile wide and hidden under three feet of ice. On top of this ice were as many feet of
(5)   snow. It was all pure white, rolling in gentle undulations where the ice jams of the freeze-up had formed. North and south, as far as the eye could see, it was unbroken white, save for a dark hairline that curved
(10)   and twisted from around the spruce-covered island to the south, and that curved and twisted away into the north, where it disappeared behind another spruce-covered island. The dark hairline
(15)   was the trail—the main trail—that led south five hundred miles to the Chilkoot Pass, Dyea, and salt water; and that led north seventy miles to Dawson, and still on to the north a thousand miles to Nulato,
(20)   and finally to St. Michael on Bering Sea, a thousand miles and half a thousand more.
But all this—the mysterious, far-reaching hairline trail, the absence of sun from the sky, the tremendous cold, and the
(25)   strangeness and weirdness of it all—made no impression on the man. It was not because he was long used to it. He was a newcomer in the land, a *chechaquo,* and this was his first winter. The trouble with
(30)   him was that he was without imagination. He was quick and alert in the things of life, but only in the things, and not in the significances. Fifty degrees below zero meant eighty-odd degrees of frost. Such
(35)   fact impressed him as being cold and uncomfortable, and that was all.

Jack London, "To Build a Fire."

TIP
To identify the main idea, read the entire passage and ask yourself, "What is the author writing about?" This is the subject. Then ask yourself, "What is the main thing the author is saying about the subject?" This is the main idea.

6. Based on this excerpt, the conflict of the story will most likely involve which of the following?

(1) a psychological struggle within the character
(2) a struggle between the character and another person
(3) a struggle between the character and society
(4) a struggle between the character and the forces of nature
(5) a struggle between the character and his destiny

7. What is the main idea of the second paragraph?

(1) The man was awed by his magnificent surroundings.
(2) The man was suffering from frostbite and hypothermia.
(3) The man did not understand the danger of the situation.
(4) The man was very experienced in dealing with cold weather.
(5) The man was cold and hungry.

8. Based on the information in the excerpt, what is the Yukon in lines 2 and 3?

(1) a vast wilderness
(2) an inland sea
(3) a frozen river
(4) a frozen trail
(5) a snow-covered prairie

9. The style of this excerpt is characterized by which of the following?

(1) complex sentence structure
(2) short choppy sentences
(3) vivid visual details
(4) minimal use of dialogue
(5) ornate and elaborate descriptions

Questions 10 through 13 refer to the following excerpt from a short story.

WHY IS THIS WOMAN WEARING BLACK?

I should have known the minute I saw her, holding court in her widow's costume, that something had cracked inside Doña Ernestina. She was in full *lato*—black from
(5) head to toe, including a mantilla. . . .
Doña Ernestina simply waited for me to join the other two leaning against the machines before she continued explaining what had happened when the news of
(10) Tony had arrived at her door the day before. She spoke calmly, a haughty expression on her face, looking like an offended duchess in her beautiful black dress. She was pale, pale, but she had a
(15) wild look in her eyes. The officer had told her that—when the time came—they would bury Tony with "full military honors"; for now they were sending her the medal and a flag. But she had said, *"No, gracias,"*
(20) to the funeral, and she sent the flag and medals back marked *Ya no vive aqui:* Does not live here anymore. "Tell the Mr. President of the United States what I say: *No, gracias."* Then she waited for
(25) our response.
Lydia shook her head, indicating that she was speechless. And Elenita looked pointedly at me, forcing me to be the one to speak the words of sympathy for all of
(30) us, to reassure Doña Ernestina that she had done exactly what any of us would have done in her place: yes, we would have all said *No, gracias,* to any president who had actually tried to pay for a son's life
(35) with a few trinkets and a folded flag.

Judith Ortiz Cofer, "Nada," *The Latin Deli: Prose and Poetry.*

TIP

Answer application questions by using the process of elimination. Read each answer choice to rule out those that do not fit the character or situation. You will then be better able to determine the right answer.

10. Why does the narrator begin to believe Doña Ernestina has "cracked"?

   (1) She spoke of her son's death too calmly.
   (2) She was dressed too beautifully for such a sad occasion.
   (3) She was dressed as a widow in mourning.
   (4) Her only son was killed in Vietnam.
   (5) She sent the flag and the medals back to the military.

11. Based on the information in this excerpt, if the president invited Doña Ernestina to a ceremony to honor war heroes, how would she <u>most likely</u> react?

   She would

   (1) wear her widow's costume to the ceremony
   (2) refuse to attend the ceremony
   (3) implore him to end the war
   (4) ask to give a speech about her son
   (5) thank the president for honoring her son

12. Which of the following descriptions <u>best</u> indicates Doña Ernestina's state of <u>mind</u>?

   (1) She was dressed in black from head to toe.
   (2) She had a haughty expression on her face.
   (3) She looked like a duchess.
   (4) She had a wild look in her eyes.
   (5) She sent the flag and medals back.

13. In this excerpt, what technique does the author use to add authenticity?

   (1) third-person narration
   (2) a president's name
   (3) formal language
   (4) Spanish phrases
   (5) figurative language

Unit 2: Understanding Fiction

Questions 14 through 17 refer to the following excerpt from a novel.

WHY IS JOHN DISTRACTED BY HIS NEW TEACHER?

When he was young, John had paid no attention in Sunday school, and always forgot the golden text, which earned him the wrath of his father. Around the time of
(5) his fourteenth birthday, with all the pressures of church and home uniting to drive him to the altar, he strove to appear more serious and therefore less conspicuous.[1] But he was distracted by his
(10) new teacher, Elisha, who was the pastor's nephew and who had but lately arrived from Georgia. He was not much older than John, only seventeen, and he was already saved and was a preacher. John stared at
(15) Elisha all during the lesson, admiring the timbre of Elisha's voice, much deeper and manlier than his own, admiring the leanness, and grace, and strength, and darkness of Elisha in his Sunday suit,
(20) wondering if he would ever be holy as Elisha was holy. But he did not follow the lesson, and when, sometimes, Elisha paused to ask John a question, John was ashamed and confused, feeling the palms
(25) of his hands become wet and his heart pound like a hammer. Elisha would smile and reprimand him gently, and the lesson would go on.
Roy never knew his Sunday school
(30) lesson either, but it was different with Roy—no one really expected of Roy what was expected of John. Everyone was always praying that the Lord would change Roy's heart, but it was John who was
(35) expected to be good, to be a good example.

----

[1] noticeable

James Baldwin, *Go Tell It on the Mountain.*

14. What does the author mean by the phrase "with all the pressures of the church and home uniting to drive him to the altar" (lines 5–7)?

   (1) The pressure from his parents is driving John from his home.
   (2) The church has been pressuring John to become a member.
   (3) John's parents have been pressuring him to join the church.
   (4) John is being pressured to become a preacher.
   (5) John is being pressured to get married.

15. Which of the following is the primary effect that Elisha has on John?

   (1) John feels inspired to work harder.
   (2) John finds it hard to concentrate on his lessons.
   (3) John tries to make himself more noticeable.
   (4) John decides to become a preacher.
   (5) John's hands sweat and his heart pounds.

16. With whom does the author compare and contrast John in this excerpt?

   (1) his father
   (2) his mother
   (3) his brother Roy
   (4) his teacher Elisha
   (5) his pastor

17. The style of this excerpt is characterized by which of the following?

   (1) use of many descriptive words
   (2) frequent use of figurative language
   (3) reliance on dialect
   (4) sprinkles of humor throughout
   (5) use of first-person narration throughout

Questions 18 through 23 refer to the following excerpt from a novel.

WHAT MANNER OF WOMAN IS THIS?

Helene Wright was an impressive woman, at least in Medallion she was. Heavy hair in a bun, dark eyes arched in a perpetual[1] query[2] about other people's

(5) manners. A woman who won all social battles with presence and a conviction of the legitimacy of her authority. Since there was no Catholic church in Medallion then, she joined the most conservative black

(10) church. And held sway.[3] It was Helene who never turned her head in church when latecomers arrived; Helene who established the practice of seasonal altar flowers; Helene who introduced the giving

(15) of banquets of welcome to returning Negro veterans. She lost only one battle—the pronunciation of her name. The people in the Bottom refused to say Helene. They called her Helen Wright and left it at that.

(20) All in all her life was a satisfactory one. She loved her house and enjoyed manipulating her daughter and her husband. She would sigh sometimes just before falling asleep, thinking that she had

(25) indeed come far enough away from the Sundown House.

So it was with extremely mixed emotions that she read a letter from Mr. Henri Martin describing the illness of

(30) her grandmother, and suggesting she come down right away. She didn't want to go, but could not bring herself to ignore the silent plea of the woman who had rescued her.

------

[1] constant [2] question [3] power

Toni Morrison, *Sula*.

18. Which of the following best describes this character?

   (1) timid
   (2) critical
   (3) accepting
   (4) wealthy
   (5) undependable

19. Based on the information in this excerpt, which of the following is most important to Helene?

   (1) helping her church
   (2) being in control
   (3) being well-dressed
   (4) honoring war veterans
   (5) keeping a tidy house

20. Why did Helene Wright have so much power in her church?

   (1) She had excellent ideas.
   (2) She was very sure of herself.
   (3) She had been a member all her life.
   (4) She had good manners.
   (5) She was very conservative.

21. Based on her personality as described in this excerpt, which of the following most likely describes Helene's house?

   (1) warm and homey
   (2) filled with artificial flowers
   (3) dirty and unkempt
   (4) tastefully decorated
   (5) spare and hardly furnished

22. According to the information in this excerpt, which of the following best describes Helene?

   (1) She is loved by the people in the Bottom.
   (2) She is submissive to her husband.
   (3) She was in trouble at some time in her past.
   (4) She does not live up to her responsibilities.
   (5) She is dissatisfied with her life.

23. Based on the excerpt, what is the narrator's attitude toward Helene Wright?

   (1) amusement
   (2) disapproval
   (3) respect
   (4) disgust
   (5) admiration

Questions 24 through 28 refer to the following excerpt from a short story.

WHAT IS THE BOY'S SECRET FEAR?

"Don't think," I said. "Just take it easy."

"I'm taking it easy," he said and looked straight ahead. He was evidently holding tight onto himself about something.

(5)   "Take this with water."

"Do you think it will do any good?"

"Of course it will."

I sat down and opened the *Pirate* book and commenced to read, but I could see

(10)   he was not following, so I stopped.

"About what time do you think I'm going to die?" he asked.

"What?"

"About how long will it be before I die?"

(15)   "You aren't going to die. What's the matter with you?"

"Oh, yes, I am. I heard him say a hundred and two."

"People don't die with a fever of one

(20)   hundred and two. That's a silly way to talk."

"I know they do. At school in France the boys told me you can't live with forty-four degrees. I've got a hundred and two."

He had been waiting to die all day, ever

(25)   since nine o'clock in the morning.

"You poor Schatz," I said. "Poor old Schatz. It's like miles and kilometers. You aren't going to die. That's a different thermometer. On that thermometer

(30)   thirty-seven is normal. On this kind it's ninety-eight."

"Are you sure?"

"Absolutely," I said. "It's like miles and kilometers. You know, like how many

(35)   kilometers we make when we do seventy miles in the car?"

Ernest Hemingway, "A Day's Wait," *The Short Stories of Ernest Hemingway.*

To draw a conclusion, list all of the facts available to you. Then think of reasonable explanations for the facts. Disregard any explanations that the facts together do not support.

24. Which of the following best describes the narrator's attitude toward the boy?

(1) anger
(2) love
(3) pity
(4) frustration
(5) resentment

25. Why does the narrator decide to read the boy a story?

(1) The boy pleaded with him to.
(2) He wants to get the boy's mind off his illness.
(3) The boy misplaced his glasses and couldn't read it himself.
(4) He wants to fulfill a fatherly role for the boy.
(5) He is bored and wants to pass the time.

26. How is the plot of the excerpt like the boy's fear?

(1) It remains mysterious throughout.
(2) It fails to reach a climax.
(3) It awakens little sympathy.
(4) It is about something trivial.
(5) It builds up and resolves.

27. What type of effect is created by the absence of descriptive images in this excerpt?

(1) cold, scientific impression
(2) dull, ho-hum feeling
(3) direct, factual impact
(4) dry, scholarly quality
(5) dreamy, poetic mood

28. Which of the following characterizes the style of this excerpt?

(1) brief and economical
(2) light and humorous
(3) complicated and challenging
(4) precise and sensual
(5) elegant and polished

WHAT DOES ROSICKY THINK ABOUT THE GRAVEYARD?

After he had gone eight miles, he came
to the graveyard, which lay just at the edge
of his own hay-land. There he stopped his
horses and sat still on his wagon seat,
(5) looking about at the snowfall. Over yonder
on the hill he could see his own house,
crouching low, with the clump of orchard
behind and the windmill before, and all
down the gentle hill-slope the rows of pale
(10) gold cornstalks stood out against the
white field. The snow was falling over the
cornfield and the pasture and the hay-land,
steadily, with very little wind—a nice dry
snow. The graveyard had only a light wire
(15) fence about it and was all overgrown with
long red grass. The fine snow, settling into
this red grass and upon the few little
evergreens and the headstones, looked
very pretty.
(20)   It was a nice graveyard, Rosicky
reflected, sort of snug and homelike, not
cramped or mournful,—a big sweep all
round it. A man could lie down in the long
grass and see the complete arch of the
(25) sky over him, hear the wagons go by; in
summer the mowing-machine rattled right
up to the wire fence. And it was so near
home. Over there across the cornstalks his
own roof and windmill looked so good to
(30) him that he promised himself to mind the
Doctor and take care of himself. He was
awful fond of his place, he admitted. He
wasn't anxious to leave it. And it was a
comfort to think that he would never have
(35) to go farther than the edge of his own
hayfield. The snow, falling over his
barnyard and the graveyard, seemed to
draw things together like. And they were
all old neighbors in the graveyard, most
(40) of them friends; there was nothing to
feel awkward or embarrassed about.
Embarrassment was the most
disagreeable feeling Rosicky knew. He
didn't often have it,—only with certain
(45) people whom he didn't understand at all.

Willa Cather, "Neighbor Rosicky," *Obscure Destinies.*

29. Based on his character as established in this excerpt, how would Rosicky most likely approach his own death?

   (1) with regret for not having lived his life to the fullest
   (2) with resignation, knowing he could do nothing about it
   (3) with denial, refusing to believe he was dying
   (4) with anger, asking why he had to die
   (5) with peace, knowing he would not leave his land

30. The graveyard and the farm are next to each other, both covered with snow. This image supports the theme of the excerpt by suggesting which of the following?

   (1) Winter is the season of death.
   (2) The snow brings death to the living things on the farm.
   (3) Everything gets buried at one time or another.
   (4) Life and death exist side by side in this world.
   (5) People will start burying their dead in the barnyard.

31. Which of the following best describes the tone of this excerpt?

   (1) comforting
   (2) mournful
   (3) upbeat
   (4) critical
   (5) mysterious

32. Which of the following best characterizes the style of this excerpt?

   (1) highly descriptive images
   (2) short active sentences
   (3) ornate language
   (4) unusual word choice
   (5) use of exaggeration

Answers start on page 309.

Cumulative Review Performance Analysis

Unit 2 ● Fiction

Use the Answers and Explanations starting on page 309 to check your answers to the Unit 2 Cumulative Review. Then use the chart to figure out the skill areas in which you need more practice.

On the chart, circle the questions that you answered correctly. Write the number correct for each skill area. Add the number of questions that you got correct on the Cumulative Review. If you feel that you need more practice, go back and review the lessons for the skill areas that were difficult for you.

Questions	Number Correct	Skill Area	Lessons for Review
2, 6, 7, 8, 14, 15, 18, 20, 24	____/9	Comprehension	10, 11, 13, 14, 16, 17, 19
1, 4, 11, 21, 29	____/5	Application	12
3, 10, 12, 16, 19, 22, 25, 26, 27, 30, 31	____/11	Analysis	10, 11, 13, 14, 15, 16, 17, 18
5, 9, 13, 17, 23, 28, 32	____/7	Synthesis	11, 15, 17, 19
TOTAL CORRECT	____/32		

UNIT 3

Understanding Poetry

Poetry is a special kind of writing in which descriptive language is used to create images or feelings. It appeals to the emotions, the senses, or the imagination of the reader. You read poems in books and magazines. You write poems to express your feelings or sometimes to tell a story. When you listen to music, you are hearing a kind of poetry in the song lyrics. While fiction and nonfiction are written in sentences and paragraphs, poetry is written in lines or groups of lines called stanzas.

Understanding poetry will help you pass the GED Language Arts, Reading Test. Questions about literature make up about 75 percent of the GED Reading Test. Some of these questions will relate to poetry.

William Carlos Williams used the shape and structure of words to create vivid imagery in his poetry.

The lessons in this unit include:

Lesson 20: **Identifying the Effects of Rhythm and Rhyme**
Poets give their poetry a particular sound by carefully arranging words in patterns. Two of these word patterns are rhythm and rhyme.

Lesson 21: **Interpreting Figurative Language**
Poets use figurative language to create pictures in the reader's mind. Much figurative language in poetry is based on making unusual comparisons. Other figurative language gives human qualities to nonhuman objects.

Lesson 22: **Interpreting Symbols and Images**
A symbol in a poem stands for an important idea. A person, an object, an event, or anything else in a poem may be a symbol. An image appeals to the reader's senses—sight, taste, touch, smell, and hearing.

Lesson 23: **Making Inferences**
Making inferences is a necessary skill for reading poetry. To appreciate a poem, you need to "read between the lines" to interpret the meaning of the poem.

Lesson 24: **Interpreting Theme**
The central idea in a work of literature is called the theme. The theme of a poem expresses a specific opinion or belief about a larger topic.

SELECTED POETS

○ Countee Cullen

○ Emily Dickinson

○ Robert Frost

○ Li-Young Lee

○ Simon J. Ortiz

○ Marge Piercy

○ Christina Rossetti

○ Walt Whitman

○ William Carlos Williams

○ Elinor Wylie

Lesson 20

GED SKILL Identifying the Effects of Rhythm and Rhyme

In poetry, sounds support meaning. The words of a poem communicate ideas; the sounds of those words communicate feelings connected to the ideas. Poets create "sound effects" by carefully choosing words and arranging them in patterns. Two word patterns are **rhythm** and **rhyme.**

All poems have rhythm, or a beat. This beat may be fast or slow, regular or irregular. Rhythm is primarily created by a pattern of stressed syllables. To understand how, slowly say the phrase "Once upon a midnight dreary." Notice that every other syllable is stressed. This creates rhythm.

Another way poets create rhythm in a poem is by the use of punctuation. Commas, periods, or the absence of punctuation both within and at the ends of lines affect the poem's sound and rhythm.

Many poems also have rhyme. Rhyme is created by repeating the sounds at the ends of words, as in *struck* and *truck*. Sometimes word endings sound similar but do not rhyme completely, as in *house* and *bounce*. Both full and partial rhymes tie parts of a poem together in a pattern. Rhythm and rhyme create the shape and feel of a poem.

Read the following excerpt from a poem and complete the exercise below.

VELVET SHOES

Let us walk in the white snow
　In a soundless space;
　With footsteps quiet and slow,
　At a tranquil pace,
　Under veils of white lace.

Elinor Wylie, *Collected Poems.*

1. Fill in the blanks with words from the poem.

   The word *space* rhymes with ＿＿＿＿＿＿ and ＿＿＿＿＿＿.

2. What effect does the punctuation have on the rhythm of the poem? Put a check mark next to your answer.
   ＿＿＿ a. It gives a jerky, abrupt rhythm.
   ＿＿＿ b. It gives a slow, peaceful rhythm.

You are correct if you answered that *space* rhymes with *pace* and *lace* for question 1. You can hear the rhyme when you say the words aloud. For question 2, you are correct if you chose *option b*.

---

rhythm
a pattern created by the rise and fall in the sounds of words as well as by the use of punctuation

rhyme
a similarity in the sounds at the ends of words that ties two or more words together

TIP

To become more aware of a poem's rhythm and rhyme, read it aloud. Do the lines move along slowly or quickly? Do any of the words have similar sounds? These patterns will help you tie ideas or feelings together.

Read the following poem and complete the exercise below.

WAS THE SPEAKER'S CHILDHOOD A HAPPY ONE?

MY PAPA'S WALTZ

The whiskey on your breath
Could make a small boy dizzy;
But I hung on like death:
Such waltzing was not easy.

(5) We romped until the pans
Slid from the kitchen shelf;
My mother's countenance
Could not unfrown itself.

The hand that held my wrist
(10) Was battered on one knuckle;
At every step you missed
My right ear scraped a buckle.

You beat time on my head
With a palm caked hard by dirt,
(15) Then waltzed me off to bed
Still clinging to your shirt.

Theodore Roethke, *The Collected Poems
of Theodore Roethke.*

1. List three pairs of words from the poem that rhyme completely. Then list two pairs of words that are partial rhymes.

   Full rhymes: _____

   Partial rhymes: _____

2. Put a check mark next to the sentence that better describes the punctuation in this poem.

   _____ a. The punctuation is regular.

   _____ b. The punctuation is irregular.

3. Put a check mark next to the sentence that better describes the effect created by the rhythmic pattern.

   _____ a. The rhythm is graceful, like a professional dancer doing the waltz.

   _____ b. The rhythm is clumsy, like a drunk person dancing.

Answers start on page 311.

Directions: Choose the one best answer to each question.

Questions 1 through 4 refer to the following poem.

WHAT DOES WINTER REPRESENT?

CHANGING AUTUMN WEATHER

SEPTEMBER
Rain sweeps across the roof
Clearing nostrils cleaning minds
Purging asphalt in the urban forest
(5)   primeval
We creatures who live under rocks
Are surprised come
morning

OCTOBER
(10)   Twilight mist smokes sad cigars
Culls candy sweetness
Passion
Paused for proffered gems
Captures facets
(15)   Pasting diamonds in the sky

NOVEMBER
Here am I
Present and accountable
I am rain standing
(20)   Wind walking
Fire sitting
Join my breathing
Here am I
I am here
(25)   I do

DECEMBER
Standing mute in timberland
The grand fall-timbred lute thrums forth
the hum
(30)   Lending credence to the season
Swirling spackled clouds dip low
As winter looms
And spirits
Sink
(35)   cold

D. George Higgins, *International Library of Poetry*.

1. Which of the following best restates the first stanza?

   (1) Rainfall is a city's primary connection to nature.
   (2) City dwellers usually have little respect for the weather.
   (3) Rainfall in cities brightens the outlook of the inhabitants.
   (4) City dwellers behave like frightened animals during storms.
   (5) Rainfall in cities bears little resemblance to rainfall in jungles.

2. What is the main method the poet uses to create rhythm in the second stanza?

   (1) He relies on a regular rhyming pattern.
   (2) He emphasizes one particular vowel sound.
   (3) He uses a pattern of stressed syllables.
   (4) He repeats the sounds at the beginnings of words.
   (5) He uses common words that are easy to pronounce.

3. What effect does the author create by using short simple lines in the third stanza?

   (1) a childlike sense of wonder
   (2) a sense of peaceful relaxation
   (3) an impression of utter despair
   (4) a sensation of brisk movement
   (5) a feeling of barely-controlled anger

4. How does the mood of the fourth stanza compare to the mood of the first stanza?

   The fourth stanza is

   (1) more gloomy
   (2) less bitter
   (3) more anxious
   (4) less tranquil
   (5) more passionate

Questions 5 through 7 refer to the following poem.

WHERE DO THESE ROADS LEAD?

THE ROAD NOT TAKEN

Two roads diverged in a yellow wood,
And sorry I could not travel both
And be one traveler, long I stood
And looked down one as far as I could
(5)   To where it bent in the undergrowth;

Then took the other, as just as fair,
And having perhaps the better claim,
Because it was grassy and wanted wear;
Though as for that the passing there
(10)   Had worn them really about the same,

And both that morning equally lay
In leaves no step had trodden black.
Oh, I kept the first for another day!
Yet knowing how way leads on to way,
(15)   I doubted if I should ever come back.

I shall be telling this with a sigh
Somewhere ages and ages hence:
Two roads diverged in a wood, and I—
I took the one less traveled by,
(20)   And that has made all the difference.

Robert Frost, *The Poetry of Robert Frost.*

5. What is the most likely meaning of "diverged"
    in "Two roads diverged in a yellow wood"
    (line 1)?

    (1) ran parallel
    (2) separated
    (3) merged
    (4) overlapped
    (5) appeared

6. Which of the following best describes the
    theme of the poem?

    (1) regrets over choices not made
    (2) the ability to accomplish anything
    (3) how decisions define people's lives
    (4) traveling as a positive experience
    (5) how walking in nature can change you

7. What would the speaker in this poem most
    likely do if he had to decide where to live?

    (1) think carefully before committing himself
    (2) ask his friends for their opinions
    (3) choose the most popular neighborhood
    (4) worry that he made the wrong choice
    (5) be unable to make up his mind

TIP Poets often use rhythm to create the mood of a poem. Think of the way music uses rhythm to make us feel sad or romantic or joyful.

Answers start on page 311.

GED Mini-Test • Lesson 20

Directions: This is a ten-minute practice test. After ten minutes, mark the last question you finished. Then complete the test and check your answers. If most of your answers were correct, but you didn't finish, try to work faster next time. Choose the <u>one best answer</u> to each question.

<u>Questions 1 and 2</u> refer to the following poem.

WHAT WAS THE FERRY RIDE LIKE?

RECUERDO

We were very tired, we were very merry—
We had gone back and forth all night on the ferry.
It was bare and bright, and smelled like a stable—
But we looked into a fire, we leaned across a table,
(5)   We lay on a hill-top underneath the moon;
And the whistles kept blowing, and the dawn came soon.

We were very tired, we were very merry,
We had gone back and forth all night on the ferry;
And you ate an apple, and I ate a pear,
(10) From a dozen of each we had bought somewhere;
And the sky went wan, and the wind came cold,
And the sun rose dripping, a bucketful of gold.

We were very tired, we were very merry,
We had gone back and forth all night on the ferry.
(15) We hailed, "Good-morrow, mother!" to a shawl-covered
     head,
And bought a morning paper, which neither of us read;
And she wept, "God bless you!" for the apples and pears,
And we gave her all our money but our subway fares.

Edna St. Vincent Millay, *Collected Poems.*

1. What is the main idea that the speaker is expressing in this poem?

   She is

   (1) thinking about a pleasurable night
   (2) recalling a time when she had little to eat but fruit
   (3) describing a trip to see her mother
   (4) complaining about an exhausting, smelly ferry ride
   (5) feeling that time passes too slowly

2. What is the effect of repeating the lines, "We were very tired, we were very merry— / We had gone back and forth all night on the ferry" (lines 1, 2, 7, 8, 13, 14)?

   It emphasizes

   (1) how boring the ferry ride was
   (2) how the rhythm of the numerous ferry rides affected the couple
   (3) what the people in the poem were doing
   (4) that there was no other means of transport
   (5) how sleepy the speaker and her companion felt

Questions 3 through 7 refer to the following poem.

WHAT MADE THIS SPEAKER SO HAPPY?

I WANDERED LONELY AS A CLOUD

I wandered lonely as a cloud
That floats on high o'er vales and hills,
When all at once I saw a crowd,
A host, of golden daffodils;
(5) Beside the lake, beneath the trees,
Fluttering and dancing in the breeze.

Continuous as the stars that shine
And twinkle on the milky way,
They stretched in never-ending line
(10) Along the margin of a bay:
Ten thousand saw I at a glance,
Tossing their heads in sprightly dance.

The waves beside them danced; but they
Outdid the sparkling waves in glee;
(15) A poet could not but be gay,
In such a jocund company;
I gazed—and gazed—but little thought
What wealth the show to me had brought:

For oft, when on my couch I lie
(20) In vacant or in pensive mood,
They flash upon that inward eye
Which is the bliss of solitude;
And then my heart with pleasure fills,
And dances with the daffodils.

William Wordsworth, "I Wandered Lonely As a Cloud."

3. Which of the following sentences best restates the main idea of the poem?

  (1) Unexpected sights can produce endless pleasure.
  (2) Daffodils are the speaker's favorite flower.
  (3) Flowers often seem to possess human qualities.
  (4) Certain images can be easily forgotten.
  (5) Wandering is a way for poets to find subject matter.

4. To what does the speaker compare the daffodils?

  (1) a lonely cloud
  (2) the stars of the milky way
  (3) a pensive mood
  (4) a heart filled with pleasure
  (5) dancing waves

5. Which of the following is the best restatement of "They flash upon that inward eye / Which is the bliss of solitude" (lines 21–22)?

  (1) The speaker often looks inward to his soul.
  (2) The daffodils remind the speaker of yellow lightning flashes.
  (3) The speaker sometimes pictures the flowers in his mind when he is alone.
  (4) Being alone brings the speaker great pleasure.
  (5) Having left the flowers, the speaker cannot picture them in his mind.

6. What is the best description of the rhythm of this poem?

  (1) pounding and insistent
  (2) cheerful and upbeat
  (3) fast-paced and energetic
  (4) slow and thoughtful
  (5) uneven and surprising

7. Based on the poem, which of the following would the speaker most likely do if he were caught in a rain shower?

He would

  (1) feel annoyed that his clothes were getting wet
  (2) be relieved that the storm was not worse
  (3) notice all the details of how the rain looked and felt
  (4) think that the rain looked like sparkling waves
  (5) conclude that nature is predictable and kind

Answers start on page 312.

Lesson 21

GED SKILL Interpreting Figurative Language

figurative language
language in which ordinary words are combined in new ways to make a point

personification
a type of figurative language that gives human qualities to non-human objects

Poetry may sometimes seem difficult to understand. One reason for this is that poetry has a language all its own—that is, it uses words in a way different from most other types of writing. One way in which poets make their writing unique is through the use of **figurative language.** Figurative language involves the use of ordinary words in unusual ways. Poets use figurative language to make a particular point. For instance, exaggeration is one type of figurative language. If a poet states that the stars of the night sky are close enough to touch, he or she is exaggerating to emphasize how close the stars appear. Poets may also use **personification** and give human qualities to animals, objects, or ideas, as in the sentence "The trees danced in the wind."

Other types of figurative language include similes and metaphors, which you learned about in Lesson 16. Paying close attention to the figurative language in a poem can help you grasp the poem's meaning.

Read the following poem and answer the question below.

HARLEM

What happens to a dream deferred?

Does it dry up
like a raisin in the sun?
Or fester like a sore—
and then run?
Does it stink like rotten meat?
Or crust and sugar over
like a syrupy sweet?
Maybe it just sags
like a heavy load.

Or does it explode?

Langston Hughes, *Collected Poems.*

TIP

If a description or comparison does not make literal sense, then it is probably figurative. Look for unusual descriptions and comparisons, then use your imagination to figure out what they mean.

What does the line "dry up / like a raisin in the sun" suggest about a dream deferred? Put a check mark next to your answer.

_____ a. It can be preserved to enjoy later.

_____ b. It shrinks and loses its strength.

You are correct if you chose *option b*. This line suggests that when a dream is put off, it can shrink and lose its power in the same way that a grape shrivels in the sun.

Read the following poem and answer the questions below.

WHO OR WHAT IS THE SPEAKER?

MIRROR

I am silver and exact. I have no preconceptions.
Whatever I see I swallow immediately
Just as it is, unmisted by love or dislike.
I am not cruel, only truthful—
(5) The eye of a little god, four-cornered.
Most of the time I meditate on the opposite wall.
It is pink, with speckles. I have looked at it so long
I think it is a part of my heart. But it flickers.
Faces and darkness separate us over and over.

(10) Now I am a lake. A woman bends over me,
Searching my reaches for what she really is.
Then she turns to those liars, the candles or the moon.
I see her back, and reflect it faithfully.
She rewards me with tears and an agitation of hands.
(15) I am important to her. She comes and goes.
Each morning it is her face that replaces the darkness.
In me she has drowned a young girl, and in me an old woman
Rises toward her day after day, like a terrible fish.

Sylvia Plath, *The Collected Poems of Sylvia Plath.*

1. Which one of the following is an example of personification? Put a check mark next to the correct answer.

    _____ a. The mirror swallows.

    _____ b. The mirror reflects.

2. What is the mirror compared to in the poem? Put a check mark next to the correct answer.

    _____ a. the candles

    _____ b. a lake

    _____ c. a young girl

3. Which of the following is suggested by the phrase "the eye of a little god" (line 5)? Put a check mark next to the correct answer.

    _____ a. The small mirror has great power over the woman.

    _____ b. The woman has turned away from her religion.

4. What rises toward the woman "day after day, like a terrible fish" (line 18)?

    The image of herself as _____.

Answers start on page 313.

Directions: Choose the <u>one best answer</u> to each question.

<u>Questions 1 and 2</u> refer to the following poem.

TO WHAT ARE HARD WORKERS COMPARED?

TO BE OF USE

The people I love the best
jump into work head first
without dallying in the shallows
and swim off with sure strokes almost out of sight.
(5) They seem to become natives of that element,
and black sleek heads of seals
bouncing like half-submerged balls.

I love people who harness themselves, an ox to a heavy cart,
who pull like water buffalo, with massive patience,
(10) who strain in the mud and the muck to move things forward,
who do what has to be done, again and again.

I want to be with people who submerge
in the task, who go into the fields to harvest
and work in a row and pass the bags along,
(15) who are not parlor generals and field deserters
but move in a common rhythm
when the food must come in or the fire be put out.

The work of the world is common as mud.
Botched, it smears the hands, crumbles to dust.
(20) But the thing worth doing well done
has a shape that satisfies, clean and evident.
Greek amphoras for wine or oil,
Hopi vases that held corn, are put in museums
but you know they were made to be used.
(25) The pitcher cries for water to carry
and the person for work that is real.

Marge Piercy, *Circles on the Water.*

1. What is meant by the line "Botched, it smears the hands, crumbles to dust" (line 19)?

   (1) Don't be afraid to get your hands dirty.
   (2) Work done quickly must often be repeated.
   (3) Wear work gloves when doing dirty work.
   (4) Work poorly done does not last.
   (5) Work is dirty, dangerous business.

2. Which of the following is the <u>best</u> restatement of "The pitcher cries for water to carry" (line 25)?

   (1) Pitchers belong in museums.
   (2) Pitchers are made to be useful.
   (3) Pitchers are like people weeping.
   (4) Pitchers are cracked and leaking.
   (5) Pitchers have been abandoned.

WHAT HAS THIS SPEAKER REALIZED?

ABEL MELVENY

I bought every kind of machine that's known—
Grinders, shellers, planters, mowers,
Mills and rakes and ploughs and threshers—
And all of them stood in the rain and sun,
(5) Getting rusted, warped and battered,
For I had no sheds to store them in,
And no use for most of them.
And toward the last, when I thought it over,
There by my window, growing clearer
(10) About myself, as my pulse slowed down,
And looked at one of the mills I bought—
Which I didn't have the slightest need of,
As things turned out, and I never ran—
A fine machine, once brightly varnished,
(15) And eager to do its work,
Now with its paint washed off—
I saw myself as a good machine
That Life had never used.

Edgar Lee Masters, *Spoon River Anthology.*

3. Which of these sentences <u>best</u> describes the similarities between the speaker and the machines?

   (1) Both must work hard before they break.
   (2) Both need constant attention to stay in good shape.
   (3) Both were meant to work hard but did not.
   (4) Both grow old gracefully.
   (5) Both are easily replaced.

4. Which of the following is the machinery in this poem <u>most</u> like?

   (1) an outdoor sculpture garden
   (2) a toaster that was never taken out of its box
   (3) useless junk piled in a landfill
   (4) objects with great sentimental value
   (5) a used car that needs a little work

5. Which of the following <u>best</u> suggests the central theme of this poem?

   The speaker

   (1) will live life to the fullest from now on
   (2) believes it is too late to live a full life
   (3) will take care of his material possessions from now on
   (4) will engage in courageous acts from now on
   (5) has moved from a life of wealth to one of poverty

Remember, poets often want to help their readers look at the world in a new way. To understand how they do this, look for ordinary words used in figurative ways.

Answers start on page 313.

Directions: This is a ten-minute practice test. After ten minutes, mark the last question you finished. Then complete the test and check your answers. If most of your answers were correct, but you didn't finish, try to work faster next time. Choose the one best answer to each question.

Questions 1 through 9 refer to the following poem.

IS THIS OFFICE A WELCOMING PLACE?

LIFE AND DEATH AMONG THE XEROX PEOPLE

It was the wrong office
    but I went in
not a soul knew me
    but they said: Sit Down
(5) they showed me corridors of paper
    and said: Begin Here

They wheeled in a machine
    a miniature electric chair
sparks flew from the earplugs
(10)   antennas sprang from my nostrils
they switched on the current
    the machine said: Marry Me

I had forgotten my numbers
    they said it could be serious
(15) they showed me the paper cutter
    it sliced like a guillotine
my head fell bloodlessly
    into the waste basket

I mined my way through stockrooms
(20)   I wrote urgent xxxxxxxxxxx's every day
to faces flat as paper
    the telephones feared nothing human
the windows were mirages
    permanently nailed shut

(25) They handed me a skin
    and said: Wear This
it was somebody else's life
    it didn't quite fit
so I left it lying there . . .
(30)   that was a queer cemetery.

Olga Cabral, *We Become New.*

1. Why does the speaker say she is in "the wrong office" (line 1)?

   (1) She did not feel comfortable there.
   (2) She was filling in for someone else that day.
   (3) She had been given incorrect directions.
   (4) She was transferred to the copy room from a different job.
   (5) She had no friends at work.

2. What does the speaker imply by saying, "my head fell bloodlessly" (line 17)?

   (1) She did not make a mess.
   (2) She felt lifeless and not human.
   (3) She was dizzy and fainted.
   (4) She is coldhearted and cruel.
   (5) She felt others were out to get her.

3. Which of the following statements best describes the speaker's circumstances?

   She is

   (1) a lost soul
   (2) a fish out of water
   (3) like a snake shedding her skin
   (4) the new kid on the block
   (5) driving the wrong way down a one-way street

4. What is the main effect of the line "the machine said: Marry Me" (line 12)?

   (1) It compares the machine to a compassionate human being.
   (2) It shows that the speaker must give her full attention to a machine.
   (3) It indicates how sophisticated the office's technology is.
   (4) It emphasizes the speaker's frequent use of understatement.
   (5) It reveals that the speaker is fantasizing about getting married.

5. Which of the following statements from the poem indicates that endless work awaits?

   (1) "faces flat as paper" (line 21)
   (2) "corridors of paper" (line 5)
   (3) "antennas sprang from my nostrils" (line 10)
   (4) "the telephones feared nothing human" (line 22)
   (5) "the windows were mirages" (line 23)

6. Which of the following is the best description of the tone of this poem?

   (1) disturbing and unreal
   (2) upbeat and cheerful
   (3) amusing and lighthearted
   (4) suspenseful and mysterious
   (5) peaceful and confident

7. Which of the following lines from the poem best describes the expectations in this office?

   (1) "but they said: Sit Down" (line 4)
   (2) "they showed me the paper cutter / it sliced like a guillotine" (lines 15–16)
   (3) "sparks flew from the earplugs" (line 9)
   (4) "I had forgotten my numbers" (line 13)
   (5) "They handed me a skin / and said: Wear This" (lines 25–26)

8. If the speaker read the poem to an audience, with which of the following phrases would she most likely begin an introduction?

   (1) Once upon a time . . .
   (2) The purpose of the following poem . . .
   (3) The reader cannot fail to appreciate . . .
   (4) A funny thing happened at work.
   (5) It was a nightmare I will never forget.

9. Which of the following best describes the speaker's opinion of offices?

   (1) They are unsafe work environments.
   (2) They rely too much on technology.
   (3) They are isolating and inhumane.
   (4) They need windows that can be opened.
   (5) They attract imaginative workers.

Answers start on page 313.

Lesson 22

GED SKILL Interpreting Symbols and Images

A **symbol** in a poem is a word or phrase that stands for an important idea, such as youth, age, life, death, or hope. A symbol is often difficult to recognize by itself. You need to look at the content of the poem to figure it out. A person, an object, an event, or anything else in a poem may be a symbol, and it may stand for one or several ideas.

An **image** appeals to the reader's senses. It recreates sensations of sight, taste, touch, smell, and hearing. A poet will create an image by using words that readers can associate with their own experience.

Read the following poem and answer the questions below.

OREAD[1]

Whirl up, sea—
whirl your pointed pines,
splash your great pines
on our rocks,
hurl your green over us,
cover us with your pools of fir.

_____

[1] the mountain nymphs in Greek mythology

H. D. (Hilda Doolittle), *Collected Poems 1912–1944.*

1. What ideas do the images in this poem suggest? Put a check mark next to the correct answer.

   _____ a. energy and movement

   _____ b. peace and quiet

2. What feeling does the line "cover us with your pools of fir" create? Put a check mark next to the correct answer.

   _____ a. a sense of the struggle between humans and nature

   _____ b. a desire to be joined with the forces of nature

Option a is the correct answer to question 1. Everything about the poem—whirling, splashing, hurling—is full of energy. *Option b* is the correct answer for question 2. Although the poem gives a sense of wildness, there is no indication of battle or struggle. The image of being covered with forest gives the feeling of being one with nature.

---

symbol
a powerful image that represents a person, place, or thing beyond the object it describes

image
a mental picture created by the imaginative use of words

TIP

To identify symbols, look for repeated or closely related images. Repetition of an image often signals that the image is symbolic.

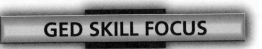

GED SKILL FOCUS

Read the following poem and complete the exercise below.

WHAT HAPPENED OUT OF THE ORDINARY?

EATING TOGETHER

In the steamer is the trout
seasoned with slivers of ginger,
two sprigs of green onion, and sesame oil.
We shall eat it with rice for lunch,
(5) brothers, sister, my mother who will
taste the sweetest meat of the head,
holding it between her fingers
deftly, the way my father did
weeks ago. Then he lay down
(10) to sleep like a snow-covered road
winding through the pines older than him,
without any travelers, and lonely for no one.

Li-Young Lee, *Rose.*

1. Why is the image of the trout and its preparation (lines 1–3) important? Put a check mark next to the correct answer.

   _____ a. It symbolizes the family members and the odd combination they represent.

   _____ b. It symbolizes the way that ordinary events in daily life continue.

2. Which of the following does the father's lying down to sleep most likely symbolize? Put a check mark next to the correct answer.

   _____ a. rest

   _____ b. death

   _____ c. loneliness

3. Write three phrases or words from the poem that appeal to the sense of taste or smell.

   _____

   _____

   _____

4. Mark the following statements *T* for true or *F* for false.

   _____ a. Getting "the sweetest meat of the head" (line 6) symbolizes being the head of the family.

   _____ b. The family is noisy and festive as they gather to eat their delicious lunch.

   _____ c. The image of the "snow-covered road" (line 10) creates a peaceful feeling.

   _____ d. The image of the travelers (line 12) symbolizes people who seek spiritual knowledge.

Answers start on page 314.

Directions: Choose the one best answer to each question.

Questions 1 and 2 refer to the following poem.

FOR WHOM DOES THE WHEEL TURN?

THE WHEEL

At the first strokes of the fiddle bow
the dancers rise from their seats.
The dance begins to shape itself
in the crowd, as couples join,
(5)   and couples join couples, their movement
together lightening their feet.
They move in the ancient circle
of the dance. The dance and the song
call each other into being. Soon
(10) they are one—rapt in a single
rapture, so that even the night
has its clarity, and time
is the wheel that brings it round.

In this rapture the dead return.
(15) Sorrow is gone from them.
They are light. They step
into the steps of the living
and turn with them in the dance
in the sweet enclosure
(20) of the song, and timeless
is the wheel that brings it round.

Wendell Berry, *The Wheel.*

1. Which of the following best describes the meaning of "The dance and the song / call each other into being" (lines 8–9)?

   (1) The song is very familiar to the dancers.
   (2) The dance and the song depend on one another.
   (3) The dancers sometimes play music.
   (4) The dancers sing a song to begin the dance.
   (5) The song and the dance are popular and well-known.

2. Which of the following best describes what the dance represents?

   (1) the cycle of life and death
   (2) a joyous occasion
   (3) the end of life
   (4) an ancient ritual
   (5) the day-to-day routine

 Trust the feelings that a poem's images and symbols convey—especially on a first reading.

WHY IS THIS BIRD SINGING?

SYMPATHY

I know what the caged bird feels, alas!
    When the sun is bright on the upland slopes;
When the wind stirs soft through the springing grass,
And the river flows like a stream of glass;
(5)   When the first bird sings and the first bud opes,
And the faint perfume from its chalice steals—
I know what the caged bird feels!

I know why the caged bird beats his wing
    Till its blood is red on the cruel bars;
(10)   For he must fly back to his perch and cling
When he fain would be on the bough a-swing;
    And a pain still throbs in the old, old scars
And they pulse again with a keener sting—
I know why he beats his wing!

(15)   I know why the caged bird sings, ah me,
    When his wing is bruised and his bosom sore,—
When he beats his bars and he would be free;
It is not a carol of joy or glee,
    But a prayer that he sends from his heart's deep core,
(20)   But a plea, that upward to Heaven he flings—
I know why the caged bird sings!

Paul Laurence Dunbar, *The Complete Poems of Paul Laurence Dunbar.*

3. Which of the following statements best explains why the bird's wing is "bruised and his bosom sore" (line 16)?

   (1) The bird has accidentally flown into the cage's bars.
   (2) The bird has hurt himself while struggling to escape his cage.
   (3) The bird is injuring himself on purpose because he is unhappy.
   (4) The bird's cage is too small for a creature of his size.
   (5) The bird's cage contains no good place on which he can land.

4. What does the word "chalice" refer to in the phrase, "faint perfume from its chalice" (line 6)?

   (1) the bird
   (2) the cage
   (3) a flower
   (4) the river
   (5) a gentle breeze

5. Which of the following ideas are most clearly contrasted in the poem?

   (1) freedom and imprisonment
   (2) fear and joy
   (3) violence and peacefulness
   (4) life and death
   (5) truth and deception

Answers start on page 314.

Directions: This is a ten-minute practice test. After ten minutes, mark the last question you finished. Then complete the test and check your answers. If most of your answers were correct, but you didn't finish, try to work faster next time. Choose the <u>one best answer</u> to each question.

<u>Questions 1 through 8</u> refer to the following poem.

WHAT GOES ON AT THE ZOO?

THE WOMAN AT THE WASHINGTON ZOO

The saris go by me from the embassies.

Cloth from the moon. Cloth from another planet.
They look back at the leopard like the leopard.

And I. . . .
(5)   This print of mine, that has kept its color.
Alive through so many cleanings; this dull null
Navy I wear to work, and wear from work, and so
To my bed, so to my grave, with no
Complaints, no comment: neither from my chief,
(10)   The Deputy Chief Assistant, nor his chief—
Only I complain . . . this serviceable
Body that no sunlight dyes, no hand suffuses
But, dome-shadowed, withering among columns,
Wavy beneath fountains—small, far-off, shining
(15)   In the eyes of animals, these beings trapped
As I am trapped but not, themselves, the trap,
Aging, but without knowledge of their age,
Kept safe here, knowing not of death, for death—
Oh, bars of my own body, open, open!

(20)   The world goes by my cage and never sees me.
And there come not to me, as come to these,
The wild beasts, sparrows pecking the llamas' grain,
Pigeons settling on the bears' bread, buzzards
Tearing the meat the flies have clouded. . . .
(25)   Vulture,
When you come for the white rat that the foxes left,
Take off the red helmet of your head, the black
Wings that have shadowed me, and step to me as man:
The wild brother at whose feet the white wolves fawn;
(30)   To whose hand of power the great lioness
Stalks, purring. . . .
                              You know what I was,
You see what I am: change me, change me!

Randall Jarrell, *The Woman at the Washington Zoo.*

1. What does the poem suggest about the speaker's job?

   (1) She is an office worker.
   (2) She is an animal keeper at a zoo.
   (3) She works for the military.
   (4) She is retired.
   (5) She works at an embassy.

2. Which of the following sentences best restates the meaning of the line "The world goes by my cage and never sees me" (line 20)?

   (1) She never has any visitors to her home.
   (2) She would like to travel more.
   (3) She feels as though her friends do not appreciate her.
   (4) She refuses to let others know her true self.
   (5) She sees life happening without her.

3. What does the speaker mean by "these beings trapped / As I am trapped but not, themselves, the trap" (lines 15–16)?

   (1) She and the animals are held captive for their own good.
   (2) She lives next to the zoo and seeing animals in cages upsets her.
   (3) She was once caught in an animal trap by accident.
   (4) She feels caged within herself just as the animals are penned in cages.
   (5) She feels as dangerous as a trapped animal.

4. Based on the information in the poem, which of the following is most likely the speaker's greatest wish?

   (1) to let the animals out of their cages
   (2) to have people notice her more often
   (3) to wear more interesting clothing
   (4) to break free of her life's routine
   (5) to get a promotion at work

5. Which of the following does the vulture mentioned in lines 25–33 most likely symbolize?

   (1) fear
   (2) life
   (3) nature
   (4) change
   (5) hunger

6. What two types of cloth are contrasted in the poem?

   (1) the colorful cloth of the saris and the dull cloth of the speaker's work clothes
   (2) cloth from the moon and cloth from another planet
   (3) the cloth that has kept its color and the dull navy cloth
   (4) the cloth of the saris and the leopard-print cloth
   (5) the cloth of the speaker's work clothes and the cloth dyed by sunlight

7. Which of the following words best describes the tone of the poem?

   (1) furious
   (2) peaceful
   (3) despairing
   (4) patient
   (5) hopeful

8. Which of the following does the phrase "for death— / Oh, bars of my own body, open, open" (lines 18 and 19) most likely mean?

   The speaker

   (1) feels trapped by her physical limitations
   (2) feels that death will release her from captivity
   (3) deeply fears growing old
   (4) wishes she lived in a more exciting city
   (5) has a great fear of death

Answers start on page 314.

GED SKILL **Making Inferences**

Some poems are similar to puzzles—you need to figure out what the poet is suggesting in order to fully understand the poem. Then you make a decision based on your own understanding of what is indirectly stated. By considering the facts and information, you can make a logical decision about what the poem is about. But sometimes the facts are not spelled out. You must then make a decision based on stated and suggested information. This is called making an **inference.**

Of course, your inference may be reasonable and still not be correct. So, when reading a poem, be sure to make inferences using all of the clues the poet provides; that is, the words the poet chooses and the images they create.

inference
an idea the reader figures out based on stated and suggested information

TIP

Take note of what is implied in the poem. Then add this to what is directly stated and make an inference based on both the direct and implied information.

Read the following excerpt from a poem and complete the exercise below.

A NARROW FELLOW IN THE GRASS

A narrow Fellow in the Grass
Occasionally rides—
You may have met Him—did you not
His notice sudden is—

The Grass divides as with a Comb—
A spotted shaft is seen—
An then it closes at your feet
And opens further on—

Emily Dickinson, *The Poems of Emily Dickinson.*

1. What does this excerpt most resemble? Put a check mark by the correct answer.

    _____ a. a riddle

    _____ b. a joke

2. What can you infer is the subject of the poem? Put a check mark by the correct answer.

    _____ a. a turtle

    _____ b. a snake

3. Circle the clues from the poem that support your answer to question 2.

Option a is the correct answer to question 1. You must deduce the subject of the poem by using clues, which makes it similar to a riddle. *Option b* is the correct answer to question 2. Clues that you may have circled for question 3 include *narrow Fellow, Grass divides,* and *A spotted shaft.*

Read the following poem and complete the exercise below.

DOES THE TEACHER UNDERSTAND HER STUDENTS?

ENGLISH AS A SECOND LANGUAGE

The underpaid young teacher
prints the letters t, r, e, e
on the blackboard and imagines
forests and gardens springing up
(5) in the tired heads of her students.

But they see only four letters;
a vertical beam weighed down
by a crushing crossbar
and followed by a hook,
(10) and after the hook, two squiggles,
arcane identical twins
which could be spying eyes
or ready fists, could be handles,
could be curled seedlings, could take root,
(15) could develop leaves

Lisel Mueller, *Second Language: Poems.*

1. From lines 1–5 of this poem, what can you infer about the teacher? Put a check mark next to the better answer.

    _____ a. She has given up on her students and fears they will never learn English.

    _____ b. She hopes to bring English to life for them and help them see its beauty.

2. Underline the words in lines 1–5 that support your answer to question 1.

3. What is being described in lines 7–10?

    _____

4. Does the poem suggest that the students could learn English? Put a check mark next to your answer.

    _____ Yes

    _____ No

5. Circle the words or phrases in the poem that support your answer to question 4.

Answers start on page 315.

Directions: Choose the one best answer to each question.

Questions 1 through 4 refer to the following poem.

WHAT IS THE GIFT THE SON RECEIVES?

THE GIFT

To pull the metal splinter from my palm
my father recited a story in a low voice.
I watched his lovely face and not the blade.
Before the story ended, he'd removed
(5)   the iron sliver I thought I'd die from.

I can't remember the tale,
but hear his voice still, a well
of dark water, a prayer.
And I recall his hands
(10) two measures of tenderness
he laid against my face,
The flames of discipline
he raised above my head.

Had you entered that afternoon
(15) you would have thought you saw a man
planting something in a boy's palm,
a silver tear, a tiny flame.
Had you followed that boy
you would have arrived here,
(20) where I bend over my wife's right hand.

Look how I shave her thumbnail down
so carefully she feels no pain.
Watch as I lift the splinter out.
I was seven when my father took my hand
(25) like this,

and I did not hold that shard
between my fingers and think,
Metal that will bury me,
christen it Little Assassin,
(30) Ore Going Deep for my Heart,
And I did not lift up my wound and cry,
Death visited here!
I did what a child does
when he's given something to keep.
(35) I kissed my father.

Li-Young Lee, *Rose.*

1. Which of the following best describes the effect of comparing the father's voice to a prayer (lines 7–8)?

   It gives

   (1) a frightened feeling
   (2) a hopeful feeling
   (3) a grateful feeling
   (4) a soothing feeling
   (5) a painful feeling

2. Based on the context of the poem, what is the most likely reason that the speaker "did not lift up [his] wound and cry, / *Death visited here!*" (lines 31–32)?

   (1) He is eager to please his father.
   (2) He is trying to appear brave.
   (3) He is fearful of dying.
   (4) He is forbidden to move his injured hand.
   (5) He is grateful for his father's help.

3. What is the most important thing the speaker is given to keep (line 34)?

   (1) the metal sliver his father had removed
   (2) the knowledge of how to painlessly remove splinters
   (3) a precious memory of kindness
   (4) freedom from the pain of the splinter
   (5) the rebuilding of a relationship

4. Which of the following best states the theme of this poem?

   (1) Be kind to others and they will be kind to you.
   (2) Tenderness can be passed from person to person.
   (3) A gentle father makes a happy son.
   (4) Men with kind fathers make gentle husbands.
   (5) Helping others can make your heart glad.

Questions 5 through 7 refer to the following poem.

HOW DOES THE SPEAKER FEEL ABOUT HIS FATHER?

MIAMI

It started with the Bay Bridge.
He couldn't take that steel vault into the blue
above the blue, so much horizon!
Then it was the road itself, the rise and fall,
(5)   the continual blind curve.
He hired a chauffeur, he took the train.
Then it was hotels, so many rooms
the same, he had to sleep with the light on.
His courage has shrunk to the size of a windowbox.

(10)   Father who scared the witches and vampires
from my childhood closets, father
who walked before me like a hero's shield
through neighborhoods where hoodlums honed their knives
on concrete, where nerve was law,
(15)   who will drive you home from Miami?
You're broke and I'm a thousand miles away
with frightened children of my own.
Who will rescue you from the garden
where jets flash like swords above your head?

Daniel Mark Epstein, *The Book of Fortune.*

5. With which of the following ideas would you expect the speaker to <u>most likely</u> agree?

   (1) Large cities can be dangerous places to drive.
   (2) Children can sometimes be a burden.
   (3) Living far away from your parents is unhealthful.
   (4) Older people should live with their children.
   (5) Parents and children eventually change roles.

6. Which of the following <u>best</u> explains the meaning of "where nerve was law" (line 14)?

   (1) where the police were nervous
   (2) where people were nervous
   (3) where people had to be brave to survive
   (4) where hoodlums made the rules
   (5) where there were no police officers

7. Which of the following ideas is <u>most</u> clearly contrasted in the poem?

   (1) respect and disrespect
   (2) intelligence and ignorance
   (3) love and hatred
   (4) fearlessness and fear
   (5) justice and injustice

TIP
To make inferences, act like a detective. Is there an underlying meaning? What do the details of the poem have in common?

Answers start on page 315.

Directions: This is a ten-minute practice test. After ten minutes, mark the last question you finished. Then complete the test and check your answers. If most of your answers were correct, but you didn't finish, try to work faster next time. Choose the <u>one best answer</u> to each question.

<u>Questions 1 through 10</u> refer to the following poem.

HOW DOES THIS MAN FEEL ABOUT NATURE?

EARTH AND RAIN, THE PLANTS & SUN

Once near San Ysidro
on the way to Colorado,
I stopped and looked.

The sound of a meadowlark
(5) through smell of fresh cut alfalfa.

Raho would say,
"Look, Dad." A hawk

sweeping
        its wings

(10) clear through
        the blue
of whole and pure
        the wind
                the sky.

(15) It is writhing
overhead.
Hear. The Bringer.
        The Thunderer.

Sunlight falls
(20) through cloud curtains,
a straight bright shaft.

It falls,
        it falls,
down
(25)   to earth,
a green plant.

Today, the Katzina[1] come.
The dancing prayers.

Many times, the Katzina.
(30) The dancing prayers.
It shall not end,
son, it will not end,
this love.
Again and again,
(35) the earth is new again.
They come, listen, listen.
Hold on to your mother's hand.
They come

O great joy, they come.
(40) The plants with bells.
The stones with voices.
Listen, son, hold my hand.

---

[1] Southwest Native American masked dancers who, during certain ceremonial rites, impersonate ancestral spirits.

Simon J. Ortiz, *Woven Stone.*

1. Which of the following is the <u>best</u> restatement of lines 1–3?

   (1) You should always take time to stop and enjoy nature while traveling.
   (2) San Ysidro is the most beautiful area on the way to Colorado.
   (3) My schedule did not allow me to stop during my previous journey.
   (4) I stopped to look at the land around San Ysidro while traveling to Colorado.
   (5) The land around Colorado is worth stopping and looking at.

2. Which of the following phrases best describes the effect of the rhythm of lines 8–14?

   It gives

   (1) a quick and anxious feeling
   (2) the feeling of gliding back and forth
   (3) the peaceful feeling of a beautiful day
   (4) a happy, excited feeling
   (5) the feeling of a storm brewing in the distance

3. In which season does the poem most likely take place?

   (1) spring
   (2) summer
   (3) winter
   (4) fall
   (5) harvest

4. Which of the following best describes the mood of the poem?

   (1) joyful
   (2) depressed
   (3) angry
   (4) surprised
   (5) disinterested

5. Based on the context, who or what is "writhing / overhead" (lines 15–16)?

   (1) a hawk and its prey
   (2) the plants in the wind
   (3) clouds filled with rain
   (4) the Katzina dancers
   (5) the falling sunlight

6. Based on the poem, what can be inferred about the speaker?

   (1) He is leaving his wife and son.
   (2) He is traveling with his family.
   (3) He is making his journey alone.
   (4) He is recalling a difficult journey.
   (5) He is waiting to see a ceremonial dance.

7. To what or whom does the phrase "they come" in line 39 refer?

   (1) the mother and son
   (2) the hawks
   (3) the plants with bells
   (4) the renewal of the plants and earth
   (5) the Katzina

8. What is the theme, or underlying message, of this poem?

   (1) A day in the country goes by quickly.
   (2) Travel with a child can be filled with pleasure.
   (3) The earth is renewed by rainfall.
   (4) The cycle of nature and plant life is wonderful.
   (5) The Katzina dancers add ritual to our lives.

9. Based on the information in the poem, if the speaker could live anywhere he wanted, which of the following locations would he most likely choose?

   (1) New York City
   (2) the suburbs
   (3) the North Pole
   (4) a space station
   (5) a forest

10. To what do the lines "The plants with bells. / The stones with voices" (lines 40–41) most likely refer?

   (1) The people have hung plants and stones with decorations.
   (2) The plants and stones make music if you listen closely.
   (3) The speaker is having a wonderful dream.
   (4) The dancers seem as if they are a part of nature.
   (5) The plants and stones have come to life.

Answers start on page 316.

Lesson 24

GED SKILL **Interpreting Theme**

If a poem started with the words "Love will scar you," you could be fairly certain that its **theme,** or central idea, would have to do with the painful side of love. If, instead, you read "love is a rosebud," you would be guided toward a different theme. The theme of a poem expresses a specific opinion or belief about a larger topic. In the examples above, the topic is love, but the theme is what the poet has to say about love. For example, a theme might be that "love is a painful experience" (the scars) or "love is delicate and full of possibilities" (the rosebud).

Typically, the theme of a poem will not be directly stated. Therefore, you will have to infer it. You infer a theme by deciding what the poem is about (its topic) and then considering what the poet has to say about that topic. What figurative language and images does the poet use to describe the topic? What comparisons are made? What senses are involved? All of these are important clues to theme.

theme
the main idea in a work of literature, or a basic comment about life that the writer wants to share

To identify the theme of a poem, ask yourself, "What is the poet saying about life?" Try to sum up the theme in a single sentence.

Read the following excerpt from a poem and answer the questions below.

THE WIND IN THE TREES

clears the morning of doves.
You remember the loneliness,
the loneliness you knew as a child
when everyone in the house was busy.

Cathy Song, *Frameless Windows, Squares of Light: Poems.*

1. Put a check mark next to the main topic of this excerpt.

   ——— a. morning

   ——— b. loneliness

2. Put a check mark next to the theme of this excerpt.

   ——— a. Adults are too preoccupied to see the loneliness of childhood.

   ——— b. Childhood is a lonely and cruel time of life.

You are correct if you answered *option b* for question 1. The word *loneliness* is repeated twice in the short excerpt, giving it great emphasis. For question 2, *option a* is the correct answer. The theme is almost directly stated in the last two lines. *Option b* is incorrect because the poem does not indicate that all of childhood is lonely, nor that it is a cruel time of life.

GED SKILL FOCUS

Read the following poem and complete the exercise below.

WHAT IS THE POEM OF THE AIR?

SNOW-FLAKES

Out of the bosom of the Air,
Out of the cloud-folds of her garments shaken,
Over the woodlands brown and bare,
Over the harvest-fields forsaken
(5) Silent, and soft, and slow
Descends the snow.

Even as our cloudy fancies take
Suddenly shape in some divine expression,
Even as the troubled heart doth make
(10) In the white countenance confession,
The troubled sky reveals
The grief it feels.

This is the poem of the air,
Slowly in silent syllables recorded;
(15) This is the secret of despair,
Long in its cloudy bosom hoarded,
Now whispered and revealed
To wood and field.

Henry Wadsworth Longfellow, "Snow-flakes."

1. What is the main topic of this poem? Put a check mark next to the correct answer.

_____ a. woods and fields

_____ b. the snow

2. What is the <u>most</u> important idea that the speaker is trying to communicate about the topic? Put a check mark next to the correct answer.

_____ a. Snow is nature's expression of sadness.

_____ b. Snow interferes with harvesting.

3. How does the second stanza contribute to the poem's theme?

_____ a. It warns of cloudy skies and approaching storms.

_____ b. It compares the snow to human expressions of grief.

4. List three words from the last two stanzas (lines 7–18) that are clues to the theme.

_____

_____

Answers start on page 317.

GED Practice • Lesson 24

Directions: Choose the <u>one best answer</u> to the following questions.

<u>Questions 1 through 3</u> refer to the following poem.

HOW DOES THIS POET FEEL ABOUT DARKNESS?

FROM THE DARK TOWER

We shall not always plant while others reap
The olden increment of bursting fruit,
Not always countenance, abject and mute,
That lesser men should hold their brothers cheap;
(5) Not everlastingly while others sleep
Shall we beguile their limbs with mellow flute,
Not always bend to some more subtle brute;
We were not made eternally to weep.

The night whose sable breast relieves the stark,
(10) White stars is no less lovely being dark,
And there are buds that cannot bloom at all
In light, but crumple, piteous, and fall;
So in the dark we hide the heart that bleeds,
And wait, and tend our agonizing seeds.

Countee Cullen, *Copper Sun.*

1. Which of the following can you infer about the speaker on the basis of this poem?

   The speaker

   (1) is unhappy with his present situation
   (2) thinks he will be sad forever
   (3) is describing someone crying
   (4) prefers night to day
   (5) feels that some deserve to work while others rest

2. Which word <u>best</u> describes the tone of this poem?

   (1) resigned
   (2) elated
   (3) anxious
   (4) hopeful
   (5) angry

3. Which of the following <u>best</u> states the theme of this poem?

   (1) Stars are not the only thing that make a night sky beautiful.
   (2) Some people reap the rewards of other people's labor.
   (3) In time, unjust situations will change for the better.
   (4) Farming is a hard life that only leads to despair.
   (5) Keeping silent is the best way to make changes.

 If the theme, or underlying message, of a poem is not stated directly, look for clues that tell you what the poem is about. A poet's tone and the images he or she chooses are two ways that the poem's theme can be expressed.

WHAT DELIGHTS THIS POET?

THE POOR

It's the anarchy of poverty
delights me, the old
yellow wooden house indented
among the new brick tenements

(5) Or a cast-iron balcony
with panels showing oak branches
in full leaf. It fits
the dress of the children

reflecting every stage and
(10) custom of necessity—
Chimneys, roofs, fences of
wood and metal in an unfenced

age and enclosing next to
nothing at all: the old man
(15) in a sweater and soft black
hat who sweeps the sidewalk—

his own ten feet of it
in a wind that fitfully
turning his corner has
(20) overwhelmed the entire city

William Carlos Williams, *Collected Poems:
1909–1939, Volume I.*

4. Which of the following best states the theme
   of this poem?

   (1) Beauty and charm can be found in what is
       considered ugly.
   (2) Fences tend to make old buildings more
       attractive.
   (3) The new tenements are better than the
       old houses in the neighborhood.
   (4) Tall buildings can make the wind
       overwhelming.
   (5) Sweeping the dirty streets is a sad,
       futile action.

5. What does the poet mean in lines 9–10 by
   describing the children's clothes as "reflecting
   every stage and custom of necessity"?

   The children are dressed in

   (1) age-appropriate, traditional clothing
   (2) colorful costumes
   (3) what is affordable and available
   (4) clothing that suits their individual needs
   (5) clothing that is not suited to the
       temperature

Answers start on page 317.

Directions: This is a ten-minute practice test. After ten minutes, mark the last question you finished. Then complete the test and check your answers. If most of your answers were correct, but you didn't finish, try to work faster next time. Choose the <u>one best answer</u> to each question.

<u>Questions 1 and 2</u> refer to the following poem.

WHAT ARE THE TOURISTS DOING?

FENCES

Mouths full of laughter,
the *turistas* come to the tall hotel
with suitcases full of dollars.

Every morning my brother makes
(5) the cool beach sand new for them.
With a wooden board he smooths
away all footprints.

I peek through the cactus fence
and watch the women rub oil
(10) sweeter than honey into their arms and legs
while their children jump waves
or sip drinks from long straws,
coconut white, mango yellow.

Once my little sister
(15) ran barefoot across the hot sand
for a taste.

My mother roared like the ocean,
"No. No. It's their beach.
It's their beach."

Pat Mora, *Communion.*

1. Which of the following <u>best</u> states the theme of the poem?

   (1) The tourists and the local people experience the beach differently.
   (2) Tourists pay such high prices that it is as if they own the beach.
   (3) Sometimes good fences are necessary to make good neighbors.
   (4) Small children are often disobedient.
   (5) A firm voice can help to control unruly children.

2. Which of the following ideas are <u>most</u> clearly contrasted in the poem?

   (1) beach and sea
   (2) freedom and restriction
   (3) maturity and childhood
   (4) misbehavior and good manners
   (5) knowledge and ignorance

WHY IS THE SPEAKER CALLING THE CHILD?

CALLING THE CHILD

From the third floor I beckon to the child
Flying over the grass. As if by chance
My signal catches her and stops her dance
Under the lilac tree;
(5) And I have flung my net at something wild
And brought it down in all its loveliness.
She lifts her eyes to mine reluctantly,
Measuring in my look our twin distress.

Then from the garden she considers me
(10) And gathering joy, breaks from the closing net
And races off like one who would forget
That there are nets and snares.
But she returns and stands beneath the tree
With great solemnity, with legs apart,
(15) And wags her head at last and makes a start
And starts her humorous marching up the stairs.

Karl Shapiro, *Collected Poems 1940–1978.*

3. What is suggested by the child's "flying over the grass" (line 2)?

    (1) The child can actually fly.
    (2) The little girl has abundant energy.
    (3) The child is playing with a model airplane.
    (4) The girl is pretending to fly.
    (5) The girl is trying not to touch the grass.

4. Which of the following best describes what the speaker means by "Measuring in my look our twin distress" (line 8)?

    (1) The child looks like the speaker.
    (2) The speaker observes happiness in the child's eyes.
    (3) The child is a twin.
    (4) The speaker and the child have similar feelings of regret.
    (5) The speaker and the child are equally reluctant to stop their play.

5. What is the effect of the image of the net in the poem?

    (1) It emphasizes the child's untamed, free nature.
    (2) It shows that the speaker is a skilled hunter.
    (3) It shows that parents trap their children.
    (4) It shows that the speaker is heartless.
    (5) It shows how movement adds meaning to the poem.

6. Which of the following best states the theme of the poem?

    (1) Adults enjoy restricting a child's freedom.
    (2) There is the spirit of a child in everyone.
    (3) A natural, free spirit is eventually tamed by adulthood.
    (4) There should be no restrictions in life.
    (5) Children find humor in everything.

Answers start on page 317.

Unit 3 Cumulative Review Understanding Poetry

Directions: Choose the one best answer to each question.

Questions 1 through 6 refer to the following poem.

WHAT MADE THE POET FEEL THIS WAY?

BREAK, BREAK, BREAK

Break, break, break,
    On thy cold gray stones, O Sea!
And I would that my tongue could utter
    The thoughts that arise in me.

(5) O well for the fisherman's boy,
    That he shouts with his sister at play!
O well for the sailor lad,
    That he sings in his boat on the bay!

And the stately ships go on
(10)   To their haven under the hill;
But O for the touch of a vanished hand,
    And the sound of a voice that is still!

Break, break, break,
    At the foot of thy crags, O Sea!
(15) But the tender grace of a day that is dead
    Will never come back to me.

Alfred, Lord Tennyson, "Break, Break, Break."

1. What rhythm and image does the poet create by repeating the word "break"?

    (1) the singing of a young sailor
    (2) the boredom of life at sea
    (3) the cries of a seagull
    (4) the pattern of the ocean's waves
    (5) the rising and setting of the sun

2. For what is the speaker in the poem longing?

    (1) the days of his childhood
    (2) his youth as a fisherman
    (3) his home by the sea
    (4) a ship he once owned
    (5) a loved one who has died

3. If this poem were set to music, which kind would be most appropriate?

    (1) scary
    (2) joyous
    (3) sad
    (4) jazzy
    (5) playful

4. What is the most important function of the image of the young people (lines 5–8)?

    (1) It contrasts with the speaker's sorrow.
    (2) It reminds the speaker of his boyhood.
    (3) It reminds the speaker of life's joys.
    (4) It provides the speaker with an audience for his story.
    (5) It symbolizes his dislike for youth.

5. Which of the following does the image of the "cold gray stones" (line 2) suggest?

    (1) rage
    (2) strength
    (3) love for nature
    (4) peace of mind
    (5) indifference

6. Which of the following best restates the meaning of "I would that my tongue could utter / The thoughts that arise in me" (lines 3–4)?

The speaker

    (1) has never been good with words
    (2) is afraid he will insult someone
    (3) hopes he can express his feelings
    (4) cannot speak over the noise of the sea
    (5) hopes others will understand him

Questions 7 through 10 refer to the following poem.

WHAT HAS HAPPENED TO THIS PLACE?

CARMEL POINT

The extraordinary patience of things!
This beautiful place defaced with a crop of suburban houses—
How beautiful when we first beheld it,
Unbroken field of poppy and lupin walled with clean cliffs;
(5)   No intrusion but two or three horses pasturing,
Or a few milch [milk] cows rubbing their flanks on the outcrop rock-heads—
Now the spoiler has come: does it care?
Not faintly. It has all time. It knows the people are a tide
That swells and in time will ebb, and all
(10)   Their works dissolve. Meanwhile the image of the pristine beauty
Lives in the very grain of the granite,
Safe as the endless ocean that climbs our cliff.—As for us:
We must uncenter our minds from ourselves;
We must unhumanize our views a little, and become confident
(15)   As the rock and ocean that we were made from.

Robinson Jeffers, *The Collected Poetry of Robinson Jeffers.*

7. What does the word "it" refer to in the phrase "It has all time" (line 8)?

    (1) the spoiler
    (2) the crop of suburban houses
    (3) development
    (4) nature
    (5) the cliffs

8. Which of the following organizations would the speaker in this poem most likely join?

    (1) the National Rifle Association
    (2) the Nature Conservancy
    (3) the National Builders Association
    (4) the Red Cross
    (5) the Chamber of Commerce

9. Which of the following statements best explains the image that people are "a tide / That swells and in time will ebb" (lines 8–9)?

    (1) All people will eventually wash out to sea.
    (2) The human population is growing at an ever-increasing rate.
    (3) The local population will move to a more distant suburb.
    (4) Populations increase and decrease in cycles.
    (5) The community might fall into the sea.

10. Which of the following best states the main theme of the poem?

    (1) Patience is a virtue in people.
    (2) People must realize their place in nature.
    (3) People rule the Earth.
    (4) Rock and ocean will destroy people.
    (5) People have destroyed the Earth.

Paying extra attention to the punctuation within and at the ends of lines can help you understand the rhythm and meaning of a poem.

WHO ARE THE MIGRANTS?

MIGRANTS

Birds obeying migration maps etched in their brains
Never revised their Interstate routes.
Some of them still stop off in Washington, D.C.

This autumn evening as the lights of the Pentagon
(5)   Come on like the glare of urgent trouble through surgery
     skylights,
Come on like a far-off hope of control,

I watch a peaceful V-sign of Canada Geese
Lower their landing gear, slip to rest on the slicky Potomac,
(10)   Break rank and huddle with the bobbing power boats.

Wings of jets beating the air, taking turns for the landing—
Pterodactyls circling the filled-in swamps under National Airport.
There is a great wild honking

Of traffic on the bridges—
(15)   The daily homing of migrants with headlights dimmed
Who loop and bank by instinct along broken white lines.

Rod Jellema, *The Eighth Day: New and Selected Poems.*

11. In lines 9–12, what image does the poet use to describe the geese?

    (1) the wings of pterodactyls
    (2) bobbing power boats
    (3) airplanes landing
    (4) the swamps by the airport
    (5) a smooth river

12. Which of the following statements best explains line 2, that the birds "Never revised their Interstate routes"?

    (1) Civilization has not changed the patterns of the geese.
    (2) Geese tend to fly over major roadways.
    (3) Geese usually stop in Washington, D.C.
    (4) Signs of civilization confuse the geese.
    (5) Geese ought to fly through less populated areas.

13. What is being compared to the geese in lines 13–16?

    (1) creatures from the dinosaur era
    (2) people driving home from work
    (3) cars with dim headlights
    (4) broken white lines on the road
    (5) traffic clogging the roadways

14. What do the "filled-in swamps under National Airport" (line 12) symbolize?

    (1) how much the environment has changed
    (2) that the airport sits in a marshy area
    (3) how muggy Washington is in the summer
    (4) that the geese will no longer land there
    (5) what a problem the geese have become

WHERE IS THIS TRAVELER HEADED?

UP-HILL

Does the road wind up-hill all the way?
    Yes, to the very end.
Will the day's journey take the whole long day?
    From morn to night, my friend.

(5) But is there for the night a resting-place?
    A roof for when the slow dark hours begin.
May not the darkness hide it from my face?
    You cannot miss that inn.

Shall I meet other wayfarers at night?
(10)   Those who have gone before.
Then must I knock, or call when just in sight?
    They will not keep you standing at the door.

Shall I find comfort, travel-sore and weak?
    Of labor you shall find the sum.
(15) Will there be beds for me and all who seek?
    Yea, beds for all who come.

Christina Rossetti, "Up-Hill."

15. What does the structure of this poem most resemble?

    (1) a song
    (2) a riddle
    (3) a conversation
    (4) a dream
    (5) a nursery rhyme

16. Which of the following best describes how rhyme is used in this poem?

    (1) to give the poem a childlike quality
    (2) to make the poem melodious
    (3) to signify the passing of time
    (4) to identify two separate voices
    (5) to give the poem a dreamlike quality

17. In this poem, what do "Those who have gone before" most likely symbolize (line 10)?

    (1) lost children
    (2) laborers on the way to work
    (3) stray sheep or goats
    (4) the innkeeper and his wife
    (5) people who have died

18. What is the best description of this poem's rhythm?

    (1) fast and jerky
    (2) galloping
    (3) slow and steady
    (4) monotonous
    (5) irregular and halting

HOW DOES THIS YOUNG WIFE FEEL?

THE RIVER MERCHANT'S WIFE: A LETTER

While my hair was still cut straight across my forehead
I played about the front gate, pulling flowers.
You came by on bamboo stilts, playing horse,
You walked about my seat, playing with blue plums.
(5)   And we went on living in the village of Chokan:
Two small people, without dislike or suspicion.

At fourteen I married My Lord you.
I never laughed, being bashful.
Lowering my head, I looked at the wall.
(10)   Called to, a thousand times, I never looked back.

At fifteen I stopped scowling.
I desired my dust to be mingled with yours
Forever and forever and forever.
Why should I climb the look out?

(15)   At sixteen you departed,
You went into far Ku-to-yen, by the river of swirling eddies,
And you have been gone five months.
The monkeys make sorrowful noise overhead.

You dragged your feet when you went out.
(20)   By the gate now, the moss is grown, the different mosses,
Too deep to clear them away!
The leaves fall early this autumn, in wind.

The paired butterflies are already yellow with August
Over the grass in the West garden;
(25)   They hurt me. I grow older.
If you are coming down through the narrows of the river Kiang,
Please let me know beforehand,
And I will come out to meet you
As far as Cho-fu-sa. (by Rihaku)

Ezra Pound, *Personae.*

19. At the beginning of the poem, what is the relationship between the couple?

    (1) They are schoolmates.
    (2) They are enemies.
    (3) They are sweethearts.
    (4) They are rivals.
    (5) They are playmates.

20. Which of the following phrases best describes the overall mood of the poem?

    (1) wistful longing
    (2) lighthearted playfulness
    (3) stormy anger
    (4) dreadful suspense
    (5) romantic passion

21. Based on the third stanza, which of the following options is the best restatement of "Why should I climb the look out" (line 14)?

    (1) It is hopeless for me to escape.
    (2) I am happy, so why look elsewhere?
    (3) My husband will not come, so why look?
    (4) My life is over, so why keep trying?
    (5) I have no enemies anymore.

22. What does the gathering moss at the gate symbolize (line 20)?

    (1) The girl is dead and speaking from the grave.
    (2) The woman has an interest in gardening.
    (3) The girl is a prisoner in her own home.
    (4) The girl is a poor housekeeper.
    (5) The husband has been away a long time.

23. Which of the following is the most likely explanation of why the yellow, paired butterflies "hurt" the woman (lines 23–25)?

    (1) They remind her that winter is on the way.
    (2) They warn her that her husband is in danger.
    (3) They symbolize her happy childhood.
    (4) They remind her that life is short and she is alone.
    (5) They taunt her because she has no children.

24. Which of the following can you infer about the couple's youthful marriage?

    (1) They fell in love with each other at age fourteen.
    (2) The girl was a servant in her husband's home.
    (3) The marriage was arranged by their two families.
    (4) No one else suitable lived in the village of Chokan.
    (5) They were desperate to marry before they got too old.

25. Which of the following best explains the function of the phrase "The monkeys make sorrowful noise overhead" (line 18)?

    To show that the monkeys

    (1) are sad creatures
    (2) make the girl sadder
    (3) echo the girl's sadness
    (4) often make sad noises
    (5) are worried about the girl

26. If the woman in this poem could give a lesson about life to a young girl, which of the following would she be most likely to say?

    (1) The course of life is unpredictable.
    (2) Always be joyful, no matter what happens.
    (3) Life is painful from beginning to end.
    (4) Marry when you are very young.
    (5) Always obey your parents.

27. Which of the following best describes the woman's emotions over the course of the poem?

    (1) sorrow to devotion to obedience to joy
    (2) playfulness to obedience to devotion to longing
    (3) obedience to sorrow to playfulness to devotion
    (4) sorrow to melancholy to peacefulness to joy
    (5) playfulness to longing to hopelessness to despair

WHAT IS ORDINARY ABOUT A MIRACLE?

MIRACLES

Why, who makes much of a miracle?
As to me I know of nothing else but miracles,
Whether I walk the streets of Manhattan,
Or dart my sight over the roofs of houses toward the sky,
(5)   Or wade with naked feet along the beach just in the edge of the water,
Or stand under the trees in the woods,
Or talk by day with any one I love,
Or sit at table at dinner with the rest,
Or look at strangers opposite me riding in the car,
(10)   Or watch honeybees busy around the hive of a summer forenoon,
Or animals feeding in the fields,
Or birds, or the wonderfulness of insects in the air,
Or the wonderfulness of the sundown, or of stars shining so quiet and bright,
Or the exquisite delicate thin curve of the new moon in spring;
(15)   These with the rest, one and all, are to me miracles,
The whole referring, yet each distinct and in its place.
To me every hour of the light and dark is a miracle,
Every cubic inch of space is a miracle,
Every square yard of the surface of the earth is spread with the same,
(20)   Every foot of the interior swarms with the same.

To me the sea is a continual miracle,
The fishes that swim—the rocks—the motion of the waves—
    the ships with men in them,
What stranger miracles are there?

Walt Whitman, "Miracles."

28. Which of the following sets up a rhythm in this poem?

(1) omitting punctuation at the end of lines
(2) repeating images of flight
(3) switching from questions to statements
(4) referring to the motion of waves
(5) repeating the word "Or"

29. What senses are most directly appealed to in line 10?

(1) hearing and taste
(2) sight and hearing
(3) sight and taste
(4) taste and touch
(5) touch and movement

30. What is the theme of this poem?

(1) The world is filled with miracles.
(2) All miracles are the same.
(3) There are no miracles.
(4) Most people ignore miracles.
(5) Only nature contains miracles.

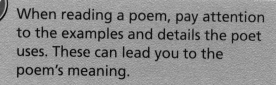

TIP
When reading a poem, pay attention to the examples and details the poet uses. These can lead you to the poem's meaning.

Answers start on page 318.

Unit 3: Understanding Poetry

Cumulative Review Performance Analysis
Unit 3 • Poetry

Use the Answers and Explanations starting on page 318 to check your answers to the Unit 3 Cumulative Review. Then use the chart to figure out the skill areas in which you need more practice.

On the chart, circle the questions that you answered correctly. Write the number correct for each skill area. Add the number of questions that you got correct on the Cumulative Review. If you feel that you need more practice, go back and review the lessons for the skill areas that were difficult for you.

Questions	Number Correct	Skill Area	Lessons for Review
2, 6, 7, 11, 19, 21	____/6	Comprehension	21, 22, 23, 24
3, 8, 26	____/3	Application	22, 23
1, 4, 5, 9, 12, 14, 16, 17, 22, 23, 24, 25, 28 29	____/14	Analysis	20, 21, 22, 23
10, 13, 15, 18, 20, 27 30	____/7	Synthesis	23, 24
TOTAL CORRECT	____/30		

UNIT 4

Understanding Drama

Drama is a type of literature that is meant to be performed by actors. The characters in drama face conflict and struggle to resolve important issues. The scenery, the music, the gestures, and the dialogue work together to create a mood and express ideas. The dialogue, or the conversation, between characters furthers the plot and reveals what the characters are like. There are also stage directions that give information about what a character is doing as he or she speaks.

In this unit, you will learn to analyze drama using both the spoken and the unspoken language of a play. The GED Language Arts, Reading Test will include drama selections to determine how well you understand this form of literature. Overall, literature is the basis for 75 percent of the questions on the GED Reading Test.

August Wilson's plays about the African-American experience have earned him the Pulitzer Prize for drama.

The lessons in this unit include:

Lesson 25: Understanding Plot
Identifying plot elements helps you to understand which events in a play are the most important and how the events are related.

Lesson 26: Inferring Character
Examining what the characters say, do, and think—and paying attention to what other characters say about them—can give you a deeper understanding of a play.

Lesson 27: Understanding Motivation
Understanding a character's motivation means understanding why the character says or does something. Analyzing the reason behind a character's actions can help you follow the plot and better understand the meaning of the play.

Lesson 28: Interpreting Theme
Interpreting the theme of a play requires answering the question "What is the most important idea the playwright is trying to get across?"

SELECTED PLAYWRIGHTS

- Lillian Hellman
- Beth Henley
- Henrik Ibsen
- Sam Shepard
- Wendy Wasserstein
- August Wilson

GED SKILL **Understanding Plot**

Like a story, a play has a beginning, middle, and end. The events in a play and the order in which they occur—from the opening of the play to the conclusion—are the **plot.**

In a typical plot, the **exposition** gives background information and introduces the setting and the characters. As the play develops, **complications** occur that create a **conflict**—a problem that needs to be resolved. The point at which the conflict reaches its peak is the **climax.** It represents the turning point of the play. Afterward, the tension decreases, and problems that were not resolved during the climax come to an end in the **resolution.**

plot
the events in a play and the order in which they are arranged

Read the following summary of a play and complete the exercise below.

Two close friends, Valentine and Proteus, fall in love with Silvia, the daughter of the Duke of Milan. The duke, however, wants his daughter to marry a man named Thurio, whom Silvia does not love. Proteus betrays his friend Valentine and causes him to be banished from the kingdom. Silvia decides she wants to be with Valentine and escapes to the forest to join him. Proteus pursues Valentine and Silvia. He catches Silvia and is about to overpower her when Valentine rescues her. Valentine then forgives Proteus for his behavior. Silvia's father arrives. The duke is impressed by Valentine's honorable conduct and gives his consent to a marriage between Silvia and Valentine. Proteus, meanwhile, realizes the error of his ways and becomes content to marry his former girlfriend, Julia.

TIP

To determine the complications in a plot, be alert to circumstances or events that make life more difficult for the characters. To identify conflicts, analyze the characters' reactions to the complications.

1. Which of the following details is from the exposition of the play? Put a check mark next to the correct answer.

    _____ a. Silvia flees to the forest.

    _____ b. Valentine and Proteus are close friends.

    _____ c. Valentine forgives Proteus.

2. Write a description of the climax of the play on the line below.

    _____

3. Which of the following details is from the resolution of the play? Put a check mark next to the correct answer.

    _____ a. Proteus catches Silvia.

    _____ b. The duke allows Silvia and Valentine to marry.

For question 1, *option b* is correct. This detail gives background information about the characters. For question 2, you may have written something such as *Valentine rescues Silvia from Proteus.* For question 3, *option b* is correct.

Read the following excerpt from a play and complete the exercise below.

MINNIE: A present? This early in the day? Can I open it?

SOPHIE: Ask Fan.

FAN: Go ahead.

MINNIE: *(Reading, but confused)* But what does it mean?

FRANK: It's a deed.

SOPHIE: It's the deed to your part of this land. You're twenty-one now.

MISS LEAH: Every colored woman ought to have a piece of land she can claim as her own.

FRANK: Do you know how much that land is worth?

SOPHIE: We're interested in buying more land, not selling what we've got.

FRANK: Well, from what that white fella told me on the train, not everybody around here feels that way. I heard some of your neighbors are considering some pretty generous offers.

MISS LEAH: Speculators!

FRANK: They're offering $500 an acre.

MISS LEAH: I can't believe it.

FRANK: Doesn't that at least make you more open to the idea? You could be a very rich woman.

SOPHIE: And I'd be standing in the middle of Kansas without any place to call home. You can't grow wheat on an acre of money.

FRANK: There's plenty of other land around from what I could see. What's the difference?

SOPHIE: The difference is we own this land. Whether they like it or not, and anybody who tries to say different is going to find himself buried on it.

Pearl Cleage, *Flyin' West.*

1. Put a check mark next to the sentences that give information from the exposition of this scene.

_____ a. Frank thinks the land should be sold for the money.

_____ b. It is Minnie's birthday.

_____ c. The present is a deed to some of the family land.

2. Name the two characters that are most in conflict with one another.

_____

_____

3. Put a check mark next to the complication developed in this scene.

_____ a. Minnie's birthday present is a piece of land.

_____ b. Minnie is opening her present early in the day.

Answers start on page 320.

Directions: Choose the one best answer to each question.

Questions 1 through 4 refer to the following excerpt from a play.

HOW DO THESE WOMEN ACT WITH EACH OTHER?

CHICK: . . . Oh! Oh! Oh! I almost forgot. Here's a present for you. Happy birthday to Lenny, from the Buck Boyles! *(She takes a wrapped package*
(5) *from her bag and hands it to LENNY.)*
LENNY: Why, thank you, Chick. It's so nice to have you remember my birthday every year like you do.
CHICK: *(modestly)* Oh, well, now, that's
(10) just the way I am, I suppose. That's just the way I was brought up to be. Well, why don't you go on and open up the present?
LENNY: All right. *(She starts to unwrap*
(15) *the gift.)*
CHICK: It's a box of candy—assorted crèmes.
LENNY: Candy—that's always a nice gift.
CHICK: And you have a sweet tooth,
(20) don't you?
LENNY: I guess.
CHICK: Well, I'm glad you like it.
LENNY: I do.
CHICK: Oh, speaking of which, remember
(25) that little polka-dot dress you got Peekay for her fifth birthday last month?
LENNY: The red-and-white one?
CHICK: Yes; well, the first time I put it in
(30) the washing machine, I mean the very first time, it fell all to pieces. Those little polka dots just dropped right off in the water.
LENNY: *(crushed)* Oh, no. Well, I'll get
(35) something else for her, then—a little toy.
CHICK: Oh, no, no, no, no, no! We wouldn't hear of it! I just wanted to let you know so you wouldn't go and
(40) waste any more of your hard-earned money on that make of dress.

Those inexpensive brands just don't hold up. I'm sorry, but not in these modern washing machines.

Beth Henley, *Crimes of the Heart.*

1. Based on the excerpt, which of the following is most likely to happen if Lenny buys Peekay a toy?

   (1) Peekay will immediately break the toy.
   (2) Lenny will criticize Peekay.
   (3) Lenny will tell Chick how much the toy cost.
   (4) Chick will criticize the toy.
   (5) Chick will refuse to give Peekay the toy.

2. With which of the following statements would Lenny be most likely to agree?

   (1) If you cannot be nice, be polite.
   (2) Honesty is the best policy.
   (3) The gift you get is never the one you want.
   (4) Bad luck is always followed by good.
   (5) Do not criticize others for your own mistakes.

3. Which of the following best explains why the playwright includes the dialogue about "the polka-dot dress" (lines 24–44)?

   (1) to express Peekay's disappointment
   (2) to demonstrate Chick's attention to detail
   (3) to show Lenny's good taste
   (4) to portray Chick as inconsiderate
   (5) to highlight Chick's knowledge of fabrics

4. What does this scene reveal about Lenny's character?

   (1) She has a mind of her own.
   (2) She prefers candy to other presents.
   (3) She often says what others want her to say.
   (4) She always remembers Chick's birthday.
   (5) She has a lot of money.

Questions 5 through 8 refer to the following excerpt from a play.

WHAT HAS NORA DONE FOR HER HUSBAND?

MRS. LINDE: . . . A wife can't borrow without her husband's consent.

NORA: *(tossing her head)* Ah, but when it happens to be a wife with a bit of a
(5)   sense of business . . . a wife who knows her way about things, then . . .

MRS. LINDE: But, Nora, I just don't understand. . . .

NORA: You don't have to. I haven't said I
(10)   did borrow the money. I might have got it some other way. *(throws herself back on the sofa)* I might even have got it from some admirer. Anyone as reasonably attractive as I am . . .

(15) MRS. LINDE: Don't be so silly!

NORA: Now you must be dying of curiosity, Kristine.

MRS. LINDE: Listen to me now, Nora dear—you haven't done anything rash,
(20)   have you?

NORA: *(sitting up again)* Is it rash to save your husband's life?

MRS. LINDE: I think it was rash to do anything without telling him. . . .

(25) NORA: But the whole point was that he mustn't know anything. Good heavens, can't you see! He wasn't even supposed to know how desperately ill he was. It was me the doctors came
(30)   and told his life was in danger, that the only way to save him was to go South for a while. Do you think I didn't try talking him into it first? I began dropping hints about how nice it would
(35)   be if I could be taken on a little trip abroad, like other young wives. I wept, I pleaded, I told him he ought to show some consideration for my condition, and let me have a bit of my own way.
(40)   And then I suggested he might take out a loan. But at that he nearly lost his temper, Kristine. He said I was being frivolous, that it was his duty as a husband not to give in to all these
(45)   whims and fancies of mine—

as I do believe he called them. All right, I thought, somehow you've got to be saved. And it was then I found a way.

Henrik Ibsen, *A Doll's House.*

5. Based on the dialogue in the scene, how can Nora's character best be described?

(1) humble and obedient
(2) hysterical and panicky
(3) arrogant and evil
(4) resourceful and determined
(5) childish and impulsive

6. Which of the following words best describes the tone expressed in the excerpt?

(1) frightened
(2) secretive
(3) hopeless
(4) upbeat
(5) humorous

7. Based on the excerpt, what would Mrs. Linde most likely do if a friend asked her to conceal an envelope containing important documents?

(1) feel very offended
(2) offer to help in some other way
(3) feel honored at the confidence
(4) agree to the request enthusiastically
(5) insist that her friend be straightforward

8. Why does Nora want to go South?

(1) She wants to do some traveling.
(2) She wants to do what is best for her husband's health.
(3) She wants to take a break from her husband's temper.
(4) She wants to save money.
(5) She wants to leave her home and start a better life.

Answers start on page 320.

Directions: This is a ten-minute practice test. After ten minutes, mark the last question you finished. Then complete the test and check your answers. If most of your answers were correct, but you didn't finish, try to work faster next time. Choose the one best answer to each question.

<u>Questions 1 through 11</u> refer to the following excerpt from a play.

CAN THIS CHILD BE TRUSTED?

MARY: *(without looking up)* I'm not lying. I went out walking and I saw the flowers and they looked pretty and I didn't know it was so late.

(5) KAREN: *(impatiently)* Stop it, Mary! I'm not interested in hearing that foolish story again. I *know* you got the flowers out of the garbage can. What I do want to know is why you feel you have to lie

(10) out of it.

MARY: *(beginning to whimper)* I *did* pick the flowers near Conway's. You never believe me. You believe everybody but me. It's always like that. Everything I

(15) say you fuss at me about. Everything I do is wrong.

KAREN: You know that isn't true. *(Goes to* MARY, *puts her arm around her, waits until the sobbing has stopped)* Look,

(20) Mary, look at me. *(Raises* MARY'S *face with her hand)* Let's try to understand each other. If you feel that you *have* to take a walk, or that you just *can't* come to class, or that you'd

(25) like to go into the village by yourself, come and tell me—I'll try and understand. *(smiles)* I don't say that I'll always agree that you should do exactly what you want to do, but I've

(30) had feelings like that, too—everybody has—and I won't be unreasonable about yours. But this way, this kind of lying you do, makes everything wrong.

MARY: *(looking steadily at* KAREN*)* I got

(35) the flowers near Conway's cornfield.

KAREN: *(looks at* MARY, *sighs, moves back toward desk and stands there for a moment)* Well, there doesn't seem to be any other way with you; you'll have

(40) to be punished. Take your recreation periods alone for the next two weeks.

No horseback-riding and no hockey. Don't leave the school grounds for any reason whatsoever. Is that clear?

(45) MARY: *(carefully)* Saturday, too?
KAREN: Yes.
MARY: But you said I could go to the boat races.
KAREN: I'm sorry, but you can't go.

(50) MARY: I'll tell my grandmother. I'll tell her how everybody treats me here and the way I get punished for every little thing I do. I'll tell her. I'll—
MRS. MORTAR: Why, I'd slap her

(55) hands! . . .
KAREN: *(turning back from door, ignoring* MRS. MORTAR'S *speech. To* MARY*)* Go upstairs, Mary.
MARY: I don't feel well.

(60) KAREN: *(wearily)* Go upstairs now.
MARY: I've got a pain. I've had it all morning. It hurts right here. *(pointing vaguely in the direction of her heart)* Really it does.

(65) KAREN: Ask Miss Dobie to give you some hot water and bicarbonate of soda.
MARY: It's a bad pain. I've never had it before.
KAREN: I don't think it can be very

(70) serious.
MARY: My heart! It's my heart! It's stopping or something. I can't breathe. *(She takes a long breath and falls awkwardly to the floor.)*

Lillian Hellman, *The Children's Hour.*

1. Which of the following phrases <u>best</u> describes Karen?

   (1) prim and proper
   (2) harsh and demanding
   (3) kind and forgiving
   (4) reasonable and firm
   (5) easily intimidated

2. Which of the following phrases best describes Mary?

   (1) lonely and misunderstood
   (2) pathetic and victimized
   (3) friendly and open
   (4) slow-witted and dull
   (5) sneaky and uncooperative

3. Based on the information in this excerpt, how would Mary most likely behave on the job?

   She would

   (1) make excuses for turning in work late
   (2) be too frightened to voice her opinion
   (3) quit after only a few days
   (4) work hard to get promoted
   (5) be able to communicate well with co-workers

4. Which of the following best describes the mood created in this scene?

   (1) harmonious
   (2) suspenseful
   (3) tense
   (4) sorrowful
   (5) lighthearted

5. Based on this excerpt, which of the following best describes Mary's attitude toward Karen?

   (1) Mary is uncertain about Karen's feelings.
   (2) Mary is not interested in Karen.
   (3) Mary is trying to manipulate Karen.
   (4) Mary wants to gain Karen's affection.
   (5) Mary does not trust Karen.

6. What does the stage direction *"looking steadily at Karen"* (line 34) suggest?

   (1) Mary feels no shame about lying.
   (2) Mary is angry about being unjustly accused.
   (3) Mary wants to calm Karen down.
   (4) Mary wants Karen to understand her better.
   (5) Mary is trying to understand Karen.

7. Which of the following is the most likely reason that Mary falls to the floor?

   (1) She is upset and has fainted.
   (2) She has a heart ailment.
   (3) She does not like what Karen said.
   (4) She does not want Mrs. Mortar to slap her.
   (5) She exhausted herself on her long walk.

8. Based on the excerpt, what would Mrs. Mortar most likely do if she were in charge of Mary?

   (1) behave towards Mary much as Karen does
   (2) treat Mary more leniently than Karen does
   (3) assign Mary an extremely harsh punishment
   (4) try her best to reason with Mary
   (5) send Mary away from the school

9. Based on the excerpt, what can be inferred about Karen's relationship with Mrs. Mortar?

   (1) Karen does not value Mrs. Mortar's opinions.
   (2) Mrs. Mortar is Karen's close and trusted friend.
   (3) Karen is careful not to hurt Mrs. Mortar's feelings.
   (4) Karen ultimately has respect for Mrs. Mortar.
   (5) Mrs. Mortar was once Karen's teacher.

10. Based on the excerpt, which of the following would Mary most likely do to get her way?

    (1) beg and plead for what she wants
    (2) tell the truth and hope for the best
    (3) pretend to be ill to get sympathy
    (4) act as if she cared about Karen
    (5) try to bargain for what she wants

11. Based on the excerpt, which of the following is Karen most likely to do next?

    (1) call Mary's grandmother
    (2) call a doctor
    (3) scold Mrs. Mortar
    (4) wait for Mary to decide to get up
    (5) ask someone to take Mary to her room

Answers start on page 321.

GED SKILL Inferring Character

Characters in drama are fictional people who take part in a play's events. The main character is called the **protagonist.** The action and main conflict of the play center on this character. The other characters that the protagonist encounters help bring about the climax.

How can you learn about a play's characters? First, you can learn about them from what they say in their **dialogue** with other characters. Dialogue may reveal what the characters feel or what they are thinking. It may also reveal details about the characters' backgrounds.

Second, you can learn about characters from their actions. The **stage directions** are words in parentheses that describe characters' gestures, movements, and expressions. Stage directions may also give details about costumes or the setting. For example, a description of a character wearing a wrinkled suit with one shoe untied helps you understand the type of person the character is.

characters
the people who participate in the events of the play

protagonist
the central character, who struggles to resolve one or more conflicts

TIP

To understand a character, examine what the character does and says. Look at the stage directions that refer to the character. Then look for clues in the dialogue of other characters; notice what they say about him or her.

Read the following excerpt from a play and complete the exercise below.

AUSTIN: I don't want to hear about it, okay? Go tell it to the executives! Tell it to somebody who's going to turn it into a package deal or something. A T.V. series. Don't tell it to me.

SAUL: But I want to continue with your project too, Austin. It's not as though we can't do both. We're big enough for that aren't we?

AUSTIN: "We"? I can't do both! I don't know about "we."

LEE: *(to SAUL)* See, what'd I tell ya'. He's totally unsympathetic.

SAUL: Austin, there's no point in our going to another screenwriter for this. It just doesn't make sense. You're brothers. You know each other. There's a familiarity with the material that just wouldn't be possible otherwise.

AUSTIN: There's no familiarity with the material! None! I don't know what "Tornado Country" is. I don't know what a "gooseneck" is. And I don't want to know! *(pointing to LEE)* He's a hustler! He's a bigger hustler than you are! If you can't see that, then—

Sam Shepard, *True West.*

Put a check mark next to the answer that best describes Austin's attitude towards Saul in this excerpt.

_____ a. defiant

_____ b. cooperative

You are correct if you chose *option a.* Austin refuses to cooperate with Saul's plan for Austin to be part of this project.

Read the following excerpt from a play and complete the exercise below.

Alejo sits to the right of the diningroom table. Orlando stands to Alejo's left. He is now a lieutenant commander. He wears an army tunic, breeches, and boots. Leticia stands to the left. She wears a dress that suggests 1940s fashion.

LETICIA: What! Me go hunting? Do you think I'm going to shoot a deer, the most beautiful animal in the world? Do you think I'm going to destroy a deer? On the contrary, I would run in the field and scream and wave my arms like a mad woman and try to scare them away so the hunters could not reach them. I'd run in front of the bullets and let the mad hunters kill me—stand in the way of the bullets—stop the bullets with my body. I don't see how anyone can shoot a deer.

ORLANDO: *(To Alejo.)* Do you understand that? You, who are her friend, can you understand that? You don't think that is madness? She's mad. Tell her that—she'll think it's you who's mad. *(To Leticia.)* Hunting is a sport! A skill! Don't talk about something you know nothing about. Must you have an opinion about every damn thing? Can't you keep your mouth shut when you don't know what you're talking about? *(Orlando exits right.)*

Maria Irene Fornes, *The Conduct of Life.*

1. Who is the protagonist in the excerpt?

   _____

2. List three details that the dialogue reveals about the protagonist.

   a. _____

   b. _____

   c. _____

3. What do the stage directions reveal about Orlando's work and way of dressing?

   _____

   _____

4. Put a check mark next to the statement that best describes Orlando.

   _____ a. a meek and insecure person

   _____ b. a kind and loving husband

   _____ c. a ruthless killer

   _____ d. an authoritative, confident man

Answers start on page 321.

Directions: Choose the <u>one best answer</u> to each question.

Questions 1 through 3 refer to the following excerpt from a play.

IS AMANDA REALLY CONCERNED ABOUT LAURA'S FEELINGS?

AMANDA: I thought that you were an adult; it seems that I was mistaken. *(She crosses slowly to the sofa and sinks down and stares at* LAURA.*)*

(5) LAURA: Please don't stare at me, Mother. (AMANDA *closes her eyes and lowers her head. Count ten.*)

AMANDA: What are we going to do, what is going to become of us, what is the

(10) future?

LAURA: Has something happened, Mother? (AMANDA *draws a long breath and takes out the handkerchief again. Dabbing process.*) Mother,

(15) has—something happened?

AMANDA: I'll be all right in a minute, I'm just bewildered— *(Count five)*—by life. . . .

LAURA: Mother, I wish that you would tell

(20) me what's happened!

AMANDA: As you know, I was supposed to be inducted into my office at the D.A.R. [Daughters of the American Revolution, a patriotic society] this

(25) afternoon. But I stopped off at Rubicam's business college to speak to your teachers about your having a cold and ask them what progress they thought you were making down there.

(30) LAURA: Oh. . . .

AMANDA: I went to the typing instructor and introduced myself as your mother. She didn't know who you were. "Wingfield," she said. "We don't have

(35) any such student enrolled at the school!"

I assured her she did, that you had been going to classes since early in January.

(40) "I wonder," she said, "if you could be talking about that terribly shy little girl who dropped out of school after only a few days' attendance?"

Tennessee Williams, *The Glass Menagerie.*

1. Based on the excerpt, why does Laura <u>most likely</u> ask her mother not to stare (line 5)?

   (1) She wants to embarrass her mother.
   (2) She is a very shy person.
   (3) She is angry at her mother.
   (4) She is upset about school.
   (5) She wants to change the subject.

2. Which of the following <u>best</u> explains why Amanda says the lines beginning "What are we going to do . . . " (lines 8–10)?

   (1) She is upset about losing Laura's tuition money.
   (2) She wants to make a dramatic effect.
   (3) She wants to comfort Laura.
   (4) She fears a tragedy has happened.
   (5) She is proud of Laura.

3. Which of the following <u>best</u> explains the function of the stage directions *"Count ten"* (line 7) and *"Count five"* (line 17)?

   These lines show that

   (1) Amanda is asking Laura to count in order to calm her down
   (2) Amanda is waiting for Laura to speak
   (3) Laura is trying to calm Amanda down
   (4) Amanda is pausing while she thinks of what to say next
   (5) Amanda feels faint and is pausing to breathe

Questions 4 through 8 refer to the following excerpt from a play.

WHAT KIND OF TEACHER IS SISTER MARY AGNES?

SISTER MARY AGNES: Well, Mary Thomas, don't you think you should get those bangs cut? I remember a story about a young lady who had a hairdo

(5) she liked so much . . . I believe you would call it a beehive. How can you see from behind all that hair? Well, she never washed her hair because she didn't want to ruin it. About two months

(10) later, she went to the doctor's . . . Eugene, could you please stop shaking him? Thank you . . .

MARIA THERESA: What happened to the girl with the beehive?

(15) SISTER MARY AGNES: Who? . . . oh . . . yes. Well, when she went to the doctor's he found bugs all in her hair and they were eating her brains out. Now we all want to see your pretty

(20) face, don't we, dear?

COLLEEN: Yeah, we all want to see her pretty face, don't we, Eddie?

MARIA THERESA: Drop dead. I think it's time to change classes, Sister.

(25) SISTER MARY AGNES: Thank you dear. Let me check.

ELIZABETH: Sister, are you looking for something? Are you looking for your glasses?

(30) SISTER MARY AGNES: I know I put them some where . . . now, just one second . . .

ELIZABETH: Sister, they are around your neck.

(35) SISTER MARY AGNES: So they are. I put them there so I wouldn't forget them. Isn't that funny?

MARIA THERESA: Hysterical, we're all dying. Let me out of here.

(40) SISTER MARY AGNES: It *is* time to change classes. Would you like me to walk you?

COLLEEN: No. It's right across the hall. Hey, Sister, thanks again. (COLLEEN

(45) *and* MARIA THERESA *exit.*)

SISTER MARY AGNES: Have a nice afternoon. Good bye, Loretta.

ELIZABETH: I said my name is Elizabeth.

Casey Kurti, *Catholic School Girls.*

4. Which of the following words best describes Sister Mary Agnes?

   (1) creative
   (2) aggressive
   (3) hopeful
   (4) efficient
   (5) absentminded

5. Based on the excerpt, if Sister Mary Agnes were to wear regular street clothes, which type would she be most likely to wear?

   (1) bright and bold clothing
   (2) fashionable clothing
   (3) neat and clean clothing
   (4) comfortable clothing
   (5) youthful clothing

6. Which of the following words best describes the mood in this scene?

   (1) lighthearted
   (2) tense
   (3) distressed
   (4) serene
   (5) joyous

7. Based on the excerpt, which of the following statements best describes what Maria Theresa wants?

   (1) to get a new hairdo
   (2) to earn Sister Mary Agnes's affections
   (3) to be liked by her classmates
   (4) to change classes
   (5) to get revenge on Eddie

8. Why does Sister Mary Agnes tell the story about the beehive hairdo?

   (1) to frighten the class
   (2) to see if she can make the class laugh
   (3) to get Maria Theresa to cut her hair
   (4) to threaten Maria Theresa
   (5) to fill up the last few minutes of class time

Answers start on page 322.

GED Mini-Test • Lesson 26

Directions: This is a ten-minute practice test. After ten minutes, mark the last question you finished. Then complete the test and check your answers. If most of your answers were correct, but you didn't finish, try to work faster next time. Choose the one best answer to each question.

Questions 1 through 10 refer to the following excerpt from a play.

WHY DO TROY AND CORY DISAGREE?

TROY: I'm through with it now. You go on and get them boards. *(Pause.)* Your mama tells me you got recruited by a college football team? Is that right?

(5) CORY: Yeah. Coach Zellman say the recruiter gonna be coming by to talk to you. Get you to sign the permission papers.

TROY: I thought you supposed to be
(10) working down there at the A&P. Ain't you suppose to be working down there after school?

CORY: Mr. Stawicki say he gonna hold my job for me until after the football
(15) season. Say starting next week I can work weekends.

TROY: I thought we had an understanding about this football stuff? You suppose to keep up with your chores and hold
(20) that job down at the A&P. Ain't been around here all day on a Saturday. Ain't none of your chores done . . . and now you telling me you done quit your job.

(25) CORY: I'm gonna be working weekends.

TROY: You damn right you are! And ain't no need for nobody coming around here to talk to me about signing nothing.

(30) CORY: Hey, Pop . . . you can't do that. He's coming all the way from North Carolina.

TROY: I don't care where he coming from. The white man ain't gonna let you get
(35) nowhere with that football no way. You go on and get your book-learning so you can work yourself up in that A&P or learn how to fix cars or build houses or something, get you a trade. That
(40) way you have something can't nobody take away from you.

You go on and learn how to put your hands to some good use. Besides hauling people's garbage.

(45) CORY: I get good grades, Pop. That's why the recruiter wants to talk with you. You got to keep up your grades to get recruited. This way I'll be going to college. I'll get a chance . . .

(50) TROY: First you gonna get your butt down there to the A&P and get your job back.

CORY: Mr. Stawicki done already hired somebody else 'cause I told him I was
(55) playing football.

TROY: You a bigger fool than I thought . . . to let somebody take away your job so you can play some football. Where you gonna get your money to take out your
(60) girlfriend and whatnot? What kind of foolishness is that to let somebody take away your job?

CORY: I'm still gonna be working weekends.

(65) TROY: Naw . . . naw. You getting your butt out of here and finding you another job.

CORY: Come on, Pop! I got to practice. I can't work after school and play football too. The team needs me.
(70) That's what Coach Zellman say . . .

TROY: I don't care what nobody else say. I'm the boss . . . you understand? I'm the boss around here. I do the only saying what counts.

August Wilson, *Fences.*

1. Of what does Troy accuse Cory?

   (1) receiving failing grades in school
   (2) refusing to speak to the recruiter
   (3) spending too much money
   (4) not doing his chores
   (5) working too many hours at the A&P

2. How does Troy feel about Cory's decision?

   (1) Troy is quite pleased with Cory's choice.
   (2) Troy is happy for Cory but worries about his studies.
   (3) Troy is opposed to Cory's desire to play football.
   (4) Troy thinks Cory does not have enough money for college.
   (5) Troy believes Cory should quit school and work full time at the A&P.

3. Which of the following best describes what Cory wants?

   (1) to become the manager of the A&P
   (2) to go to college
   (3) to marry his girlfriend
   (4) to do whatever Troy thinks is best
   (5) to find another job

4. Which of the following phrases best describes the overall mood of the excerpt?

   (1) resigned and depressed
   (2) angry and bitter
   (3) forbidding and frightening
   (4) sorrowful and painful
   (5) tense and disharmonious

5. Based on the excerpt, which of the following is most likely to happen?

   (1) Cory's mother will tell the recruiter not to visit.
   (2) Mr. Stawicki will fire Cory from the A&P.
   (3) Corey will decide to stop doing his chores.
   (4) Troy will change his mind and talk to the recruiter.
   (5) Cory will try to reason with Troy.

6. Who is the central character in the excerpt?

   (1) Mr. Stawicki
   (2) Cory
   (3) Cory's coach
   (4) Cory's mother
   (5) Troy

7. Which of the following most likely causes Troy to make the statement, "The white man ain't gonna let you get nowhere with that football no way" (lines 34–35)?

   (1) Troy will say anything to persuade Cory to return to his job at the A&P.
   (2) Troy knows Coach Zellman and knows he is unfair.
   (3) Troy knows from experience that playing college sports gets students nowhere.
   (4) Troy has been treated unfairly in the past and is warning Cory.
   (5) Troy fears that Cory is not talented enough to make the team.

8. Which piece of advice is Troy most likely to give his son?

   (1) A parent must be hard on a child to avoid spoiling him or her.
   (2) A leader often does not know any more than the person following.
   (3) What is good for one person is good for everyone.
   (4) A true friend is always available to help you.
   (5) Seeking immediate gain can cost you later on.

9. What is the main reason Troy wants Cory to continue working at the A&P?

   (1) because he cannot afford Cory's tuition
   (2) so Cory can continue to do his chores
   (3) so Cory will have a job that cannot be taken away
   (4) so Cory will not waste time going to college
   (5) because football is a dangerous sport

10. Which of the following best describes Mr. Stawicki's attitude toward Cory?

    (1) amused
    (2) unappreciative
    (3) skeptical
    (4) displeased
    (5) supportive

Answers start on page 322.

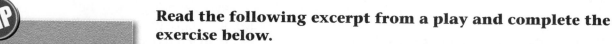

Lesson 27

GED SKILL Understanding Motivation

motivation
the reason a character does or says something

Motivation is the reason a character behaves a certain way. A character's motivation tells who he or she really is. One way in which plays differ from novels and short stories is that plays are told entirely through dialogue and action. In a play, the characters' thoughts are not directly revealed to the reader or audience. As a result, the motivations of the characters are sometimes more difficult to identify.

To understand what motivates the characters in a play, pay attention to what they say. Ask yourself why a character makes certain statements and what he or she hopes to achieve by making them. Characters' motivations can be found not only in what they say, however, but also in what they do. Stage directions, which may describe a character's actions, can also provide clues to motivation.

Read the following excerpt from a play and complete the exercise below.

JESSIE *(Standing behind* MAMA *now, holding her shoulders):* Now, when you hear the shot, I don't want you to come in. First of all, you won't be able to get in by yourself, but I don't want you trying. Call Dawson, then call the police, and then call Agnes. And then you'll need something to do till somebody gets here, so wash the hot-chocolate pan. You wash that pan till you hear the doorbell ring and I don't care if it's an hour, you keep washing that pan.
MAMA: I'll make my calls and then I'll just sit. I won't need something to do. What will the police say?

Marsha Norman, *'night, Mother.*

TIP

Discover a character's motivation by asking yourself, "Why is this character behaving this way?" Then try to figure out the true reason behind the character's words or actions.

1. Put a check mark next to the <u>most likely</u> motivation for the daughter to tell her mother to wash the pan.

   _____ a. She does not want her mother to hear the police arriving.

   _____ b. She does not want her mother to think about the shot.

   _____ c. She does not want her mother to get into trouble.

2. Put a check mark next to the statement that better describes the daughter's feelings toward her mother.

   _____ a. She cares about her mother.

   _____ b. She feels her mother is too nosy.

You were correct if you chose *option b* for question 1 and *option a* for question 2. The daughter seems to care about her mother. This is indicated both by her gesture of holding her mother's shoulders and by her words, which show concern for her mother's well-being.

Unit 4: Understanding Drama

GED SKILL FOCUS

Read the following excerpt from a play and complete the exercise below.

GUSTA: *(suddenly)* Eddie, there's a bird on the ceiling.

EDDIE: It's a *flamingo.*

GUSTA: All right, I'll believe you; it's a flamingo. Why is it on the ceiling?

EDDIE: Gonna be like a *symbol* for us, Gloria, for the place; like I was tellin' Joey: Borden's got a cow, Billingsley's got a stork, Firestone—

GUSTA: How much did the dopey bird cost?

EDDIE: It just so happens this hand-made, hand-crafted, sixty-eight-light Flamingo Chandelier is the only one of its kind in the world.

GUSTA: Two is hard to imagine. *(She goes to Kitchen stove; Eddie continues, high with "Opening Day" fever)*

EDDIE: Gloria, I'm talkin' to Joey this mornin', somethin' *come* to me—somethin' for the *place,* somethin' we never *tried* before—a *word, one* word, a magic word's gonna make all the difference!

GUSTA: Fire.

EDDIE: Advertising!

GUSTA: We'll burn it down and get the insurance. The Moose *alone* puts us in clover. *(Exits deep into Kitchen, out of sight)*

EDDIE: *Advertising!* Advertising, kiddo! *(Exits into Kitchen, pursuing her, inspired; we hear his voice from inside, his enthusiasm building)* I'm talkin' about a small ad, classy, in there with the Clubs, Gloria—just a picture of a flamingo, one word: *"Lounge,"* under it; under that "Six Eighty-One Canal"—like everybody *knows* already, like it's *in,* Gloria—

CHARLIE: *(during above, rising from booth, moving towards Kitchen)* Leave her alone, Pop, leave her *alone,* it's never gonna *happen*—

Herb Gardner, *Conversations With My Father.*

1. Match the name of each character to his or her main motivation for speaking by writing the correct letter in the space provided.

   a. Eddie   b. Gusta   c. Charlie

   _____ wants to express doubt about someone else's behavior

   _____ is determined to prevent someone from taking a certain action

   _____ hopes to persuade someone to share a certain viewpoint

2. When Gusta asks Eddie how much the flamingo cost, he does not answer her question directly. What motivates him to answer the way he does? Place a check mark next to the two <u>most likely</u> reasons.

   _____ a. He wants to hide from her exactly how expensive the flamingo was.

   _____ b. He wants to suggest that he has plenty of money left over.

   _____ c. He wants to prove to her that the flamingo was worth the price he paid.

Answers start on page 323.

Directions: Choose the <u>one best answer</u> to each question.

<u>Questions 1 through 4</u> refer to the following excerpt from a play.

HOW CAN ANNIE AND HELEN WORK TOGETHER?

ANNIE: It's hopeless here. I can't teach a child who runs away.

KELLER: *(nonplused)* Then—do I understand you—propose—

(5) ANNIE: Well, if we all agree it's hopeless, the next question is what—

KATE: Miss Annie. I am not agreed. I think perhaps you—underestimate Helen.

ANNIE: I think everybody else here does.

(10) KATE: She did fold her napkin. She learns, she learns, do you know she began talking when she was six months old? She could say "water." Not really— "wahwah." "Wahwah," but she meant

(15) water, she knew what it meant, and only six months old, I never saw a child so—bright, or outgoing—It's still in her, somewhere, isn't it? You should have seen her before her illness, such

(20) a good-tempered child—

ANNIE: *(agreeably)* She's changed.

KATE: Miss Annie, put up with it. And with us.

KELLER: Us!

(25) KATE: Please? Like the lost lamb in the parable, I love her all the more.

ANNIE: Mrs. Keller, I don't think Helen's worst handicap is deafness or blindness. I think it's your love.

(30) And pity.

KELLER: Now what does that mean?

ANNIE: All of you here are so sorry for her you've kept her—like a pet, why, even a dog you housebreak. No wonder

(35) she won't let me come near her. It's useless for me to try to teach her language or anything else here. I might as well—

KATE: *(cuts in)* Miss Annie, before you

(40) came we spoke of putting her in an asylum.

William Gibson, *The Miracle Worker.*

1. Which of the following best explains why Kate says, "She did fold her napkin" (line 10)?

   (1) She is jealous of Helen.
   (2) She doesn't want Annie to leave.
   (3) She does not want to care for Helen.
   (4) She is angry at Mr. Keller.
   (5) She is disappointed in Helen.

2. Based on what the other characters say about Helen, which of the following words <u>best</u> describes her behavior?

   (1) uncooperative
   (2) shy
   (3) enthusiastic
   (4) helpful
   (5) friendly

3. Which of the following lines from the excerpt <u>best</u> indicates that Annie thinks there is hope for Helen?

   (1) "I think everybody else here does." (line 9)
   (2) "She's changed." (line 21)
   (3) "Mrs. Keller, I don't think Helen's worst handicap is deafness or blindness." (lines 27–29)
   (4) "I can't teach a child who runs away." (lines 1–2)
   (5) "No wonder she won't let me come near her." (lines 34–35)

4. Which of the following statements about children with disabilities would Annie <u>most likely</u> agree?

   (1) They cannot be taught language.
   (2) They should be given what they want.
   (3) They must be taught, not pitied.
   (4) They are often better off in an asylum.
   (5) They should be treated like pets.

Questions 5 through 9 refer to the following excerpt from a play.

WHAT DO THESE MEN HAVE IN COMMON?

LUKE: You play piano like I dreamed you
would.
DAVID: I been finding out lately you was
pretty good. Mama never let us keep a
(5)   phonograph. I just didn't never hear
any of your records—until here lately.
You was right up there with the best,
Jellyroll Morton and Louis Armstrong
and cats like that. . . . You never come
(10)   to look for us. Why?
LUKE: I started to. I wanted to. I thought of
it lots of times.
DAVID: Why didn't you never do it? Did
you think it was good riddance we was
(15)   gone?
LUKE: I was hoping you wouldn't never
think that, never.
DAVID: I wonder what you expected me to
think. I remembered you, but couldn't
(20)   never talk about you. I use to hear
about you sometime, but I couldn't
never say, That's my daddy. I was too
ashamed. I remembered how you used
to play for me sometimes. That was
(25)   why I started playing the piano. I used
to go to sleep dreaming about the way
we'd play together one day, me with my
piano and you with your trombone.
LUKE: David. David.
(30) DAVID: You never come. You never come
when you could do us some good. You
come now, now when you can't do
nobody any good. Every time I think
about it, think about *you,* I want to
(35)   break down and cry like a baby. You
make me—ah! You make me feel
so bad.
LUKE: Son—don't try to get away from
the things that hurt you. The things that
(40)   hurt you—sometimes that's all you
got. You got to learn to live with those
things—and—use them.

James Baldwin, *The Amen Corner.*

5. What does David seem to want most?

    (1) to learn why his father became a musician
    (2) to forget about his father for good
    (3) to be a better musician than his father
    (4) to find out what his father thinks of him
    (5) to understand his father's absence

6. What does David most likely mean when he says, "You was right up there with the best" (line 7)?

    (1) Luke was one of David's heroes.
    (2) Luke lived in a good neighborhood.
    (3) Luke was a great musician.
    (4) Mama hid Luke's records among the others.
    (5) Mama admired Luke a great deal.

7. What is the most likely reason that David started playing piano?

    (1) He had a natural talent for it.
    (2) He needed to occupy his free time.
    (3) He wanted to be a famous musician.
    (4) He was encouraged by his mother.
    (5) He wanted to be connected to his father.

8. Which of the following attitudes best describes David's feelings toward his father?

    (1) admiring and respectful
    (2) hurt and angry
    (3) indifferent and numb
    (4) hopeful and questioning
    (5) ashamed and embarrassed

9. What is the overall mood of this piece?

    (1) calm and comforting
    (2) violent and disruptive
    (3) gloomy and mournful
    (4) lighthearted and playful
    (5) emotional and earnest

Answers start on page 323.

Directions: This is a ten-minute practice test. After ten minutes, mark the last question you finished. Then complete the test and check your answers. If most of your answers were correct, but you didn't finish, try to work faster next time. Choose the one best answer to each question.

Questions 1 through 11 refer to the following excerpt from a play.

WHAT IS ESPERANZA SEARCHING FOR?

ESPERANZA: . . . Ramón, we're not getting weaker. We're stronger than ever before. *(He snorts with disgust.)* They're getting weaker. They thought
(5) they could break our picket line. And they failed. And now they can't win unless they pull off something big, and pull it off fast.

RAMÓN: Like what?

(10) ESPERANZA: I don't know. But I can feel it coming. It's like . . . like a lull before the storm. Charley Vidal says . . .

RAMÓN: *(exploding)* Charley Vidal says! Don't throw Charley Vidal up to me!

(15) ESPERANZA: Charley's my friend. I need friends. *(She looks at him strangely.)* Why are you afraid to have me as your friend?

RAMÓN: I don't know what you're talking
(20) about.

ESPERANZA: No, you don't. Have you learned nothing from this strike? Why are you afraid to have me at your side? Do you still think you can have dignity
(25) only if I have none?

RAMÓN: You talk of dignity? After what you've been doing?

ESPERANZA: Yes. I talk of dignity. The Anglo bosses look down on you, and
(30) you hate them for it. "Stay in your place, you dirty Mexican"—that's what they tell you. But why must you say to me "Stay in *your* place"? Do you feel better having someone lower than you?

(35) RAMÓN: Shut up, you're talking crazy. *(But ESPERANZA moves right up to him, speaking now with great passion.)*

ESPERANZA: Whose neck shall I stand on, to make me feel superior? And
(40) what will I get out of it? I don't want anything lower than I am. I'm low

enough already. I want to rise. And push everything up with me as I go. . . .

RAMÓN: *(fiercely)* Will you be still?

(45) ESPERANZA: *(shouting)* And if you can't understand this you're a fool— because you can't win this strike without me! You can't win *anything* without me! *(He seizes her shoulder
(50) with one hand, half raises the other to slap her. ESPERANZA'S body goes rigid. She stares straight at him, defiant and unflinching. RAMÓN drops his hand.)*

(55) ESPERANZA: That would be the old way. Never try it on me again—never.

Michael Wilson, *Salt of the Earth.*

1. Based on the excerpt, what does dignity mean to Esperanza?

    (1) having good friends
    (2) walking a picket line
    (3) having self-respect
    (4) being independent
    (5) having power over others

2. If Esperanza were a business executive, with which of the following statements would she most likely agree?

    It is important for a business

    (1) to be successful no matter whom it hurts
    (2) to grow without driving others out of business
    (3) to be stronger than its competitors
    (4) to avoid conflict
    (5) to avoid partnerships with other companies

3. To which of the following does Esperanza compare the way Ramón treats her?

   to the way

   (1) adults treat children
   (2) the workers treat the bosses
   (3) the Anglos treat the Mexicans
   (4) humans treat animals
   (5) the Mexicans treat the Anglos

4. Based on this excerpt, what can you infer about Ramón's beliefs?

   (1) No one should go on strike.
   (2) Workers and bosses are allies.
   (3) Men and women cannot be friends.
   (4) Women should express themselves.
   (5) Men and women together will win the strike.

5. Which of the following statements best expresses the theme of this excerpt?

   (1) Human dignity is worth defending.
   (2) People should try to avoid disputes.
   (3) Strikes should be handled reasonably and fairly.
   (4) Winning can seem like the most important goal.
   (5) Ramón and Esperanza disagree on fundamental issues.

6. Which of the following is Ramón most likely referring to when he says, "You talk of dignity? After what you've been doing?" (lines 26–27)?

   (1) Esperanza has been doing work that is not respected.
   (2) Esperanza has recently embarrassed herself.
   (3) Esperanza is not a serious person.
   (4) Esperanza is not trustworthy.
   (5) Esperanza is friends with disreputable people.

7. What decision does Esperanza make in lines 55–56?

   (1) She will leave Ramón soon.
   (2) She will use others to help her get ahead.
   (3) She will urge the workers to end the strike.
   (4) She will not allow Ramón to hit her.
   (5) She will become Ramón's friend.

8. Which of the following is most likely to happen in Ramón and Esperanza's future?

   (1) Ramón and Esperanza's relationship will change.
   (2) The strike will fail because they cannot agree.
   (3) Ramón will become friends with the Anglos.
   (4) Esperanza will become mentally unstable.
   (5) Ramón and Esperanza will continue with the old way of doing things.

9. Which of the following best represents Esperanza's attitude toward the strike?

   (1) She has doubts about its effectiveness.
   (2) She firmly supports it and its goals.
   (3) She opposes it under any conditions.
   (4) She believes the opposing side is getting stronger.
   (5) She believes that Ramón could win it alone.

10. What is the tone of the excerpt?

    (1) heated
    (2) annoyed
    (3) conversational
    (4) respectful
    (5) inquisitive

11. Based on the stage directions for Ramón, which of the following images best describes his personality?

    (1) a brewing pot of coffee
    (2) an active volcano
    (3) an exhausted animal
    (4) a gust of wind in a sail
    (5) an old shoe

Answers start on page 324.

Lesson 28

GED SKILL Interpreting Theme

theme
the central idea in a piece of literature

TIP

To identify theme, ask yourself, "What does this play say about human nature? What is the most important point the playwright is trying to make?"

The central idea in a play is called the **theme.** The theme is the underlying meaning that the playwright wants the reader or audience to understand about the play. An example of a theme is "Friendship is based on understanding." It is not enough to say that the theme is friendship. You have to go one step further and answer the question, "What is it about friendship that the playwright is trying to say?" Usually, the playwright does not state the theme directly, so it is up to the reader or audience to decide what it is.

Remember, the theme is different from the general topic or a plot summary of the play. For example, imagine a play with two main characters—John, a Republican, and Cynthia, a Democrat. The general topic might be a romance between the two characters. But the theme of this play might be "Love can overcome any differences."

Read the following excerpt from a play and complete the exercise below.

PETER: Are you in love?
SCOOP: Excuse me?
PETER: I like to think that when two people our age get married, they are in love.
HEIDI *(takes Peter's arm):* Peter's very romantic.
SCOOP: I see. Are you an item now?
HEIDI: No.
PETER *(louder):* Yes.
SCOOP: Makes sense. Lisa marries a nice Jewish lawyer; Heidi marries a warm Italian pediatrician. It's all interchangeable, isn't it? To answer your question am I in love, sure, why not?
HEIDI *(squeezes Peter's hand):* Why not?

Wendy Wasserstein, *The Heidi Chronicles.*

Put a check mark next to the statement that <u>best</u> identifies the theme of this excerpt.

_____ a. Scoop and Heidi are old friends.

_____ b. Peter is too outspoken.

_____ c. Reacting defensively with friends is not productive.

_____ d. Love is a delicate subject between some friends.

You were correct if you chose *option d.* The friends seem to want to talk about their love lives, but also seem cautious about revealing too much. This is the underlying message of the excerpt.

Read the following excerpt from a play and complete the exercise below.

AMBASSADOR: . . . Axel, most fathers start their sons in the mail room and let them work their way up. I started you on top and you worked your way to the mail room. This Embassy is a clean start for you. If it's not run letter perfect, I'll fire you and if your own father fires you—it's the end of the line. Goodbye. *(Exits.)*

MAGEE: Have a good flight, Dad. *(Crosses to door and calls.)* Mr. Kilroy!

KILROY: *(Entering.)* You called?

MAGEE: For the next two weeks I am in charge of this Embassy. Business will go on as usual and it would mean a great deal to me to have your full cooperation.

KILROY: Your father should have known better than to leave in charge a man who was asked to leave Africa.

MAGEE: That's not fair. Some of the best men in the foreign service have at one time or another been recalled from a country.

KILROY: Africa is a continent. You've been recalled from an entire continent. And what about Japan, you never mention that, or the Soviet Union—you managed to cover that up, too.

MAGEE: You know I've had some bad breaks careerwise.

KILROY: *(Accusatory.)* And you were hung in effigy in Panama!

MAGEE: I admitted I was!

KILROY: Yes, but you didn't say it was by our own Embassy! *(Phone rings.* KILROY *lets* MAGEE *get it.)*

MAGEE: *(Into phone.)* Yes? Yes, this is the American Embassy. . . .

Woody Allen, *Don't Drink the Water.*

1. Put a check mark next to the statement that best expresses the theme of this excerpt.

   _____ a. The conflict between Magee and Kilroy will never be resolved.

   _____ b. Magee's father reprimands his son at the Embassy.

   _____ c. An incompetent employee can cause unfortunate but humorous situations.

   _____ d. The U.S. foreign service made mistakes by continuing to hire Magee.

2. Write two details from the excerpt that support the theme.

   _____

   _____

3. Put a check mark next to the phrase that better identifies the topic of this excerpt, as opposed to the theme.

   _____ a. father-son relationships

   _____ b. inability to perform a job

Answers start on page 325.

Directions: Choose the one best answer to each question.

Questions 1 through 5 refer to the following excerpt from a play.

IS MRS. DUDGEON PLEASED?

MRS. DUDGEON: . . . Oh, it's you, is it, Mrs. Anderson?

JUDITH: (very politely—almost patronizingly) Yes. Can I do anything
(5)   for you, Mrs. Dudgeon? Can I help to get the place ready before they come to read the will?

MRS. DUDGEON: (stiffly) Thank you, Mrs. Anderson, my house is always ready
(10)   for anyone to come into.

JUDITH: (with complacent amiability) Yes, indeed it is. Perhaps you had rather I did not intrude on you just now.

MRS. DUDGEON: Oh, one more or less
(15)   will make no difference this morning, Mrs. Anderson. Now that you're here, you'd better stay. If you wouldn't mind shutting that door! (JUDITH smiles, implying "How stupid of me!" and shuts
(20)   it with an exasperating air of doing something pretty and becoming.) That's better. I must go and tidy myself a bit. I suppose you don't mind stopping here to receive anyone that
(25)   comes in until I'm ready.

JUDITH: (graciously giving her leave) Oh yes, certainly. Leave that to me, Mrs. Dudgeon; and take your time. (She hangs up her cloak and bonnet.)

(30) MRS. DUDGEON: (half sneering) I thought that would be more in your way than getting the house ready.

George Bernard Shaw, The Devil's Disciple.

1. Based on this excerpt, what do Mrs. Dudgeon's words and actions indicate?

   (1) She is patient and long-suffering.
   (2) She is gentle and easygoing.
   (3) She is pure and high-minded.
   (4) She is stingy and tightfisted.
   (5) She is rude and touchy.

2. Based upon the stage directions, which of the following is the best description of Judith?

   (1) sweet and self-sacrificing
   (2) smug and self-satisfied
   (3) high-strung and sensitive
   (4) depressed and withdrawn
   (5) angry and defensive

3. Which of the following best states the main idea of this excerpt?

   (1) Judith has arrived very early for a party at Mrs. Dudgeon's.
   (2) Judith is an unexpected guest for the reading of a will.
   (3) Judith and Mrs. Dudgeon are trying to become friends.
   (4) Judith's politeness has made an awkward meeting easier.
   (5) Mrs. Dudgeon is pleased that Judith has come to help.

4. Which of the following best describes the mood of this excerpt?

   (1) mournful
   (2) tense
   (3) lighthearted
   (4) suspenseful
   (5) tender

5. What is the most likely reason that Mrs. Dudgeon says, "I thought that would be more in your way than getting the house ready" (lines 30–32)?

   (1) She did not hear Judith's offer to help clean.
   (2) She thinks Judith is excellent at greeting people.
   (3) She believes Judith is untidy.
   (4) She thinks Judith was insincere about wanting to clean.
   (5) She wants to be kind to Judith.

Questions 6 through 10 refer to the following excerpt from a play.

WHAT PROBLEM DOES THIS FAMILY HAVE?

JOSEPHINE: Good morning, dear. (EVEYLN *turns on stove to heat coffee,* THAYER *takes a large mixing bowl and pours cornflakes in it, then*
(5)   *adds milk and sugar*) What do you think I did? I overslept! Haven't slept past six-thirty in I don't know how long.
EVELYN: You were up late.
JOSEPHINE: Oh, I usually am. I go to bed
(10)   with a good book and I can't stop for hours. Funny, isn't it? Puts most people to sleep. Your grandfather couldn't turn two pages before his eyes would close. But not me. I get wide
(15)   awake with excitement—even books I've read before—isn't that the limit?
EVELYN: Did you see any shooting stars?
JOSEPHINE: Don't recall any. (THAYER *exits to porch with his bowl of*
(20)   *cornflakes*)
EVELYN: I saw four or five on the way up here Friday night. I stopped to look.
JOSEPHINE: My, that's a lot of wishes! I guess I'm too old for wishes. I haven't
(25)   looked for a shooting star in many years.
EVELYN: You did last night.
JOSEPHINE: Oh no. (*shakes her head as if the idea is absurd*)
(30) EVELYN: (*puzzled, can't really believe that* JOSEPHINE *doesn't remember*) We all stayed in here talking, and you went outside. You said you were looking for shooting stars.
(35) JOSEPHINE: (*confused*) Is that right?
EVELYN: You don't remember, do you?
JOSEPHINE: You know, I don't.
EVELYN: You were telling us about how Grandfather used to rehearse his
(40)   arguments and everybody'd get in on it. (JOSEPHINE *chuckles*) You remember that, don't you?

Elizabeth Diggs, *Close Ties.*

6. What is Evelyn's attitude toward Josephine?

    (1) She is upset with Josephine.
    (2) She is fond of Josephine.
    (3) She is insensitive to Josephine.
    (4) She is indifferent to Josephine.
    (5) She is amused by Josephine.

7. Which of the following conclusions can you make about Josephine?

    (1) She tells stories that are not true.
    (2) She bores Evelyn with her stories.
    (3) She is Thayer's mother.
    (4) She is usually an early riser.
    (5) She is worried about something.

8. If Evelyn asks Josephine about her childhood, what will Josephine most likely do?

    (1) choose to talk about another topic
    (2) tell Evelyn the subject is none of her business
    (3) enjoy telling stories about her youth
    (4) not recall many memories
    (5) say she would rather read a book

9. Which of the following topics is most closely related to the theme of the excerpt?

    (1) a mother-and-daughter relationship
    (2) one of the problems of aging
    (3) a family breakfast scene
    (4) the joy of reading
    (5) wishing on shooting stars

10. How does Josephine respond to Evelyn's insistence that Josephine watched shooting stars the previous evening?

    (1) with disbelief
    (2) with humor
    (3) with fear
    (4) with anger
    (5) with indifference

Answers start on page 325.

Directions: This is a ten-minute practice test. After ten minutes, mark the last question you finished. Then complete the test and check your answers. If most of your answers were correct, but you didn't finish, try to work faster next time. Choose the <u>one best answer</u> to each question.

<u>Questions 1 through 11</u> refer to the following excerpt from a play.

DOES MEDVEDENKO LOVE MASHA?

MEDVEDENKO: Why do you always wear black?

MASHA: I am in mourning for my life. I'm unhappy.

(5) MEDVEDENKO: You unhappy? I can't understand it. Your health is good, and your father is not rich but he's well enough off. My life is much harder to bear than yours. I get twenty-three

(10) roubles a month, and that's all, and then out of that the pension fund has to be deducted, but I don't wear mourning. (They sit down.)

MASHA: It isn't a question of money. Even

(15) a beggar can be happy.

MEDVEDENKO: Yes, theoretically he can, but not when you come right down to it. Look at me, with my mother, my two sisters and my little brother, and my

(20) salary twenty-three roubles in all. Well, people have to eat and drink, don't they? Have to have tea and sugar? Have tobacco? So it just goes round and round.

(25) MASHA: (Glancing towards the stage) The play will begin soon.

MEDVEDENKO: Yes. The acting will be done by Nina Zaretchny and the play was written by Constantine

(30) Gavrilovitch. They are in love with each other, and today their souls are mingled in a longing to create some image both can share and true to both. But my soul and your soul can't find any

(35) ground to meet on. You see how it is. I love you; I can't stay at home because I keep wishing so for you; and so every day I walk four miles here and four miles back and meet with nothing but

(40) indifference on your side. That's only natural. I've got nothing, we're a big family. Who wants to marry a man who can't even feed himself?

MASHA: Fiddlesticks! (She takes snuff)

(45) Your love touches me, but I can't return it, that's all. (Offers him snuff) Help yourself.

MEDVEDENKO: I'd as soon not. (A pause.)

(50) MASHA: My, how close it is! It must be going to storm tonight. All you do is philosophise or talk about money. You think the worst misery we can have is poverty. But I think it's a thousand

(55) times easier to go ragged and beg for bread than—But you'd never understand that—

Anton Chekov, *The Sea Gull.*

1. Which statement best describes Medvedenko's father?

   (1) He is usually at home with the family.
   (2) He is out of town on business.
   (3) He works hard all day.
   (4) He is sick at home.
   (5) He does not live with the family.

2. Which of the following phrases <u>best</u> describes Medvedenko?

   (1) sincere and lonely
   (2) moody and arrogant
   (3) lighthearted and sweet
   (4) dull and uneducated
   (5) pathetic and victimized

3. What does Masha mean when she says that Medvedenko's love touches her (line 45)?

   (1) She is beginning to love him back.
   (2) She appreciates his feelings.
   (3) She is angry that he will not leave her alone.
   (4) She is struggling to keep her love hidden.
   (5) She is trying to give him hope for their future.

4. Which of the following best describes the relationship between Masha and Medvedenko?

    (1) one-sided love
    (2) secret love
    (3) deep friendship
    (4) mutual respect
    (5) friendly acquaintanceship

5. Which of the following statements best describes the theme developed in the excerpt?

    (1) Happiness does not depend on money.
    (2) Love is often unexpected.
    (3) Persistence will win you the one you love.
    (4) Opposite personalities attract one another.
    (5) Money makes life easier.

6. How does the statement "It must be going to storm tonight" (lines 50–51) contribute to the mood of the excerpt?

    It suggests

    (1) restlessness
    (2) ease
    (3) danger
    (4) sudden freedom
    (5) unearthly power

7. Based on the excerpt, what is the most likely meaning of "I can't stay at home because I keep wishing so for you" (lines 36–37)?

    (1) Medvedenko is unhappy at home and has abandoned his family.
    (2) Medvedenko hates himself and feels he does not deserve his home.
    (3) Medvedenko feels compelled by love to visit Masha.
    (4) Medvedenko is so cheap he will not share his wealth with his family.
    (5) Medvedenko feels guilty for seeing Masha.

8. Which of the following reasons is the most likely motivation for Medvedenko's mentioning that the actress and the playwright are in love with each other?

    (1) He thinks it will give additional meaning to the play.
    (2) He hopes the information will change Masha's feelings.
    (3) He enjoys gossiping about wealthy and famous people.
    (4) He thinks Masha will enjoy the information.
    (5) He contrasts their relationship with his relationship with Masha.

9. Why does Medvedenko think Masha will not marry him?

    (1) because she dislikes him
    (2) because he is poor
    (3) because they have nothing in common
    (4) because she is too unhappy
    (5) because he worries too much

10. Which of the following is the most likely reason that Medvedenko refuses the snuff?

    (1) He does not like to use it.
    (2) He knows the play is about to begin.
    (3) He prefers to continue the conversation.
    (4) He is upset that Masha doesn't love him.
    (5) He doesn't want to appear to be a beggar.

11. If Medvedenko were a traveling shoe salesman, what kind would he most likely be?

    (1) He would be persistent and try to win over customers.
    (2) He would be shy and not want to bother people.
    (3) He would complain about the customers.
    (4) He would make more sales than anyone else.
    (5) He would refuse to travel long distances.

Answers start on page 326.

Unit 4 Cumulative Review Understanding Drama

Directions: Choose the <u>one best answer</u> to each question.

Questions 1 through 3 refer to the following excerpt from a play.

WHAT DOES ALCESTE THINK OF THE POEM?

ALCESTE: *(going toward the Officer).* Well, then what do you want? Come in, sir.

THE OFFICER: Sir, two words with you.

(5) ALCESTE: You may speak out, sir.

THE OFFICER: Their honors, the Marshals of France, whose commands I bear, summon you to appear before them immediately, sir.

(10) ALCESTE: Who? Me, sir?

THE OFFICER: You.

ALCESTE: And what for?

PHILINTE: *(to Alceste).* About that silly business of yours with Oronte.

(15) CÉLIMÈNE: *(to Philinte).* What?

PHILINTE: Oronte and he had some words over a certain little poem he didn't approve of. The Marshals want to nip the affair in the bud.

(20) ALCESTE: Well, *I'll* show no base compliance.

PHILINTE: You'll have to obey orders. Come, get ready.

ALCESTE: What understanding can they

(25) bring us to? Will these gentlemen condemn me to find merit in the poem we quarrel over? I won't retract a jot of what I've said of it. I find it terrible.

PHILINTE: But a little more gentleness—

(30) ALCESTE: I'll not yield an inch. The poem is execrable.

PHILINTE: You might be a little more elastic. Come on.

ALCESTE: I'm coming. But nothing will

(35) make me retract.

PHILINTE: Let's go and find out.

ALCESTE: Unless an express command from the King requires my liking the lines that cause all this trouble, by

(40) Heaven! I shall maintain that they are bad, and that any man ought to be hanged for composing them.

(To Clitandre and to Acaste who are laughing.) Damn it, gentlemen, I didn't

(45) imagine I was being so amusing!

CÉLIMÈNE: Quickly! Go where you have to go.

ALCESTE: I'm going, madam, and I'll be back here to resume our discussion.

Molière, *The Misanthrope.*

1. What is Alceste's initial reaction to being summoned by the Marshals?

   (1) anger
   (2) disbelief
   (3) joy
   (4) anxiety
   (5) fear

2. What does Philinte mean when he says to Alceste, "But a little more gentleness—" (line 29)?

   (1) Try to be a little nicer to people.
   (2) Be less indignant about the poem.
   (3) Show respect for the Marshals.
   (4) Change your mind about the poem.
   (5) Recognize the poem's gentle qualities.

3. If Alceste were the judge of a pie-baking contest, what kind of judge would he be?

   (1) He would have difficulty making a decision about the winning pie.
   (2) He would be persuaded by the choices of the other judges.
   (3) He would confidently choose the one pie that he was convinced was best.
   (4) He would pretend that all the pies were great, even if some were not.
   (5) He would choose the pie made by the person who had tried hardest.

Questions 4 through 7 refer to the following excerpt from a play.

WHAT IS THE MOTHER UPSET ABOUT?

Bridegroom's home.
BRIDEGROOM: Mother.
MOTHER: Yes.
BRIDEGROOM: I'm away now.
(5) MOTHER: Where are you going?
BRIDEGROOM: The vineyard.
MOTHER: Wait a minute.
BRIDEGROOM: What is it?
MOTHER: Take something to eat.
(10) BRIDEGROOM: Leave it mother. I'll eat grapes. Give me the knife.
MOTHER: The knife?
BRIDEGROOM: To cut the grapes.
MOTHER: The knife, the knife! Damn the
(15) knife, damn all knives, damn the devil who created knives.
BRIDEGROOM: Enough of that, mother.
MOTHER: And guns and pistols, even the tiniest little knife, even pitchforks and
(20) mattocks.
BRIDEGROOM: Yes, yes.
MOTHER: Anything that can pierce and cut a man's body. A glorious man, an angel, his mouth like a flower, who
(25) goes out to his vines or his olives, to look after them, to care for them because they are his passed down to him from his fathers—
BRIDEGROOM: Mother, that is enough.
(30) MOTHER: And he never comes back. Or he comes back only to be laid out with a palm leaf over him and a plateful of rough salt to stop him swelling in the heat. How can you carry that knife on
(35) you? Why do I keep that snake in the kitchen?
BRIDEGROOM: Have you finished?
MOTHER: If I live another hundred years I shall never be finished. First your
(40) father, fresh as a carnation, and I had him for three short years. Then your brother. How is it that something as small as a pistol or a knife can do away with a man who is like a bull? I shall
(45) never be quiet.

The months pass and the despair makes my eyes raw, it makes my hair harsh—
BRIDEGROOM: Shall we stop now,
(50) mother?

Federico García Lorca, *Blood Wedding.*

4. Which of the following statements best expresses the theme of this excerpt?

   (1) Knives are just as dangerous as other weapons.
   (2) Sons often ignore their mothers' advice.
   (3) Inherited land can bring trouble.
   (4) The mother and father loved each other.
   (5) The violent loss of family causes sadness.

5. Based on the information in this excerpt, which of the following best describes the mother's concern?

   (1) that knives and guns are dangerous
   (2) that she will never forget her tragedy
   (3) that she cannot forgive her son
   (4) that she did not really love her husband
   (5) that her second son will also be killed

6. Which of the following best describes the son's attitude towards his mother?

   (1) indifference
   (2) impatience
   (3) empathy
   (4) anger
   (5) sarcasm

7. What is the overall mood of this excerpt?

   (1) forgiving
   (2) loving
   (3) hopeful
   (4) anguished
   (5) tense

DO THESE ROOMMATES AGREE ABOUT MOST THINGS?

FELIX: . . . (Gets down on his knees, picks up chips and puts them into box.) Don't forget I cook and clean and take care of this house. I save us a lot of money,
(5) don't I?

OSCAR: Yeah, but then you keep me up all night counting it.

FELIX: (Goes to table and sweeps chips and cards into box.) Now wait a
(10) minute. We're not always going at each other. We have some fun too, don't we?

OSCAR: (Crosses to couch.) Fun? Felix, getting a clear picture on Channel Two
(15) isn't my idea of whoopee.

FELIX: What are you talking about?

OSCAR: All right, what do you and I do every night? (Takes off sneakers, dropping them on floor.)

(20) FELIX: What do we do? You mean after dinner?

OSCAR: That's right. After we've had your halibut steak and the dishes are done and the sink has been Brillo'd and
(25) the pans have been S.O.S.'d and the leftovers have been Saran-wrapped— what do we do?

FELIX: (Finishes clearing table and puts everything on top of bookcase.) Well,
(30) we read . . . we talk . . .

OSCAR: (Takes off pants and throws them on floor.) No, no. I read and you talk! . . . I try to work and you talk. . . . I take a bath and you talk. . . . I go to
(35) sleep and you talk. We've got your life arranged pretty good but I'm still looking for a little entertainment.

FELIX: (Pulling upstage kitchen chairs away from table.) What are you
(40) saying? That I talk too much?

OSCAR: (Sits on couch.) No, no. I'm not complaining. You have a lot to say. What's worrying me is that I'm beginning to listen. . . .

Neil Simon, *The Odd Couple*.

8. Which of the following sayings comes closest to stating the theme of this excerpt?

   (1) Opposites attract.
   (2) Beauty is only skin deep.
   (3) Silence is a virtue.
   (4) Home is where the heart is.
   (5) Every rose has its thorn.

9. Which of the following would Felix probably enjoy least?

   (1) trying a new recipe
   (2) napping in the afternoon
   (3) organizing his dresser drawers
   (4) balancing his checkbook
   (5) dusting his furniture

10. Which of the following statements comes closest to what Oscar means when he tells Felix, "Yeah, but then you keep me up all night counting it." (lines 6–7)?

   (1) Felix stays up too late at night.
   (2) Oscar and Felix share a bedroom.
   (3) Felix talks about the cleaning he does.
   (4) Felix talks about the money he saves.
   (5) Oscar has a bad case of insomnia.

11. Based on the information given in the excerpt, which of the following describes Oscar's fear?

   (1) Felix will stop cooking and cleaning.
   (2) Felix is not saving them money.
   (3) Felix will move somewhere else.
   (4) Oscar is getting used to Felix.
   (5) Oscar is starting to act like Felix.

 TIP A character's motivation can be revealed by the way he or she treats the other characters. Does the character speak to the other characters respectfully? Or is he or she unfriendly?

WHAT IS GERTRUDE'S RELATIONSHIP TO THE OTHER CHARACTERS?

GERTRUDE: *(Springing to her feet, and addressing the Spanish people).* I thought we were going for a stroll up the beach after lunch. *(There is* (5) *apprehension behind her words.)* You'll never digest lying on your backs, and besides you're sure to fall asleep if you don't get up right away. *(She regains her inner composure as she gives her* (10) *commands.)*

MRS. LOPEZ: *(groaning)* ¡Ay! ¡Caray! Why don't you sleep, Miss Eastman ¿Cuevas?

GERTRUDE: It's very bad for you, really. (15) Come on. Come on, everybody! Get up! You too, Alta Gracia and Quintina, get up! Come on, everybody up! *(There is a good deal of protesting while the servants and the* SOLARES *family* (20) *struggle to their feet)* I promise you you'll feel much better later on if we take just a little walk along the beach.

VIVIAN: *(Leaping to* GERTRUDE's *side in one bound)* I *love* to walk on the (25) beach! (MOLLY *too has come forward to be with her mother.)*

GERTRUDE: *(Pause. Again stifling her apprehension with a command)* You children stay here. Or take a walk along (30) the cliffs if you'd like to. But be careful!

FREDERICA: I want to be with my mother.

GERTRUDE: Well, come along, but we're only going for a short stroll. What a baby you are, Frederica Lopez.

(35) MR. SOLARES: I'll run the car up to my house and go and collect that horse I was telling you about. Then I'll catch up with you on the way back.

GERTRUDE: .You won't get much of (40) a walk.

Jane Bowles, *In the Summer House.*

TIP

Ask yourself what details bring a character to life. Does the character cover his mouth when he sneezes?

12. What is one of the reasons Gertrude gives for encouraging the others to take a walk?

   (1) She wants them to see Mr. Solares' horse.
   (2) She wants to show them the beach.
   (3) She wants to keep them from being bored.
   (4) They need to respect her wishes.
   (5) They need to get exercise.

13. Based on the information in the excerpt, who are Vivian and Molly?

   (1) Mrs. Lopez's children
   (2) Miss Solares' children
   (3) Miss Eastman's sisters
   (4) Gertrude's children
   (5) Frederica's cousins

14. Based on this excerpt, which of the following statements best describes Gertrude?

   (1) pushy and uncaring
   (2) lighthearted and kind
   (3) insecure and demanding
   (4) secretive and loyal
   (5) successful and arrogant

15. Which of the following words best describes the overall mood of the excerpt?

   (1) serious
   (2) uneasy
   (3) suspenseful
   (4) joyful
   (5) thoughtful

16. Which of the following statements best describes Gertrude's attitude toward the children?

   (1) Gertrude does not like children.
   (2) Gertrude thinks children should not associate with adults.
   (3) Gertrude would prefer to walk without the children.
   (4) Gertrude feels children are bored by adults.
   (5) Gertrude thinks children complain too much.

IS THIS MAN ACTING LIKE AN ADULT?

WALTER: I'm going out!
RUTH: Where?
WALTER: Just out of this house somewhere—
(5) RUTH: *(Getting her coat)* I'll come too.
WALTER: I don't want you to come!
RUTH: I got something to talk to you about, Walter.
WALTER: That's too bad.
(10) MAMA: *(Still quietly)* Walter Lee—*(She waits and he finally turns and looks at her)* Sit down.
WALTER: I'm a grown man, Mama.
MAMA: Ain't nobody said you wasn't
(15) grown. But you still in my house and my presence. And as long as you are—you'll talk to your wife civil. Now sit down.
RUTH: *(Suddenly)* Oh, let him go out and
(20) drink himself to death! He makes me sick to my stomach*! (She flings her coat against him)*
WALTER*: (Violently)* And you turn mine too, baby! (RUTH *goes into their*
(25) *bedroom and slams the door behind her)* That was my greatest mistake—
MAMA: *(Still quietly)* Walter, what is the matter with you?
WALTER: Matter with me? Ain't nothing
(30) the matter with *me!*
MAMA: Yes there is. Something eating you up like a crazy man. Something more than me not giving you this money. The past few years I been
(35) watching it happen to you. You get all nervous acting and kind of wild in the eyes—
(WALTER *jumps up impatiently at her words)* I said sit there now, I'm talking
(40) to you!
WALTER: Mama—I don't need no nagging at me today.

Lorraine Hansberry, *A Raisin in the Sun.*

17. Which of the following best describes the overall mood of this excerpt?

  (1) sorrowful
  (2) tense
  (3) tolerant
  (4) courageous
  (5) playful

18. Based on this excerpt, which of the following phrases best describes Walter's mother?

  (1) patient and long-suffering
  (2) hard and domineering
  (3) passive and easygoing
  (4) whiny and complaining
  (5) strong and caring

19. Which of the following best describes the relationship between Ruth and Walter?

  (1) Ruth is devoted and loving to Walter.
  (2) Walter does not want to be with Ruth.
  (3) Ruth is thinking about leaving Walter.
  (4) The couple is tired of Mama's interference.
  (5) Walter prefers his mother to Ruth.

20. If Walter were to ask Ruth to go with him, what would Ruth's response most likely be?

  (1) to refuse to speak to Walter
  (2) to get sick to her stomach
  (3) to accompany Walter and talk with him
  (4) to ask if his mother could come along
  (5) to nag at Walter regarding his behavior

21. What is Walter referring to when he says, "That was my greatest mistake—" (line 26)?

  (1) getting married to Ruth
  (2) allowing Ruth to slam the door
  (3) drinking too much
  (4) letting his mother nag him
  (5) not earning enough money

Questions 22 through 24 refer to the following excerpt from a play.

WHAT DECISION HAS MRS. BROOKS MADE AND WHY?

RUBY: (RUBY and MRS. BROOKS enter through the front door.) Girl, I sure wish I could get my hands on whoever that is keeps pushing every one of them

(5) buttons on the elevator before they get off. The old elevator door banging shut on every floor just about drove me out of my mind. I don't see how you can be so good-natured about it, Gladys.

(10) MRS. BROOKS: Sometimes I think that's my trouble, I'm too good-natured about everything.
RUBY: Ah, girl.
MRS. BROOKS: It's true, and you know it.

(15) I just let everybody push me around.
RUBY: Don't be so hard on yourself, Gladys.
MRS. BROOKS: But, girl, this morning I made up my mind, I'm leaving Mr.

(20) Brooks.
RUBY: Gladys, it's not that bad, is it? Remember it ain't the easiest thing in the world to leave a man after all these years.

(25) MRS. BROOKS: Humph. Telling me I couldn't buy a new dress for Gail's wedding; that was the last straw.
RUBY: You know, Gladys, there is such a thing as going from the refrigerator into

(30) the frying pan.
MRS. BROOKS: Oh, Ruby, be serious.
RUBY: I am just as serious as cancer. I mean, it's not as though the man won't work. Everybody knows that he ain't

(35) known to mess up a piece of money.
MRS. BROOKS: A lot of good it does me. Everything in the house is in his name. My name don't appear on nothing except the income tax deductions. . . .

(40) MRS. BROOKS: Last week I overspent buying groceries, and talking about a man carrying on! You'd have thought that seventeen cents was going to cause a panic down on Wall Street.

(45) RUBY: Now, Gladys, you know sometimes he does have good intentions.

MRS. BROOKS: My granny always said that the road to hell is paved with good intentions.

(50) RUBY: My granny always said that there's some good in everybody.
MRS. BROOKS: If there's some good in Mr. Brooks he's done done a Houdini with it, and made it disappear. 'Cause

(55) you sure can't see it.

Charlie Russell, *Five on the Black Hand Side.*

22. Which of the following sentences best describes what Mrs. Brooks' grandmother meant by "the road to hell is paved with good intentions" (lines 48–49)?

(1) Never trust people who say that they mean well.
(2) Bad things can result even when someone means well.
(3) It is obvious that Mr. Brooks was always an evil person.
(4) Spending too much money will get you into trouble.
(5) All good things will eventually disappear.

23. Based on this excerpt, which of the following statements can you infer about Mrs. Brooks?

(1) She has thought for a long time about leaving Mr. Brooks.
(2) She needs Ruby's approval before she will leave Mr. Brooks.
(3) She will not leave Mr. Brooks until she has found a job.
(4) She probably will not leave Mr. Brooks at all.
(5) She will probably move in with Ruby.

24. Which of the following best describes the theme of this excerpt?

(1) Spouses sometimes complain unnecessarily.
(2) People who work hard often do not like to spend money.
(3) Disagreements over money can affect relationships.
(4) Friends are not always supportive.
(5) Wealthy people have problems too.

Questions 25 through 27 refer to the following excerpt from a play.

WHAT IS LANE'S OPINION OF MARRIAGE?

ALGERNON: Did you hear what I was playing, Lane?

LANE: I didn't think it polite to listen, sir.

(5) ALGERNON: I'm sorry for that, for your sake. I don't play accurately—any one can play accurately—but I play with wonderful expression. As far as the piano is concerned, sentiment is my forte. I keep science for Life.

(10) LANE: Yes, sir.

ALGERNON: And, speaking of the science of Life, have you got the cucumber sandwiches cut for Lady Bracknell?

(15) LANE: Yes, sir. (Hands them on a salver.)

ALGERNON (inspects them, takes two, and sits down on the sofa) Oh . . . by the way, Lane, I see from your book that on Thursday night, when Lord

(20) Shoreman and Mr. Worthing were dining with me, eight bottles of champagne are entered as having been consumed.

LANE: Yes, sir; eight bottles and a pint.

(25) ALGERNON: Why is it that at a bachelor's establishment the servants invariably drink the champagne? I ask merely for information.

LANE: I attribute it to the superior quality

(30) of the wine, sir. I have often observed that in married households the champagne is rarely of a first-rate brand.

ALGERNON: Good heavens! Is marriage

(35) so demoralizing as that?

LANE: I believe it is a very pleasant state, sir. I have had very little experience of it myself up to the present. I have only been married once. That was in

(40) consequence of a misunderstanding between myself and a young person.

ALGERNON: (languidly) I don't know that I am much interested in your family life, Lane.

(45) LANE: No sir; it is not a very interesting subject. I never think of it myself.

ALGERNON: Very natural, I am sure. That will do, Lane, thank you.

LANE: Thank you, sir. (Goes out.)

(50) ALGERNON: Lane's views on marriage seem somewhat lax. Really, if the lower orders don't set us a good example, what on earth is the use of them? They seem, as a class, to

(55) have absolutely no sense of moral responsibility.

Oscar Wilde, *The Importance of Being Earnest.*

25. If Lane were to overhear Algernon's last comment (lines 50–56), how would he most likely respond?

He would

(1) angrily walk away
(2) try to correct Algernon
(3) try to set a better example
(4) tell the other servants
(5) pretend he did not hear it

26. On the basis of this excerpt, what most likely happened to the champagne if the servants did not drink it?

(1) Lane returned it because it was of poor quality.
(2) The servants broke several bottles.
(3) The books are incorrect and less champagne was consumed.
(4) Algernon and his dinner guests drank it.
(5) Lane is keeping the bottles for himself.

27. Later in the play, Algernon speaks with his friend, Jack, about the "business" of marriage proposals. Based on this information and on the excerpt, what is the best description of Algernon's attitude towards marriage?

(1) unromantic
(2) impractical
(3) uninterested
(4) hopeful
(5) respectful

Answers start on page 327.

Cumulative Review Performance Analysis
Unit 4 • Understanding Drama

Use the Answers and Explanations starting on page 327 to check your answers to the Unit 4 Cumulative Review. Then use the chart to figure out the skill areas in which you need more practice.

On the chart, circle the questions that you answered correctly. Write the number correct for each skill area. Add the number of questions that you got correct on the Cumulative Review. If you feel that you need more practice, go back and review the lessons for the skill areas that were difficult for you.

Questions	Number Correct	Skill Area	Lessons for Review
1, 5, 11, 12, 13, 19, 23	____/7	Comprehension	25, 26, 27
3, 9, 10, 20, 25	____/5	Application	27
2, 6, 8, 14, 16, 18, 21, 22, 26	____/9	Analysis	25, 26, 27
4, 7, 15, 17, 24, 27	____/6	Synthesis	28
TOTAL CORRECT	____/27		

About the Posttest and Simulated Test

Now that you have finished the instructional and practice pages for the book, you're ready to take the first of two tests that are found in the back of this book.

Posttest

The Posttest will let you assess how well you have mastered the content area and skills that have been reinforced throughout the units. Compare your Posttest results with your Pretest results. It is likely that some of your scores show an improvement.

However, by following the directions on the Posttest Performance Analysis chart, you can easily identify areas that you may want to review. It is common to do better in some areas than others. You can make effective use of your study time by concentrating on areas where you need more practice.

Simulated Test

The Simulated Test gives you another chance to practice your content and cognitive skills as well as your test-taking skills before you take the actual GED Test. For the Simulated Test, you may want to time yourself so you can better mimic the situation of the actual GED testing situation.

Allow some time to pass between taking the Posttest and subsequent review of selected areas before you try the Simulated Test. Doing so can provide you with useful information about how well you have learned the skills.

Complete Answers and Explanations are provided for both the Posttest and Simulated Test in order to give you useful and relevant feedback.

LANGUAGE ARTS, READING
Directions

The Language Arts, Reading Posttest consists of excerpts from fiction, nonfiction, poetry, and drama. Each excerpt is followed by multiple-choice questions about the reading material.

Read each excerpt first and then answer the questions that follow. Refer to the reading material as often as necessary in answering the questions.

Each excerpt is preceded by a "purpose question." The purpose question gives a reason for reading the material. Use these purpose questions to help focus your reading. You are not required to answer these purpose questions. They are given only to help you concentrate on the ideas presented in the reading material.

You should spend no more than 65 minutes answering the 40 questions on this posttest. Work carefully, but do not spend too much time on any one question. Do not skip any items. Make a reasonable guess when you are not sure of an answer. You will not be penalized for incorrect answers.

When time is up, mark the last item you finished. This will tell you whether you can finish the real GED Test in the time allowed. Then complete the test.

Record your answers to the questions on a copy of the answer sheet on page 348. Be sure that all required information is properly recorded on the answer sheet.

To record your answers, mark the numbered space on the answer sheet that corresponds to the answer you choose for each question on the test.

Example:

It was Susan's dream machine. The metallic blue paint gleamed, and the sporty wheels were highly polished. Under the hood, the engine was no less carefully cleaned. Inside, flashy lights illuminated the instruments on the dashboard, and the seats were covered by rich leather upholstery.

What does "It" most likely refer to in this excerpt?

(1) an airplane
(2) a stereo system
(3) an automobile
(4) a boat
(5) a motorcycle   ① ② ● ④ ⑤

The correct answer is "an automobile"; therefore, answer space 3 would be marked on the answer sheet.

Do not rest the point of your pencil on the answer sheet while you are considering your answer. Make no stray or unnecessary marks. If you change an answer, erase your first mark completely. Mark only one answer space for each question; multiple answers will be scored as incorrect. Do not fold or crease your answer sheet.

When you finish the test, use the Performance Analysis Chart on page 258 to determine whether you are ready to take the real GED Test, and, if not, which skill areas need additional review.

Adapted with permission of the American Council on Education.

Directions: Choose the one best answer to each question.

Questions 1 through 6 refer to the following excerpt from a novel.

WHAT DOES SCROOGE SEE AND HEAR AT THE CHRISTMAS PARTY?

There was first a game of blind-man's bluff. And I no more believe Topper was really blinded than I believe he had eyes in his boots. Because the way in which he
(5) went after that plump sister in the lace tucker was an outrage on the credulity of human nature. Knocking down the fire-irons, tumbling over the chairs, bumping up against the piano, smothering himself
(10) among the curtains, wherever she went, there went he. He always knew where the plump sister was. He wouldn't catch anybody else. If you had fallen up against him, as some of them did, he would have
(15) made a feint of endeavoring to seize you, which would have been an affront to your understanding; and would instantly have sidled off in the direction of the plump sister.
(20) "Here is a new game," said Scrooge. "One half hour, Spirit, only one!"
It was a Game called Yes and No, where Scrooge's nephew had to think of something, and the rest must find out what;
(25) he only answering to their questions yes or no as the case was. The fire of questioning to which he was exposed, elicited from him that he was thinking of an animal, rather a disagreeable animal, a savage animal,
(30) an animal that growled and grunted sometimes, and talked sometimes, and lived in London, and walked about the streets, and wasn't made a show of, and wasn't led by anybody, and didn't live in
(35) a menagerie, and was never killed in a market, and was not a horse, or an ass, or a cow, or a bull, or a tiger, or a dog, or a pig, or a cat, or a bear. At every new question put to him, this nephew burst
(40) into a fresh roar of laughter; and was so inexpressibly tickled, that he was obliged to get up off the sofa and stamp. At last the plump sister cried out:
"I have found it out! I know what it is,
(45) Fred! I know what it is!"
"What is it?" cried Fred.
"It's your uncle Scro-o-o-oge!"
Which it certainly was. . . .
"He has given us plenty of merriment, I
(50) am sure," said Fred, "and it would be ungrateful not to drink his health. Here is a glass of mulled wine ready to our hand at the moment; and I say, 'Uncle Scrooge!'"
"Well! Uncle Scrooge!" they cried. . . .
(55) Uncle Scrooge had become so gay and light of heart, that he would have pledged the unconscious company in return, and thanked them in an inaudible speech, if the Ghost had given him time. But the whole
(60) scene passed off in the breath of the last word spoken by his nephew; and he and the Spirit were again upon their travels.

Charles Dickens, *A Christmas Carol.*

1. Which of the following words or phrases <u>best</u> describes Topper?

   (1) athletic
   (2) single-minded
   (3) resigned
   (4) dangerous
   (5) respectable

2. Based on the information in the excerpt, if Topper went horseback riding, which of the following would he <u>most likely</u> do?

   (1) ride off by himself to get some peace and quiet
   (2) politely invite the plump sister to go with him
   (3) organize a group of riders that included the plump sister
   (4) try to spook the plump sister's horse so she would fall
   (5) challenge the other riders to a race

3. Why does Fred drink a toast to Scrooge?

   (1) Everyone at the party genuinely likes Scrooge.
   (2) Scrooge has given the party and set up the games.
   (3) Scrooge has made them laugh by being the object of a game.
   (4) Everyone is glad that Scrooge is finally dead.
   (5) He is glad that Scrooge has become lighthearted.

4. Which of the following is revealed about Scrooge in the last paragraph of the excerpt?

   He is

   (1) invisible
   (2) clumsy
   (3) furious
   (4) drunk
   (5) disguised

5. Which of the following pairs of words <u>most</u> accurately compares how Scrooge behaves during the excerpt with how the people playing the game view him?

   (1) resentful and amusing
   (2) sad and happy
   (3) playful and serious
   (4) timid and bold
   (5) joyful and unpleasant

6. Which of the following phrases <u>best</u> describes the author's style?

   (1) simple and direct
   (2) dry and scholarly
   (3) wordy but lively
   (4) solemn but profound
   (5) flat and unemotional

WHY DID MICHAEL FUREY DIE?

Her hand was warm and moist: it did not respond to his touch, but he continued to caress it just as he had caressed her first letter to him that spring morning.

(5)   —It was in the winter, she said, about the beginning of the winter when I was going to leave my grandmother's and come up here to the convent. And he was ill at the time in his lodgings in Galway and

(10)   wouldn't be let out, and his people in Oughterard were written to. He was in decline, they said, or something like that. I never knew rightly.

She paused for a moment and sighed.

(15)   —Poor fellow, she said. He was very fond of me and he was such a gentle boy. We used to go out together, walking, you know, Gabriel, like the way they do in the country. He was going to study singing only

(20)   for his health. He had a very good voice, poor Michael Furey.

—Well; and then? asked Gabriel.

—And then when it came to the time for me to leave Galway and come up to the

(25)   convent he was much worse and I wouldn't be let see him, so I wrote a letter saying I was going up to Dublin and would be back in the summer and hoping he would be better then.

(30)   She paused for a moment to get her voice under control and then went on:

—Then the night before I left I was in my grandmother's house in Nun's Island, packing up, and heard gravel thrown up

(35)   against the window. The window was so wet I couldn't see so I ran downstairs as I was and there was the poor fellow at the end of the garden, shivering.

—And did you not tell him to go back?

(40)   asked Gabriel.

—I implored of him to go home at once and told him he would get his death in the rain. But he said he did not want to live. I can see his eyes as well as well! He was

(45)   standing at the end of the wall where there was a tree.

—And did he go home? asked Gabriel.

—Yes, he went home. And when I was only a week in the convent he died and he

(50)   was buried at Oughterard where his people came from. O, the day that I heard that, that he was dead!

She stopped, choking with sobs, and, overcome by emotion, flung herself face

(55)   downward on the bed, sobbing in the quilt. Gabriel held her hand for a moment longer, irresolutely, and then, shy of intruding on her grief, let it fall gently and walked to the window.

James Joyce, "The Dead," *Dubliners.*

7. Based on the excerpt, what are Gabriel's feelings toward the woman?

   (1) He is in love with her.
   (2) He fears for her sanity.
   (3) He thinks her grief over Michael Furey is silly.
   (4) He is jealous of her relationship with Michael Furey.
   (5) He hopes that she will forget about Michael Furey.

8. What was the woman's response to Michael Furey's last visit?

   (1) She told him she loved him.
   (2) She sent him away for his own good.
   (3) She decided to leave the convent.
   (4) She planned to run away with him.
   (5) She rejected him for Gabriel.

9. What was the immediate cause of Michael Furey's death?

   (1) He had been in ill health.
   (2) He was hit by lightning.
   (3) He swam out to Nun's Island.
   (4) He stayed out in the rain.
   (5) He walked all the way to Dublin.

10. What was most likely the underlying cause of Michael Furey's death?

   (1) He had failed to become a well-known singer.
   (2) He liked to go for long walks during the night.
   (3) He did not want to live without the woman he loved.
   (4) He wanted to get back at the world for his misfortune.
   (5) He suffered from a fatal disease that finally overcame him.

11. What is the main effect of the last two sentences in the excerpt (lines 53–59)?

   (1) to show that these two people will never get along
   (2) to contrast the stormy feelings of the woman with the quiet feelings of the man
   (3) to emphasize the tragedy of Michael Furey's death
   (4) to hint that the woman is not really grieving over Michael Furey
   (5) to suggest that the woman might kill herself over Michael Furey

12. How does the woman change during the excerpt?

   She becomes

   (1) more responsive to Gabriel's touch as she tells her story
   (2) more emotional about the story she tells
   (3) angrier with Michael Furey for leaving her
   (4) more pleased with her decision to join a convent
   (5) less interested in the man she is talking to

13. Which of the following words best describes the overall mood of the excerpt?

   (1) mournful
   (2) anxious
   (3) comforting
   (4) calm
   (5) suspenseful

WHAT TYPES OF PAY INCENTIVES DO EMPLOYERS OFFER?

Years ago, the only employees offered incentive plans were sales personnel, piece workers, and top executives. Today, most large companies and many smaller

(5) firms offer an incentive package to all of their employees.

Commissions

Commissions are paid to salespeople. They are usually based on a percentage of

(10) actual sales made. Salespeople typically receive a base salary or draw that guarantees them a minimum income, which is especially important during periods when commissions might be below

(15) average. In years past, most salespeople were paid on commission. Now, most salespeople are compensated through some combination of salary and incentive bonus plan.

(20) ### Bonus plans

Bonus plans follow many different models. There may be a company-wide bonus plan wherein each employee receives the same or differing bonuses if certain criteria, such

(25) as profitability or sales goals, are met during a specific period of time—typically on an annual or monthly basis. The bonus amount is usually based on a set percentage of each employee's base

(30) salary.

Most bonuses are awarded periodically unless an exceptional achievement has been accomplished. Some bonuses are awarded upon completion of preset goals.

(35) ### Salary at-risk plans

Salary at-risk plans are widely used. They are primarily a way of shifting an existing work force or sales force to a more incentive-based remuneration plan. As an

(40) incentive, however, it doesn't necessarily work, and many participants in a salary at-risk plan aren't happy with their lot.

Essentially, in a salary at-risk plan, a base salary is not guaranteed. To earn a base

(45) salary, an individual employee or the company as a whole must reach a set sales or profit goal, or come within a range that is typically set around 85 percent. If 100 percent of the goal is reached,

(50) participants receive a bonus above the base salary. Most salary at-risk plans offer higher bonus levels for achieving higher goals.

Profit sharing

(55) Profit-sharing plans are generally applicable on a company-wide basis and are made available to all full-time employees who have been with the company for a preset amount of time.

(60) Usually the company will contribute a small percentage of its profitability to a pool, which is then divided among the eligible employees. Division is typically pro-rated according to the base salary of

(65) each participant. Profit sharing is generally, but not always, determined on an annual basis. Many companies will not make contributions to the pool unless profits reach a certain predetermined level.

Bob Adams, "Incentive Pay Options," *Streetwise Small Business Start-Up.*

14. Based on the excerpt, why are salespeople usually paid a base salary and incentive bonus instead of just a commission?

    (1) Commission amounts can vary significantly.
    (2) Earning a commission requires many long hours.
    (3) Earning a commission requires being with a company for several years.
    (4) Earning a commission requires that a company reach a certain profit level.
    (5) Commission amounts are only awarded periodically.

15. Which of the following statements best summarizes the "criteria" (line 25) that affect a bonus plan?

    (1) Employees get bonuses if the company makes money.
    (2) Employees get bonuses on a certain date each year.
    (3) Most employees are awarded bonuses automatically.
    (4) Each employee receives a bonus based on the number of hours worked.
    (5) Employees who have been with a company longer will receive larger bonuses.

16. Which of the following sentences best explains a salary at-risk plan?

    (1) Employees must reach their previous sales levels to maintain their salary.
    (2) Base salary levels depend only on individual performance.
    (3) A base salary is guaranteed to all employees.
    (4) Employees must reach a sales goal to earn a base salary.
    (5) Reaching sales goals has no effect on bonus amounts.

17. Based on the information in this excerpt, which of the following companies would a high-achieving salesperson most likely choose to work for?

    a company that

    (1) always reaches 50% of its sales goal
    (2) offers a salary at-risk bonus plan
    (3) provides a low base salary
    (4) offers bonuses that are not based on preset goals
    (5) offers all employees the same bonus

18. Which of the following phrases best describes the overall purpose of the excerpt?

    (1) to prove that incentive plans are ineffective
    (2) to provide information about incentive plans
    (3) to discourage the use of incentive plans
    (4) to promote profit-sharing incentive plans
    (5) to show that all incentive plans are equal

Questions 19 through 24 refer to the following poem.

HOW DOES THE SPEAKER FEEL?

I AM THE ONLY BEING WHOSE DOOM

I am the only being whose doom
No tongue would ask, no eye would mourn;
I never caused a thought of gloom,
A smile of joy, since I was born.

(5)   In secret pleasure, secret tears,
This changeful life has slipped away,
As friendless after eighteen years,
As lone as on my natal day.

There have been times I cannot hide,
(10) There have been times when this was drear,
When my sad soul forgot its pride
And longed for one to love me here.

But those were in the early glow
Of feelings since subdued by care;
(15) And they have died so long ago,
I hardly now believe they were.

First melted off the hope of youth,
Then fancy's rainbow fast withdrew;
And then experience told me truth
(20) In mortal bosoms never grew.

'Twas grief enough to think mankind
All hollow, servile, insincere;
But worst to trust to my own mind
And find the same corruption there.

Emily Brontë, "I am the only being whose doom."

19. Which of the following sentences best summarizes the first stanza?

The speaker

(1) would not be missed if she died
(2) wonders who would miss her if she died
(3) wishes people were kinder to her
(4) caused many people unhappiness
(5) has been unhappy since she was born

20. If the speaker visited her hometown, which of the following would most likely happen?

She would

(1) not have any friends to stay with
(2) take a friend along with her
(3) stop by to see a few close friends
(4) not have time to see all of her friends
(5) try to avoid her old friends

21. What does the speaker most likely mean by the phrase "worst to trust to my own mind / And find the same corruption there" (lines 23–24)?

(1) She refuses to trust herself.
(2) She wants to trust herself.
(3) She fears that she is corrupt.
(4) She finds others very corrupt.
(5) She knows she is not corrupt.

22. Which of the following sentences best describes the speaker's attitude towards humanity?

(1) She believes she is better than the rest of humanity.
(2) She wonders whether the majority of people are happy.
(3) She envies those people who are happy.
(4) She holds a very low opinion of humanity.
(5) She hopes humanity will change.

23. Which of the following phrases best describes the change in the speaker's emotions from youth through adulthood?

(1) skeptical, then optimistic
(2) hopeful, then unhappy
(3) satisfied, then fearful
(4) innocent, then hostile
(5) loving, then manipulative

24. Another poem by the same poet is entitled "Alone I sat; the summer day." Based on that title and on the information in "I am the only being whose doom," which of the following best describes the mood of Brontë's poems?

(1) angry
(2) inquisitive
(3) anxious
(4) content
(5) disillusioned

WHY IS MARY'S FATHER UPSET WITH HER?

Who knows who called my parents, Doc or Miss Presson. "We have to have a talk," said Daddy in his lowest voice, guiding me with a pinch of the back of my neck into
(5) the den. "It looks like, Mary Meade, that we need to talk some economics tonight."

"Yes sir," I said.

"Do you know what I mean?"

"No sir."

(10) "Economics is a big word for, uh, hmmm. Uh, money. Things about money."

I remember his hemming and hawing more than his exact words. But Daddy always kept you standing for a long time,
(15) getting to the point, and I remember that word "economics" so well from that evening that even today it gives me a catch in the stomach.

"I've been letting you charge a dollar
(20) here and there at Connell's—figured it would teach you something—but it looks like you been at it every week. And I would like to ask just why you need so many dollars. I know about the shows at the
(25) Buckhead and all, but you also have your allowance, and your money for sitting with Robert."

"Yes."

"Yes what."

(30) "Yes sir."

"I mean yes, what are you doing with the money, Mary Meade?"

I looked at Daddy and opened my mouth. Probably the only two times I've
(35) ever been as terrified as that was the time with Carson and the day before my wedding when I told Clifford Sealew that I could not go through with it. Without planning to, I had lied to Clifford, told
(40) him there was someone else.

"Well?" said my father

From my opened mouth the words slipped easy as a prayer. "I gave the money to Queen Esther."

(45) Unlike Cliff, Daddy didn't explode or break down. He said something along the lines of "I thought so" and went on to question me about Queen Esther going in Connell's with me and trying to cash
(50) checks. Then he came back around to my lie. He asked me if she'd forced me to give her money.

"Oh, no, no, no!" I saw immediately what I'd gotten into. I saw his angry look
(55) gathering, and I knew it was directed at her. "No, Daddy. I wanted to give it to her. She can't get real money for your checks. She tried, and she can't."

He said something like "So I heard" and
(60) changed into being real sweet to me. He praised me that night, which I'll always remember, and my fears subsided. We hugged and kissed and I was sent on somewhere, having learned that lying
(65) pays, while Daddy stayed in the den in his leather armchair. . . .

Elizabeth Seydel Morgan, "Economics," *Downhome*.

25. Why does Mary Meade's father think she did something wrong?

(1) She charged too much at Connell's.
(2) She spoke disrespectfully to him.
(3) She canceled her wedding to Clifford.
(4) She spent her entire allowance.
(5) She took checks from Queen Esther.

26. Which of the following best describes the father?

He is

(1) mean-spirited
(2) indecisive
(3) easily deceived
(4) a strict disciplinarian
(5) grateful to his daughter

27. How do Mary's feelings change during the course of the conversation with her father?

(1) from fear to relief
(2) from fear to regret
(3) from respect to love
(4) from respect to anger
(5) from fear to anger

28. Which of the following best describes the theme of the excerpt?

(1) Lying should rarely be forgiven.
(2) Lying sometimes has its benefits.
(3) Lying can get you more money.
(4) Lying can destroy relationships.
(5) Lying to help others is not a good idea.

29. Based on the information in this excerpt, if Mary were to learn that a friend accidentally put a dent in someone else's car, what advice would she most likely give her friend?

(1) Offer an explanation before you are confronted.
(2) Say that you were not the driver.
(3) Tell the owner exactly what happened.
(4) Talk to a lawyer before you admit guilt.
(5) Say that you swerved to avoid a child.

30. Later in the story Queen Esther is fired from her job as maid to Mary's family. Based on this information and on the excerpt, which of the following descriptions of Queen Esther is most likely true?

(1) Mary's father thinks she is untrustworthy.
(2) She is not a very good employee.
(3) She is a bad influence on Mary.
(4) She has been lying to Mary's family.
(5) Mary's father thinks she is greedy.

WHAT ARE LINDA AND WILLY ARGUING ABOUT?

LINDA: *(taking the jacket from him)* Why don't you go down to the place tomorrow and tell Howard you've simply got to work in New York?

(5) You're too accommodating, dear.

WILLY: If old man Wagner was alive I'd a been in charge of New York now! That man was a prince, he was a masterful man. But that boy of his, that Howard,

(10) he don't appreciate. When I went north the first time, the Wagner Company didn't know where New England was!

LINDA: Why don't you tell those things to Howard, dear?

(15) WILLY: *(encouraged)* I will, I definitely will. Is there any cheese?

LINDA: I'll make you a sandwich.

WILLY: No, go to sleep. I'll take some milk. I'll be up right away. The boys in?

(20) LINDA: They're sleeping. Happy took Biff on a date tonight.

WILLY: *(interested)* That so?

LINDA: It was so nice to see them shaving together, one behind the other, in the

(25) bathroom. And going out together. You notice? The whole house smells of shaving lotion.

WILLY: Figure it out. Work a lifetime to pay off a house. You finally own it, and

(30) there's nobody to live in it.

LINDA: Well, dear, life is a casting off. It's always that way.

WILLY: No, no, some people—some people accomplish something. Did Biff

(35) say anything after I went this morning?

LINDA: You shouldn't have criticized him, Willy, especially after he just got off the train. You mustn't lose your temper with him.

(40) WILLY: When the hell did I lose my temper? I simply asked him if he was making any money. Is that a criticism?

LINDA: But, dear, how could he make any money?

(45) WILLY: *(worried and angered)* There's such an undercurrent in him. He became a moody man. Did he apologize when I left this morning?

LINDA: He was crestfallen, Willy. You know

(50) how he admires you. I think if he finds himself, then you'll both be happier and not fight any more.

WILLY: How can he find himself on a farm? Is that a life? A farmhand? In the

(55) beginning, when he was young, I thought, well, a young man, it's good for him to tramp around, take a lot of different jobs. But it's more than ten years now and he has yet to make

(60) thirty-five dollars a week!

LINDA: He's finding himself, Willy.

WILLY: Not finding yourself at the age of thirty-four is a disgrace!

Arthur Miller, *Death of a Salesman.*

31. What is Willy's attitude towards his son, Biff?

    He thinks Biff

    (1) is wasting time
    (2) has many talents
    (3) treats him well
    (4) will be a good farmer
    (5) should join his company

32. If Linda had Willy's job as a salesperson, what would her attitude towards the job most likely be?

    (1) overeager
    (2) disorganized
    (3) apprehensive
    (4) even-tempered
    (5) exhilarated

33. Which of the following words best describes Willy?

    (1) dissatisfied
    (2) easy-going
    (3) generous
    (4) greedy
    (5) loving

34. What is Biff's attitude towards his father?

    (1) Biff appreciates his sense of humor.
    (2) Biff feels little respect for him.
    (3) Biff is hurt by his comments.
    (4) Biff is angry at him.
    (5) Biff feels very close to him.

35. Earlier in the play, Linda thinks about Willy's "massive dreams" as well as "the turbulent longing within" Willy. Based on this information and on the excerpt, what is Willy most likely longing for?

    (1) to work in New York
    (2) to have his boys live with him again
    (3) for a life in the country
    (4) for his accomplishments to have meaning
    (5) for Biff to choose a good career

WHAT MAKES A GOOD DOCTOR?

The latest offering in this genre is *Second Opinions,* by Jerome Groopman, a professor at Harvard Medical School, chief of experimental medicine at Beth

(5) Israel Deaconess Medical Center, and a staff writer for the *New Yorker.* The eight vignettes in this brief book are, as the subtitle indicates, "stories of intuition and choice in the changing world of medicine."

(10) Groopman's writing is lucid and engaging, free of the jargon that makes medical journals inaccessible to nonspecialists. He writes of patients— including friends and family members—

(15) who experience the terror wrought by terrible diseases and who, for better or for worse, are largely reliant on their physicians to guide them on an uncertain and unwanted journey. At such times,

(20) Groopman suggests, one needs doctors who are not just medically knowledgeable, but also wise and caring.

One of Groopman's more touching stories relates his grandfather Max's

(25) descent into dementia and, ultimately, death. Here the nemesis is not so much the disease that is untreatable by "slash, burn, or poison" (the author's slang for surgery, radiation, or drugs), but a cold-

(30) hearted neurologist who sees the once-vigorous old man as mere grist for a research paper on subtypes of Alzheimer's disease. The neurologist brusquely asked the failing man a few diagnostic questions,

(35) conducted a day's worth of tests, then shipped him in a van to a nursing home. The family was not even given the chance to accompany Max to the home. Such stories should spur medical schools to

(40) require every student to take courses in humility, sensitivity, and compassion—and inspire many a dissatisfied patient to give a copy of *Second Opinions* to doctors they know.

(45) Another story tells of a middle-aged woman whose doctor in Hyannis diagnosed her problem as asthma and treated her accordingly. Unfortunately, she had acute leukemia. The doctor, working under the

(50) penny-pinching strictures of an HMO, had conducted only limited testing. He had prescribed the "usual" treatment for the symptoms noted and later never apologized for his error and his rudeness.

(55) After Groopman and his Boston colleagues corrected her course of treatment, she became well enough to resume treatment in Hyannis. But the die was cast: Despite undergoing an expensive course of

(60) experimental chemotherapy (paid for not by the HMO but by the federal government), she succumbed quickly. Such occurrences, which probably take place by the thousands every day of

(65) the year, should motivate concerned policymakers to bend every effort to reform this country's healthcare system—which is fabulous as long as we are healthy.

One of the book's important messages

(70) is that patients with serious medical conditions need to protect themselves from physicians who don't listen or are too quick to treat.

Michael F. Jacobson, "The Body Politic," *Boston Magazine.*

36. The reviewer suggests that the nation's healthcare system works best under what circumstances?

    (1) if the patient remains in good health
    (2) if the doctor is trained in the appropriate specialty
    (3) if the illness does not require hospitalization
    (4) if the illness is easy to diagnose
    (5) if the patient needs a second opinion

37. On the basis of this excerpt, which of the following would the reviewer most likely do if he became ill?

    (1) Rely only on his own judgment in making medical decisions.
    (2) Refuse to ask family members to help him.
    (3) Choose a doctor who has published many papers.
    (4) Consult a doctor who practices at a research hospital.
    (5) Find a doctor who has a good bedside manner.

38. What is the point of view expressed by the reviewer?

    (1) Doctors should usually perform more tests.
    (2) Doctors need to practice being compassionate.
    (3) Patients rarely need to seek second opinions.
    (4) Doctors should avoid working for HMOs.
    (5) Patients can manage their own health care.

39. Which ideas are most clearly contrasted in the review?

    (1) knowledge and ignorance
    (2) trust and fear
    (3) skill and incompetence
    (4) truth and deception
    (5) caring and indifference

40. Later in the review, the reviewer says, "There was also the too-frequent theme (in the book) that your doctor is not as good as . . . a Harvard doctor." Based on this information and on the excerpt, what is the reviewer's overall opinion about the book?

    (1) The book makes a good argument about medical care, but not every point made is valid.
    (2) The book's focus is too narrow and should include discussion of country doctors.
    (3) The book makes a good point but uses too much medical terminology.
    (4) The book's personal stories are effective and prove that highly skilled doctors are rare.
    (5) The book shows that certain medical schools produce more compassionate doctors.

Answers start on page 329.

Posttest Performance Analysis Chart
Language Arts, Reading

This chart can help you determine your strengths and weaknesses on the content and skill areas of the GED Language Arts, Reading Posttest. Use the Answers and Explanations starting on page 329 to check your answers to the test. Then circle on the chart the numbers of the test items you answered correctly. Put the total number correct for each content area and skill area in each row and column. Look at the total items correct in each column and row and decide which areas are difficult for you. Use the page references to study those areas. Use a copy of the Study Planner on page 31 to guide your review.

Thinking Skill Content Area	Comprehension	Application	Analysis	Synthesis	Total Correct
Nonfiction (Pages 32–97)	14, 16, 36	17, 37	15	18, 38, 39, 40	_____/10
Fiction (Pages 98–167)	3, 8, 9, 25	2, 29	1, 4, 7, 10, 11, 26	5, 6, 12, 13, 27, 28, 30	_____/19
Poetry (Pages 168–207)		20	19, 21, 22	23, 24	_____/6
Drama (Pages 208–241)		32	31, 33, 34	35	_____/5
Total Correct	_____/7	_____/6	_____/13	_____/14	_____/40

1–32 → Use the Study Planner on page 31 to organize your review.
33–40 → Congratulations! You're ready for the GED! You can get more practice with the Simulated Test on pages 259–274.

For additional help, see the *Steck-Vaughn GED Language Arts, Reading Exercise Book.*

LANGUAGE ARTS, READING
Directions

The Language Arts, Reading Simulated Test consists of excerpts from fiction, nonfiction, poetry, and drama. Each excerpt is followed by multiple-choice questions about the reading material.

Read each excerpt first and then answer the questions that follow. Refer to the reading material as often as necessary in answering the questions.

Each excerpt is preceded by a "purpose question." The purpose question gives a reason for reading the material. Use these purpose questions to help focus your reading. You are not required to answer these purpose questions. They are given only to help you concentrate on the ideas presented in the reading material.

You should spend no more than 65 minutes answering the 40 questions on this Simulated Test. Work carefully, but do not spend too much time on any one question. Do not skip any items. Make a reasonable guess when you are not sure of an answer. You will not be penalized for incorrect answers.

When time is up, mark the last item you finished. This will tell you whether you can finish the real GED Test in the time allowed. Then complete the test.

Record your answers to the questions on a copy of the answer sheet on page 348. Be sure that all required information is properly recorded on the answer sheet.

To record your answers, mark the numbered space on the answer sheet that corresponds to the answer you choose for each question on the test.

Example:

It was Susan's dream machine. The metallic blue paint gleamed, and the sporty wheels were highly polished. Under the hood, the engine was no less carefully cleaned. Inside, flashy lights illuminated the instruments on the dashboard, and the seats were covered by rich leather upholstery.

What does "It" most likely refer to in this excerpt?

(1) an airplane
(2) a stereo system
(3) an automobile
(4) a boat
(5) a motorcycle

The correct answer is "an automobile"; therefore, answer space 3 would be marked on the answer sheet.

Do not rest the point of your pencil on the answer sheet while you are considering your answer. Make no stray or unnecessary marks. If you change an answer, erase your first mark completely. Mark only one answer space for each question; multiple answers will be scored as incorrect. Do not fold or crease your answer sheet.

When you finish the test, use the Performance Analysis Chart on page 274 to determine whether you are ready to take the real GED Test, and, if not, which skill areas need additional review.

Adapted with permission of the American Council on Education.

Directions: Choose the one best answer to each question.

Questions 1 through 6 refer to the following excerpt from a review.

HOW DOES PURA FE MAKE A NEW KIND OF MUSIC?

The scene is Brooklyn's Prospect Park amphitheater: the summer night is cool, the moon an elegant silver. Across the stage waft clouds of sage as members of
(5) Pura Fe, a Native American jazz-fusion ensemble, prepare for a performance, burning herbs and circling together backstage in prayer. Dressed in beads, vests and other traditional garb, the seven
(10) musicians look as if they're pioneer folk, but their music—plaintive Indian chants jazzily arranged for three female voices and syncopated with flutes, drums, rattles and bells—sounds surprisingly hip; in fact,
(15) many of their tunes could easily slip onto the pop charts, sandwiched somewhere between Ladysmith Black Mambazo's South African gospel and the more jazz-oriented licks of Take 6. Their lyrics,
(20) however, set Pura Fe apart from the mainstream. With an ear tuned to history, they have adapted songs and chants they learned from their grandparents, from other elders at powwows, and even from
(25) their own visions and dreams. "We are not relics . . . not souvenirs . . . not echoes of the past" goes one song. ". . . We are here and now/proud Indian nation/with ancestor spirits . . . together the power
(30) of prayer/brings the medicine back."

Ten years ago, an Indian-arts group like Pura Fe—grounded in tradition but artistically progressive—would have been unthinkable in contemporary America.
(35) Victimized by a racial repression that proved nearly fatal, whole generations of Native Americans either denied their identity out of shame or retreated into tribal separatism. It wasn't until 1978 that the
(40) American Indian Religious Freedom Act even allowed native peoples to practice— in public or in private—their spiritual rituals. But the youngest generation of Native American performance artists,
(45) actively challenging stereotypes and discrimination, are finding new ways to connect with their heritage and still remain urban. By establishing themselves as caretakers of a culture that has been
(50) all but lost, they have become a bridge between two seemingly incongruous worlds.

The music of the Pura Fe ensemble is not just by Indians for Indians, insists
(55) Frank Menusan, who came to perform the music of his ancestry only after an in-depth study of music and instruments from other cultures. Among the instruments he plays professionally are the East Indian sitar and
(60) vina, the Turkish oud and string lutes from Afghanistan, as well as all kinds of Latin percussion. While the Pura Fe group uses only authentic Indian instruments such as peyote rattles, tree-trunk drums, pre-
(65) Columbian ocharinas and Amerindian flutes, it's Menusan's wide-ranging musicianship that brings a freshness to the group's arrangements. "We are trying very hard to keep the integrity of our music,"
(70) he says, "while opening it up to be more universal. A lot of people, even Indians, have stereotyped their own music as a monotonous drumbeat with a lot of wailing. But we received the blessings from elders
(75) of many tribal affiliations who believe in what we're doing and condone it. If it touches them, they say, they're sure it will touch others."

Pamela Bloom, "Keeping the Faith," *Taxi*.

1. What is one of the ways that Pura Fe creates a new form of Native American music?

    (1) by using only traditional Indian instruments
    (2) by singing plaintive chants
    (3) by using jazzy arrangements
    (4) by rejecting syncopation
    (5) by using the Asian sitar

2. What is the most likely reason the author compares Pura Fe to Ladysmith Black Mambazo and Take 6 (lines 17–19)?

    (1) to indicate that Pura Fe is better than both groups
    (2) to give an idea of what Pura Fe's music sounds like
    (3) to suggest to Pura Fe the sounds they should imitate
    (4) to ridicule Pura Fe's attempts to sound hip
    (5) to tell whose music Pura Fe has adapted as their own

3. The author of this review finds Pura Fe's music interesting. Which of the following details from the excerpt best supports that conclusion?

    (1) "Their lyrics . . . set Pura Fe apart from the mainstream." (lines 19–21)
    (2) "Ten years ago, an Indian-arts group like Pura Fe . . . would have been unthinkable. . . ." (lines 31–34)
    (3) "A lot of people . . . have stereotyped their own music as a monotonous drumbeat. . . ." (lines 71–73)
    (4) ". . . they have adapted songs and chants they learned from their grandparents. . . ." (lines 22–23)
    (5) "We are trying very hard to keep the integrity of our music. . . ." (lines 68–69)

4. On the basis of the review, what would Pura Fe most likely do if they heard a traditional Native American chant they had not heard before?

    They might

    (1) play it using Turkish and Afghani instruments
    (2) arrange it in a more modern style
    (3) teach it to their grandparents and other elders
    (4) play it to educate the audience about Native American history
    (5) play it only for an audience of other Native Americans

5. What is the author's main reason for including information about recent Native American history?

    (1) to explain why Pura Fe has been prohibited from performing until now
    (2) to cause the reader to feel sympathy for Pura Fe
    (3) to explain how Pura Fe developed a unique style
    (4) to show that Pura Fe's music is primarily intended for other Native Americans
    (5) to show how Pura Fe is representative of the youngest generation of Native Americans

6. How is the excerpt organized?

    (1) A specific list of topics relating to the music is followed by an in-depth argument.
    (2) A series of general statements about the music is presented without specific support.
    (3) The merits of the music are contrasted with its faults.
    (4) A description of the music is followed by historical background and personal stories.
    (5) An analysis of Native American culture moves from the past to the present.

IS YOUTH ACCESSIBLE IN OLD AGE?

HOW TO BE OLD

It is easy to be young. (Everybody is,
at first.) It is not easy
to be old. It takes time.

Youth is given; age is achieved.
(5) One must work a magic to mix with time
in order to become old.
Youth is given. One must put it away
like a doll in a closet,
take it out and play with it only
(10) on holidays. One must have many dresses
and dress the doll impeccably
(but not to show the doll, to keep it hidden.)

It is necessary to adore the doll,
to remember it in the dark on the ordinary
(15) days, and every day congratulate
one's aging face in the mirror

In time one will be very old.
In time, one's life will be accomplished.
And in time, in time, the doll—
(20) like new, though ancient—will be found.

May Swenson, *To Mix with Time, New and Selected Poems.*

7. According to the poem, what does the doll represent?

   (1) magic
   (2) time
   (3) appearances
   (4) youth
   (5) old age

8. What is the main effect of the description of the doll (lines 7–12)?

   (1) It emphasizes how precious youth is.
   (2) It emphasizes the playfulness of life.
   (3) It shows the futility of fighting old age.
   (4) It shows how the speaker felt as a girl.
   (5) It shows how helpless older people are.

9. According to the poem, what is true of age?

   It must be

   (1) worked for
   (2) fought off
   (3) treated like a doll
   (4) put into a closet
   (5) found

10. How would the speaker's feelings about her old age be most likely to affect her interactions with her grandchildren?

   She would

   (1) be overly disappointed when they make mistakes
   (2) consider their problems to be more important than her own
   (3) be distant and uninvolved in their lives
   (4) encourage them to act more grown-up
   (5) enjoy participating in their games

11. Which of the following is the speaker most concerned about?

   (1) hiding her past
   (2) saving her old dolls
   (3) growing old gracefully
   (4) forgetting her youth
   (5) dressing to look younger

WHAT KIND OF LIVES DO MARTY AND ANGIE LEAD?

ANGIE: Well, what do you feel like doing tonight?

MARTY: I don't know. What do you feel like doing?

(5) ANGIE: Well, we're back to that, huh? I say to you: "What do you feel like doing tonight?" And you say to me: "I don't know, what do you feel like doing?" And then we wind up sitting around the

(10) house with a couple of cans of beer, watching Sid Caesar on television. Well, I tell you what I feel like doing. I feel like calling up Mary Feeney. She likes you. (MARTY *looks up quickly*

(15) *at this.*)

MARTY: What makes you say that?

ANGIE: I could see she likes you.

MARTY: Yeah, sure.

ANGIE: *(Half rising in his seat)* I'll call

(20) her up.

MARTY: You call her up for yourself, Angie. I don't feel like calling her up. (ANGIE *sits down again. They both return to reading the paper for a*

(25) *moment. Then* ANGIE *looks up again.*)

ANGIE: Boy, you're getting to be a real drag, you know that?

MARTY: Angie, I'm thirty-six years old. I been looking for a girl every Saturday

(30) night of my life. I'm a little, short, fat fellow and girls don't go for me, that's all. I'm not like you. I mean, you joke around, and they laugh at you, and you get along fine. I just stand around like

(35) a bug. What's the sense of kidding myself? Everybody's always telling me to get married. Get married. Get married. Don't you think I wanna get married? I wanna get married. They

(40) drive me crazy. Now, I don't wanna wreck your Saturday night for you, Angie. You wanna go somewhere, you go ahead. I don't wanna go.

ANGIE: Boy, they drive me crazy too. My

(45) old lady, every word outta her mouth, when you gonna get married?

Paddy Chayefsky, *Marty, The Collected Works of Paddy Chayefsky: The Screenplays.*

12. On the basis of the excerpt, what is Marty's main problem?

(1) He is thirty-six years old.
(2) He is short and fat.
(3) He is not popular with women.
(4) He stands around like a bug.
(5) He is not like Angie.

13. Which of the following words best describes Angie?

(1) optimistic
(2) frustrated
(3) bitter
(4) content
(5) charming

14. Which of the following words best describes Marty?

(1) angry
(2) resourceful
(3) defeated
(4) manipulative
(5) humble

15. Based on the information in the excerpt, how would Marty most likely spend his time if he unexpectedly had a week off from work?

(1) trying to get a date
(2) thinking about the joys of marriage
(3) sitting around his house
(4) arguing with Mary Feeney
(5) exercising to lose weight

16. Which of the following best states the theme of this excerpt?

(1) Marriage is a natural desire for everyone.
(2) Saturday nights can be boring for many people.
(3) Marty is missing many good opportunities.
(4) Two people cannot decide what to do on Saturday night.
(5) Lonely people sometimes stop being socially active.

17. In what way does Angie differ from Marty?

(1) Angie is less determined to change his life than Marty is.
(2) Angie is more comfortable with women than Marty is.
(3) Angie is more annoyed by his mother than Marty is.
(4) Angie wants to get married more than Marty does.
(5) Angie is less willing to call women on the telephone than Marty is.

IS RAZUMIHIN HELPFUL TO THE FAMILY?

Raskolnikov was the first to open the door; he flung it wide and stood still in the doorway, dumbfounded.

(5) His mother and sister were sitting on his sofa and had been waiting an hour and a half for him. Why had he never expected, never thought of them, though the news that they had started, were on their way and would arrive immediately, had been

(10) repeated to him only that day? They had spent that hour and a half plying Nastasya with questions. She was still standing before them and had told them everything by now. They were beside themselves with

(15) alarm when they heard of his "running away" today, ill and, as they understood from her story, delirious! "Good heavens, what had become of him?" Both had been weeping, both had been in anguish for that

(20) hour and a half.

A cry of joy, of ecstasy, greeted Raskolnikov's entrance. Both rushed to him. But he stood like one dead; a sudden intolerable sensation struck him like a

(25) thunderbolt. He did not lift his arms to embrace them, he could not. His mother and sister clasped him in their arms, kissed him, laughed and cried. He took a step, tottered and fell to the ground,

(30) fainting.

Anxiety, cries of horror, moans . . . Razumihin who was standing in the doorway flew into the room, seized the sick man in his strong arms and in a

(35) moment had him on the sofa.

"It's nothing, nothing!" he cried to the mother and sister—"it's only a faint, a mere trifle! Only just now the doctor said he was much better, that he is perfectly well!

(40) Water! See, he is coming to himself, he is all right again!"

And seizing Dounia by the arm so that he almost dislocated it, he made her bend down to see that "he is all right again".

(45) The mother and sister looked on him with emotion and gratitude, as their Providence. They had heard already from Nastasya all that had been done for their Rodya during his illness, by this "very competent young

(50) man . . ."

Fyodor Dostoevsky, *Crime and Punishment.*

18. How does Raskolnikov react to his family's visit?

He is

(1) pleased
(2) unhappy
(3) resentful
(4) emotionless
(5) shy

19. What is the relationship between Raskolnikov and Razumihin?

(1) Razumihin is Raskolnikov's doctor.
(2) They are business partners.
(3) Razumihin is Raskolnikov's brother.
(4) They know each other well.
(5) They are recent acquaintances.

20. Based on their behavior in the excerpt, how would the mother and sister most likely react if Raskolnikov were to recover from his illness?

(1) They would be angry with Raskolnikov for getting so ill in the first place.
(2) They would feel that Razumihin is partially responsible for Raskolnikov's recovery.
(3) They would be grateful that Raskolnikov followed the doctor's orders while sick.
(4) They would be angry with Razumihin for not telling them about the illness sooner.
(5) They would feel that Raskolnikov's recovery was destined from the beginning.

21. Which of the following best describes the mood of this excerpt?

(1) sinister
(2) angry
(3) peaceful
(4) gloomy
(5) agitated

22. Later in the story, Razumihin pleads with the mother and sister, "If you stay . . . you'll drive him to a frenzy, and then goodness knows what will happen!" Based on the information in the excerpt, what is Razumihin's most likely motivation in making this statement?

(1) He has selfish reasons for keeping Raskolnikov's family away from him.
(2) He prefers to have a doctor take care of Raskolnikov while he is sick.
(3) He knows that Raskolnikov dislikes his family and wants them to leave.
(4) He distrusts Raskolnikov's family and does not want them around.
(5) He believes that the mother and sister are too fragile to see Raskolnikov in this state.

IS QUICK WAX A GOOD PRODUCT?

TO: Aileen Rosen, Director of Sales
FROM: Patricia Phillips, Territory 12

(5) Since it was introduced in January of 1993, Quick Wax has been unsuccessful in Territory 12 and has not affected the sale of our Easy Shine. Discussions with customers and my own analysis of Quick Wax suggest three reasons for its failure to compete with our product.

(10) 1. Quick Wax has not received the promotion necessary for a new product. Advertising—primarily on radio—has been sporadic and has not developed a clear, consistent image for the product.
(15) In addition, the Quick Wax sales representative in Territory 12 is new and inexperienced; he is not known to customers, and his sales pitch (which I once overheard) is weak. As far as I
(20) can tell, his efforts are not supported by phone calls or mailings from his home office.

(25) 2. When Quick Wax does make it to the store shelves, buyers do not choose it over our product. Though priced competitively with our product, Quick Wax is poorly packaged. The container seems smaller than ours, though in fact it holds the same eight ounces. The
(30) lettering on the Quick Wax package (red on blue) is difficult to read, in contrast to the white-on-green lettering on the Easy Shine package.

(35) 3. Our special purchase offers and my increased efforts to serve existing customers have had the intended effect of keeping customers satisfied with our product and reducing their inclination to stock something new.

(40) Copies: L. Goldberger, Director of Marketing
L. MacGregor, Customer Service Manager

"Bigelow Wax Company," *The Little, Brown Handbook.*

23. Based on the information in the memo, why might customers tend to choose a larger-looking package?

Because it

(1) appears to contain more of the product
(2) has a label that is easier to read
(3) is more convenient to carry
(4) is more appealing to the eye
(5) is easier to locate on the store shelf

24. On the basis of the memo, which of the following is a reason for Easy Shine's success?

(1) special purchase offers
(2) red lettering
(3) small containers
(4) new salespeople
(5) pursuit of new customers

25. If the Director of Marketing for Easy Shine were to market bath soap, what approach would she most likely take?

She would

(1) hire all new sales representatives
(2) spy on her competitor's sales department
(3) create small, compact packaging
(4) place only a few advertisements on the Internet
(5) ensure that the lettering on the package is easy to read

26. How is the excerpt organized?

It presents a series of

(1) strategies for preparing an ad campaign
(2) rules for selling a product
(3) factual statements supported by evidence
(4) advantages and disadvantages of two products
(5) arguments followed by descriptive stories

27. Which of the following best describes the purpose of this memo?

(1) to argue
(2) to examine
(3) to persuade
(4) to instruct
(5) to congratulate

28. Based on the information in this memo, what is the best description of the relationship between Quick Wax and Easy Shine?

(1) They are equally balanced enemies.
(2) They are working partners.
(3) They rely on each other for sales.
(4) They are longtime competitors.
(5) They share similar goals.

WHAT IS LANCE'S PASSION?

It appeared with time at any rate to be to the brush that Lance had been born; for Mrs. Mallow, one day when the boy was turning twenty, broke it to their friend, who
(5) shared, to the last delicate morsel, their problems and pains, that it seemed as if nothing would really do but that he should embrace the career. It had been impossible longer to remain blind to the
(10) fact that he was gaining no glory at Cambridge, where Brench's own college had for a year tempered its tone to him as for Brench's own sake. Therefore why renew the vain form of preparing him for
(15) the impossible? The impossible—it had become clear—was that he should be anything but an artist.

"Oh dear, dear!" said poor Peter.

"Don't you believe in it?" asked Mrs.
(20) Mallow, who still, at more than forty, had her violet velvet eyes, her creamy satin skin and her silken chestnut hair.

"Believe in what?"

"Why in Lance's passion."

(25) "I don't know what you mean by 'believing in it.' I've never been unaware, certainly, of his disposition, from his earliest time, to daub and draw; but I confess I've hoped it would burn out."

(30) "But why should it," she sweetly smiled, "with his wonderful heredity? Passion is passion—though of course indeed *you,* dear Peter, know nothing of that. Has the Master's ever burned out?"

(35) Peter looked off a little and, in his familiar formless way, kept up for a moment a sound between a smothered whistle and a subdued hum. "Do you think he's going to be another Master?"

(40) She seemed scarce prepared to go that length, yet she had on the whole a marvelous trust. "I know what you mean by that. Will it be a career to incur the jealousies and provoke the machinations
(45) that have been at times almost too much

for his father? Well—say it may be, since nothing but claptrap, in these dreadful days, *can,* it would seem, make its way, and since, with the curse of refinement and
(50) distinction, one may easily find one's self begging one's bread. Put it at the worst— say he *has* the misfortune to wing his flight further than the vulgar taste of his stupid countrymen can follow. Think, all the same,
(55) of the happiness—the same the Master has had. He'll *know.*"

Peter looked rueful. "Ah but *what* will he know?"

Henry James, "The Tree of Knowledge."

29. Who is the Master?

    (1) Peter
    (2) Mrs. Mallow's father
    (3) Lance's brother
    (4) Lance's father
    (5) Lance

30. What is being referred to in the lines "he should embrace the career" (lines 7–8)?

    (1) the career Peter wants Lance to follow
    (2) a career as a painter
    (3) an academic career
    (4) the career Lance's father wants for him
    (5) a career as an architect

31. Which of the following statements best explains the meaning of the phrase "to wing his flight further . . ." (lines 52–53)?

    Lance might

    (1) travel to distant lands
    (2) paint images of birds in flight
    (3) be ahead of his time
    (4) do better than expected
    (5) become very wealthy

32. What point of view about art is expressed in the excerpt?

    (1) Art created by people of refinement is usually very good.
    (2) Great art does not always lead to great wealth.
    (3) Refinement is more important than artistic talent.
    (4) Refined people usually find great success.
    (5) The upper class often prefers cheap artwork.

33. What is the tone of this excerpt?

    (1) joyful
    (2) gossipy
    (3) comical
    (4) sullen
    (5) suspenseful

34. Earlier in the story the narrator says, "The Master's idea, . . . had in almost any case, even after years, remained undiscoverable to Peter." Based on this information and the excerpt, which of the following best describes Peter?

    (1) unappreciative of the Master's art
    (2) skilled at spotting artistic talent
    (3) jealous of the Master's artistic ability
    (4) a better artist than the Master
    (5) an overly critical friend

CAN JAMES FORGIVE PEGGY?

Every now and then, though, I would have a run-in with a patron who demanded something preposterous. Maybe they wanted me to immediately hand over a
(5) book so popular that others had been waiting months for it; maybe they wanted to supply a page-long shopping list of books so I could pull them off the shelves. Maybe they wanted not to be charged a
(10) penny for their enormous fines because they had been too busy to get to the library. (The most unmanageable patrons always told me how *busy* they were.) I'd say, politely, no. They'd say yes. I got firm;
(15) they got insulting. I'd start to explain my position in depth, they'd ask to see a manager—and then I'd bow my head (I *loved* this moment) and say, "I am Miss Cort, the director of the library." It was not
(20) a title I ever otherwise claimed.

I longed to say, Listen: in my library, as in the Kingdom of Heaven, the rude and busy are not rewarded. We honor manners, patience, good deeds, and grave
(25) misfortune only.

And one of two things happened: the patrons returned, and either thought I'd forgotten what had happened or had forgotten themselves, and were amazed
(30) when I politely, smilingly remembered them by name.

Or they never came back.

James and I had not argued, but I'd felt I'd done something much worse in so
(35) misunderstanding what he'd wanted, in giving him *Medical Curiosities* [an outdated book about physical extremes]. I could forgive myself social clumsiness, my occasional crippling shyness, a sharp
(40) tongue at the wrong time. I could not forgive sloppy library work, and that is what I was guilty of: a patron—my best, most beloved patron—needed help in finding something, and I'd jumped to a
(45) conclusion and given him books that were worse than useless. He'd asked me a straightforward question and I had not come close to providing an answer.

(50) But he returned the next Friday, with a different question. I still remember: he wanted to know what an anti-Pope was.

Maybe it was forgiveness, and maybe it was just teenage obliviousness, but the sight of James that afternoon seemed
(55) miraculous. *You came back,* I said to him as I sent him to the card catalog ("Look under Catholic Church—history") and he said, *Sure, Peggy, where else would I go?*

Elizabeth McCracken, *The Giant's House.*

35. What does the word *position* mean in the phrase "explain my position" (lines 15–16)?

   (1) point of view
   (2) job description
   (3) physical location
   (4) advice about books
   (5) politely phrased insult

36. According to the excerpt, how would Peggy most likely respond to a patron who lost a library book because the patron's house burned down?

   (1) buy the patron a similar book
   (2) make the patron pay for the book
   (3) ask the patron to recommend the book
   (4) tell the patron not to worry about the book
   (5) bar the patron from checking out another book

37. What do lines 40–42 suggest about Peggy's character?

   "I could not forgive sloppy library work, and that is what I was guilty of: . . ."

   (1) She is patient and polite.
   (2) She takes pride in her work.
   (3) She has very little self-confidence.
   (4) She is greatly concerned with neatness.
   (5) She doubts that she is in the right profession.

38. What is the main function of the first half of the excerpt, from the beginning to "Or they never came back" (lines 1–32)?

   (1) to provide a mental image of the layout of the library
   (2) to detail the rules for borrowing books from the library
   (3) to explain why James continued to check out library books
   (4) to describe the personalities of the library's various patrons
   (5) to show why Peggy worried that James might stop coming to the library

39. Which of the following best describes Peggy's attitude toward patrons who do not follow the library rules?

   (1) They are impatient people who deserve to be insulted.
   (2) They are forgetful people who deserve to be excused.
   (3) They are unfortunate people who deserve to be helped.
   (4) They are rude people who deserve to be embarrassed.
   (5) They are straightforward people who deserve to be answered.

40. Earlier in the novel, the author states that James is 16 years old and 7 feet, 5 inches tall. How does this information support Peggy's feeling that the book she gave him, *Medical Curiosities,* is "worse than useless" (line 46)?

   (1) Peggy fears that James will find the book insulting.
   (2) Peggy believes that James will think the book is uninteresting.
   (3) Peggy discovers that the book cannot answer James' question.
   (4) Peggy realizes that James is too young to understand a technical book.
   (5) Peggy finds that the book only contains information about average heights.

Answers start on page 332.

Simulated Test Performance Analysis Chart
Language Arts, Reading

This chart can help you determine your strengths and weaknesses on the content and skill areas of the GED Language Arts, Reading Simulated Test. Use the Answers and Explanations starting on page 332 to check your answers to the test. Then circle on the chart the numbers of the test items you answered correctly. Put the total number correct for each content area and skill area in each row and column. Look at the total items correct in each column and row and decide which areas are difficult for you.

Thinking Skill / Content Area	Comprehension	Application	Analysis	Synthesis	Total Correct
Nonfiction (Pages 32–97)	1, 23, 24	4, 25	2, 3, 5	6, 26, 27, 28	_____/12
Fiction (Pages 98–167)	29, 35	20, 36	18, 19, 30, 31, 37, 38	21, 22, 32, 33, 34, 39, 40	_____/17
Poetry (Pages 168–207)	7, 9	10	8	11	_____/5
Drama (Pages 208–241)	12	15	13, 14	16, 17	_____/6
Total Correct	_____/8	_____/6	_____/12	_____/14	_____/40

1–32 → You need more review.
33–40 → Congratulations! You're ready for the GED!

For additional help, see the *Steck-Vaughn GED Language Arts, Reading Exercise Book.*

Answers and Explanations

PRETEST (Pages 15–29)

1. **(2) the feelings that pass between people** (Analysis) The excerpt states that the songs appeal to Helen not for abstract artistic reasons, but because the songs are about the daily joys and struggles of life. In this case, the word "currency" refers to something that is exchanged between people—specifically, feelings and emotions. Although "currency" usually refers to money, there is no evidence to support that meaning here; therefore, options (1), (3), and (5) are incorrect. There is no evidence to support option (4).

2. **(1) Helen should not have abandoned music.** (Analysis) Helen's music fills her life with joy and richness, and the narrator asks, "oh why did you leave it, Helen?" (lines 11–12). There is no evidence to support options (2), (4), or (5). Although the narrator does approve of and admire Helen's singing, there is not enough evidence to suggest that he thinks she is the best singer of her time, option (3).

3. **(2) feels emotions deeply** (Synthesis) The excerpt describes Helen as experiencing the joy and sadness evoked by decades of songs about life. The phrase given in the question emphasizes these emotions. The excerpt states that Helen's request to sing represents her reentry into the music world, so option (1) is incorrect. There is no evidence to support options (3) or (4). Francis does make Helen happy; however, the phrase in question refers to both positive and negative emotions. An "unbearable memory" is one that is painful. Therefore, option (5) is not the best choice.

4. **(5) happily stay with Francis** (Application) Helen loves Francis and seems loyal to him. She was also loyal to her first love until he ended the relationship. That loyalty indicates that she would not leave Francis. There is no evidence to support options (1), (3), or (4). There is no evidence that she feels the need to ask Francis's permission for anything, so option (2) is incorrect.

5. **(4) nostalgic** (Synthesis) The focus of the excerpt is on Helen's memories and on the songs that she associates with those memories. Although the songs evoke feelings of melancholy, option (1), and joy, option (3), each of these feelings is only part of the mood of the excerpt. There is no evidence to support option (2). The emotions displayed in the excerpt are too extreme and varied to be best described as pleasant, option (5).

6. **(4) He is threatening Lee Chong.** (Analysis) These are veiled statements that indicate to Lee Chong that Mack and his friends might harm Lee's property if Lee does not allow them to move in. There is no evidence to support options (1), (2), (3), or (5).

7. **(3) try to help put out the fire** (Application) Mack's deal with Lee allows him and his friends to live in the Abbeville place. Therefore, it is in their best interest to protect the place and put out the fire. If fire destroyed the house, they would have to move out, option (1). However, since they would not move out unless they had to, option (1) is not the best choice. Mack implies that he and his friends would burn the place only if he does not get what he wants; since he is getting what he wants, option (2) is incorrect. There is no support for option (4). Although there is some indication that Lee Chong thinks Mack and his friends are capable of theft, they do not actually steal anything in the excerpt; therefore, option (5) is not the best choice.

8. **(1) useful** (Analysis) Both parties get what they need: Mack and his friends have a place to live, and Lee Chong is assured that his place will not be destroyed. Although Mack's behavior may be considered immoral, option (2), Lee Chong's behavior probably would not be. The situation might have become dangerous only if Lee Chong did not agree to let Mack live in the place, so option (3) is incorrect. There is no evidence to support options (4) and (5).

9. **(2) fair prices to ensure many repeat customers** (Application) Judging from his behavior in the excerpt, Lee Chong is a practical man who keeps an eye on the long-term benefit more than short-term gain; therefore, he would probably choose an approach that would be the most likely to benefit him in the long run. There is no evidence that he shows favoritism to his friends; friendship is not part of the deal that he and Mack make; therefore, option (1) is incorrect. There is no evidence to support option (3). He does not seem to be unfair to customers at the grocery store; therefore, options (4) and (5) are incorrect.

10. **(4) power and practicality** (Synthesis) The group exerts its power over Lee Chong by threatening his property, so Lee Chong responds with a practical approach to protecting it. There is no support for options (1), (2), or (5). Although Mack and his friends do receive the benefit of living in the Abbeville place, the granting of that favor is not entirely voluntary on Lee's part. Therefore, option (3) is not the best answer.

11. **(3) Weighing risks helps in making good decisions.** (Synthesis) Lee Chong thinks carefully about the negative and positive consequences before deciding to agree to Mack's proposal. Lee decides to work with the group rather than risk danger to his house. Since Lee Chong's saving face was the result of taking the path that would cause the least amount of damage to his property, it is not a weak approach. Therefore, option (1) is not the best choice. Mack and Lee are not friends; in fact, Mack is forcing Lee Chong to let him use the property, so option (2) is incorrect. Lee Chong does use negotiation skills to protect his interests; therefore, option (4) is incorrect. Mack is gaining a place to live by being unfair to Lee Chong; therefore, option (5) is also incorrect.

12. **(3) tense** (Synthesis) Lee Chong is not pleased with his visit from Mack, and the conversation between the two men is tense. There is no evidence to support options (1) or (2). Neither Mack nor Lee Chong expresses anger; therefore, option (4) is incorrect. There may be a superficial friendliness, option (5), but this choice does not address the underlying conflict of the situation.

13. **(2) to show what the stories have in common** (Analysis) The stories in the book are interrelated and illustrate some important effects of the war on soldiers. To give a sense of these effects, the reviewer discusses more than one story. In particular, he mentions two stories in which embarrassment plays a role in motivating soldiers. The reviewer is not the focus of this review, so options (1) and (4) are incorrect. There is no evidence to support option (3). Although the book's author appears to have disliked the war, option (5) does not explain the structure of the review.

14. **(3) It examines the soldiers' feelings.** (Comprehension) The reviewer indicates that this book is unique because it discusses not only the horror of war, but also the soldiers' courage, fear, and shame. The review does not describe soldiers' routines, so option (1) is incorrect. The fact that the book is composed of short stories is not emphasized as one of its particular strengths, so option (2) is incorrect. There is no evidence to support option (4). The review focuses on the author's description of battles; therefore, option (5) is incorrect.

15. **(2) be criticized for not going to war** (Comprehension) The book describes embarrassment as the reason that the author, and perhaps others, served in the war—specifically embarrassment that they would be thought of as unpatriotic. There is no evidence to support the other options.

16. **(3) it should be read in addition to The Things They Carried** (Comprehension) The reviewer applauds this novel, too. He describes both of O'Brien's books as "essential fiction about Vietnam" (lines 7–8). He does not indicate that it is better than The Things They Carried, so option (1) is incorrect. There is no evidence to support options (2), (4), or (5).

17. **(5) admiring** (Synthesis) The reviewer states that the book is "high up on the list of best fiction about any war" (lines 19–20) and that the author examines the soldiers' feelings about the war "with sensitivity and insight" (lines 13–14). Although the subject of the book is harsh, the review of the book is not; therefore, option (1) is incorrect. There is no evidence to support options (2) or (3). The author is very enthusiastic about O'Brien's book; therefore, option (4) is not strong enough to be the best description of the review's tone.

18. **(2) the experience of war** (Synthesis) The majority of the review describes the specifics of the war experience as written about in O'Brien's book. Although some of the stories may be based on the author's experiences, the review states that the stories are fictional; therefore, option (1) is incorrect. Particular battles are not discussed, so option (3) is incorrect. There is no evidence to support options (4) or (5).

19. **(4) Filmmakers are limited to depicting a novel's basic meaning and mood.** (Comprehension) The word "you" in the quotation refers to filmmakers, and "adaptation" refers to the filmed version of a novel. By the phrase "faithful in spirit," Goldman means being true to the basic meaning and mood of a novel; therefore, option (4) is the best answer. Option (1) is incorrect because the quotation does not indicate whether adaptations of novels are usually successful. Options (2) and (5) may be true, but they do not restate the meaning of the lines. Although option (3) is implied by the quotation, it does not restate Goldman's words and is therefore incorrect.

20. **(4) represents a practical option for filmmakers attempting to cover entire novels** (Analysis) According to the author, one way in which novels can be simplified for filming is by combining two or more characters into one. There is no evidence to support option (1). Although the author does mention alterations to a novel's plot, he does not imply that this technique is preferable to creating composite characters. For this reason, option (2) is incorrect. The author does not suggest that the use of composite characters will necessarily lead to the success or failure of a film; therefore, options (3) and (5) are incorrect.

21. **(5) has a rather simple plot structure**
(Application) According to the author, the main problems involved in filming a novel are that a film cannot be as long or explore topics in as much depth as a novel can. To help a beginning filmmaker avoid these problems, the author would likely advise him or her to choose a novel with a simple plot. There is no direct evidence in the excerpt to support option (1). The author believes that a novel with a large number of characters, option (2), or that takes place over an extended period of time, option (3), is more difficult to film, not easier. Therefore, neither of these options is the best answer. The author specifically states that the filmmaker's job is easier when the audience has read the book, making option (4) incorrect.

22. **(3) has a style that is less academic than that of the rest of the excerpt**
(Synthesis) The styles of the two writers are quite distinct. Compare the informal language of the quotation—"you're talking a little, teeny slice" (lines 25–26)—with the more academic language of the rest of the excerpt—"the rather severe limitations imposed on the length of a film" (lines 1–2). Neither passage makes much use of figurative language, and both express similar ideas; therefore, options (1) and (2) are incorrect. Although the quotation does offer a specific example, the rest of the excerpt does not present statistics. For this reason, option (4) is not the best answer. Option (5) is incorrect because the quotation assumes readers are unfamiliar with at least some aspects of the movie industry, such as the length of a screenplay.

23. **(2) to explain some of the difficulties involved in basing a film on a novel**
(Synthesis) The excerpt focuses on the problems faced by filmmakers when filming novels (such as limits related to time and complexity). Option (1) has no support from the excerpt. The author does not suggest that novels are poor sources for films, only that they can present challenges; for this reason, option (3) is not the best answer. Although the author does state that characters are sometimes combined and that subplots may be eliminated in filmed versions of novels, neither of these ideas is the author's central focus; therefore, options (4) and (5) are also incorrect.

24. **(3) Both have a librarian friend.**
(Comprehension) The upstairs neighbor was a librarian, and she was friends with the librarian in the speaker's former town. There is no evidence to support option (1). The upstairs neighbor and the librarian friend are from South Dakota; the speaker, however, is not, so

option (2) is incorrect. There is no evidence that the upstairs neighbor has just moved in; therefore, option (4) is incorrect. There is some support for option (5), in that the upstairs neighbor would not have come down to visit if she did not like talking. In addition, the speaker does not seem to dislike talking to the people in her apartment. However, there is little direct evidence that the speaker enjoys talking to neighbors in general; therefore, option (5) is not the best choice.

25. **(2) The installer's wife is very busy.**
(Analysis) The installer indicates he has elderly parents and that his wife could use some help in caring for them. Therefore, the line is an expression meaning that the installer's wife works hard. There is no evidence to support the other options.

26. **(3) the speaker's neighbor** (Comprehension) The speaker mentions that the upstairs apartment brought cake. Therefore, she is referring to the person who lives in the apartment, not the apartment itself. Option (1) is a literal interpretation of figurative language; therefore, it is incorrect. None of the people mentioned in options (2), (4), and (5) brought cake; therefore, these options also are incorrect.

27. **(1) She has faith in humanity.** (Analysis) The speaker's statement suggests that people are more dependable than objects. There is no evidence to support the other options.

28. **(4) helpful** (Synthesis) The installer is generous with his offers to help, the students are helping the speaker move in, and the neighbor brings cake. Therefore, options (1) and (2) are incorrect. There is no evidence to support options (3) or (5).

29. **(1) conversational** (Synthesis) The speaker seems to be almost chatting about her experiences moving into her new apartment. Although she does seem happy, celebratory is too strong a word to describe the tone of this poem; therefore, option (2) is not the best choice. The speaker acts pleased and friendly; therefore, options (3) and (5) are incorrect. There is no support in the poem for option (4).

30. **(1) He had run out of ideas.**
(Comprehension) Ethan had asked for an advance on his payment and had been turned down. He was not able to think of another way to get the advance, so he bid Hale farewell and left. There is no indication in the excerpt that Ethan was not calm, option (2), or out of a job, option (3). Ethan does not at any point admit to Hale that he does, in fact, really need the advance. He does not stop pretending; therefore, option (4) is incorrect. If Ethan does lose respect

for Hale, he shows no sign of it; therefore, option (5) is incorrect.

31. **(2) They are connected through business.** (Analysis) Hale is Ethan's employer; they seem to have a cordial employer/employee relationship. There is no evidence of dislike, option (1). Although there is some evidence that they have been acquainted for a number of years, Ethan's uneasiness suggests that they are not good friends; therefore, option (3) is incorrect. There is no evidence to support option (4). Hale knows how long Ethan has been married, which indicates that they have been acquainted for some time. Therefore, option (5) is incorrect.

32. **(3) independent** (Analysis) Ethan cannot bring himself to admit that he needs the money or Hale's help. This indicates that he is an independent person. There is no evidence to support the other options.

33. **(4) pride and honesty** (Synthesis) Ethan is too proud to admit that he really needs the money; in other words, he is too proud to be completely honest. Although Ethan's request is rejected, neither character behaves generously; therefore, option (1) is not the best choice. The men are not close friends, and although Ethan does not admit how badly he needs the money, he does not lie to Hale; therefore, option (2) is incorrect. Neither confidence nor insecurity is emphasized in the excerpt; therefore, option (3) is incorrect. Although Ethan is in need of money, there is little evidence that Hale himself is a wealthy man other than the fact that he is Ethan's employer. On the contrary, he actually suggests that he might need an extension in order to pay Ethan; therefore, option (5) is not the best answer.

34. **(4) impractical** (Synthesis) Hale is building a house for Ned and Ruth; it is costing so much that he is suggesting that he perhaps might be a little late in paying Ethan. Hale's wearing a diamond stud in his shirt also indicates that he perhaps lives slightly beyond his means and is therefore impractical in his spending habits. Hale seems somewhat interested in Ethan and his situation; therefore, option (1) is incorrect. Although Hale might want an extension in which to pay Ethan, there is no indication that he is miserly, option (2). There is no evidence in the excerpt that Hale is skilled with money; therefore, option (3) is incorrect. He might be slightly selfish since he wants to pay Ethan late in order to build a house for Ned and Ruth. However, he does ask whether Ethan has money problems, and Ethan realizes that if he were to admit his financial hardship, Hale would be more likely to help him. Those details indicate that Hale is not completely selfish; therefore, option (5) is not the best answer.

35. **(5) She is glad that she married him.** (Comprehension) Mrs. X. states that he is "a good, dear husband" (line 54). The excerpt mentions that a woman tried to seduce Mrs. X.'s husband, but there is no evidence that he was flirting with her, so option (1) is incorrect. Although Mrs. X. mentions her husband's anger, she does not complain about it; therefore, option (2) is incorrect. There is no evidence to support options (3) or (4).

36. **(5) manipulative** (Analysis) Mrs. X. claims she did not "intrigue" Miss Y. out of the Grand Theatre, but her protestations are not quite believable. Mrs. X. may appear friendly, but she frightens Miss Y. with the gun and makes fun of her husband, indicating that the friendliness is not genuine. Therefore, option (1) is not the best answer. There is no evidence to support option (2). Mrs. X. does seem somewhat threatening, but her behavior is not extreme enough to call her "vindictive" or "sinister"; therefore, options (3) and (4) are not the best choices.

37. **(3) Mrs. X. thinks Miss Y. resents her.** (Comprehension) According to Mrs. X., Miss Y. thinks that Mrs. X. tried to remove her from the Grand Theatre. For this reason, Mrs. X. believes that Miss Y. resents her. Miss Y. may actually hate Mrs. X., option (1), but there is no direct evidence in the excerpt to support this. There is no evidence in the excerpt to support options (2) or (5). Mrs. X. and Miss Y. may be enemies, but even if they are, there is no evidence that their rivalry is longstanding; therefore, option (4) is not the best answer.

38. **(3) guarded** (Analysis) Miss Y. is very cautious about being direct with Mrs. X.; Mrs. X. is convinced that Miss Y. holds a grudge against her. Any warmth between the two is purely superficial, so option (1) is incorrect. Mrs. X. does seem to want to show off in front of Miss Y. However, since Miss Y. does not demonstrate similar behavior, option (2) is incorrect. Neither woman is openly unfriendly to the other, but both appear to be hiding something; therefore, options (4) and (5) are incorrect.

39. **(3) I know more about you than you think I do.** (Application) Miss Y. knows that Mrs. X. likely forced her out of the Grand Theatre. In addition, Miss Y. laughs when Mrs. X. says her husband has been faithful, as if she knows something Mrs. X. does not. There is reason to believe that Miss Y. cared about the Grand Theatre, so option (1) is incorrect. Miss Y. laughs at the imitation of Mr. X., so option (2) is incorrect. Miss Y.'s feelings seem to go beyond mere amusement, so option (4) is not the best

choice. There is no evidence to support option (5).

40. **(1) cunning** (Synthesis) A cat at a mouse hole is sly enough to wait silently for its prey to emerge. Similarly, Miss Y. sits silently in the excerpt, allowing Mrs. X. to talk and reveal information. There is no support in the excerpt for options (2), (4), or (5). Miss Y. is not indifferent, as evidenced by the attention she pays Mrs. X. and by her laughter at Mrs. X.'s jokes. Therefore, option (3) is incorrect.

UNIT 1: INTERPRETING NONFICTION
Lesson 1
GED Skill Focus (Pages 36–37)

1. **b.** Television is not as respected as the movie business.

2. **a.** Movie stars and top directors often refuse to work in it.
   b. They rarely admit to watching it.
   c. Movie agents advise clients that it's the last resort for careers in distress.
   d. Writers and intellectuals patronize it.

3. **b.** no

4. **c.** Television is often far better than the movies.

5. **a.** It is stated directly.

6. In the central circle labeled "main idea" you should have written something like *Television is often far better than the movies.*

   In the surrounding circles you may have listed the following supporting details:
   - *Some TV shows are vivid, powerful, or funny.*
   - *There are at least one or two good shows on every night.*
   - *Television has no problem finding shows to nominate for awards.*
   - *Television is a writer's medium.*

7. Your answer may be similar to the following: *If the television industry has no trouble finding shows to nominate for awards, then the overall quality of television must be high.*

GED Practice (Pages 38–39)

1. **(2) the way words united the author's family** (Comprehension) The excerpt focuses on how the sounds of spoken Spanish brought the author's family closer together. Option (1) is incorrect because the author does not discuss his culture in general, only his particular family. Because the excerpt does not discuss the author's efforts to learn English, option (3) is incorrect. There is no direct evidence to support option (4). Although the author describes the family's invention words, this activity is not the main focus of the excerpt; therefore, option (5) can be ruled out.

2. **(1) celebratory** (Synthesis) The author is recalling joyful memories in a way that lets the reader share his experience. Option (2) is contradicted by the emotions expressed in the excerpt. Although some of the events the author describes may be fanciful (such as the invention of words), his language in the excerpt is not; in fact, some sentences are quite scholarly. Therefore, option (3) is incorrect. The author does not express regret that his childhood is past, nor does he urge the reader to action. Therefore, options (4) and (5) are also incorrect.

3. **(5) it has close ties to the sense of touch** (Analysis) The author's description of speaking Spanish makes it seem as though the words can be physically touched with the tongue. Although options (1) and (2) may be true of the author's attitude, the excerpt does not support them. There is no evidence to suggest that option (3) is correct. The author does suggest that the sound of Spanish itself has a meaning to him and his family. However, the statement in the question is related to the "feel" of the language rather than the sound, making option (4) incorrect.

4. **(3) language that conveys private emotions** (Synthesis) In the excerpt, the author describes how the language spoken by his family brought them together and made them feel part of a unique and private group. Based on the excerpt, option (1) is too broad to describe what the author means by "family language." Options (2) and (5) do not make sense in the context of the statement quoted in the question. Although the author's family sometimes ignored the rules of grammar by inventing words, option (4), this choice is too narrow to fit the author's definition of "family language."

5. **(4) Attention to editorial quality may help improve journalism.** (Comprehension) The lines preceding the quote in the question are "Wall Street doesn't care much about editorial quality; journalists do and others should" (lines 1–3). The quotation in the question is a continuation of this thought—that people should care about editorial quality because journalism is not perfect. This implies that attention to quality can help improve journalism. Option (1) is the opposite of what is stated in the excerpt. Option (2) may be true but is not discussed in the excerpt. There is no support in the excerpt for options (3) and (5).

6. **(5) News magazines summarize and analyze the news.** (Analysis) The paragraph discusses the place and function of news magazines in "the food chain of journalism" (lines 6–7). It says that the "news magazine comes along to summarize and analyze" (lines 11–12) and describes what it takes to do

this. Options (1), (3), and (4) may be true but are not discussed in the excerpt. Option (2) is a detail from the paragraph, not the main idea.

7. **(3) It reminds the reader of having an upset stomach from overeating.** (Analysis) The figurative suggestion compares receiving too much information to the discomfort of overeating. Option (1) has no support. Option (2) might be true in general, but other media besides television are part of the problem discussed. Option (4) would only add to the problem. Option (5) is not suggested.

8. **(1) time order—explaining the order in which the media cover the news** (Synthesis) In the second paragraph, when describing the "food chain," the author uses the words "first" when discussing radio news, "then" when referring to television news, and "finally" when referring to the news magazine. This indicates the use of a sequence, or time order, pattern.

GED Mini-Test (Pages 40–41)

1. **(3) A judge may award a prize based upon some small point.** (Comprehension) The preceding paragraph raises the question of how to choose between two good entries. This paragraph containing the quote explains how the judge makes that choice: She focuses on a detail in one of the garments that the other does not have—the covered buttons. There is no evidence that the senior judge is, in general, a picky person, so option (1) is incorrect. Option (2) is incorrect because there is no evidence that all garments need covered buttons. They only became important when everything else was equal. Option (4) is true, but is not suggested by the word "nitpicking," so it is incorrect. "Nitpicking" suggests the opposite of option (5), so it is incorrect.

2. **(3) its covered buttons** (Analysis) The fact that the judge states that in "Highland County, covered buttons are *it*" (lines 27–28) suggests that the buttons are an important factor in the decision. There is no evidence that options (1), (2), and (5) are outstanding features of the jumper, so they are incorrect. The fact that the judges get nitpicky, or look at very small details, suggests that this is not the reason, so option (4) is incorrect.

3. **(4) The judge is dissatisfied with this year's crop.** (Analysis) A sigh can show regret or displeasure. Option (1) may be true but has no support in the excerpt. Options (2) and (5) may be true, but the excerpt does not indicate that the judge is sighing because she is bored or because she is not being paid. There is no evidence for option (3).

4. **(2) informal and casual** (Synthesis) The dialogue in the excerpt as well as the subject of the article, a county fair, both support the description of the writing as informal and casual. None of the other options accurately describe the style of the writing.

5. **(5) as an international star** (Comprehension) Because Hemingway presented himself more as a celebrity than as a writer, people began to think of him as a star. His literary skill, option (1), took second place. Options (2), (3), and (4) are factual but are not mentioned in the excerpt.

6. **(3) an early Hemingway story** (Application) The reviewer expresses a preference for Hemingway's early work in lines 20–22. Options (1), (2), (4), and (5) are about Hemingway's life, about which the reviewer does not write favorably.

7. **(3) to introduce a discussion of Hemingway's life and style of writing** (Analysis) The first paragraph provides an example of Hemingway's style of writing and describes an important event in his life. Options (1) and (4) are not mentioned in the excerpt. The first paragraph does not criticize Hemingway's behavior, option (2), or explain why he became a celebrity, option (5).

Lesson 2
GED Skill Focus (Page 43)

1. **b.** the employees of Peerless Laminating

2. **a.** The electronic mail system at Peerless Laminating Service is a business tool.

3. You may have written something such as *The company doesn't want employees to waste time with personal e-mails while they are on the job. It also doesn't want employees to use company e-mail to write offensive messages, because such behavior is bad for the company's image.*

4. **c.** Use and Misuse of the Company's E-mail System
   e. Guidelines for Appropriate Use of the E-mail System

GED Practice (Pages 44–45)

1. **(3) how to search the Web** (Comprehension) The excerpt describes how confusing it can be to try to find information on the Web and gives some hints and information about using search engines. Option (1) is a detail from the excerpt but does not describe the main idea, and so is incorrect. Options (2) and (5) are not supported by the excerpt and so are incorrect. Option (4) is incorrect because the excerpt tells how to use a search engine, not how to create one.

2. **(3) food service opportunities** (Application) The words *food service* indicate that this option has to do with cooking, and the word *opportunities* suggests jobs. Options (1) and (4) would give information about cooking and learning to cook, but not about jobs; therefore, they are incorrect. Option (2) would give you information about all types of jobs. Because this information would not be specific to cooking, this is not the best option. Option (5) would give information about businesses that provide food, not about jobs, and so is incorrect.

3. **(3) The Web is an electronic library.** (Analysis) The excerpt describes the Web as "the greatest resource of information the world has ever known" (lines 1–3), which suggests that it is an enormous electronic library. Option (1) is not a true statement and so is incorrect. Options (2) and (4) are not supported by the excerpt and so are incorrect. Option (5) is the opposite of what is stated in the article and so is incorrect.

4. **(3) a title containing a few important words from the page** (Application) The excerpt states that in doing a search, search engines try to find documents that contain the searchers' keywords in the title (lines 34–37). Therefore, to make it easy for interested searchers to find the document, the page's title should include two or three important key words. Because different searchers may use different words as keywords, it makes sense to put more than one important word in the title. Options (1), (4), and (5) would not enable search engines to find the document effectively; therefore, they are incorrect. Option (2) would attract some interested searchers, but using only one word would limit the number of searchers who would find the page.

5. **(5) theft of a computer** (Comprehension) The excerpt states that terminated employees are eligible for coverage under most circumstances except "gross misconduct" (line 16). Options (1) and (2) are problems with the company, not with the employee's conduct, and therefore would not disqualify the employee. Options (3) and (4) are described in the excerpt as situations in which the employee would qualify for benefits; therefore, they are incorrect.

6. **(3) Qualified ex-employees and their dependents can retain their health insurance.** (Comprehension) Option (1) is too general to describe the main idea of the excerpt and therefore is incorrect. Option (2) is true but is incomplete because the excerpt also describes how the dependents of ex-employees can retain insurance. Option (4) is too general. Option (5) is not covered in the excerpt.

7. **(2) Companies with fewer than 20 employees are exempt.** (Analysis) The excerpt states that Jetstream Airways is required by law to provide the coverage described because it is "an employer of more than 20 people" (line 4). You can infer from this statement that companies with fewer than 20 employees are not required to provide this coverage. There is no support in the excerpt for the other options.

GED Mini-Test (Pages 46–47)

1. **(3) An employer-sponsored program is available to help troubled employees.** (Comprehension) Lines 20–24 introduce the EARS program as one that helps employees resolve personal problems. The rest of the excerpt goes on to describe this program. Options (1), (4), and (5) are true statements, but they do not summarize the entire excerpt. Option (2) is an opinion that is not expressed by the excerpt.

2. **(2) can help with many types of problems** (Comprehension) The first sentence of the paragraph introduces the topic. Then the writer lists the kinds of problems that can affect job performance, and then states that the EARS program is designed to help employees resolve such problems. None of the other options are true about the excerpt.

3. **(4) make it difficult to excel at work** (Comprehension) The first paragraph states that unresolved difficulties at home can follow an employee to work. This suggests that they can prevent the employee from performing up to his or her ability. Option (1) is too strong in the context of this statement and is therefore incorrect. Option (3) cannot be assumed or inferred from the statement and so is incorrect. Options (2) and (5) are not supported by the information in the excerpt.

4. **(4) feeling overwhelmed by a project** (Application) The program as described is set up to deal with emotional problems. Feeling overwhelmed is an emotional reaction that could be helped by counseling. Options (1), (2), and (3) do not involve emotions and so are incorrect. Option (5), although involving emotions, is not necessarily a problem and so is incorrect.

5. **(3) They want their employees to function well.** (Analysis) The excerpt states that outside problems can interfere with "an employee's ability to perform well" (lines 9–10). The excerpt suggests the opposite of option (1). Option (2) may be true but is not stated or implied in the excerpt. Option (4) is incorrect because the excerpt states that the company knows that this is often not possible. Option (5) is the opposite of the first course of action recommended by the company.

6. **(3) will not cover costs it considers to be too high** (Analysis) In the context of the sentence, the words "reasonable" and "customary" mean charges that are not excessive and that most medical professionals would expect a patient to pay. Options (1), (2), (4), and (5) are neither stated nor implied by the information in the excerpt.

7. **(2) Employees might not seek help if the program were not confidential.** (Analysis) The excerpt implies that the employer wants employees to get help because their personal problems can affect their work. Employees might not get help if they thought other people, especially employers, might find out about their personal problems. Options (1), (4), and (5) might be true but do not explain why an employer would want the program to remain confidential. Therefore, they are incorrect. Option (3) is not supported by the excerpt and so is incorrect.

8. **(1) straightforward and matter-of-fact** (Synthesis) The excerpt is written in clear, straightforward language that the average employee can understand; the purpose of EARS is frankly discussed. None of the other options accurately describes the style in which the excerpt is written.

9. **(4) by introducing a problem and offering a solution** (Synthesis) The excerpt begins by introducing the topic of personal problems and their effect on an employee's performance. It then describes the types of problems that employees experience and offers a solution to help employees resolve them. This clearly demonstrates the problem/solution organizational pattern. Although the excerpt does discuss the steps involved in EARS counseling, this is just one small part of the excerpt and does not describe it as a whole. Therefore, option (1) is incorrect. Option (2) is not supported by the information in the excerpt. The help available to address problems is as important as the problems themselves; therefore, option (3) is incorrect. Although problems may be more familiar to readers than potential help, option (5) does not effectively describe the organizational pattern of the excerpt.

Lesson 3
GED Skill Focus (Page 49)

1. **d.** Six Logical Steps to Plan a Business Letter

2. identify your objective

3. picture your reader in your mind

4. The effectiveness of your letter depends on the quality of your preparation.

5. Your answer should be similar to the following: *Planning is the most important step in writing a business letter.*

GED Practice (Pages 50–51)

1. **(1) Gates is worth more, so his time is more valuable.** (Comprehension) The excerpt describes how, in 1986, it was not worth Bill Gates's time to pick up a $5 bill, whereas now it is not worth his time to pick up a $500 bill. The excerpt does not indicate that Bill Gates will have to work more; therefore, option (2) is incorrect. Option (3) may be true, but is not suggested by the excerpt. There is no support in the excerpt for option (4). Option (5) is true, but it does not restate the lines given in the question and therefore is not the correct choice.

2. **(5) humorous** (Synthesis) The author uses humor to describe the immense amount of money that Bill Gates earns. For instance, he creates an image of Bill Gates wasting his time by picking up a $500 bill. The author does not seem to be congratulating Bill Gates, nor does he seem envious or critical of him; therefore, options (1), (2), and (3) are incorrect. There is also no evidence that the author is disgusted by Gates's wealth, option (4).

3. **(4) Modest wealth seems like pocket change to Gates.** (Analysis) This section of the excerpt is devoted to comparing what money means to an average American with what that same amount of money means to Bill Gates. There is no support in the excerpt for the option (1). Although options (2) and (5) may be true, they do not restate the lines from the excerpt. The author suggests that Gates could spend fortunes without a second thought, but there is not evidence that he does so.

4. **(2) He would make comparisons.** (Application) The author uses comparisons throughout the excerpt to emphasize both how much money Bill Gates makes as well as how his earning power has increased over the years. Therefore, he would probably use comparisons to describe a great distance, such as that from Earth to the moon. The author does use technical language to describe a top-of-the-line computer, but most of the language in the excerpt is nontechnical; therefore, option (1) is incorrect. The author does not exaggerate Gates's wealth, option (3), nor does he describe different viewpoints, option (4). The author does not simply state facts about Gates's wealth; instead he goes out of his way to make sure the reader understands just how large Gates's fortune is. Therefore, option (5) is not the best choice.

5. **(2) The warranty applies only to manufacturing defects.** (Comprehension)

The paragraph describes in detail all of the circumstances under which the company is not responsible for defects or damage; these include anything that happens after manufacturing, including damage incurred during shipping. A person with this warranty would already have bought the item in question, so option (1) is incorrect. Option (3) is true, but is only a detail from the paragraph and so is incorrect. Option (4) is the opposite of what the paragraph states and so is incorrect. Option (5) is a matter of opinion, not an idea given in the paragraph, and so is incorrect.

6. **(1) to describe the conditions under which the company will replace or repair the product** (Comprehension) The purpose of the warranty is stated in the first sentence of the first paragraph. Option (2) is true only in certain circumstances. Options (3) and (5) are not stated in the warranty. Option (4) is not true based on the information in the warranty statement.

7. **(2) furnish proof of the date of purchase** (Analysis) The warranty applies only up to one year after the original purchase. Therefore, although it is not specified in the warranty statement, it is reasonable to expect the purchaser to provide proof of the date of purchase for the company to comply with the terms of the warranty agreement. Options (1), (3), and (5) would not likely be criteria that a purchaser should meet for a manufacturer to honor a warranty agreement. Option (4) could be a criterion, but there is no reference made to such a requirement in the excerpt.

8. **(5) formal and legal** (Analysis) The agreement uses legal terminology such as "thereof," "herein," and "exclusions." The sentences are long and complex. Whether or not the style is boring is a matter of opinion, so option (4) is not the best answer. None of the other options is supported by the details in the warranty statement.

GED Mini-Test (Pages 52–53)

1. **(3) All auto insurance contracts have certain basic features.** (Comprehension) The key idea of the excerpt is stated in the first sentence, *Even the most basic auto insurance policies contain a number of key provisions.* Options (1), (2), and (4) are opinions not expressed in the excerpt. Option (5) is a true statement, but does not state the main idea of the excerpt.

2. **(3) you, while driving a car borrowed from your neighbor** (Application) The excerpt states that liability coverage covers the insured when driving another car with permission. Option (1) is incorrect because your son has to be driving your car to be covered. Option (2)

is incorrect because your son did not have permission to borrow the car and so is not covered. Options (4) and (5) are incorrect because, according to this excerpt, liability insurance does not cover friends.

3. **(3) the greatest amount the insurance company will pay if you injure someone** (Analysis) The excerpt states that the declarations include the limits—that is, the maximum amounts for which you are covered (lines 28–29). The other options are not mentioned in the description of declarations.

4. **(2) is responsible for damage** (Comprehension) The excerpt states that liability is "damage for which you are legally responsible" (lines 10–11) and then discusses what this includes. Options (1), (3), and (5) are too specific and are therefore incorrect. There is no support in the excerpt for option (4).

5. **(1) liability** (Analysis) The excerpt states that liability insurance pays for "emergency first aid to the injured" (line 23). Medical coverage pays for medical treatment only for the "insured, covered passengers, and covered family members" (lines 43–45) and so would not cover a pedestrian. Therefore, option (2) is incorrect. Option (3) is incorrect because medical coverage pays for damage inflicted upon the insured and his or her property, not the other way around. Options (4) and (5) are incorrect because they deal with damage to the car, not to a pedestrian.

6. **(5) collision and comprehensive** (Analysis) The excerpt states that collision coverage pays for damages to the insured's car resulting from an accident with another car or object and that comprehensive coverage applies to most other damage to the insured's car. It also states that the amount paid to repair the car is based on its age, use, and wear and tear. You can infer that for an older car, this amount would likely be less than it would cost to repair the car and less than the amount of accumulated premiums.

7. **(3) comprehensive and collision** (Analysis) A car serves as collateral for the loan that finances its purchase. Therefore, it is in the loan company's best interest to ensure that comprehensive and collision coverage is kept in place so that the car can be repaired in the event of damage. This allows the company to maintain its claim on the vehicle until the loan is paid.

8. **(2) It might lower your insurance payment.** (Synthesis) The more the insured is willing to pay in deductibles to cover a loss, the less the insurer has to pay. This would tend to make the insurance payments, or premiums, lower. Option (1) is probably the opposite effect

that an increased deductible has on coverage. Option (3) is not necessarily true. Option (4) is true, but it benefits the insurance company more than it benefits the insured. Option (5) is incorrect because the amount of the deductible has nothing to do with a driver's risk of having an accident.

9. **(3) explaining features in order of their importance** (Synthesis) In introducing the types of coverages, the excerpt begins with the most important—liability coverage. Then it describes less important coverages, such as medical payments and underinsured/uninsured motorists coverage. It ends with those that are the most expendable, collision and comprehensive.

Lesson 4
GED Skill Focus (Page 55)
1. **c.** Plants can die from fungus infections.

2. Sample answer: Tropical areas have both high temperatures and high humidity for long periods of time. Both of these factors put plants at risk of incurring fungus infections.

3. Sample answer: A person's hands can pass fungus infections to plants if the person was handling a plant that was already infected with a fungus, or by handling a pot in which an infected plant used to grow.

4. **a.** An ounce of prevention is worth a pound of cure.

5. Sample answer: By spending a little time preventing a problem right now, you will avoid spending a great deal of time fixing the problem later.

GED Practice (Pages 56–57)
1. **(1) the insurance plan pays** (Comprehension) The last sentence of the second paragraph defines the coinsurance provision as 90 percent of the covered charges that the network (to which the insurance plan belongs) pays.

2. **(2) Up to 6 months' leave is granted if the father is to be the primary caretaker.** (Application). The excerpt states that the company is progressive and employee friendly. This would be consistent with a generous paternity leave. Options (1), (4), and (5) are not generous and so are incorrect. Option (3) is far too generous; it would be impractical for any company to offer an unlimited amount of time.

3. **(3) Their use helps to control insurance costs.** (Analysis) Cost containment is a compelling reason for employers to encourage the use of certain healthcare providers. There is

nothing in the excerpt to suggest that approved eyecare professionals are more qualified than those that are not approved. Therefore, option (1) is incorrect. Option (4) implies that out-of-network eyecare professionals overcharge their patients, a generalization that is unfounded. Options (2) and (5) are not supported by the facts in the excerpt.

4. **(4) to increase efficiency and productivity** (Comprehension) The first line of the excerpt states, "Used correctly, voice mail is a tool to enhance your personal effectiveness and your company's productivity." Options (1), (2), and (3) are not benefits of the technology that are mentioned in the excerpt. Option (5) is a benefit that is cited but is not the chief purpose of voice mail as stated at the beginning of the excerpt.

5. **(1) a cash (ATM) machine** (Application) ATM machines decrease the workload of busy bank tellers and also help customers get their banking done more efficiently. This is similar to the role voice mail plays as described in the excerpt; it reduces the workload of receptionists and secretaries and helps the people with whom they come in contact. Options (2) and (3) have some aspects in common with voice mail: both are technological advances and both make some tasks quicker and more efficient. However, neither replaces the need for a person to do the work as effectively as either voice mail or ATM machines and therefore are not the best choices. Options (4) and (5) have little in common with voice mail and therefore are incorrect.

6. **(1) choosing to leave a voice mail message rather than speaking to a person directly** (Application) According to the author, the purpose of voice mail is to enable a person to leave a message when he or she cannot reach an individual, not to avoid talking to the person. Options (2) through (5) are acceptable uses of voice mail based on the information in the excerpt.

7. **(2) direct** (Synthesis) The excerpt discusses the benefits and appropriate uses of voice mail in a clear, easy-to-understand manner. None of the other options is supported by the excerpt.

GED Mini-Test (Pages 58–59)
1. **(4) revising** (Comprehension) The entire focus of the article is on the importance of revision. None of the other steps in the writing process is discussed in the same detail.

2. **(3) artist** (Comprehension) Paragraph five of the excerpt recommends that writers develop the mindset of painters and musicians who look forward to revising their work and consider it an important step. Options (1), (2), and (5) are

Answers and Explanations

not supported by the excerpt. Option (4) is mentioned as an attitude that writers should avoid, not develop, and therefore is incorrect.

3. **(3) perfecting** (Comprehension) In contrasting the business letter writer's attitude toward revision with that of the painter's, the authors describe the painter's final touchups to a painting as perfecting it. It is suggested that by carefully reviewing a business letter for mistakes, a writer can perfect it as well.

4. **(1) Revision in Five Easy Steps** (Analysis) The excerpt details the revision process by giving writers five quick steps to follow. The first paragraph of the excerpt implies that revising may take as little as five minutes; therefore, it is only a part of the writing process, making option (2) incorrect. Option (3) may be a true statement about the process of writing but is not the emphasis of the excerpt. Option (4) addresses only one aspect of the process of revision—writers' distaste for it. Option (5) is incorrect because the excerpt does not suggest that revision is the first step in rewriting.

5. **(2) Step 2** (Application) Twain's statement refers to word use, and Step 2 of the excerpt addresses the words used in a letter or memo. Option (1) refers to the main idea of the message, option (3) refers to the letter's coherence, option (4) refers to surface errors, and option (5) refers to the way the letter looks on the page.

6. **(3) It will not detect context errors.** (Analysis) Spell-check corrects words that are misspelled. However, it cannot detect correctly spelled words that are used in the wrong contexts. Option (1) does not address the question. No evidence in the excerpt supports option (2). Option (4) is a true statement but does not explain why the spell-check function is not foolproof. Option (5) describes an error made by a writer, not a problem with the spell-check mechanism.

7. **(4) Dress for success.** (Application) Step 5 concerns the look of the document on the page. It implies that a document that "looks" good will be more effective in the same way that a person who is nicely dressed may be more effective in business.

8. **(1) friendly and informal** (Synthesis) The authors refer to the reader in the first person throughout the excerpt and describe the revision process in lighthearted terms. None of the other options accurately describe the style of the excerpt.

9. **(3) posing a problem and giving a solution** (Synthesis) The excerpt presents the problem in the first two paragraphs—the failure of writers to

review their work with an eye toward revising it. The rest of the excerpt is devoted to providing solutions to the problem.

Lesson 5
GED Skill Focus (Page 61)
1. **a.** dance

2. **c.** Tharp has little money to spend to put on performances.

3. **d.** Due to the economy, the future of Tharp's art is bleak.

4. **a.** There is no money for stage props.
   b. Dancers wear practice clothes rather than costumes.
   c. The music is taped.
   d. Ticket prices are scaled down.

You may also have listed that Tharp is working without her own company and without a permanent base of support.

GED Practice (Pages 62–63)
1. **(2) believes that he was self-serving** (Comprehension) The author describes how Johnson befriended an older man at college and flattered him in order to gain power. This suggests that Johnson was out to use other people in order to get what he wanted. Johnson's skill at campaigning is not mentioned in the excerpt, so option (1) is incorrect. Options (3), (4), and (5) are not supported by the facts in the excerpt.

2. **(4) He was a flatterer.** (Comprehension) The author uses a form of the word *flatter* three times in one sentence (lines 22–23). This indicates that the author feels strongly that Lyndon Johnson used flattery to get what he wanted. Options (1) and (2) are not used to describe Johnson. Option (3) is used to describe Johnson's flattery, not Johnson himself. Option (5) is used to describe Johnson, but does not explain how he attained power.

3. **(2) He tried to become friends with men who could help him.** (Analysis) The author describes how Johnson became friends with older men who helped him acquire power. Although Johnson did befriend powerful men, there is no evidence in the excerpt to suggest that he did not form other types of friendships. Therefore, option (5) is incorrect. There is no support in the excerpt for the other options.

4. **(2) Johnson could wheel and deal.** (Synthesis) To get programs passed by Congress, presidents must be able to successfully persuade legislators to support them, a form of wheeling and dealing. Option (1) is incorrect because this would likely make it more difficult to get

legislation passed. Although being shameless could possibly help in getting bills passed, it is not a strong enough characteristic to get legislation passed. Therefore, option (3) is incorrect. Option (4) is incorrect because the excerpt suggests that the only people Johnson cared about pleasing were those who could help him. Option (5) is an opinion that is not supported by the excerpt.

5. **(4) The benefits of preservation can't always be measured in dollars and cents.** (Comprehension) The phrase "economic benefits" pertains to making money. From the context of the sentence, you can infer that the word *intangible* means "not measurable by money." None of the other options make sense in the context of the excerpt.

6. **(3) making profits from new building projects** (Analysis) The writer states that developers are often willing to duplicate a certain style and implies that they describe some historic buildings as not achieving their "highest tax-generating potential" (lines 35–36). This suggests that developers are more concerned about making money than preserving historic neighborhoods. Option (1) might be true, but would not be real estate developers' chief concern. They are trying to make a profit and do not work for the city. Options (2) and (5) are not mentioned in the excerpt. Option (4) is the concern of the author of the editorial, not the real estate developers.

7. **(1) to raise awareness about the importance of preserving historic buildings** (Synthesis) The entire editorial focuses on the importance of preserving historic buildings that serve as a unique glimpse into the city's past. None of the other options reflect the overall purpose of the editorial.

GED Mini-Test (Pages 64–65)

1. **(2) a train** (Comprehension) The details in the excerpt lead the reader to infer that the "Demon" is a train: it travels on tracks, it gives off smoke, and it stops at a station. Options (1) and (3) are incorrect because they refer to people. Options (4) and (5) are incorrect because the description of the "Demon" clearly refers to a train, not a trolley car or a boat.

2. **(1) as if the author knows what Ishi is thinking** (Analysis) The biographer is writing as if she sees through Ishi's eyes. Option (2) is incorrect because Ishi is not telling his own story. Options (3) and (5) have no support. The author seems to know Ishi well, so option (4) is incorrect.

3. **(3) sympathetic** (Analysis) The description of the man's nervousness shows understanding.

Option (1) might refer to Ishi at one point, but not to the author. There is no support for options (2), (4), and (5).

4. **(2) It emphasizes that the train seemed alive.** (Analysis) The words in the description refer to the train as if it had human characteristics. There is no support for option (1). Option (3) is suggested by calling the train a demon, but the author is saying that Ishi sees trains as powerful and frightening, not evil. There is no support for option (4). Option (5) has nothing to do with the excerpt.

5. **(4) He had never expected to ride a train.** (Comprehension) The excerpt as a whole suggests this idea. For example, it is supported by Ishi's mother telling him that trains had nothing to do with Indians. Option (1) might be true, but it is not suggested in the excerpt. Option (2) is the opposite of what is suggested. There is no support for options (3) and (5).

6. **(4) the hooting of the train's whistle** (Analysis) This phrase refers to the noise the train makes as it comes into the station. Option (1) is incorrect because it is the train's noise being referred to, not that of people. Option (2) is incorrect because a clank is different from a moan. The noise is not Ishi's, so option (3) is incorrect. A cloud does not make a sound, so option (5) is incorrect.

7. **(2) excitement at another new experience** (Application) Because Ishi enjoyed the train ride and described the ferry and trolley rides as "wonders," it is likely that he would be excited to experience a taxi cab ride. Therefore, option (1) is incorrect. Option (3) is incorrect because, although Ishi finds the train's speed exciting, it is not a major part of his feelings about his travels. Options (4) and (5) are not discussed in the excerpt.

8. **(3) It lets him experience the journey of rivers and creeks.** (Comprehension) In lines 57–66, Ishi notes that now he can see how creeks and rivers from home reach the sea. No one he knew had ever seen this route. It is not clear that Ishi will not ride a train again, so option (1) is incorrect. Option (2) is not stated in the excerpt. While option (4) may be true, it is not indicated by the author as the reason for the route's importance to Ishi. Option (5) is true but does not indicate why the route is important to Ishi.

9. **(4) Ishi did not want the Demon to follow him.** (Analysis) Ishi's mother told him that the Demon followed white men but never bothered Indians. You can draw the conclusion that Ishi wants the Demon to know he is Indian so it

will not follow him. There is no support in the excerpt for the other options.

Lesson 6
GED Skill Focus (Page 67)
1. **b.** conversational

2. **c.** sincere

3. Sure, I'm lucky; that's something; when you have . . .

4. **b.** informal

GED Practice (Pages 68–69)
1. **(4) understanding poetry** (Comprehension) For Frost, "coming close to poetry" means understanding "what it [is] all about" (line 23). There is no evidence for options (1), (2), (3), and (5).

2. **(1) Both are inexact and unscientific.** (Comprehension) The fact that, for Frost, the best indication of a student's grasp of poetry is a "right remark" (line 28) shows how inexact and unscientific both teaching it and understanding it are. There is no evidence for options (2), (3), (4), and (5).

3. **(3) Grading a student's understanding of poetry is difficult and circumstantial.** (Analysis) From the excerpt, you can conclude that Frost believes that grading a person's understanding of poetry is not a simple task. Frost says that a passing grade may depend on only one remark, providing it is a good one. Option (1) is incorrect because Frost says he doesn't believe everyone should write poetry. Option (2) is incorrect because it can be inferred that, for Frost, grading a student's understanding of poetry is neither exact nor simple. Option (4) is a misreading of the excerpt. Option (5) is true of Frost's grading system, but it is not the best summary of his ideas.

4. **(5) serious and conversational** (Synthesis) The subject, understanding poetry, is serious, but the author writes about it as though he is having a conversation with the reader, frequently referring to himself, using "I." Option (1) is incorrect because the language used is not formal. Options (2), (3), and (4) do not characterize the style in which the excerpt is written.

5. **(2) step up their efforts to end apartheid** (Comprehension) In the first paragraph, the speaker says it is "time to intensify the struggle on all fronts" (lines 3–4) and that "the sight of freedom looming on the horizon should encourage [his people] to redouble [their] efforts" (lines 6–8). This means that they must step up their efforts to end apartheid. The speaker

believes that universal suffrage (voting rights) is important, but suffrage is not the focus of the speech. Therefore, option (1) is incorrect. Options (3) and (4) are the opposite of what the speaker is asking. Mandela asks for the help of other nations, but he is not appealing to his supporters to ask for this help. Therefore, option (5) is incorrect.

6. **(5) in view** (Analysis) Mandela says throughout the excerpt that freedom is within reach but that everyone must work together to attain it. Because freedom is within reach, option (1) is incorrect. Although option (2) may be true, it is not the intended meaning of the speaker's phrase and therefore is incorrect. Options (3) and (4) are incorrect because they give the impression that people do not need to work to attain freedom.

7. **(2) It emphasizes the need to work together.** (Analysis) The speaker's frequent use of the word "we" emphasizes the fact that ending apartheid is a common struggle that all South Africans must participate in to win their freedom. Option (1) is incorrect because nothing in the excerpt suggests that the speaker is not one of the common people. Options (3) and (4) are not the main effects of Mandela's use of the pronoun. Option (5) characterizes the speaker but does not explain the effectiveness of his repeated use of "we."

8. **(4) impassioned** (Synthesis) The speaker makes an emotional appeal to the people to continue the struggle against apartheid. The last paragraph, in which he dedicates his life to the cause, conveys his passion. None of the other options effectively describes the tone of the speech.

GED Mini-Test (Pages 70–71)
1. **(4) It has an easygoing, chatty tone.** (Synthesis) The author's chatty, conversational style is typical of an informal essay. There is no evidence for options (1), (2), (3), and (5).

2. **(2) Civilization would have come to the lake.** (Comprehension) "The tarred road" is a highway (civilization) that found its way to the lake. The author fears that the lake is no longer a secluded spot. There is no support for options (1) and (3). Options (4) and (5) are the opposite of what worried the author.

3. **(4) His son had never swum in a lake.** (Comprehension) The author states that he took his son along to the lake because his son had never experienced a lakeside vacation. There is no support for options (1) and (2). Option (3) is incorrect because the author implies that his son has experienced salt water. Option (5) may be true, but the author's references to salt water suggest the opposite.

4. **(3) The more things change, the more they stay the same.** (Application) In lines 28–39, the author wonders whether time has changed his summer vacation spot. In lines 72–78, he says that when he and his son settled into a camp near a farmhouse, he could tell that it would be pretty much the same as it had been before, even though he is now grown with a child of his own. There is some evidence to support options (1), (2), and (4), but option (3) is the expression that most strongly captures the main idea of the excerpt. Option (5) has no relationship to the excerpt.

5. **(3) He longs to recapture the joys of his youth.** (Analysis) In line 24 the author refers to visiting old haunts. In lines 39–57 he reviews memories obviously dear to him and wonders wistfully if things will still be the same. His fear that things may have changed suggests how much he wants to recapture his youth. There is some evidence to support options (1), (2), (4), and (5), but option (3) is the implication that is best supported by the excerpt.

6. **(2) He was experiencing the lake from both his own and his father's perspectives.** (Analysis) Because the author's son has developed similar behaviors to those the author had when he was a boy, the author realizes that his experience at the lake involves identifying not only with his childhood memories but also with his father. Options (1) and (4) are incorrect because they are literal interpretations of the author's words. The author does not indicate a conflict between his feelings toward the sea and the lake; therefore, option (3) is incorrect. Option (5) may be true, but it is not what the author is referring to.

7. **(5) He felt himself turning into the man his father once was.** (Analysis) The excerpt states that "suddenly it would be not I but my father who was saying the words or making the gesture" (lines 91–93) as a reason for the creepy sensation. There is no support in the excerpt for the other options.

8. **(1) to introduce the basic situation that the essay will address** (Synthesis) The first paragraph provides the background and tells the reader what the author will address in the essay. Option (2) might result from introducing the basic situation, but is not the purpose of the first paragraph. Option (3) is incorrect because the paragraph does not go into great detail about the relationship between the author and his father. Option (4) is incorrect because the theme is developed in the essay's succeeding paragraphs. Option (5) is incorrect because the author's son is not introduced in the first paragraph.

Lesson 7
GED Skill Focus (Page 73)
1. **c.** Collins handles Armstrong's money.

2. **a.** Collins demands payment from the promoter.
   b. Armstrong waited for the matter to be settled.
   d. The promoter went to his office to get the money.

3. **a.** The word "cheque" is a spelling of "check" not used in the United States.
   c. The promoter came back with several bags of half-crowns of silver.
   e. The speaker thought that Collins did not know how to count the money.

GED Practice (Pages 74–75)
1. **(3) Show runners are among the most important people in television.** (Analysis) The author states that the show runner is more influential than screenwriters or heads of production companies; therefore, option (1) is incorrect. Because the excerpt does not state that production companies always intrude, option (2) is incorrect. Option (4) is the opposite of what is implied in the excerpt. There is no support in the excerpt for option (5).

2. **(1) writing the pilot for a related new show** (Application) The excerpt defines the responsibilities of the show runner for a series that is already in production. It does not suggest that the show runner is responsible for a new show based on an existing series; therefore, it is probable that this is something the show runner would delegate to someone else. All the other options are responsibilities described as belonging to the show runner.

3. **(2) The guiding force behind *E.R.* is largely unknown to viewers.** (Synthesis) One would expect that the most influential person involved in the production of a popular TV series would be a high-profile person such as the producer or director; in reality, however, it is a person whom most viewers have never heard of. Option (1) is not true based on the excerpt. Option (3) is neither stated nor implied in the excerpt. Options (4) and (5) do not illustrate irony.

4. **(3) People were reacting to the tornado's effects.** (Comprehension) This option includes the actions of all the people in the excerpt. Options (1), (2), (4), and (5) refer to details in the excerpt, not to the general situation.

5. **(5) She did not understand why her husband had contacted her.** (Comprehension) Mrs. Miller had not worried about her husband because she did not realize there was anything to worry about. Option (1) is

highly unlikely. Most people find tornadoes very frightening. There is no evidence to support options (2) and (3). Although Mrs. Miller clearly did not know about the tornado, there is no evidence that she slept through it, option (4).

6. **(1) suspenseful** (Synthesis) The first paragraph describes the aftereffects of the tornado and ends with the anticipation of a possible second tornado, creating suspense. The suspense is sustained in the second paragraph when the narrator says that he did not know his companion's whereabouts. Options (2) and (5) are inappropriate to describe the tone of such a devastating event. Option (3) is incorrect because although the tornado was unfortunate, it is not described as a tragedy. Option (4) is incorrect because there is no mention of death resulting from the tornado.

7. **(3) an eyewitness account** (Synthesis) The excerpt is narrated in the first person and relates the events from one person's perspective. This is similar to an eyewitness account. Option (1) is incorrect because there is no evidence that the events described in the excerpt are exaggerated or untrue. A newspaper article would not be written in the first person, so option (2) is incorrect. A television interview would consist of questions and answers; therefore option (4) is incorrect. There is no evidence in the excerpt that suggests the speaker is relating his story to the police, so option (5) is also incorrect.

GED Mini-Test (Pages 76–77)

1. **(4) The people were as violent as the weather.** (Comprehension) The excerpt states that the country was wild and describes instances of harsh and violent weather. It then goes on to describe the people as angry and violent. Options (1) and (3) have nothing do with the land. Option (2) is incorrect because the way people look is not described in the excerpt. Option (5) is true but does not answer the question.

2. **(2) preparing a special ceremony** (Comprehension) The excerpt states that the person was "almost sure to be shot or ground-sluiced" (lines 22–23) and refers to his "broken body" (lines 23–24). This indicates that the potlatch in his memory is some type of funeral ceremony. Options (1), (4), and (5) all refer to happy occasions, not the sad occasion of death, and so are incorrect. There is no support for option (3).

3. **(2) The white man invaded native lands.** (Analysis) The white man "came tearing through" (lines 27–28) after the discovery of gold and is described as being mean as a bear. Therefore, you can conclude that the white man

invaded land inhabited by Indians and Eskimos. Options (1) and (4) might be true but they are not mentioned in the excerpt. While option (3) might be a logical inference, there is no evidence to support it. Lines 29–34 mention the white man's cruelty, so option (5) is not supported by the excerpt.

4. **(3) is located in a very remote region** (Analysis) The location in the excerpt is described as a long day's walk north of the Arctic Circle, an area of the Earth near the North Pole. Option (1) is not stated or implied in the excerpt. Although the writer mentions that people did sometimes get lost, the excerpt does not imply that the land was easy to get lost in, making option (2) incorrect. There is no evidence in the excerpt to support options (4) and (5).

5. **(3) He had varied interests.** (Comprehension) "[A]ll knowledge as his sphere" (line 20) means that he had a desire for knowledge. Da Vinci's genius was not limited to one area. The review refers to "an aptitude for all manner of achievement" (lines 5–6) and states that "all things, human and divine, were fit subjects . . ." (lines 47–48). Although option (1) may be true, it is not the meaning of line 20. Options (2), (4), and (5) suggest qualities not supported by the review.

6. **(3) This quality is common to da Vinci's style.** (Comprehension) The excerpt states that the poetic sense in the painting is a da Vinci quality and that many of da Vinci's paintings are mysterious. There is no support in the excerpt for option (1). Option (2) is incorrect because this phrase is used to describe the *Last Supper*, not the *Mona Lisa*. Option (4) may be true but does not explain why the painting is mysterious, and option (5) is the opposite of what is described in the excerpt.

7. **(2) He is a knowledgeable art critic.** (Analysis) The author knowledgeably evaluates two of da Vinci's most famous paintings—the *Last Supper* and the *Mona Lisa*, praising one and criticizing the popular opinion of the other. This suggests that the author is an art critic. There is no evidence to support the other options.

8. **(4) The *Mona Lisa* is a good painting; the *Last Supper* is a great one.** (Analysis) The author states that the *Mona Lisa* is overrated but still has a "balance of monumental form and lyrical feeling" (lines 37–38). This indicates that he thinks the *Mona Lisa* is a good painting, although not as good as many people think; this contrasts with his very high opinion of the *Last Supper*—"one of the finest instances of a rigid geometric enclosure" (lines 27–28). Option (1) is

incorrect because both paintings are known worldwide. Option (2) is incorrect because it does not contrast the two paintings. Option (3) is incorrect because the author does not seem to think the *Mona Lisa* is a bad painting; only that it is overrated. There is no support in the excerpt for option (5).

Lesson 8
GED Skill Focus (Page 79)
1. **b.** the real world

2. **a.** real taxi drivers
   b. TV taxi drivers

3. but

4. **c.** Television and real life contain many of the same places and things.

GED Practice (Pages 80–81)
1. **(1) Burr killed the aging Hamilton.** (Comprehension) The excerpt states that Burr sealed his fate with one bullet and that Hamilton could not care for his family (lines 41–44); this indicates that Burr shot and killed Hamilton. There is no support in the excerpt for the other options.

2. **(4) Both men sought power.** (Analysis) The excerpt describes both men as being excessively ambitious. Option (1) is incorrect because only Burr came close to winning the presidency. Option (2) is incorrect because only Burr was considered a pariah, or outcast. Option (3) is incorrect because both men are described as being potentially dangerous to the nation, and option (5) is incorrect because only Hamilton was a Federalist.

3. **(4) He is sympathetic toward both men.** (Analysis) The third paragraph credits Fleming with portraying both Burr and Hamilton accurately while at the same time making them likeable (lines 13–15). This suggests that he was sympathetic to both subjects. None of the other options is supported by the information in the excerpt.

4. **(5) analytical** (Synthesis) The author examines the changing perception of beauty in the recent history of photography in an intellectual and analytical manner. She is not argumentative; therefore, option (1) is incorrect. She does express opinions and offers evidence to support them; however, she does not seem to be trying to persuade readers. Therefore, option (2) is incorrect. She describes her perception of how ideas of beauty have changed; however, her discussion goes much deeper than a mere description; therefore, option (3) is not the best choice. Although she does explain certain ideas, option (4), this is not her main focus.

5. **(3) to photograph everyday subjects** (Comprehension) The excerpt states that ambitious photographers "conscientiously [explore] plain, tawdry, or even vapid material" (lines 14–15). The photographs resulting from this exploration may be beautiful or lyrical, but beauty or lyricism is not the photographers' main goal; therefore, option (1) is incorrect. There is no support for option (2). The excerpt states that these photographers explore plain and vapid subjects but not that the resulting photographs are themselves plain and vapid; therefore, option (4) is incorrect. The photographers probably do want their photographs to get into museums, but the excerpt does not indicate that this is their primary aim; therefore, option (5) is incorrect.

6. **(5) feeling is to indifference** (Synthesis) The excerpt describes American experience "as catalogued with passion by Whitman and as sized up with a shrug by Warhol" (lines 41–43). The two important words in this statement are "passion" and "shrug"; they suggest the idea that Whitman is filled with feeling and Warhol is indifferent. The other options contain words that relate to ideas in the excerpt, but not to descriptions of the two men.

7. **(1) Every being has dignity and worth.** (Application) The excerpt mentions Whitman's beliefs that every subject has beauty and that each person's actions and ideas are important. Therefore, he is likely to believe that all things and beings have dignity and are valuable. There is no evidence in the excerpt to support the other options.

GED Mini-Test (Pages 82–83)
1. **(5) Both come across as big spenders.** (Analysis) Lines 24–30 state that the New Hampshire Republican chairman wrote a press release that claimed both men "spent the entire $1 trillion dollar surplus in 60 minutes on national television." This statement characterizes both candidates as big spenders. Options (1), (2), (3), and (4) are not true.

2. **(2) Bradley is reserved; Gore is friendly.** (Analysis) The excerpt says that Bradley was "as usual, quiet almost to the point of diffidence" (lines 32–34), which suggests reserve, and that Gore interacted with the audience to make an impression, which indicates a friendly personality. Option (1) is incorrect because, according to the author, the tags "outsider" and "insider" do not accurately describe the candidates' experience. Option (3) is incorrect because the excerpt states that Gore worked much harder to make an impression than Bradley—not that Bradley did not work to make

an impression. There is no evidence in the excerpt to support options (4) and (5).

3. **(1) their choice of political role models** (Comprehension) The author states that the most revealing moment attracted almost no attention. He then goes on to describe the candidates' role models. Option (2) is not mentioned in the excerpt and therefore is incorrect. Options (3) and (4) are mentioned but not emphasized or discussed in detail and therefore are incorrect. Option (5) is discussed at length but is not described as offering the most insight into the candidates' characters; therefore, it is incorrect.

4. **(3) Gore wanted to appear accessible to the public.** (Analysis) Gore was answering the public's questions; the author implies that Gore did this so people would feel that he was listening to them. There is no support in the excerpt for options (1), (2), and (5). The author states that "Gore worked much harder to make an impression" (lines 35–36), showing that Gore was not being particularly spontaneous or genuine; therefore, option (4) is incorrect.

5. **(4) Gore often goes too far.** (Comprehension) To leave well enough alone means to recognize when things are going well and not overdo them. There is no support in the excerpt for options (1), (2), (3), or (5).

6. **(5) inoffensive** (Analysis) The author describes Gore's choices of Lincoln, Roosevelt, and Johnson as safe, predictable, unoriginal, and without risk of offending anyone. Options (1), (2), (3), and (4) do not accurately fit this description.

7. **(2) paragraphs 3 and 4** (Analysis) Paragraph 3 describes the candidates as having nearly equal experience in Washington. Paragraph 4 suggests that both would spend the projected budget surplus on expensive federal programs. The other options are incorrect because one or both of the paragraphs do not focus on the candidates' similarities .

8. **(2) The contrast between the candidates was not as sharp as expected.** (Synthesis) Lines 1–4 suggest that the lack of clear-cut distinctions between the candidates made it difficult to set the men apart. Options (1), (3), (4), and (5) cannot be supported based on the information presented in the excerpt.

Lesson 9
GED Skill Focus (Page 85)

1. **b.** He is a frequent watcher of weather reports.

2. **a.** fascinated and awed

3. **c.** He finds them interesting, yet a bit artificial.

4. Your answers may include the following details from the excerpt:

The author compares reporters who cover the weather to reporters who cover celebrities.
The author is very familiar with the satellite images of hurricane Floyd shown on television news.
Based on his own experience, the author states that television news cannot communicate to viewers the actual size and power of a hurricane.

GED Practice (Pages 86–87)

1. **(3) It is an entertaining film.** (Analysis) The reviewer's opinion can be found in lines 36–38. Although option (1) is an opinion expressed by the reviewer, option (3) better describes his opinion of the movie as a whole. Options (2) and (4) are opinions not held by the reviewer. Option (5) is a fact, not an opinion.

2. **(2) Branagh is perfect for the role of Henry V.** (Analysis) The paragraph describes how Branagh identifies with the role, is involved in many aspects of the movie, and looks and sounds perfect for the part. Options (1) and (3) are not supported by the paragraph. Options (4) and (5) are details from the paragraph but not the main idea.

3. **(1) Shakespeare's play *Henry V* is criticized.** (Synthesis) In the first paragraph, the reviewer refers to *Henry V* as not one of Shakespeare's best. In the last paragraph, he describes the last 10 minutes of the movie in which Henry courts his future wife as needlessly cute, assigning part of the fault for the weakness to Shakespeare. Option (2) is incorrect because only the final paragraph summarizes a scene from the movie. Options (3), (4), and (5) are not true of the review.

4. **(1) It is an appealing, though flawed, love story.** (Comprehension) The reviewer points out several appealing elements of the movie, including the strong cast, the smooth direction, and the interesting subject. However, he also indicates several failings, such as its glossy characters, their predictable struggles, and the awkward plot structure. Taken together, these points suggest that the film, though appealing, is flawed. Option (2) is not stated or implied by the reviewer. Option (3) is not true; the reviewer does not imply that the movie is a complete failure. Options (4) and (5) are too positive; neither takes into account the many flaws mentioned in the review.

5. **(2) It suggests that there is a slow, plodding pace to the movie.** (Analysis) By emphasizing how long it took for the lovers to get together, the reviewer suggests that the pace of the movie is too slow. Option (1) is incorrect because the reviewer is not that enthusiastic about the film. There is no support in the excerpt

for options (3) and (5). Option (4) indicates an effect opposite to the one intended.

6. **(5) if the plot were structured differently** (Application) One of the reviewer's main criticisms of the film is that the plot is awkwardly structured. This suggests that the film might have been improved if the plot had been structured differently. None of the other options are supported by the details in the review.

GED Mini-Test (Pages 88–89)

1. **(5) The Discovery Channel** (Analysis) In the third paragraph the author states that the programs "on the Discovery Channel are continually interesting" (lines 34–35) and goes on to discuss particular programs at length. This suggests that this may well be the author's favorite. There is little or no support in the excerpt for the other options.

2. **(5) in the first and last paragraphs** (Synthesis) Only paragraphs 1 and 5, the first and last paragraphs of the excerpt, express the author's viewpoint that a comprehensive weekly teleguide with in-depth listings in any given area would be a great help to viewers.

3. **(2) would like more interest-focused, detailed program guides** (Comprehension) The commentary discusses the limitations of most program guides and the need for a more "encompassing" (line 61) guide. Options (1) and (3) are details in the excerpt, not the most important ideas, and so are incorrect. There is no support for option (4). Option (5) is incorrect because the author discusses his own habits in order to make his point; he is not trying to convince others to copy his behavior.

4. **(3) Its program guide is a waste of money.** (Analysis) Lines 43–47 discuss how the large number of repeats on A&E means that its A&E program guide is not worth the extra price. Option (2) is the opposite of this idea; therefore, it is incorrect. Option (1) is incorrect because it contradicts what is implied by the excerpt. There is no support for option (4). Although the author is critical of A&E, option (5) cannot be inferred from the excerpt.

5. **(1) informative** (Synthesis) The author supplies the information in a straightforward and informative manner. Option (2) is incorrect because the author seems frustrated but not angry. The author does not use humor in his discussion; therefore, option (3) is incorrect. Option (4) is incorrect because the author is annoyed rather than overwhelmed. The author is not pleased by the available television listings, so option (5) is incorrect.

6. **(4) They introduce his discussion of the virtues and limitations of *TV Guide*.** (Analysis) This author uses the story of removing the inserts as an introduction to the strengths and weaknesses of *TV Guide's* listings. Option (1) is incorrect because the author lists other limitations. The author's reference to the inserts as "obstacles" indicates that he dislikes them; therefore, option (2) is incorrect. There is no support for options (3) and (5).

7. **(3) methodical** (Synthesis) The author sets forth his argument by explaining methodically how he uses *TV Guide*. He describes the different channels and the programs that they air and the way in which these programs are listed. His word choice in describing the process and the careful way in which he addresses the subject help to categorize his writing style as serious and methodical. None of the other options accurately describe the style in which the commentary is written.

8. **(3) *TV Guide* does not have room to describe every show on every channel.** (Analysis) The excerpt states that it is frustrating to check the schedule because of the "numbers of channels chronicled" (lines 11–12). It also states that this is not the fault of *TV Guide* (line 24). These clues imply that there are so many channels that there is not enough room to list everything. There is no support in the excerpt for options (1) and (2). Options (4) and (5) are true, but do not explain why the listings are not complete.

9. **(3) superficial** (Comprehension) The author states that *TV Guide* merely lists the titles of programs for many channels. This is a superficial, or shallow, treatment of listings. There is no support in the excerpt for options (1) and (5). Option (2) is the opposite of what is suggested in the excerpt. Option (4) may be true but is not the focus of the discussion in the excerpt.

Unit 1 Cumulative Review (Pages 90–96)

1. **(4) the balls on the pool table and birds about to be hit** (Analysis) In this case the writer is mixing literal language, the description of the balls, with figurative language, comparing the balls to crows. Option (1) includes the cue stick, so it is incorrect. There is no evidence to support options (2) and (5). Option (3) is incorrect because it mistakes figurative language for literal language.

2. **(3) He is ferocious toward his prey.** (Analysis) Mosconi treats his opponents in a similar manner as a shark with prey. The second half of the excerpt reveals his impatience, so option (1) is incorrect. Option (2) has no support

in the excerpt. Option (4) confuses literal language with figurative language. While option (5) may be correct, it has no relationship to the comparison of Mosconi to a shark.

3. **(2) Mosconi is having fun.** (Analysis) The simile refers to a child at play. Hitting something with a slingshot is difficult, so option (1) is incorrect. Options (3) and (4) have no support in the excerpt. Option (5) confuses the figurative with the literal.

4. **(3) Celebrity status does not automatically qualify someone to sell a product.** (Synthesis) Mosconi's rude behavior toward the inexperienced woman followed by his realization of his purpose for being there support this generalization. Option (1) is incorrect because there is no evidence that Mosconi's appearance drew a crowd, which the excerpt says included passersby and escalator riders. Options (2) and (5) are opinions that are not supported by the facts in the excerpt. Option (4) is incorrect because Mosconi is not described as being comfortable playing more than one role.

5. **(2) is an umbrella for a number of other industries** (Comprehension) Lines 2–4 state that the temporary help industry is actually an industry consisting of many industries, meaning that it can be compared to an umbrella that has other industries under it. Option (1) is incorrect because the two industries are not the same. Options (3), (4), and (5) are not stated or implied in the excerpt.

6. **(5) the temporary service for which he works** (Application) The excerpt states that a "temporary employee is *never* the employee" of the location where he or she is on assignment (lines 24–27) and "*always* the employee of the temporary help firm" (lines 28–30). Therefore, it is sensible to bring the complaint to the employer—the temporary help service. Based on this, the other options are incorrect because they do not involve the worker's employer.

7. **(5) It offers opportunities for almost any profession.** (Analysis) The excerpt describes the four categories of temporary employment and the many types of jobs these categories include. There is no support in the excerpt for the other options.

8. **(3) Renters insurance policies can protect renters in a number of ways.** (Comprehension) The excerpt describes renters insurance, the terms associated with it, and the perils that it can protect policyholders against. Option (1) is incorrect because the excerpt does not discuss homeowners insurance. Option (2) is an opinion that is not supported in the excerpt.

Option (4) is a sales pitch, and option (5) is a claim that cannot be substantiated based on the information in the excerpt.

9. **(1) replacement cost coverage renters insurance** (Application) The excerpt states that this type of insurance will pay to replace the lost property "with comparable new property" (line 23). Option (2) is incorrect because this type of coverage pays replacement cost minus depreciation. The fact that the records are old might mean that this type of insurance would pay very little for their loss. Option (3) is incorrect because a deductible is a feature of many types of insurance, not a type of policy itself. Option (4) is incorrect because this type of insurance is for claims brought against the insured, not losses incurred by the insured. Option (5) covers only a single type of peril.

10. **(4) All renters should consider buying renters insurance.** (Analysis) The excerpt states that many renters overlook this commodity (line 2) and goes on to describe the many things it can cover. There is no support in the excerpt for options (1) and (5). Option (2) may be true of people who have experienced losses, but it is not mentioned or implied in the excerpt. Therefore, it is incorrect. Option (3) is mentioned in the excerpt but is not recommended; therefore, it is incorrect.

11. **(2) informative and direct** (Synthesis) The excerpt defines terms commonly used in renters insurance policies and explains the different types of coverage in a straightforward manner. None of the other options accurately describes the style in which it is written.

12. **(2) They think of telephone calls as social.** (Comprehension) Lines 7–9 say that "For most of us, using the telephone is a social skill, not a business skill." None of the other options is mentioned in the excerpt as reasons for failing to plan a telephone call.

13. **(5) They determine how successful the exchange will be.** (Comprehension) Lines 24–26 state that the first ten to fifteen seconds of a phone call set the tone for the conversation. This is the same as saying that this brief period of time determines how successful the exchange will be. None of the other options is stated in the excerpt.

14. **(4) Tips for Answering the Telephone Effectively** (Comprehension) The excerpt provides suggestions for the effective use of the telephone for business. Option (2) is incorrect because the excerpt discusses only one aspect of telephone etiquette. None of the other options is discussed in the excerpt.

15. **(3) conversational** (Synthesis) The author uses the first person throughout, which gives the excerpt a conversational, friendly tone. None of the other options accurately describes the style in which the excerpt is written.

16. **(2) It is hard to capture the beauty of Cather's writing on television.** (Comprehension) Throughout the excerpt, the reviewer discusses the difficulty of adapting Cather's prose to television. While option (1) is true, it did not prevent Cather's work from being adapted. There is no support for option (3). Options (4) and (5) are incorrect because the reviewer states that Cather's novels have been a "staple of American literature courses" (lines 9–10).

17. **(1) Some viewers will feel comfortable and familiar with the story.** (Analysis) This is suggested in the last paragraph of the excerpt. The other options may be true, but none of these is what lines 37–38 are suggesting.

18. **(4) She is a towering figure in American literature.** (Synthesis) Porter's words used to describe Cather, such as "immovable," "monumental virtue," and "symbol" all suggest a towering presence in American literature. Option (1) is not correct because it is a negative assessment, which Porter does not hold. There is no basis in the excerpt for options (2) and (3). Porter suggests that Cather's work was neglected, but does not go as far as to say that she is a symbol of the neglected American female writer, option (5).

19. **(3) His clients do not always want his best effort.** (Comprehension) The example suggests that customers are more interested in saving or making money; the author is more interested in quality. Options (1) and (2) are incorrect because money is not his main concern and because the reader does not learn how much money he makes or needs. There is no evidence for option (4). Option (5) is not true.

20. **(4) They are a little dishonest.** (Analysis) The author says that his employer "commonly asks which will give him the most land, not which is most correct" (lines 8–9). Employers do not criticize his work, option (1), or underpay him, option (3). Options (2) and (5) are not supported by the excerpt.

21. **(2) turn down the job** (Application) Based on his statements in lines 26–28, the narrator would refuse to do a job before doing work he didn't love. Money is apparently not important to the narrator, so option (1) is incorrect. Option (3) is incorrect because the narrator is obviously proud of his work. There is no support for options (4) and (5).

22. **(4) Thoreau prefers accuracy, and his employers prefer money.** (Synthesis) Thoreau seems to want to do the type of surveying that is "most correct" (line 9); also, he invented a rule for measuring wood, but it was rejected because it was too accurate. One of Thoreau's employers, on the other hand, wants the type of surveying "which will give him the most land" (lines 8–9), a signal that the employer is most interested in personal gain. Options (1), (3), and (5) are incorrect because there is no evidence in the excerpt that Thoreau's employers are not hardworking, do not like their work, or steal Thoreau's ideas. Option (2) is incorrect because it states a likeness and does not make a contrast.

23. **(3) Workers should do what they love and be paid well for it.** (Comprehension) The last paragraph of the excerpt states that the best worker to hire is one who "does it for love of it" (line 28). It also states that towns should pay laborers well. Option (1) is not clearly stated in the excerpt and so is incorrect. Option (2) is a detail in the paragraph but not the complete main idea and so is incorrect. Option (4) may be somewhat suggested by the paragraph but is not the main idea. Option (5) is not suggested by the paragraph; the word "moral" is used to refer to the feeling a well-paid worker might have toward his or her job.

24. **(3) well-known slavery opponents** (Comprehension) Lines 29–30 refer to Garrison, Lovejoy, and others agitating for freedom. This suggests that the two men were abolitionists seeking to overthrow the institution of slavery. There is no evidence in the excerpt to support options (1), (2), (4), and (5).

25. **(2) impressed with it** (Analysis) The author states that he could never understand how the slaves "were able to keep themselves so accurately and completely informed" (lines 25–27). This shows he was impressed. Options (1), (3), and (4) are incorrect because his attitude toward the slaves' understanding is clearly positive. Option (5) overstates the author's attitude and so is incorrect.

26. **(3) a person-to-person means of transmitting information** (Analysis) Lines 35–42 refer to "late-at-night whispered discussions" that the author heard his mother and other slaves indulge in, indicating that they "understood the situation." This suggests that "'grape-vine' telegraph" is another term for word-of-mouth communication. None of the other options makes sense in the context of the term.

27. **(4) the author's deep interest in education** (Synthesis) Lines 5–8 state that "The picture of several dozen boys and girls in a schoolroom

engaged in study made a deep impression upon [the author]." This suggests that the impression was long lasting and very likely motivated him to pursue a career in education. Options (1) and (5) would have no bearing on the author's pursuit of a career in education. There is no support in the excerpt for option (2). Option (3) might inspire a desire for learning but would not necessarily correlate with the pursuit of a career in education.

UNIT 2: UNDERSTANDING FICTION
Lesson 10
GED Skill Focus (Page 101)
1. **a.** unending
   b. endlessly

2. styles of design

3. **a.** little towers
   b. The turrets were "raised high above the other roofs," which hints that they are towers.

4. Your answers may include the following: shared, same, brown.

GED Practice (Pages 102–103)
1. **(2) drafted** (Comprehension) Although all five choices are definitions of "drawn," only option (2) makes sense in the context of the sentence.

2. **(3) the disagreement between parties over a treaty** (Analysis) The Senate battle was over the ratification of Jay's treaty. No evidence supports options (1), (4), or (5). The excerpt implies that the colonies have already rebelled against England; therefore, option (2) is incorrect.

3. **(2) telling the story through one character** (Analysis) The story is being narrated by Burr, the main character. No dialogue, dialect, or flashbacks are used in the excerpt. The conflict is between two political parties.

4. **(2) opinionated** (Analysis) Burr's description of Jay's treaty as being clumsily drawn and to the United States' disadvantage indicates his strong opinions. Options (1), (3), (4), and (5) are not supported by the excerpt.

5. **(3) positions on the relationship between the states and the central government** (Synthesis) The excerpt states "One wanted a loose confederation of states, the other a strong central administration" (lines 14–16). None of the other options are supported by the excerpt.

6. **(4) burning a house filled with books** (Comprehension) The excerpt describes the man burning a home (lines 14–16), and describes the books that are burning (lines 20–24). Option (1) is incorrect because the hose sprays kerosene, not water. Options (2), (3), and (5) have no support in the excerpt.

7. **(3) demolition worker** (Application) The man enjoys destroying things by burning them. A demolition worker also destroys things. Options (1) and (2) relate to construction or repair—the opposite of destruction. Option (4) is not supported and refers only to the mention of books in the excerpt. Option (5) is not related in any way to the excerpt.

8. **(1) detailed imagery** (Analysis) The author paints a picture of the man, the house, and the books. Options (2), (3), (4), and (5) do not occur in the excerpt.

9. **(2) The flames immediately engulfed the house.** (Comprehension) The kerosene-coated house has been ignited. Option (1) is incorrect because the flames are rising, not descending. Option (3) is incorrect because the house itself, not just the lawn, is on fire. The fire has just started, so options (4) and (5) are also incorrect.

10. **(3) a hose that is suggestive of a snake** (Comprehension) The word "nozzle" points to the conclusion that this is a figurative way of describing a hose. Options (1) and (2) are incorrect because the phrase "in his fists" shows that the character is holding the "great python." Option (4) is not supported; it merely mentions fire. Option (5) is incorrect because the hose contains kerosene, not water.

GED Mini-Test (Pages 104–105)
1. **(2) He is persistent.** (Synthesis) Although the networks may have found Hadden annoying, there is nothing in the excerpt to support options (1) and (3). There is also nothing in the excerpt to support option (5), and option (4) is the opposite of how he is portrayed.

2. **(4) television programs** (Comprehension) The excerpt states "the programs that were their nominal vehicles." This phrase clearly shows that the programs and the nominal vehicles are the same thing. Option (1) is incorrect because the ads were louder than the nominal vehicles, so they could not be the nominal vehicles. Options (2) and (3) are incorrect because there is no mention of anything to do with cars in the excerpt, indicating that "vehicle" has more than one meaning. Option (5) is the opposite of what the excerpt states.

3. **(1) a device that silences TV commercials** (Analysis) The first sentence says that Hadden had invented a module that automatically muted the sound when a commercial appeared. This information tells you that the product Adnix silences TV commercials. None of the other options support this conclusion.

4. **(3) Television networks do not have viewers' best interests at heart.** (Synthesis) Hadden kept attempting to thwart the networks' advertisements, which indicates that he believed the networks did not have viewers' best interests at heart. If Hadden believed in options (1), (4), or (5), he probably would not have built his device. Option (2) is not supported by the excerpt.

5. **(2) the undesirable nature of commercials** (Synthesis) The excerpt describes a character who invents a device that renders TV commercials mute. Based on this fact and the fact that people felt a sense of relief when freed from commercials, you can infer that the theme concerns the negative effects of commercial television. Option (1) is too broad a statement; option (2) is not implied by the information in the excerpt; option (4), though it may be inferred from the excerpt, is not the theme; and option (5) is the opposite of what the excerpt portrays.

6. **(4) the acceptance of "infomercials" to promote products** (Application) Of the options listed, only option (4) concerns commercials, the target of Hadden's inventions.

7. **(4) The U.S. government wanted to take over production and use of Hadden's chip.** (Analysis) Option (1) refers to an earlier trial. Options (2) and (3) are incorrect because the excerpt does not say that Hadden was involved in industrial espionage and military intelligence. Option (5) is incorrect because there is no mention of the U.S. government's wanting Hadden's muting device.

Lesson 11
GED Skill Focus (Page 107)

1. It takes place in Salem village, at the threshold of young Goodman Brown's house.

2. It takes place at dusk. You may also mention that the excerpt seems to take place a long time ago, because Faith's manner of speaking is not the manner in which people usually speak now.

3. Your answers may include the following: pretty, young, fearful, faithful.

4. **a.** The wife is afraid to be left alone.
   b. The wife begs her husband to stay.
   c. The husband leaves as darkness falls.

GED Practice (Pages 108–109)

1. **(1) selfish** (Analysis) *Selfish* means putting your own desires ahead of everyone else's. The grandmother does not want to go to Florida, so she tries to manipulate the family into doing what she wants. Option (2) is incorrect because she is mentioning The Misfit not because she is worried but because she doesn't want to go to

Florida. There is no support in the excerpt for options (3), (4), or (5).

2. **(2) They ignore her for the most part.** (Analysis) When her son doesn't answer her, the grandmother addresses her daughter-in-law, who acts as if she does not hear her. The little boy is the only one to make a comment, and he merely suggests that she stay home. There is no support in the excerpt for the other options.

3. **(2) a meeting in which a boss tries to change his staff's mind about an issue** (Application) The grandmother is trying very hard to change her family's mind about where to vacation. None of the other options are supported by the excerpt.

4. **(5) dialogue in which her manner of speaking is shown** (Analysis) The dialogue reveals the grandmother to be a pushy and self-centered woman. The excerpt contains no information about what she looks like or details about her heritage or her preferred reading matter; therefore, options (1), (2), and (3) are incorrect. The excerpt implies that the other characters find the grandmother tiresome, but there is no actual explanation of this; therefore, option (4) is incorrect.

5. **(3) caring** (Analysis) The woman's promise to wash the boy's face (line 42) suggests that she is a caring person who is concerned about the boy's welfare even though he tried to steal from her. Options (1) and (4) are suggested by the excerpt but are not the best descriptions of the woman's character. Options (2) and (5) are not supported by the excerpt.

6. **(1) take him to her house and feed him** (Application) Lines 43–45 indicate that the boy has no one at home to care for him. If the woman is willing to take the boy home to wash his face, it is believable that she would give him something to eat. Options (2) through (5) are not supported by the excerpt.

7. **(5) The woman helps the boy make something of himself.** (Synthesis) The story's title is "Thank You, M'am," and in the excerpt the woman says she will take the boy to her house to wash him. These details suggest that the woman will help the boy and that the boy will be thankful. Although the other options are possible, the details point most strongly to option (5).

GED Mini-Test (Pages 110–111)

1. **(2) They are close to one another.** (Analysis) The discussion between the two women indicates that though they differ in age, they are very familiar with each other. There is no direct

evidence for option (1). Based on their discussion, you can infer that the women sometimes do not agree and have had different experiences, but that they do respect each other. Therefore, options (3), (4), and (5) are incorrect.

2. **(1) They have different ideas about love.** (Analysis) Esther believes that imagination is important in a relationship, but her mother does not agree. This indicates that a conflict between the two women exists. None of the other options are supported by the excerpt.

3. **(2) She is afraid that Esther will make the same mistakes she made.** (Analysis) By stating her regrets (lines 34–37), Naomi is hoping to dissuade Esther from following in her footsteps. There is no evidence to support options (1) and (5). Although option (3) may be true, there is little direct evidence to support it. Option (4) is incorrect because even though Naomi complains about an attitude she thinks Esther picked up in college, there is no indication that she is not supportive of her daughter's education.

4. **(2) try to persuade Esther to talk to him** (Application) Based on Naomi's refusal to lie to Bruce on the telephone (lines 16–17), it can be inferred that she would invite him in and try to persuade Esther to talk to him. Therefore, option (1) is incorrect. There is no indication that Naomi dislikes Bruce, so option (3) is incorrect. Option (4) is incorrect because Naomi is afraid that Esther will get married too young. There is no support for option (5).

5. **(3) Esther and Naomi decide to respect their differences.** (Analysis) The origin of the conflict is the differences between the women. If they recognized and accepted those differences and made peace with each other, a satisfying resolution to the conflict would occur. There is no direct evidence that options (1), (2), or (5) would resolve the conflict between them. There is also no evidence that Esther's deciding never to marry, option (4), would resolve anything.

6. **(4) youth and experience** (Synthesis) The excerpt contrasts Naomi's life experience and Esther's youth, both of which are the source of the conflict between the two women. Although Naomi's unwillingness to lie is contrasted with her daughter's behavior, option (3) is not the central contrast of the excerpt. There is no support in the excerpt for options (1), (2), and (5).

7. **(2) daughter-in-law** (Analysis) The excerpt opens with the character Mike Senior, whom Janet calls "Pop." In lines 13 and 14, she says that Mike should be back any minute and invites Mike Senior to get reacquainted with Shawn, who is most likely a child. These are all clues that

"Mike" is Mike Junior and that Janet is Mike Senior's daughter-in-law.

8. **(3) The family has fallen on hard times.** (Analysis) They are not having turkey on Thanksgiving. This points to the family's not having enough money to pay for a proper Thanksgiving meal. There is no real support for options (1), (2), (4), and (5).

Lesson 12
GED Skill Focus (Page 113)

1. **b.** She would wish for the best and hope that her daughter wins

2. **b.** encouraging members of her household to register to vote

3. Prosperity is just around the corner.
   Things could be much worse than they are.
   It is always darkest before dawn.

4. Your answers may include the following statements:
   "There were so many ways for things to get better."
   "But she never looked back with regret."

GED Practice (Pages 114–115)

1. **(1) think the bone soup was responsible** (Application) Lines 23–26 state that the mother hoped that the bone soup would perform the miracle of detaching Caroline from her Bahamian fiancé. This suggests that the mother believed that it had special powers. None of the other options are supported by the details in the excerpt.

2. **(3) They like to poke fun at their mother's beliefs.** (Analysis) The excerpt states that the narrator was teasing when she asked Caroline if she had had some soup; this indicates that the narrator was making fun of their mother's belief that the soup could cure all kinds of ills. There is no support in the excerpt for options (1) and (2). Options (4) and (5) may be true, but are not why the narrator asked the question.

3. **(4) She cares about her daughters' futures.** (Synthesis) The mother is excited about the passport and the possibilities it holds; she is also worried about Caroline's engagement. These details show that she is quite concerned about her daughters' futures. There is no evidence in the excerpt to support options (1), (2), or (5). Option (3) is incorrect because the mother clearly does not support Caroline's decision to marry.

4. **(4) priests** (Analysis) In lines 31 and 32, the mother says, "He must know what he can become." The father says, "A priest. . . . For your brothers." This suggests that Antonio's uncles are priests. Although there are indicators that the

uncles do indeed farm the bottomland of El Puerto, they seem to own the land. There is no indication that they are hired help; therefore, option (2), farmhands, is not supported. There is no evidence to support the remaining options.

5. **(3) selling their land and moving near the river** (Application) The wife criticizes her husband for not buying land near the river in the first place. There is no support for options (1), (2), or (5). Option (4) is not supported because the mother is proud of her Mexican heritage.

6. **(4) impractical** (Analysis) The mother's statement implies that the land is not productive enough to feed the children, but the father prizes the freedom of the llano nonetheless. This suggests that he is impractical. None of the other options are supported by the details in the excerpt.

7. **(3) an emphasis on dialogue** (Synthesis) The excerpt is a dialogue between the mother and the father. Options (1), (2), (4), and (5) do not characterize the author's style in this excerpt.

GED Mini-Test (Pages 116–117)

1. **(2) father** (Comprehension) This option is correct based on Feather calling the narrator "Daddy" at the beginning of the excerpt.

2. **(1) She is happy to see him when she wakes up in the morning.** (Comprehension) This is the most likely reason. The excerpt states that Feather was excited to see the narrator after so many hours asleep. There is no reason to think that she has negative feelings toward Jesus, so options (2) and (5) are incorrect. Option (3) is not a reason for such a strong response. Since Feather only dreamed a strange man was in the house, option (4) is incorrect.

3. **(2) quiet** (Analysis) The impression given by the phrase "silent as mist" is one of soundless movement. There is nothing to imply that Jesus is sneaky as in option (1) or scared as in option (5). While the excerpt does say that he is helpful, option (3), and small, option (4), these characteristics have nothing to do with the description in question.

4. **(3) He has chosen not to speak to other people.** (Comprehension) The excerpt states that "The doctors said that he was healthy, that he could talk if he wanted to" (lines 15–16). This refutes option (1) that his vocal cords were damaged. Just because he took over making breakfast does not mean that he is responsible for all of the household chores, option (3). Options (4) and (5) are not supported by the excerpt.

5. **(4) The narrator provides a home for Jesus.** (Analysis) The excerpt states that the narrator has known Jesus for thirteen of his

fifteen years (lines 7 and 11–12), so options (1) and (2) are incorrect. Jesus clearly lives with the narrator, so option (3) is very unlikely. Since the narrator is the provider and responsible adult (lines 13–15), option (5) is also very unlikely. Jesus seems like a member of the household, so option (4) is the correct choice.

6. **(5) responsible** (Comprehension) In the excerpt, Jesus takes over making breakfast while the narrator takes care of Feather. He also takes responsibility for informing the narrator about events and needs at school. Options (1), (2), and (3) are not supported by the excerpt. Although he is a track star, there is no other evidence to support that he is ambitious, option (4).

7. **(4) She had a scary dream.** (Analysis) While Feather has been excitable about several everyday occurrences as in options (1), (2), and (3), it becomes clear that she is very worried by her dream about a scary man in the house, option (4). The excerpt does not support option (5).

8. **(2) a single-parent family** (Application) Since there is no functioning mother in the household, option (2) is the best choice. There is no evidence that they are a foster family, option (1). They seem to function very well, the opposite of option (3). They are a small family unit, unlike option (4), and there is no evidence that they are isolated, as in option (5).

9. **(3) shows a softer, nurturing side to him** (Synthesis) Option (3) is the most likely choice. The author wants to create a counterpoint between the rough, violent world of criminals and a nurturing household where the same private detective is a single parent to a little girl and a mute boy. The other options are not as likely based on the information in the question and the excerpt.

Lesson 13

GED Skill Focus (Page 119)

1. **b.** She does not want to travel in November with small children.
   d. She does not want to miss the celebration.

2. **a.** She ran off to get married.

3. **a.** The baby is the first male born in the family in two generations.
   b. The baby was to be named after the grandfather.

4. Your answers may include the following: She and her father are on speaking terms once again. Her father has visited twice. Her father's name will continue in a new country.

GED Practice (Pages 120–121)

1. **(1) They left it bare of leaves.** (Analysis) The result is described in the last paragraph. The

color in option (2) refers to a swarm of locusts, not the land. Options (3), (4), and (5) are not mentioned in the excerpt.

2. **(4) the swarm of locusts** (Analysis) The locusts are referred to in line 9 as an army; after Stephen sees the red smear which thickens and spreads, He says, "There goes the main army" (line 14). The excerpt states that the sky is blue, so options (1) and (3) are incorrect. There is no mention of either actual soldiers or crop dusters, so options (2) and (5) are incorrect.

3. **(4) people versus nature** (Synthesis) Old Stephen and Margaret's farm has been ruined by locusts, which are a part of nature. None of the other options are supported by the excerpt.

4. **(1) color** (Synthesis) The author mentions several colors in the excerpt to describe the attack: blue, green, red, reddish brown, brownish red, black.

5. **(3) They have contracted a contagious disease.** (Comprehension) Lines 6–8 state that there were many sick and dying but that the number of new victims had gone down. This, and the reference to the "rage of the white-scabs," indicates that the people have contracted a contagious disease. The excerpt does not support options (1) and (5). Option (2) is incorrect because the phrase "thirteenth sleep of sickness" means the thirteenth day that the sickness had set in. Option (4) is incorrect because the people did leave their lodges to walk in the sun or to sit.

6. **(3) a person wearing a face mask in the hospital to avoid germs** (Application) The villagers are avoiding one another in order to keep from getting sick; a person wearing a face mask to avoid germs is also trying to keep from getting sick. Options (1) and (5) concern people actually getting sick, so these are incorrect. The excerpt does not mention villagers disliking each other, so option (2) is incorrect. Option (4) is incorrect because the villagers leave the path to avoid other villagers, not because they want to walk in the woods.

7. **(2) the presence of a bad spirit** (Analysis) Lines 20–22 mention families hit hard by the bad spirit. This implies that the people believed a bad spirit caused the epidemic. The other options are not supported by the details in the excerpt.

8. **(1) They were disheartened and sad.** (Analysis) Several clues in the excerpt point to this answer. The people do not greet each other, there was none of the usual bustle, and the wailing old woman made the people realize how much they had lost. All of these point to depression and sadness. Option (2) may be

correct, but it wouldn't cause them to be a different people. There is no support for options (3), (4), or (5).

9. **(2) It helps readers understand how the characters feel.** (Synthesis) This approach gives the reader a sense of being inside the situation and can therefore help give the reader a fuller understanding of the views and feelings of the villagers. Option (1) is incorrect because it is the opposite of what occurs. There is no support in the excerpt for option (3). Options (4) and (5) are incorrect because there is no mention in the excerpt of either the white man or outsiders.

GED Mini-Test (Pages 122–123)

1. **(1) attraction** (Comprehension) Elizabeth's disappointment over Mr. Darcy's inattention to her (lines 26–38) suggests that she is attracted to him.

2. **(5) more sure of herself** (Analysis) This is supported by Jane's speech in lines 44–50. There is no evidence in the excerpt for options (1), (2), and (3). Option (4) could be said to apply to Elizabeth, not Jane.

3. **(2) Mr. Darcy has ignored her.** (Comprehension) Elizabeth's thoughts supply this information. There is no evidence in the excerpt for options (1), (3), and (4). Only Elizabeth is disappointed; thus option (5) is incorrect.

4. **(2) Mr. Darcy had earlier shown interest in Elizabeth.** (Analysis) Elizabeth thinks he no longer cares, implying that he did before. Option (1) overdramatizes Mr. Darcy's behavior. Option (3) is incorrect because lines 55–57 refer to someone other than Mr. Darcy. There is no support for option (4). There is no evidence of flirtation, so option (5) is incorrect.

5. **(2) She will be preoccupied with thoughts about Mr. Darcy.** (Application) She tells herself not to think about him, suggesting that she will anyway. She feels that Mr. Darcy is the one who acted rudely, so option (1) is incorrect. There is no support for the other options.

6. **(3) close and affectionate** (Analysis) The dialogue between the sisters shows their close and loving relationship; additionally, at the beginning of the excerpt, Elizabeth found relief from her misery by seeing her sister's good fortune. This shows that the two are close and want the best for each other. There is no support for options (1), (4), and (5). Option (2) is only partially correct—the sisters are polite but not distant.

7. **(3) She is questioning Jane's claims of indifference.** (Analysis) Elizabeth suggests that

Jane is not indifferent when she continues by warning Jane to be careful. Although Elizabeth seems to be agreeing with Jane, her meaning is quite the opposite; therefore, option (1) is incorrect. Since Elizabeth is commenting on Jane's behavior, options (2), (4), and (5) are incorrect.

8. **(4) Mr. Darcy's** (Analysis) In paragraphs 3–7, the author shares Elizabeth's thoughts as she reflects on Mr. Darcy's behavior. In the first paragraph, the author shares Jane's and her visitor's thoughts, describing their impressions of each other. In the second paragraph, the author shares Mrs. Bennet's thoughts when she mentions her intent to invite the men to dinner. Therefore, options (1), (2), (3), and (5) are incorrect. Mr. Darcy is the only character whose thoughts are hidden from the reader.

9. **(1) Neither is very talkative on the day of the visit.** (Synthesis) Elizabeth comments on Mr. Darcy's silence, and Jane is described as talking less than usual. Although Jane is cheerful after the visit, the reader does not learn of Mr. Darcy's reaction, so option (4) is incorrect. Only Mr. Darcy's behavior is described as teasing, and this does not seem intentional, so option (5) is also incorrect. There is no support for options (2) and (3).

Lesson 14
GED Skill Focus (Page 125)
1. **a.** She has pent-up nervous energy.

2. **a.** Frankie feels left out because Jarvis and Janice are getting married.

3. Frankie indicates that she wishes that her name started with the letters *J A*, like Jarvis' and Janice's. This shows that she doesn't feel included but wishes she were.

4. **b.** It contrasts the emotions of Frankie and Berenice.

GED Practice (Pages 126–127)
1. **(2) She is very tense.** (Comprehension) A strained flag is one that is stretched tight by the wind or held tense and taut. The excerpt does not support the other options.

2. **(4) confidently, with her head held high** (Application) Miss Emily speaks straightforwardly and holds her head erect. This shows that she is a confident, proud woman. There is no evidence in the excerpt to support options (1), (2), (3), or (5).

3. **(5) She intimidates other people.** (Synthesis) Miss Emily does not state the purpose for which the arsenic will be used and stares at the druggist until he wraps it up. This indicates that she intimidates him. In addition, she also constantly interrupts the druggist, which can also be a

method of intimidation. Her insistence on buying arsenic rules out option (1), that she cannot make up her mind. There is no evidence in the excerpt to support options (2), (3), and (4).

4. **(3) Miss Emily is forceful, but the druggist is accommodating.** (Synthesis) Option (1) is incorrect because Miss Emily does not seem terribly grumpy, although she does seem determined. The druggist can be said to be accommodating because he gives Miss Emily the arsenic without making her say why she wants it. Options (2), (4), and (5) are not supported by the excerpt.

5. **(2) She is much sicker than she says she is.** (Analysis) The description of how her bones felt and how her vision was affected suggests that she is very ill, as does the conversation between Cornelia and Doctor Harry. Therefore, options (1) and (4) are incorrect. There is no evidence to support option (3), and option (5) is incorrect because she has nothing good to say about Cornelia.

6. **(1) understanding but firm** (Analysis) The effect of the doctor's words is soothing but carries a hint of warning. The words he uses are informal and simple, so option (2) is incorrect. Although "gentle" might be an appropriate description, the doctor is sure of himself, so option (3) is incorrect. Option (4) is too extreme, even though the doctor warns Granny. Because of the warning, option (5) is also incorrect.

7. **(2) what she says** (Synthesis) Granny Weatherall's words, option (2), are featured throughout the excerpt. What she has to say effectively shows her proud and somewhat cantankerous character. Each of the other options names something that actually does give some information about Granny Weatherall's character, but not nearly as much as option (2). Therefore, none of the remaining options is the best choice.

GED Mini-Test (Pages 128–129)
1. **(4) normal and natural** (Comprehension) Grandpa Blakeslee says that death is not always awful and that it is part of God's plan. He also wants no fuss made over his death. These facts support the idea that he thinks death is normal and natural. There is no evidence to support options (1) and (2). Option (3) is incorrect because he thinks that funerals, not death, are a waste of money. Option (5) is the opposite of what Grandpa Blakeslee thinks.

2. **(4) unconcerned with what society thinks** (Analysis) Option (1) is incorrect because his plans are unconventional. Option (2) is incorrect because his plans for his funeral do not suggest

vanity. Option (3) is unlikely because Grandpa Blakeslee apparently tends to ignore others' expectations. There is no specific support for option (5).

3. **(2) spending a quiet evening at home** (Application) Grandpa Blakeslee's simple and quiet tastes are illustrated throughout the excerpt. Options (1), (3), and (4) are examples of activities that Grandpa Blakeslee would avoid either because they require an expenditure of money or demand that he change his way of doing things. Option (5) is incorrect because he specifically asks for there not to be a sermon at his funeral.

4. **(1) Grandpa Blakeslee does not want a fuss made at his funeral.** (Comprehension) All of the details of the will are about avoiding anything fancy at the burial. Options (2), (3), and (5) are details that help to suggest that idea. Grandpa Blakeslee may believe funerals should be simple but does not care about dignity, so option (4) is incorrect.

5. **(4) It provides specific details that support the main idea of the excerpt.** (Analysis) The second paragraph concerns the problem of wasting money, a specific example of making too much fuss. Option (1) suggests that the main ideas of the two paragraphs are contradictory, which is incorrect. Options (2) and (5) are not related to the idea of money. The second paragraph does state that he wants to be taken straight to the cemetery, but this is not the main idea, so option (3) is incorrect.

6. **(2) They thought Grandpa Blakeslee's comments and wishes were strange.** (Analysis) It is the very unusual nature of his requests that is shocking. There is no support for options (1) and (4). Options (3) and (5) are details given in the excerpt.

7. **(1) a general storekeeper** (Analysis) Grandpa Blakeslee mentions a pine box that he has been saving upstairs at the store and requests that only his family and those at the store that want to come attend his burial. These details suggest that Grandpa Blakeslee was a general storekeeper. There is no evidence to support options (2), (4), and (5). Option (3) is incorrect because he only mentions having a vegetable patch, not a farm.

8. **(5) plainspoken** (Synthesis) Grandpa Blakeslee's wishes as written in his will are expressed in simple language that reflects his common sense. Although his wishes are expressed humorously, option (1) is incorrect because of the seriousness of the occasion. Options (2) and (3) are incorrect because Grandpa Blakeslee viewed death as a natural event that is not always awful. Option (4) is incorrect because Grandpa Blakeslee expresses his wishes in a humorous way.

9. **(2) having him "speak from the grave"** (Synthesis) The reader learns about Grandpa Blakeslee's character through the wishes he expressed in his own words. These words are being read aloud after he has died. None of the other options are used by the author in this excerpt to establish Grandpa Blakeslee's character.

10. **(5) a humorous criticism of the funeral industry** (Synthesis) Grandpa Blakeslee makes comments about not wanting a trip to Birdsong's Emporium, dressing the dead to look alive, wanting to be taken straight from home to the cemetery, and not wanting a tombstone with the word "sleeping." All of these suggest that funerals make death into something artificial and are an unnecessary expense. None of the other options are supported by the details in the excerpt.

11. **(4) It makes it seem as though Grandpa Blakeslee is actually speaking.** (Synthesis) The tone of his will is so conversational and informal that it seems as though Grandpa Blakeslee is in the room with the other characters. Grandpa Blakeslee seems to be a thoughtful and perceptive man, so option (1) is incorrect. There is no support in the excerpt for options (2) and (3). Although Grandpa Blakeslee does seem to be a practical man, it is not his nonstandard usage of English that gives this impression, so option (5) is incorrect.

Lesson 15
GED Skill Focus (Page 131)
1. **b.** defensive

2. **b.** "you can take my side or theirs"
   d. "It's my word against Eunice's and Olivia-Ann's"

3. **a.** He may not be completely reliable.

4. You may have written that he got married after knowing Marge for only four days, which is not a responsible thing to do; that he is only sixteen or seventeen years old; and that now he has no idea why he married Marge.

GED Practice (Pages 132–133)
1. **(4) a man of honor who respects his son's beliefs** (Comprehension) His response illustrates that he respects Carter's decision, even though he does not agree with it; therefore, option (2) is incorrect. Option (1) is incorrect because the excerpt indicates the father's stated concern for his wife and his unstated concern for his son. There is no evidence for option (3). The first paragraph states that Carter is the son of wealthy parents, so option (5) is incorrect.

2. **(3) keeping a difficult promise** (Application) Carter is clearly an honest and honorable man, so if he made a promise, he would keep it. It is not in his character as described in the excerpt to do what is suggested by options (1), (2), and (5). Because he has made the decision to enter the Union Army in the face of opposition, option (4) is unlikely.

3. **(2) formal** (Analysis) The father and son address each other in a formal manner, and the author uses formal language such as "cultivation," "leonine," and "perilous" in his descriptions. Options (1), (3), (4), and (5) are not supported by the details in the excerpt.

4. **(3) The war divided even the closest families.** (Synthesis) One of the tragedies of the Civil War was that family members sometimes fought on opposing sides. The father's statement that Druse is a traitor to Virginia when he joins the Union regiment emphasizes this fact. Options (1), (2), (4), and (5) are all true but do not involve Druse's decision.

5. **(2) food to feed everyone** (Comprehension) The narrator has been surprised by the unexpected guests and does not have enough food. The context clue "hot stove" indicates that option (4) is incorrect. The narrator does not seem particularly concerned with pleasing other people, so option (1) is also incorrect. Although options (3) and (5) may be true, the phrase in the question is referring to the food, not space or time.

6. **(4) make room for a sixth person at the table** (Application) Based on the details in the excerpt, it is clear that the narrator still has feelings for Mr.Whitaker; also, she stretches the chickens to feed everyone who has shown up, so she probably would do the same for Mr. Whitaker. There is not enough evidence in the excerpt to support the other options.

7. **(5) irritable** (Analysis) The narrator's comments show that she is annoyed and irritated with her sister; therefore, option (5) is correct. None of the other options are supported by the details in the excerpt.

8. **(2) resentful** (Synthesis) In the first line, the narrator says that the family was getting along fine until Stella-Rondo came back home. This indicates her resentment. Options (1), (3), (4), and (5) are the opposite of how the narrator feels toward her sister.

GED Mini-Test (Pages 134–135)
1. **(1) fearful** (Comprehension) Lines 36–37 describe the daughters as "trembling and in silence" which shows their fear. There is no support for options (2), (3), or (4). Option (5)

may be true of the women but there is no direct evidence in this excerpt to support this option.

2. **(5) walked carefully** (Comprehension) In the previous paragraph, Mr. Osborne walked (strode) downstairs. In the following paragraph, the seemingly frightened women are quietly following him. From this you can infer that they are walking carefully and quietly behind Mr. Osborne. There is no evidence that the women are falling; therefore, options (1) and (3) are incorrect. Although the women are whispering, the phrase "tripped gingerly" refers to the way they are moving, not the way they are speaking; therefore, option (2) is incorrect. There is no support for option (4).

3. **(4) He may be losing money on his investments.** (Comprehension) Although all of the answer options may be possible explanations for Mr. Osborne's behavior, only option (4) is specifically mentioned by one of the characters. In line 35, Miss Wirt says, "I suppose the funds are falling," suggesting that Mr. Osborne is losing money.

4. **(2) He would dismiss her without seeing her.** (Application) Mr. Osborne's rash decision to fire the cook and his impatience with George's tardiness for dinner support the idea that he would dismiss one of his daughters for failing to keep an appointment. Options (1), (4), and (5) are incorrect because Mr. Osborne is not characterized as being nervous, forgiving, or patient. There is not enough evidence in the excerpt to support option (3).

5. **(4) tense** (Synthesis) The words "scowling," "roared," "violently," "growled," "gruffly," and "trembled" establish a tense mood. Mr. Osborne's words and actions put everyone on edge. There is no support for the other options.

6. **(3) Mr. Osborne did not seem satisfied with the fish.** (Analysis) The word "curt" (line 58) means "sharp" or "annoyed," so Mr. Osborne was not happy with the fish. Additionally, he had already stated his strong dissatisfaction with the cook's soup, so he was probably not happy with her cooking in general. The excerpt implies that Mr. Osborne's remarks are criticisms of the fish, not commands that it should be eaten; therefore, option (1) is incorrect. There is no evidence in the excerpt to support options (2) and (4). Mr. Osborne does not appear to be the sort of man who would try to make conversation, so option (5) is incorrect.

7. **(3) the reference to Amelia's fear when she sits next to him** (Analysis) Osborne does not show any warmth toward anyone, and everyone seems frightened by him. Options (1) and (2) refer to his position in the family, a role

traditionally given to fathers in the past. Option (4) does not indicate lack of warmth. Option (5) is incorrect because he does refer to Jane, one of his daughters, by name.

8. **(1) He is extremely intolerant.** (Analysis) This behavior is suggestive of a person who is intolerant of others' shortcomings. It is not a good example of alarm, rendering option (4) incorrect. Options (2), (3), and (5) are not supported by the text.

9. **(4) one of Jane's siblings** (Analysis) The way Jane speaks of George, using his first name and saying he'll be back to dinner, as well as the way the butler calls him "Mr. George" (line 16), indicates that he is a family member. This familiarity rules out options (1), (2), and (5). There is no support in the excerpt for option (3).

10. **(5) a terrible man** (Synthesis) Lines 43–44, "for she was next to the awful Osborne," reveal the narrator's attitude toward Mr. Osborne. Mr. Osborne is depicted as cruel and violent, so option (1) is not the best choice. Mr. Osborne is depicted as neither admirable nor patient, so options (2) and (3) are incorrect. Although Mr. Osborne is certainly grumpy, this word is too mild to capture his cruelty, so option (4) is not the best choice.

Lesson 16
GED Skill Focus (Page 137)
1. **a.** tractors and insects

2. **b.** simile

3. **a.** crawled

4. monsters

5. **c.** to show how the machines resemble living creatures

6. **a.** as a symbol of destruction

GED Practice (Pages 138–139)
1. **(4) a room in an attic** (Comprehension) The excerpt refers to a "dormer window set high in the slanting room" (lines 14–15). This is a description of an attic, a room immediately below a slanting roof. There is no support for the other options.

2. **(3) He would care for the cat.** (Application) The excerpt shows Mr. Fischelson's concern for insects when he waves them away from the candle. If he shows such concern for insects, it can be inferred that he would show similar concern for a stray cat. The other options do not reflect his concern for living creatures.

3. **(1) nose and eyes** (Comprehension) The excerpt describes his nose as crooked as a beak and his eyes as being large, dark, and fluttering like those of some huge bird.

4. **(3) ominous** (Synthesis) Dr. Fischelson is dressed uncomfortably and is pacing back and forth. The insects are burning in the candle flame, and Dr. Fischelson finds this troubling. These details give the reader the feeling that something bad is going to happen. There is no support for options (1), (2), and (4). Although the insects die a painful and violent death, this detail does not characterize the overall tone of the excerpt.

5. **(5) to show the receiver she loves him** (Comprehension) The letter writer says that when her spirit is with the receiver, he will feel her love in his heart. There is no support in the excerpt for the other options.

6. **(1) stuff them in a garbage can** (Application) The wife refers to flowers as "sentimental trash," (lines 26–27) so she probably would not appreciate receiving a dozen roses. There is no evidence to support option (2) (financial concerns). She would be more likely to burn the roses, like the faded bunch of flowers, than to display them near the fireplace, so option (3) is incorrect. Options (4) and (5) suggest that the wife would be gracious (thanking or sharing), which is unlikely for someone who responds to her husband with "ineffable disdain" (lines 23–24).

7. **(5) He may be more sentimental than his wife.** (Analysis) The "long, quivering breath" (line 32) suggests that the husband may have some sentimental regrets about the letter writer. This also makes Options (2) and (3) incorrect. The wife clearly remembers not sending the flowers, so option (1) is incorrect. Nothing in the excerpt indicates that either the husband or wife have much imagination, which rules out option (4).

8. **(5) The letter writer is sentimental, while the wife is haughty.** (Synthesis) Options (1) and (2) are not correct because the excerpt contains no evidence of the letter writer's work habits, or the wife's religious views. Although the letter writer is attentive to detail, there is nothing to suggest whether the wife is forgetful, which makes option (3) incorrect. Option (4) must also be incorrect, because the letter writer is not shy about expressing her emotions. The wife responds to her husband with "ineffable disdain" (lines 23–24), which suggests haughtiness and makes option (5) the correct choice.

9. **(4) the letter writer** (Synthesis) The letter writer says, "Keep them always in remembrance of me, . . ." and encourages the receiver to kiss the flowers, "and I will be with you in spirit, . . ." (lines 7–11). The excerpt contains no evidence to support the other options.

GED Mini-Test (Pages 140–141)

1. **(4) early evening** (Comprehension) The excerpt describes the sky as being a dark color—jade-green—and mentions flowers that "seemed to lean upon the dusk" (line 11). These are clues that the scene takes place in the early evening.

2. **(3) green** (Analysis) The sky is described as being jade-green, and the character plans to wear jade beads, green stockings, and green shoes. The springtime setting also suggests green as the dominant color.

3. **(2) She is overcome with emotion.** (Analysis) Before she began to feel dizzy, Bertha was thinking of all of the advantages she had that contributed to her happiness. This suggests that she was overcome with emotion. Option (1) is incorrect because the statement that she felt quite drunk is figurative, not literal. Although Bertha does think that the jonquils have a strong odor, she believes that it is not too strong, so option (3) is incorrect. Bertha says that the cats are "creepy," but this does not explain her dizziness, so option (5) is incorrect. There is no support for option (4).

4. **(1) visiting art galleries** (Application) Among the things that make her happy, Bertha's mention of friends who are painters indicates that she would likely visit art galleries. Option (2) is not supported by the details in the excerpt, and option (3) is incorrect because she reacts negatively to cats. Option (4) is incorrect because she is quite well off and unlikely to do her own housework, and option (5) is incorrect because she has a cook.

5. **(4) sensory words** (Analysis) The excerpt is characterized by vivid, colorful descriptions that appeal to the senses of sight and smell. The excerpt contains no dialogue except Bertha's occasional statements to herself, so option (1) is incorrect. Option (2) does not apply to the use of verbs in this excerpt. The excerpt seems full of emotion, so option (3) is incorrect. Finally, the excerpt contains a variety of sentence types, so option (5) does not characterize the excerpt as a whole.

6. **(1) It seems perfect, just as her circumstances do.** (Analysis) The pear tree is described as being "in fullest, richest bloom" (lines 4–5). Bertha compares the tree to her life, which she also sees as being in its fullest perfection. Option (2) is incorrect because the excerpt does not mention Bertha's physical attributes. Option (3) is incorrect because there is no indication in the excerpt that Bertha will be giving birth. Bertha makes no reference to growing and changing, so option (4) is incorrect. Option (5) is incorrect because Bertha is not described as being calm.

7. **(2) uneasiness** (Analysis) The cats' intrusion onto a scene that symbolizes the character's happiness is unsettling and gives the feeling that something is not quite right in this otherwise perfect scene. There is no evidence in the excerpt to support the other options.

8. **(1) The colors she planned to wear matched her surroundings.** (Analysis) Before she went upstairs to dress, Bertha realized that the colors she had chosen to wear were the same as those reflected in the garden, the pear tree, and the sky. The statement indicates that the correlation was coincidental and not planned. None of the other options is supported by details from the excerpt.

9. **(5) It suggests that something is missing from Bertha's life.** (Analysis) Bertha protests too strongly that her life is perfect and that she has everything, which gives the feeling that the opposite is true—something is missing. Options (1) and (2) are what Bertha says about her life but do not describe the effect that the repetition creates. There is no support in the excerpt for options (3) and (4).

10. **(2) It contributes to the feeling of unreality.** (Synthesis) The setting of the story in spring, when growing things are usually new, perfect, and unblemished, contributes to the story's mood of unreal, almost surreal, perfection. The excerpt does not discuss newness or new beginnings, so options (1) and (5) are incorrect. The excerpt is not particularly joyous or playful, so option (3) is incorrect. Option (4) refers to a detail from the excerpt and not the overall mood and so is incorrect.

11. **(2) naïve** (Synthesis) The character's statement that she is too happy, her reflection on her good fortune, and her dizzy and drunken feelings, all suggest an emotional state that is not likely to last. The character's apparent ignorance of her true feelings suggests her naiveté. The author's choice of words does not support the other four options.

Lesson 17
GED Skill Focus (Page 143)

1. **c.** Ayah cannot read.

2. **c.** Ella and Danny have a dangerous disease.

3. The grandmother died of this same disease. The disease is serious enough that the doctors want to take the children away. You might also have noted that there is not enough information in this excerpt to support the other possible answers.

4. "The whites lie."
   "I want a medicine man first."

1. **(2) reform him** (Comprehension) The excerpt refers to the widow putting the narrator into new clothes, having him say grace before eating, teaching him about Moses, and refusing to let him smoke. These are all efforts to reform him. There is no support in the excerpt for options (1), (3), (4), and (5).

2. **(3) a bowl of beef stew** (Application) The narrator says, "In a barrel of odds and ends it is different; things get mixed up, and the juice kind of swaps around, and the things go better" (lines 13–16). Of the choices, a bowl of stew is the only food that fits that description.

3. **(5) conversational** (Analysis) The narrator of the story relates his experiences as if he were talking to another person; therefore, the tone is conversational. The excerpt supports none of the other options.

4. **(1) It gives clues about the time and place.** (Synthesis) The use of slang and nonstandard English is true to the era and place where this story takes place—the South in the 1800s. Option (2) is incorrect because the widow's speech is not revealed. Options (3) and (4) might be true but are not the reasons that it is effective. Option (5) is an opinion and cannot be supported by the excerpt.

5. **(2) He never finished high school.** (Comprehension) The uncle says that the narrator's father thinks he is too good for the rest of the family because he finished high school and has a good job in town. This implies that Uncle Luis did not finish high school himself. There is no evidence in the excerpt to support options (1), (3), (4), and (5).

6. **(3) He would calmly justify his position.** (Application) The father's politeness to his brother during the outburst suggests that he would justify his position in a calm way. There is no evidence in the excerpt to support options (1), (2), (4), and (5).

7. **(4) the grandmother's** (Analysis) The grandmother's reaction is most unexpected because she supports her son's decision even though the family has lived in Los Rafas for generations and everyone else expects him to build a house next to hers.

8. **(1) tradition and self-determination** (Synthesis) The father's decision to move away from his family represents a break with the past in favor of determining his own future. None of the other options are supported by the details in the excerpt.

1. **(4) She was envious of the new soloist.** (Comprehension) This answer is suggested by the fourth paragraph. There is no evidence for option (1). Option (2) is incorrect because the church has already hired a new soloist. Option (3) is incorrect because Candace no longer sings at church. Option (5) is incorrect because she is forced to retire against her will.

2. **(2) Alma was prepared to conquer her fear.** (Comprehension) The sentence describes her lack of confidence and fear in a figurative way—as a mountain—and says that her nerves were braced for its ascent. This means she was prepared to conquer her fear. There is no evidence in the excerpt to support options (1), (3), (4), and (5).

3. **(5) The women were partially horrified.** (Comprehension) The sentence says that they were "half aghast, half smiling." This suggests that *aghast* is being contrasted with, and is therefore the opposite of, *smiling* and *amused*, so option (3) is incorrect. There is no support for options (1), (2), and (4).

4. **(4) She felt weak from the strain of having to compete with Candace's singing.** (Analysis) The fifth and sixth paragraphs describe Alma's reaction to Candace's interruption; therefore, options (1) and (2) are incorrect. The man looked at her after she felt faint, so option (3) is incorrect. Candace was removed from her job as soloist because of her flawed voice, so option (5) is incorrect.

5. **(2) try to get reinstated as the choir's soloist** (Application) The reasons for Candace's removal from the choir and her jealousy toward Alma indicate that she is unwilling to give up her status as soloist; therefore, option (1) is incorrect. Option (3) is incorrect because it is obvious that Candace considers Alma a rival and would probably not want to sing with her. There is no clear support for options (4) and (5).

6. **(3) "All the people stared at her and turned their ears critically." (lines 2–3)** (Analysis) Only option (3) contributes to the atmosphere, or general feeling, in the church. Options (1), (2), (4), and (5) are details that describe the characters and not the setting of the story.

7. **(1) She is willing to face a challenge.** (Analysis) Alma is nervous, but she sings well anyway. Option (2) is incorrect because she is not thinking about her looks. There is no support for the other options.

UNIT 2

8. **(4) informal and serious** (Analysis) The language is not technical, so option (1) is incorrect. Option (2) is incorrect because the author describes the emotions of the characters. There is little suggestion of humor, so option (3) is incorrect. The language is direct and informative, so option (5) is incorrect.

9. **(5) a crow's voice and a canary's** (Synthesis) Candace's voice is described as being cracked, shrill, and clamoring, which could be seen as comparable to a crow's caw. Alma's voice is described as being "piercingly sweet" (line 35) and canaries are noted for their sweet and beautiful song. The cry of an eagle, the silence of a hummingbird, and the hoot of an owl are not comparable to either Candace's voice or Alma's voice as described in the excerpt; therefore, options (1), (2), (3), and (4) are incorrect.

Lesson 18
GED Skill Focus (Page 149)
1. **b.** They work at the same place.

2. They both liked to come into town on Saturday afternoons and wander through the streets.

3. "In his nature he was as unlike Hal Winters as two men can be unlike" (lines 5–6).

4. Ray
   a. has a wife and children
   b. is about fifty
   c. is round shouldered
   d. is quiet, rather nervous, and serious

   Hal
   a. is a woman-chaser
   b. is younger than Ray
   c. is broad shouldered
   d. is a fighter and a "bad one"

GED Practice (Pages 150–151)
1. **(3) They have been stranded.**
   (Comprehension) In lines 36–37, Piggy asks, "When'll your dad rescue us?" This suggests that the boys are stranded. There is no evidence to support the other options.

2. **(4) suffer in silence** (Application) In lines 17–18, Piggy responds to Ralph's comment about his asthma "with a sort of humble patience." This supports option (4). There is nothing in the excerpt that would support options (1), (2), (3), and (5).

3. **(3) Both believe Ralph's father will rescue them.** (Synthesis) Ralph directly states that his father will come get them. Piggy asks when this will happen, suggesting that he believes what Ralph says. Options (2) and (5) are only true of Piggy, and option (4) is true only of Ralph. There is no evidence that either boy envies the other, so option (1) is also incorrect.

4. **(4) inhabitants** (Comprehension) Probably the only ones who would really notice the dissimilarities between the islands would be the people who lived or stayed there. None of the other options make sense in this context.

5. **(2) They are the same shape and size.** (Analysis) Options (1) and (4) are not true. Option (3) describes the contrast between the islands, not the islands themselves. There is no support for option (5).

6. **(2) two sides of the same town, one side upper class, the other side middle class** (Application) West Egg and East Egg are right next to each other; and the excerpt states that West Egg is the less fashionable of the two islands. This implies that East Egg is more fashionable and probably wealthier than its neighbor. Option (1) is incorrect because no mention is made in the excerpt of customs. Option (3) is incorrect because there is no mention of conflict in the excerpt. The narrator lives on one of the Eggs and does not seem to be wealthy; therefore, option (4) is incorrect. There is nothing in the excerpt to support option (5).

7. **(2) They are rented only part of the year.** (Comprehension) Lines 21–23 state that the narrator was squeezed between two huge places that rented for twelve or fifteen thousand a season. This suggests that the mansions are rented during part of the year. Options (1), (3), and (5) are not supported by the details in the excerpt. Option (4) refers only to the description of the house to the right of the narrator's.

8. **(2) vividly descriptive detail** (Synthesis) The narrator uses vivid visual images to describe the two islands. None of the other options are supported by the excerpt.

GED Mini-Test (Pages 152–153)
1. **(3) Miss Brooke's poor dress made her beauty all the more noticeable.**
   (Comprehension) The expression "to throw in relief" means to emphasize due to sharpness in contrast. The phrase from the excerpt means that her poor dress contrasted sharply with her beauty. Although option (1) may be true, it is not the meaning of the lines from the excerpt. None of the other options make sense in the context of the excerpt.

2. **(4) Appearances can be deceiving.**
   (Comprehension) This phrase states that the human mind is different than the outward appearance of a person, which is another way of saying that you cannot judge a person by how he or she looks. There is no support in the excerpt for options (1), (2), (3), and (5).

3. (2) a fine quotation (Comprehension)
Lines 9–12 state that "her plain garments, which by the side of provincial fashion gave her the impressiveness of a fine quotation."

4. (3) They try to dress like ladies. (Analysis)
The statement "The pride of being ladies had something to do with it" (lines 24–25) as well as the statement that the sisters "regarded frippery as the ambition of a huckster's daughter" (lines 35–36) support the idea that the sisters thought conservative, plain clothing was appropriate for ladies from a "good" family. There is no support in the excerpt for options (1), (2), and (4). They do seem to live in a rural area, but this does not explain their plain dress, so option (5) is incorrect.

5. (4) think it was a mistake (Application) The excerpt describes Miss Brooke as "not in the least self-admiring" (lines 48–49) and mentions how she only looked at men as possible matches for her sister. This implies that she would not think she were worthy of an offer of marriage. There is no evidence in the excerpt to support options (1), (2), (3), and (5).

6. (3) modest (Analysis) The excerpt describes Miss Brooke as being not in the least self-admiring. This means that she is modest. None of the other options fit her character.

7. (5) impractical (Analysis) To imply that a person lacks common sense suggests that he or she is impractical or unrealistic. None of the other adjectives accurately describe Dorothea's character.

8. (1) Dorothea is more innocent than Celia. (Analysis) The excerpt states that although Celia looked more innocent, Celia was more knowing and worldly wise than Dorothea. The other options are the opposite of ideas given in the excerpt.

9. (4) a distinguished minister (Analysis) The sisters' family is "good" and has included some clergymen, so a minister would probably be considered a good choice for a husband. Lines 29–30 state that you "would not find any yard-measuring or parcel-tying forefathers," indicating that the family is not working class and does not include merchants. Because the family seems to be quite class-conscious, family members would not want to marry a merchant or someone who works with his hands, eliminating options (1), (2), (3), and (5).

10. (1) long, complex sentences (Synthesis) None of the other options is true, based on this excerpt.

11. (3) sympathetic (Synthesis) The narrator's sympathy for Dorothea is revealed in the statement "Poor Dorothea!" (line 43), which implies that Dorothea is misunderstood.

Lesson 19
GED Skill Focus (Page 155)
1. **b.** angry

2. **c.** indifferent

3. **c.** nature does not care about human beings

4. **a.** Human beings are like grains of sand on a beach.

5. "nature does not regard him as important"

GED Practice (Pages 156–157)
1. **(3) She was thankful that Richmond had not been attacked.** (Comprehension) The first paragraph in the excerpt states that "Richmond was saved" (line 6). This seems the most likely reason for Lutie's prayers. If she had been praying for the soldiers who had died, they would probably not have been prayers of thanksgiving; therefore, option (1) is incorrect. The excerpt does not state that the war was over, so option (2) is incorrect. Even though Richmond had not been attacked, it had clearly been touched by death; therefore, option (4) is incorrect. There is no support in the excerpt for option (5).

2. **(2) a bulldozer** (Application) Lutie's final image is of a large destructive machine. Options (1) and (5) are not related to Lutie's final image. Although a fan does have blades, it is not destructive, so option (3) is incorrect. Option (4) is modern but has nothing to do with death.

3. **(5) McClellan seemed incapable of moving his forces.** (Analysis) The author makes the comparison to show that McClellan was not moving his troops. Lines 5–6 state that McClellan "seemed imprisoned by his own weight," much like a frog would be if it were full of heavy shot. The other options are not implied by the comparison.

4. **(3) War is an instrument of death.** (Synthesis) The excerpt refers to the fact that death touched everyone during the war, no matter what their station in life. Option (1) is incorrect because the excerpt does not discuss equal opportunities, only that death touched everyone equally. The excerpt does not say that the war was about to end, so option (2) is incorrect. Options (4) and (5) are minor details in the excerpt and are not the theme.

5. **(4) The woman is afraid of someone she knows.** (Comprehension) Option (1) is incorrect; there is no suggestion that the woman is really allergic to paint. There is no evidence for option (2). Options (3) and (5) are supported in the excerpt, but they do not restate the main idea.

6. **(2) move out of the apartment** (Application) It can be inferred from the woman's reluctance to return to her apartment after a week (lines 17–21) that she would move if she could. There is no support for options (1), (3), and (5). Since the garage is the only place the woman feels safe, option (4) is incorrect.

7. **(1) fears for her life** (Analysis) The woman buys a chain for her door and does not go out after work. These actions suggest her fear. None of the other options are supported by evidence in the excerpt.

8. **(2) anxious** (Synthesis) The narrator describes the effect that the man has on her, using the words "cold sweat" and "nervous" and she discusses her precautions against his return.

9. **(4) conversational** (Synthesis) The author writes as though she is speaking directly to the reader, using first person narration throughout the excerpt. None of the other adjectives accurately describe the style of writing.

GED Mini-Test (Pages 158–159)

1. **(5) A person's worldview is shaped by key events.** (Comprehension) This idea is stated in the last sentence of the first paragraph. There is no evidence for options (1) and (4). Options (2) and (3) may be true but are not supported by the excerpt.

2. **(4) Every few months something shocking occurs.** (Comprehension) The narrator gives the example of Mussolini's death, which was a shocking event because he "had almost seemed one of the eternal leaders" (lines 51–52). There is no support in the excerpt for options (1), (2), and (3). Although the narrator refers to a shortage of supplies, there is no mention that this occurs every few months, so option (5) is incorrect.

3. **(4) The historical era affects the individual.** (Application) The statement is similar to the author's belief that a person is affected by certain events in life. People's experiences are directly affected by the time and place in history during which they live; therefore, individuals' understanding of how the world works will be affected by this as well. Option (1) is not suggested by the excerpt. Option (2) suggests that the present is more important than the past, but the author is talking about the importance of the past. Option (3) is too general, and option (5) has nothing to do with what the author is saying.

4. **(2) by talking about the war as if it were happening now** (Analysis) The present tense makes the war seem more immediate, as close as it seems to the author. Options (1) and (3) are mentioned but do not help to explain the author's feelings. Options (4) and (5) are false.

5. **(1) to recall events that took place during his adolescence** (Analysis) From the perspective of a sixteen-year-old, the narrator describes in detail the effects the war had on Americans. Option (2) is incorrect because not all of the realities that the narrator experienced affect Americans today. Option (3) is incorrect because the excerpt does not address the present. Option (4) is incorrect because the narrator does not recall many pleasant times during the war; and option (5) is incorrect because the excerpt describes the American way of life during the war, not the horrors of war.

6. **(1) He was young and impressionable.** (Analysis) He seems to have seen the events from a youthful point of view; sixteen is an age when emotions are easily influenced. Option (2) may be true but is not supported. Options (3) and (4) are mentioned, but they were not the cause of the narrator's feelings. Option (5) is incorrect because the narrator says that he did not foresee himself becoming a soldier.

7. **(5) serious** (Analysis) The entire excerpt describes the difficult realities of living through the war years. This description is presented in a serious manner. Option (1) is incorrect because the narrator doesn't criticize; he presents the realities as they were. Option (2) is the opposite of the tone of the excerpt. Option (3) is incorrect because it implies warm feelings that the narrator does not express, and option (4) is incorrect because the focus is on the past and not the future.

8. **(4) matter-of-fact and repetitive** (Synthesis) The narrator describes the effect of the war primarily in short sentences with very little description, and he repeatedly uses the word "always" (lines 18–33). None of the other options accurately describe the style in which the excerpt is written.

9. **(4) indicate the monotony imposed by war** (Synthesis) The style of the excerpt is characterized mainly by short sentences presented in a repetitive pattern that reflect the monotony and regimentation of wartime. Option (1) is incorrect because the excerpt does not promote patriotism. Option (2) is incorrect because it does not discuss the war directly. Option (3) may be a result of reading about the hardships of war but would not affect the style in which the author chose to write. Option (5) is incorrect because it was written by an adult and does not truly reflect the mindset of a sixteen-year-old.

10. (3) The "good old days" were not always good. (Synthesis) The narrator is recounting the negative effects that the war had on the America he knew during his youth. None of the other statements are supported by the details in the excerpt.

Unit 2 Cumulative Review (Pages 160–166)

1. (4) gladness (Application) From the excerpt, you can conclude that the narrator wants to be friends with his son. Though he may not understand some of his son's choices, the father takes him seriously and says that he is not unsympathetic to him. Therefore, options (1) and (2) are incorrect. The father's tone is primarily serious, so option (3) is incorrect. Option (5) is not supported by the excerpt.

2. (4) He did not follow in his father's footsteps. (Comprehension) In lines 24–26, the narrator says that "Business was just as much out of the question for me as politics had been for my father." The excerpt also says something about the family still having a few political connections. You can infer from this that someone, likely the narrator's grandfather, was in politics and that the narrator's father didn't go into it. This implies that neither the narrator nor his father before him followed his father's career paths. There is not enough evidence in the excerpt to support options (1), (2), (3), and (5).

3. (1) It emphasizes that the narrator wanted to escape into a safer world. (Analysis) The narrator notes that business could cause suffering and alludes to negative family history that makes an ivory tower appealing. The image of an ivory tower is one of being raised up above it all, something like an escape. The reference is not to Jack, so options (3) and (4) are incorrect. Option (5) is incorrect because the excerpt shows how little the father and son have in common. There is no evidence for option (2).

4. (5) He would do his best to accept Jack's views. (Application) Based on the tone of the excerpt, it is apparent that the father seeks to reconcile with his son. This suggests that he would try to accept his son's views even if he did not share them. Option (1) is incorrect because it does not describe the behavior of a father seeking to make friends with a son. There is no basis of support for options (2), (3), and (4).

5. (2) serious (Synthesis) The narrator states that he is not trying to make crude jokes and refers to himself as a serious man. This rules out options (4) and (5). The narrator says he is not unsympathetic to his son's views, so options (1) and (3) are incorrect.

6. (4) a struggle between the character and the forces of nature (Comprehension) The excerpt describes the harsh environment in detail and suggests that the man does not appreciate its severity. This is a clue that the conflict likely will involve the man's fight for survival against nature. No internal struggle is hinted at in this excerpt, no other characters are introduced, society is not mentioned, and the character's destiny is not mentioned or hinted at, so options (1), (2), (3), and (5) are incorrect.

7. (3) The man did not understand the danger of the situation. (Comprehension) The preceding paragraph explains the magnificence of the man's surroundings in order to reveal how unmoved he is by them, so option (1) is incorrect. Option (2) has no support. Option (4) is incorrect because while there is no mention of other characters, there is also no mention that the man desires company. Option (5) might be true, but it is not the main idea of the paragraph.

8. (3) a frozen river (Comprehension) The excerpt states that the "Yukon lay a mile wide" (lines 2–3) and that it rolled in "gentle undulations where the ice jams of the freeze-up had formed" (lines 5–7), suggesting that it was frozen water. Because the details indicate that the Yukon is water that is only a mile wide, the other options are not supported.

9. (3) vivid visual details (Synthesis) The author's use of descriptive words helps the reader to visualize the landscape. Options (1) and (2) do not describe the writer's style, which really contains both a mix of shorter and longer, more complex sentences. Option (4) is incorrect because dialogue is not used. Option (5) is incorrect because the descriptions are not excessive.

10. (3) She was dressed as a widow in mourning. (Analysis) Widow's dress is appropriate for a woman who has lost her husband, not her child, so this would be an indication that the character is becoming mentally imbalanced. Options (1) and (2) do not suggest mental instability. Option (4) is incorrect because the fact that her child was killed is not evidence that she had lost her mind. Option (5) is incorrect because although the flag and medals insult rather than comfort her, this reaction is not unusual enough to be evidence that she was losing her mind.

11. (2) refuse to attend the ceremony (Application) Doña Ernestina's response of "*no, gracias*" to the military's offer to give her son a military funeral suggests that she would not attend the ceremony. Option (1) is incorrect because the excerpt makes it clear that she would not attend. Option (3) is incorrect because she does not discuss the war in the excerpt. Option (4) is incorrect because it is not characteristic of her based on the way she is described in the excerpt. Option (5) is incorrect because it is the opposite of her feelings toward the president and the military.

12. **(4) She had a wild look in her eyes.** (Analysis) This description of Doña Ernestina is the best clue to her state of mind. Option (1) might suggest her state of mind but it is not as telling as her physical description. Options (2) and (3) are descriptions that do not reflect mental instability. Option (5) indicates her sense of hurt and betrayal more than mental instability.

13. **(4) Spanish phrases** (Synthesis) The excerpt features the use of such Spanish words and phrases as *"lato,"* *"Ya no vive aqui,"* and *"No, gracias."* Although the author does use third-person narration, this technique does not add to the excerpt's authenticity, so option (1) is incorrect. Options (2), (3), and (5) are not true of the style of this excerpt.

14. **(4) John is being pressured to become a preacher.** (Comprehension) The word "altar" is used figuratively in the excerpt to stand for the church. Therefore, the phrase implies that both the church and his parents were pushing him toward becoming a preacher. Options (1) and (5) are incorrect because there is no evidence to support them. Options (2) and (3) are incorrect because it is clear that John is already a member of the church.

15. **(2) John finds it hard to concentrate on his lessons.** (Comprehension) The excerpt describes how John was distracted by his new teacher and how sometimes he did not follow the lessons. There is no support in the excerpt for options (1) and (4). Option (3) is incorrect because it is the opposite of John's intent. Option (5) is incorrect because the excerpt says that it occurred only when Elisha asked John a question.

16. **(3) his brother Roy** (Analysis) The last paragraph of the excerpt says that although Roy never knew his Sunday school lesson either, he was treated differently from John and that not as much was expected of him as was expected of John.

17. **(1) use of many descriptive words** (Synthesis) The author uses many descriptive words to describe John's admiration of Elisha such as "deeper," "manlier," "leanness," "grace," "strength," and "darkness." None of the other options are true of this excerpt.

18. **(2) critical** (Comprehension) The excerpt describes the character as having "dark eyes arched in a perpetual query about other people's manners" (lines 3–5). This description indicates that she is critical of others. Options (1), (3), and (5) are the opposite of the woman's character as described. The character might be wealthy, option (4), but there is not enough evidence in the excerpt to support the inference.

19. **(2) being in control** (Analysis) Lines 5–7 state that she was a "woman who won all social battles with presence and a conviction of the legitimacy of her authority." This implies that being in control was most important to her. Option (1) is true, but based on the way she is described in the excerpt, it would not be as important to her as being in control. There is no evidence to support options (3), (4), and (5).

20. **(2) She was very sure of herself.** (Comprehension) The excerpt states that she had a conviction of the legitimacy of her authority. This means that she was very sure of herself. Option (1) might be true but would not account for the power she wielded. Option (3) is incorrect because the excerpt states that Helene had come far away from Sundown House, suggesting that she has not always lived in Medallion. Options (4) and (5) have no relationship to the power she had.

21. **(4) tastefully decorated** (Application) Helene is described in the excerpt as being responsible for putting flowers on the altar at her church. This implies that she cares about the appearance of her surroundings. There is not enough evidence in the excerpt to suggest that her home is warm and homey, option (1). If she puts fresh flowers on the altar at church, it seems unlikely that she would display artificial flowers in her home, so option (2) is incorrect. Based on the way she is described in the excerpt, option (3) would not be plausible. There is not enough evidence in the excerpt to support option (5).

22. **(3) She was in trouble at some time in her past.** (Analysis) The last line of the excerpt says she could not ignore the silent plea of the woman who had rescued her. This implies that she was in trouble at some time in her life. Option (1) is incorrect because the refusal of the people to pronounce her name correctly indicates that she was not loved. Option (2) is incorrect because the excerpt says that she manipulated her husband and daughter. Option (4) is incorrect because she is described as a woman who took responsibility for a number of duties at her church. Option (5) is false because the excerpt says that to her, life was satisfactory.

23. **(2) disapproval** (Synthesis) The narrator introduces the character as being impressive to the people in Medallion and then describes her

in a somewhat unflattering way. This suggests that the narrator does not approve of the character's behavior. There is no support in the excerpt for options (1), (3), and (5). Option (4) is too strong a word to describe the narrator's attitude based on the way in which the character is depicted.

24. **(3) pity** (Comprehension) The fact that the narrator says "Poor old Schatz" (lines 26–27) shows that he feels sorry for the boy. There is no evidence for options (1), (4), and (5). Option (2) might be true but the excerpt gives no indication that the author is feeling this emotion.

25. **(2) He wants to get the boy's mind off his illness.** (Analysis) In line 1, the narrator tells the boy not to think and to take it easy, meaning he is trying to get his mind off being sick. Reading a book to the boy would distract the boy's attention. There is no evidence in the excerpt to support options (1), (3), (4), and (5).

26. **(5) It builds up and resolves.** (Analysis) The underlying structure of the excerpt matches the buildup and resolution of the boy's fear. Options (1), (2), (3), and (4) are incorrect because the fear is explained in lines 11 and 12, reaches a climax in lines 21–23, awakens the reader's sympathy, and concerns fear of death, which is not trivial.

27. **(3) direct, factual impact** (Analysis) Because the excerpt consists of little more than dialogue, the revelation of the boy's secret fear comes as a shock. The tense and down-to-earth nature of the scene rules out options (1), (2), (4), and (5).

28. **(1) brief and economical** (Synthesis) The excerpt is characterized by brief exchanges of dialogue requiring the use of few words. None of the other options accurately describe the style in which this excerpt is written.

29. **(5) with peace, knowing he would not leave his land** (Application) Lines 30–36 describe his fondness for the land, saying that he was not anxious to leave it and that it was a comfort to him to think that he would never have to go farther than the edge of his own hayfield. None of the other options accurately describe his feelings about his eventual death.

30. **(4) Life and death exist side by side in this world.** (Analysis) The closeness of the graveyard, a symbol of death, and the farm, a symbol of life, indicates that both exist at once in the world. Options (1) and (2) are incorrect because the excerpt does not focus solely on death. Option (3) does not address the topics of life and death. There is no support for option (5) in the excerpt.

31. **(1) comforting** (Analysis) The excerpt describes the narrator's attachment to his land and expresses his comfort in knowing that he will be with the land even in death. Option (2) is

incorrect because the narrator describes the graveyard as "not cramped or mournful." Option (3) is too extreme to describe his reflections about the land. Options (4) and (5) are not suggested by the excerpt.

32. **(1) highly descriptive images** (Synthesis) The author relies on vivid imagery to describe the land and the graveyard, using such descriptions as "pale gold cornstalks," "white field," and "long red grass." None of the other options accurately describe the style in which the excerpt is written.

UNIT 3: UNDERSTANDING POETRY
Lesson 20
GED Skill Focus (Page 171)
1. Possible answers:
   Full: breath/death; knuckle/buckle; head/bed; dirt/shirt; wrist/missed is very close to a full rhyme
   Partial: dizzy/easy; pans/countenance.

2. **b.** The punctuation is irregular.

3. **b.** The rhythm is clumsy, like a drunk person dancing.

GED Practice (Pages 172–173)
1. **(3) Rainfall in cities brightens the outlook of the inhabitants.** (Comprehension) The poet says that rainfall surprises those who live in cities and "cleans" their minds, suggesting that the rainfall brightens their moods. Although the author does suggest that rainfall connects a city to nature, he does not suggest that it is the *only* connection, option (1). There is no evidence to support option (2). Option (4) refers to only a single line of the stanza—"creatures who live under rocks" (line 5); therefore, it is not the best choice. The poet seems to suggest that city rainfall does resemble rainfall in jungles; therefore, option (5) is also incorrect.

2. **(4) He repeats the sounds of the beginnings of words.** (Analysis) The poet repeats *s* sounds ("smokes sad cigars"), *k* sounds ("Culls candy"), and *p* sounds ("Passion/Paused") at the beginnings of words. Options (1) and (3) are incorrect because the stanza does not contain rhyme or a regular pattern of stressed syllables. The poet uses a wide variety of short and long vowel sounds; therefore, option (2) is incorrect. Option (5) is incorrect because some of the words, such as "Culls" and "proffered," are not common in everyday speech.

3. **(4) a sensation of brisk movement** (Analysis) The short lines encourage the reader to read quickly. In addition, many of the simple words in the stanza suggest motion: "wind," "rain," "fire," "walking." Although some of the vocabulary may be childlike, the ideas expressed

in the stanza are not; therefore, option (1) is incorrect. Option (2) is incorrect because the stanza's structure encourages the reader to speed up, rather than slow down. There is no support for options (3) and (5).

4. **(1) more gloomy** (Synthesis) The correct answer can be seen by comparing the more cheerful lines "We . . ./Are surprised come/ morning" from the first stanza to the more gloomy lines "winter looms/And spirits/Sink" from the fourth stanza. The mood of neither stanza is particularly bitter, anxious, or passionate, ruling out options (2), (3), and (5). The fourth stanza, in which the narrator stands quietly among trees, is more (not less) tranquil than the first stanza, which includes a storm; therefore, option (4) is incorrect.

5. **(2) separated** (Comprehension) This point is made by the poet's description of being able to look down each road at the same time, therefore option (1) is incorrect. Options (3) and (4) are the opposite of what the poet describes. There is no direct evidence for option (5).

6. **(3) how decisions define people's lives** (Analysis) In lines 16–20, the speaker indicates the effects of his decisions on his life. The speaker does not express regret regarding his choices; therefore, option (1) is incorrect. Options (2) and (4) are not supported by the poem. The changes the speaker experiences occur as a result of his decisions in life rather than as a result of a literal walk in the woods. For this reason, option (5) is incorrect.

7. **(1) think carefully before committing himself** (Application) The speaker is likely to make a decision about where to live in the same way that he chooses a road in the woods. In the poem, the speaker thought for a while and then made a confident decision. The speaker clearly makes the decision by himself without relying on friends; therefore, option (2) is incorrect. The speaker does not choose the road that is more popular; therefore, option (3) is incorrect. Option (4) is incorrect because there is no evidence that the speaker worries about his decision. The speaker took some time to make his decision, but he made a definite choice and followed it; therefore, option (5) is incorrect.

GED Mini-Test (Pages 174–175)

1. **(1) thinking about a pleasurable night** (Comprehension) The speaker describes being tired and merry and having a series of pleasurable experiences. Option (2) is incorrect because the poem does not indicate that the speaker had nothing to eat but pears and apples. Although the poem's speaker calls out "mother," this is most likely just a greeting to an old woman that accompanied the gift of the fruit

and money; therefore, option (3) is incorrect. Although the speaker is tired and the ferry does smell, the ride is a pleasant memory; therefore, option (4) is incorrect. The ferry ride does not seem to pass too slowly for the speaker; therefore, option (5) is incorrect.

2. **(2) how the rhythm of the numerous ferry rides affected the couple** (Analysis) Repetition of these lines mimics the back and forth motion of the ferry ride as well as the lengthiness of the ride—all night long. The speaker shows no sign of boredom or need for another means of transport; therefore, options (1) and (4) are incorrect. The literal fact of a ferry ride could be expressed without the repetition; therefore, option (3) is incorrect. The speaker is sleepy, but this is not emphasized by the repetition as much as option (2); therefore, option (5) is incorrect.

3. **(1) Unexpected sights can produce endless pleasure.** (Comprehension) The sight of the daffodils was unexpected and the memory of this sight often brings pleasure to the speaker. There is no evidence to support options (2) and (5). Although the speaker does describe the flowers as "dancing" (line 6) and "Tossing their heads" (line 12), these are details, not the main idea. Therefore, option (3) is incorrect. Option (4) is the opposite of what is implied by the poem.

4. **(2) the stars of the milky way** (Analysis) It is the speaker who wanders lonely as a cloud, the speaker who experiences a pensive mood, and the speaker whose heart is filled with pleasure; therefore, options (1), (3), and (4) are incorrect. Option (5) is incorrect because the speaker contrasts the flowers with the sparkling waves; he emphasizes the difference between the two.

5. **(3) The speaker sometimes pictures the flowers in his mind when he is alone.** (Analysis) The phrase "inward eye" makes reference to what the author can see inside his head, or in his imagination. There is no support for option (2). There is no direct evidence for options (1) and (4). Option (5) is the opposite of what occurs in the poem and therefore is incorrect.

6. **(2) cheerful and upbeat** (Synthesis) The rhythm of the poem gives a happy feeling of flowers dancing. Option (1) overstates the regular rhythm of the poem; therefore, it is incorrect. This steady but active rhythm is thoughtful but not slow; nor could it be called fast-paced; therefore, options (3) and (4) are incorrect. The rhythm is fairly even; therefore, option (5) is incorrect.

7. **(3) notice all the details of how the rain looked and felt** (Application) The speaker notices so many details about the daffodils that

Answers and Explanations

he can replay them in his mind's eye. Therefore, he is likely to remember the details of a rain shower. There is no support in the poem for option (1). Options (2) and (4) might be true, but there is no evidence in the poem to support them. The speaker does not seem to feel that nature is predictable; therefore, option (5) is incorrect.

Lesson 21
GED Skill Focus (Page 177)

1. **a.** The mirror swallows.

2. **b.** a lake

3. **a.** The small mirror has great power over the woman.

4. an old woman

GED Practice (Pages 178–179)

1. **(4) Work poorly done does not last.** (Comprehension) This line from the poem describes the worthlessness of work poorly done: work that is "botched" will crumble into dust. Option (1) may be an idea in the poem but does not explain the line in question; therefore, it is incorrect. There is no mention of repeating work in the poem; therefore, option (2) is incorrect. There is no support in the poem for options (3) and (5).

2. **(2) Pitchers are made to be useful.** (Analysis) The next line in the poem reads, "and the person for work that is real." This line indicates that the pitcher is a metaphor for a person's desire for useful work. Option (1) is the opposite of the meaning of this line—a pitcher in a museum would not be used—and therefore is incorrect. Option (3) is incorrect because it restates only the first part of line 25. There is no evidence for options (4) and (5).

3. **(3) Both were meant to work hard but did not.** (Analysis) The speaker describes the machines that sit idle outside his window. He then compares himself to a good machine that once was "eager to do its work" (line 15) but had never been used. Option (1) is incorrect because there is no evidence that the machines break or are broken. There is no evidence that the machines or the speaker needs constant attention—perhaps just regular use; therefore, option (2) is incorrect. Option (4) is contradicted by information in the poem. There is no evidence to support option (5).

4. **(2) a toaster that was never taken out of its box** (Application) The machinery was never used, much like a toaster that was never removed from its box. There is no support in the poem for options (1) and (4). The machinery may be useless junk now, but it was once potentially

useful; therefore, option (3) is incorrect. The machinery was never used and may be beyond repair at this point; therefore, option (5) is incorrect.

5. **(2) believes it is too late to live a full life** (Synthesis) The poet is expressing sadness at realizing his life is almost over and he has done so little with it. There is no support for options (1), (4), and (5). Option (3) is too literal and therefore is incorrect.

GED Mini-Test (Pages 180–181)

1. **(1) She did not feel comfortable there.** (Comprehension). Everything in the poem points to how uncomfortable and alienated she feels. There is no evidence to support the other options.

2. **(2) She felt lifeless and not human.** (Comprehension) There is nothing warm or human in the poem; also, the speaker feels herself almost becoming a machine in lines 7–10. Options (1) and (5) are too literal. There is no support in the poem for options (3) and (4).

3. **(2) a fish out of water** (Application) The speaker feels as though she does not belong in that office, much like a fish does not belong out of water. The speaker knows who she is and leaves the office, so option (1) is incorrect. The image of being handed someone else's skin sounds similar to option (3), but it is someone else's skin, not her own, that she leaves behind. Although she is new to the office, this is not the focus of what goes on in the poem; therefore, option (4) is incorrect. Although the office may be a one-way street, option (5) suggests she is going the wrong way. However, the poem ends with her going the right direction by leaving the job.

4. **(2) It shows that the speaker must give her full attention to a machine.** (Analysis) That the machine says "Marry me" indicates that she is supposed to devote herself to it. Options (1) and (4) are the opposite of what is conveyed in this poem. Option (3) may be true but doesn't address the machine's request. Option (5) has no support in the poem.

5. **(2) "corridors of paper" (line 5)** (Analysis) Option (2) evokes images of stacks and stacks of paper. That the speaker was shown this paper and told to "Begin here" indicates endless work is in store. The remaining options pertain to the atmosphere of the office, not the speaker's job duties.

6. **(1) disturbing and unreal** (Synthesis) The poem describes an unpleasant and frightening experience. Options (2), (3), and (5) suggest that

the speaker in the poem is happy or pleased, but the poem contains many violent and painful images. Option (4) is incorrect because although the poem is eerie, it doesn't set up a mystery to be solved.

7. **(5) "They handed me a skin/and said: Wear This" (lines 25–26)** (Analysis) Option (5) is the only option that is broad enough to imply that the speaker is asked to become someone she is not. Options (1) and (4) are details that do not indicate what is expected of the speaker. Options (2) and (3) are imaginative images that better indicate the poem's tone than the office's expectations.

8. **(5) It was a nightmare I will never forget.** (Application) The poem includes nightmarish images such as a guillotine and electric chair. Option (1) sounds like a charming fairy tale and therefore is incorrect. Options (2) and (3) seem too formal to introduce a description of such a personal experience and therefore are incorrect. Option (4) suggests the tone of the poem is humorous, which is not the case.

9. **(3) They are isolating and inhumane.** (Synthesis) The speaker feels alone and dehumanized in the poem. Lack of safety is not the reason for the poem's violent images; therefore, option (1) is incorrect. Offices do rely on technology, but that is not the speaker's central point; therefore, option (2) is incorrect. Option (4) refers to the windows' being nailed shut, which is only a detail in the poem. Option (5) has no support in the poem.

Lesson 22
GED Skill Focus (Page 183)
1. **b.** It symbolizes the way that ordinary events in daily life continue.

2. **b.** death

3. Words or phrases that appeal to the sense of taste include *trout, ginger, green onion, sesame oil, rice, lunch, sweetest meat.* Many of the same words and phrases that appeal to the sense of smell: *trout, ginger, green onion, sesame oil, rice, lunch, sweetest meat,* as well as *pines.*

4. **a.** *True:* Getting "the sweetest meat of the head" (line 6) symbolizes being the head of the family.
   b. *False:* The family is noisy and festive as they gather to eat their delicious lunch. (The family is in fact quiet because the father has died.)
   c. *True:* The image of the "snow-covered road" (line 10) creates a peaceful feeling.
   d. *False:* The image of the travelers (line 12) symbolizes people who seek spiritual knowledge. (This image and that of the snow-covered road symbolizes death.)

GED Practice (Pages 184–185)
1. **(2) The dance and the song depend on one another.** (Analysis) The lines that follow (lines 9–11) emphasize the importance of the combination of dance and song, stating that they are one. There is no support for options (1), (3), (4), and (5) in the poem.

2. **(1) the cycle of life and death** (Analysis) Both the living and the dead participate in the dance. One clue to this is in the phrase "ancient circle" (line 7). Option (2) ignores the solemn nature of the poem. Option (3) refers only to a portion of the dance. Option (4) is too literal a meaning to be correct. Option (5) has no support in the poem.

3. **(2) The bird has hurt himself while struggling to escape his cage.** (Comprehension) The focus of this poem is on the bird's struggle and inability to escape the bonds of its cage. Although options (1) and (4) may be true, these are not the best explanations of this line. There is no support in the poem for options (3) and (5).

4. **(3) a flower** (Comprehension) The "its" from line 6 refers to the flower bud of line 5; therefore, the flower's perfume would be its smell. There is no support in the poem for option (4). While details of options (1), (2), and (5) appear in the poem, they are not discussed with regard to their smell.

5. **(1) freedom and imprisonment** (Synthesis) The bird struggles with being held captive in a cage and wanting to be free. Although joy is expressed at the idea of freedom, there is no mention of fear in the poem; therefore, option (2) is incorrect. Although the bird does injure itself on its cage and the scene outside the cage does seem peaceful, the contrast between violence and peacefulness is not the central idea of the poem; therefore, option (3) is incorrect. The issues in the poem are of freedom and lack of freedom, not life and death. Death is not discussed in this poem; therefore, option (4) is incorrect. There is no support for option (5) in the poem.

GED Mini-Test (Pages 186–187)
1. **(1) She is an office worker.** (Comprehension) She wears conservative clothing and works for a boss who also has a boss—this sounds as though she likely has an office job. Options (2) and (3) are possible answers, but there is more support for option (1) in the context of the poem. There is no support for option (4); it is contradicted by the statement "I wear to work" (line 7). Option (5) is incorrect. It is not the speaker who has any connection with an embassy but the people who wear saris.

Answers and Explanations

2. **(5) She sees life happening without her.** (Comprehension) The caged animals are visited by other animals and also the human visitors to the zoo. Even though they are caged, life is happening to them and around them. This is not the way the speaker feels about her life. Options (1) and (2) may be true but are not supported in the poem. Option (3) is incorrect because there is no mention of the woman's friends in the poem. Option (4) is incorrect because there is no evidence that the speaker is refusing to let others know her. Instead, the poem suggests that others ignore her.

3. **(4) She feels caged within herself just as the animals are penned in cages.** (Analysis) Her own life is the trap, not something done to her by someone else. There is no evidence for the other options.

4. **(4) to break free of her life's routine** (Synthesis) The speaker is stuck and unhappy in her current life; nothing new ever happens to her. There is no support for options (1) and (5). Options (2) and (3) may be true but do not have as much support as option (4).

5. **(4) change** (Analysis) The woman pleads with the vulture to change her. Earlier in the poem, she asks to be freed from her body; in other words, she wishes to be transformed by death. Therefore, the vulture is a symbol of change in this poem (specifically change from life to death). A further clue to the meaning of this symbol is the fact that vultures sometimes are associated with death because they eat dead animals. There is no evidence that the woman is afraid; therefore, option (1) is incorrect. There is no support in the poem for options (2) and (5). Although vultures are certainly a part of nature, this connection to nature is not heavily emphasized; therefore, option (3) is incorrect.

6. **(1) the colorful cloth of the saris and the dull cloth of the speaker's work clothes** (Analysis) These are the only two types of cloth mentioned in the poem, and they create a vivid contrast. The cloths mentioned in option (2) are both figurative references to the cloth of the saris. The descriptions in option (3) both pertain to the cloth of the speaker's work clothes and so do not create a contrast. Options (4) and (5) include cloth not mentioned in the poem and therefore are incorrect.

7. **(3) despairing** (Synthesis) The speaker seems lonely, sad, and almost hopeless; even the animals in the zoo have more visitors. There is no support for the other options.

8. **(2) feels that death will release her from captivity** (Analysis) The speaker brings up the topic of death in the previous line when she comments on how the animals are ignorant of it. The speaker also indicates that she feels trapped by her life. Therefore, when the speaker asks for release from the cage of her body, the most direct interpretation of this request is that she desires release from her body and her life through death. There is no support in the poem for options (1), (3), and (5). Option (4) may be true, but does not explain the phrase or the reference to the speaker's body, and therefore is incorrect.

Lesson 23
GED Skill Focus (Page 189)
1. **b.** She hopes to bring English to life for them and help them see its beauty.

2. You should have underlined "imagines forests and gardens springing up in the tired heads of her students."

3. the letters that spell "tree"

4. Yes

5. You should have circled "could be curled seedlings," "could take root," "could develop leaves."

GED Practice (Pages 190–191)
1. **(4) a soothing feeling** (Analysis) The comparison helps to create a comforting feeling that gives the impression that the speaker will be fine. Options (1) and (5) are the opposite of the feeling created by the comparison and so are incorrect. Although the feeling created by the comparison is positive, there is no allusion to hope in the stanza in which it appears. For this reason, option (2) is incorrect. Option (3) describes the feeling the boy most likely had for his father but does not describe the effect of the comparison; therefore, it is incorrect.

2. **(5) He is grateful for his father's help.** (Analysis) Lines 33–35 show that the boy is focusing on his father's kindness and not on his wound. There is no evidence to support option (4). Although options (1), (2), and (3) may be true, these are not supported by the theme of the poem, which is the gift of kindness the son receives from his father.

3. **(3) a precious memory of kindness** (Analysis) The entire poem is about the kindness his father showed him. The boy was given the metal sliver that his father had removed, but this is only a detail in the poem and is not the most important thing that the boy received; therefore, option (1) is not the best answer. Options (2) and (4) may be true, but they are small details that are relatively unimportant in the poem. Therefore, these options are incorrect. There is no evidence that there was ever any problem with the relationship between the boy and his father; therefore, option (5) is incorrect.

4. **(2) Tenderness can be passed from person to person.** (Synthesis) The speaker's father was kind and tender to him; the speaker was later kind and tender to his wife. This shows kindness being passed from person to person. Option (1) describes people exchanging favors, which is a somewhat different idea; therefore, option (1) is incorrect. Option (5) may be true, but the speaker does not refer to his own happiness when he discusses helping his wife; therefore, option (5) is incorrect. The other options may be true but do not describe the content or theme of the poem.

5. **(5) Parents and children eventually change roles.** (Application) This point is made by the speaker's discussion of how his father used to protect him and now needs protection himself. The speaker's father may feel cities are dangerous, but there is no evidence that the speaker feels this way; therefore, option (1) is incorrect. There is no evidence in the poem that the speaker feels his children are a burden or that his father found him to be a burden; therefore, option (2) is incorrect. There is no evidence to suggest that the speaker would agree with options (3) and (4).

6. **(3) where people had to be brave to survive** (Analysis) Having "nerve" can be the same as having courage, and "law" refers to what was respected by otherwise lawless people. Options (1) and (2) have nothing to do with nerve. Option (4) may be true but is the reason that courage and nerve were required in the first place and not the meaning of the line from the poem. There is no support for option (5).

7. **(4) fearlessness and fear** (Synthesis) The fear of the speaker's elderly father is contrasted with the father's fearlessness when the speaker was a child. There is no evidence to support options (1), (2), (3), and (5).

GED Mini-Test (Pages 192–193)

1. **(4) I stopped to look at the land around San Ysidro while traveling to Colorado.** (Comprehension) The poem specifically states that this is in fact what the speaker did. Although option (1) may be true, it cannot be inferred from the lines. There is not enough evidence in the poem to support option (2). Option (3) is incorrect because the lines indicate that the speaker did stop. Option (5) may be true, but this is not where the speaker stopped.

2. **(2) the feeling of gliding back and forth** (Analysis) The rhythm of these lines glides and then pauses, much like the swooping hawk described in these lines. The rhythm is not quick or strong enough for options (1), (4), or (5) to be correct. There is too much movement in these lines to support option (3).

3. **(1) spring** (Comprehension) The earth is described as "new again," so spring is the season in which the events of the poem are most likely to occur. Therefore, options (2), (3), and (4) are incorrect, as they are seasons which are not "new again." Option (5) is incorrect because the harvest season would be in the fall, not the spring.

4. **joyful** (Analysis) Lines 34–42 indicate the happiness that the speaker feels about the plants and earth. There is no direct evidence for options (2), (3), (4), and (5).

5. **(3) clouds filled with rain** (Analysis) The word "overhead" indicates that the lines refer to something in the sky, and the words "The Thunderer" later in the stanza suggest the idea of rain coming. There is no mention of the hawk's prey; therefore, option (1) is incorrect. Options (2) and (4) do not refer to something overhead and so are incorrect. The sunlight falls in a straight shaft; therefore, option (5) does not fit the definition of the word "writhing" and so is incorrect.

6. **(5) He is waiting to see a ceremonial dance.** (Comprehension) There is a time shift in the poem at line 27. The first part of the poem describes his recollection of a stop on a journey when he appreciated the beauty of the Earth, and the last part describes his eager anticipation of the Katzina and their ceremony of the Earth's renewal. There is no support for options (1) and (4). Options (2) and (3) make sense only if the speaker is still traveling, and it is not clear that he is.

7. **(5) the Katzina** (Comprehension) Line 27 states that "Today, the Katzina come." This is what the speaker is referring to. There is no support for options (1) or (2). Option (3) has some support because the bells refer to the Katzina, but it is not as complete an answer as option (5). The Katzina are coming to do a ceremonial dance about the renewal of the plants and earth, so there is also some support for option (4). However, the "plants with bells" and "stones with voices" in lines 40–41 refer to the masked dancers, not to literal plants and stones. Therefore, when the speaker uses the word "they" in the previous line, he is referring to the Katzina, not to the arrival of spring.

8. **(4) The cycle of nature and plant life is wonderful.** (Synthesis) This is the essence of the speaker's observations about the land. There is no evidence to support options (1) and (2). Option (3) may be true, but rainfall is not the central focus of the poem. Option (5) is incorrect because the speaker is less concerned with the ritual itself than with what that ritual represents—the celebration of the Earth's renewal.

9. **(5) a forest** (Application) The speaker feels joy in nature and in the growth of plants. New York City is a large city with relatively little plant life and natural surroundings; therefore, option (1) is incorrect. Option (3) is a natural environment but too barren to provide much, if any, plant growth; therefore, this is not the best option. Options (2) and (4) are not natural environments and therefore are incorrect.

10. **(4) The dancers seem as if they are a part of nature.** (Analysis) The dancers are celebrating nature in a ceremonial dance; therefore, this option makes the most sense. There is no support in the poem for the other options.

Lesson 24
GED Skill Focus (Page 195)
1. **b.** the snow

2. **a.** Snow is nature's expression of sadness.

3. **b.** It compares the snow to human expressions of grief.

4. You should have listed: *troubled, grief, despair*

GED Practice (Pages 196–197)
1. **(1) is unhappy with his present situation** (Comprehension) The first stanza of the poem suggests both the speaker's unhappiness and his hopes for change. Options (2), (4), and (5) make statements that are not implied in the poem. There is no support for option (3).

2. **(4) hopeful** (Synthesis) The first line indicates that the speaker in the poem has hope: "We shall not always plant while others reap." Option (1) represents the opposite of this belief and is therefore incorrect. There is no evidence to support options (2) and (3). The speaker may be angry, but this word does not describe the overall tone of the poem. Therefore, option (5) is incorrect.

3. **(3) In time, unjust situations will change for the better.** (Analysis) In the first stanza, the poet offers examples of mistreatment; in the second stanza he suggests that a change will come eventually. Options (1) and (2) refer to details of the poem. There is no support for options (4) and (5).

4. **(1) Beauty and charm can be found in what is considered ugly.** (Comprehension) The general topic of the poem is poverty; the poet suggests the beauty in what is not normally seen as beautiful. Option (2) is a detail that supports the theme. There is no support for options (3) and (4) in the poem. Option (5) is incorrect because the poem details positive aspects of the city.

5. **(3) what is affordable and available** (Analysis) This point is made by the poet's emphasis on necessity. Options (1) and (4) may be correct, but are not sufficiently supported by the details in the poem to be correct answers. There is no support for options (2) and (5).

GED Mini-Test (Pages 198–199)
1. **(1) The tourists and the local people experience the beach differently.** (Comprehension) The tourists and their children are having a wonderful time, while the speaker is not even allowed to go on the beach. Option (2) may be the attitude of the local people, but it expresses only a part of the whole poem and so is incorrect. The fence is not keeping everyone happy as implied in option (3). Options (4) and (5) may be true, but these are generalizations without adequate support in the poem.

2. **(2) freedom and restriction** (Synthesis) The tourists are free to enjoy the beach while the speaker and her family are not. It is not the beach and sea that are contrasted in this poem but the people on either side of the fence; therefore, option (1) is incorrect. Childhood is mentioned in the poem, but maturity is not emphasized, so option (3) is incorrect. Good manners are not emphasized in this poem, so option (4) is incorrect. There is no support for option (5).

3. **(2) The little girl has abundant energy.** (Analysis) The word "flying" suggests that the girl is running and leaping. Options (1), (3), and (4) assume the word is meant literally. Option (5) is incorrect because it suggests the girl was trying to avoid the grass; however, she was having fun.

4. **(4) The speaker and the child have similar feelings of regret.** (Analysis) The speaker's use of "twin distress" indicates both his regret at interrupting the child's play and the child's regret at being interrupted. There is no mention of an actual twin or a resemblance to the speaker; therefore, options (1) and (3) are incorrect. The child is observing the speaker's eyes, not the reverse; therefore, option (2) is incorrect. Option (5) is incorrect because the speaker does not say he was playing.

5. **(1) It emphasizes the child's untamed, free nature.** (Analysis) A net is usually used to catch butterflies. Options (2) and (4) would be correct only if you take the image literally, but it is figurative language. Option (3) is clearly not what is meant. Option (5) has nothing to do with the image of the net.

6. **(3) A natural, free spirit is eventually tamed by adulthood.** (Comprehension) The child is running free, unencumbered by

UNIT 3

restrictions. The speaker remembers how it feels to be a child even though he no longer behaves that way. He regretfully signals the child that it is time to stop playing and come inside. The other options are not supported by the poem.

Unit 3 Cumulative Review (Pages 200–206)

1. **(4) the pattern of the ocean's waves** (Analysis) By repeating the word *break*, the poet suggests the repeating in-and-out pattern of waves hitting the shore. Both times he uses this phrase, it is closely linked, in the next line, with the sea. Though the singing of a young sailor is mentioned in the poem—option (1)—it would be unlikely to have this steady repeating pattern. There is no evidence to support options (2), (3), or (5).

2. **(5) a loved one who has died** (Comprehension) Lines 11–12 state that he has lost someone he loved and still longs for that person. Though he mentions a young boy and his sister and a "sailor lad," there is no evidence that he is longing for his own youth, as mentioned in options (1) and (2). The poem offers no support for options (3) or (4).

3. **(3) sad** (Application) Because the poem is about longing, this answer makes the most sense. Nothing in the poem suggests a scary tone, so option (1) is incorrect. Options (2), (4), and (5) are almost the opposite of the mood suggested by the poem.

4. **(1) It contrasts with the speaker's sorrow.** (Analysis) Though the young people may remind the speaker of days gone by and remind him that life holds pleasures—options (2) and (3)—their real importance is as a contrast to his own feelings. This effect is underscored by the phrase "O well" at the beginning of lines 5 and 7, suggesting that though he notices their lightheartedness, he doesn't feel it. Nothing in the poem suggests options (4) or (5).

5. **(5) indifference** (Analysis) The hardness, coldness, and colorlessness of this image all suggest a lack of concern for the speaker's feelings. Nothing in the poem suggests the other options.

6. **(3) hopes he can express his feelings** (Comprehension) Though the other options are all possible interpretations, option (3) makes the most sense in the context of this poem: a person trying to find a way to express a deep and sorrowful feeling. Option (1) is not the best answer because there is no indication in the poem that the speaker generally has trouble finding the right words; only that he is having trouble expressing these particular thoughts and feelings. Although it is certainly implied that the speaker would like others to understand his thoughts, he does not mention other people in these lines; therefore, option (5) is not the best answer.

7. **(4) nature** (Comprehension) The reader has to infer the meaning of "it" from the poem's context. Since the message of the poem is that the beauties of nature will outlast the "crop of suburban houses" that have spoiled it, options (1), (2), and (3) are incorrect; they are the very things that will be outlasted by natural beauty. Option (5), the cliffs, also have "all time," but they are only part of nature and not broad enough to stand for the "it" expressed in line 8.

8. **(2) the Nature Conservancy** (Application) This is the most likely answer, as the speaker is most concerned in the poem with the beauties of nature and their preservation. Nothing in the poem suggests that the speaker would have an interest in options (1) or (4). Because he is so concerned with the beauty of nature, he would be less likely to join an organization that promotes building, option (3), or commercial development, option (5).

9. **(4) Populations increase and decrease in cycles.** (Analysis) The comparison of people with tides implies an ebb and flow, or high and low levels, occurring in a regular pattern. Option (1) is incorrect because it is a literal interpretation of figurative language. Option (2) is incorrect because it only acknowledges one part of the cycle. The poem does not support options (3) or (5).

10. **(2) People must realize their place in nature.** (Synthesis) This theme is first introduced in lines 8–9, when the speaker suggests that humans are subject to the same forces as the oceans and tides. In addition, it is stated almost directly in the last three lines of the poem. Although patience is mentioned in line 1 of the poem, option (1) is incorrect because patience is linked with nature, not with people. Options (3) and (5) are almost the opposite of the poem's message about nature's endurance. Nothing in the poem supports option (4).

11. **(3) airplanes landing** (Comprehension) The poet uses the phrases "Wings of jets," "landing gear," and "taking turns for landing" to evoke an image of the geese as airplanes landing. Although the poet also compares the geese to pterodactyls, he does not compare them to pterodactyl wings, so option (1) is incorrect. The geese land by the boats, but the poet does not compare the two; therefore, option (2) is incorrect. Geese are not compared to swamps or the river, so options (4) and (5) are incorrect.

12. **(1) Civilization has not changed the patterns of the geese.** (Analysis) You must infer this answer from the context. The idea that migration maps are "etched in their brains" tells you that their flight pattern has become part of their instinct and is thus not subject to change. Also, Washington, D.C., a big city, symbolizes the changes of civilization—not the best resting place for wild creatures like geese. Nothing in the poem suggests options (2) or (4), so they are incorrect. Option (3) is incorrect because it goes beyond what the poem says—that is, that "Some [geese] still stop off in Washington, D.C." Though option (5) may be true, it does not explain line 2 of the poem.

13. **(2) people driving home from work** (Synthesis) You can infer this from several images in the last stanza: "traffic on the bridges" (cars), "daily homing" (people going home), "migrants with headlights dimmed" (drivers of cars with headlights), "along broken white lines" (the lines along the highway). The drivers are described with words that could also apply to geese ("homing," "migrants," "loop and bank"). The poem creates the comparison by layering all of these images. Option (1) is incorrect because the dinosaur-era comparison is made in the fourth stanza, not the final one. Though options (3) and (4) are mentioned in the last stanza, neither is being compared to geese. There is no support for option (5) as a comparison to geese.

14. **(1) how much the environment has changed** (Analysis) With that image, the poet pushes the reader to imagine what the region was like before humans built an airport there; he pushes the reader even further back in time by starting that line with the image of "Pterodactyls circling." The poem states that the swamp has been filled in, so option (2) is incorrect. There is no support in the poem for the other options.

15. **(3) a conversation** (Synthesis) In alternating lines, one voice asks a question, and the other voice answers it. Of the options given, this is the most precise description of the poem's structure.

16. **(4) to identify two separate voices** (Analysis) Rhyme is used to indicate two distinct voices. The questions in each stanza have an end rhyme, as do the answers in each stanza. There is no support for options (1), (2), (3), or (5).

17. **(5) people who have died** (Analysis) The poem's images of darkness, night, resting, and inevitability all support this answer. There is no support in the poem for options (1), (2), (3), or (4).

18. **(3) slow and steady** (Synthesis) The repeating pattern of questions and answers, each line a complete "sentence," keeps the rhythm slow and steady. The pattern is too regular for options (1) or (5) to be correct. Although the poem has a regular rhythmic pattern, it also has variety in the rhythm of each line and from one line to the next, so options (2) and (4) are incorrect.

19. **(5) They are playmates.** (Comprehension) School is not mentioned, so option (1) is incorrect. Lines 2–6 describe a happy, friendly relationship, so options (2) and (4) are incorrect. There is no evidence for option (3).

20. **(1) wistful longing** (Synthesis) The references to past happiness and passing seasons give the poem a sense of longing. There is no support for options (2), (3), and (4). Although the speaker expresses her love, most of the poem is not romantic or passionate, so option (5) is incorrect.

21. **(2) I am happy, so why look elsewhere?** (Comprehension) Lines 11–13 reveal that at age fifteen, the girl fell in love with her husband. Her happiness with him rules out options (1) and (4). At this point in the poem (line 14), the husband has not yet left, so option (3) is incorrect. The poem makes no mention of enemies, so option (5) is incorrect.

22. **(5) The husband has been away a long time.** (Analysis) The image suggests that enough time has passed for moss to gather in the husband's absence. There is no support for options (1), (2), (3), or (4).

23. **(4) They remind her that life is short and she is alone.** (Analysis) The appearance of the paired butterflies reminds her that time is passing, she is getting older, and she is by herself. Option (1) is incorrect because it doesn't address the fact that the butterflies are paired. There is no support in the poem for options (2), (3), or (5).

24. **(3) The marriage was arranged by their two families.** (Analysis) The man and woman were children who lived in the same village. She was fourteen when they married and bashful around her husband; therefore it's logical that the marriage between the two was arranged. The woman was not in love when she married, so option (1) is incorrect. There is no support for options (2), (4), or (5).

25. **(3) echo the girl's sadness** (Analysis) This is what the woman notices, so it gives a clue as to her inner feelings. There is no support for the other options.

26. **(1) The course of life is unpredictable.** (Application) She might say this because of all the unpredictable changes in her own life. She herself is sorrowful, so she would be unlikely to support option (2). She has had joy in her life, so option (3) is also unlikely. Although the woman did marry very young herself, there is nothing in

the poem to suggest that she would recommend this to someone else. Therefore, option (4) is incorrect. There is no support in the excerpt for option (5).

27. **(2) playfulness to obedience to devotion to longing** (Synthesis) She was playful as a child (lines 1–3), obediently married (lines 6–10), then became devoted to her husband (lines 11–14), and finally longed for him while he was gone. The poem does not support the other options.

28. **(5) repeating the word "Or"** (Analysis) This pattern establishes a rhythm in a long section of the poem. All the lines of the poem have end punctuation, so option (1) is incorrect. Repeating images generally contribute more to theme than to rhythm, and this poem does not have a large number of references to flight, so option (2) is incorrect. The poem begins and ends with a question, but this is not sufficient to set up a rhythm, so option (3) is incorrect. Nor is the one reference to waves (line 22) sufficient to establish a rhythm.

29. **(2) sight and hearing** (Analysis) You can see the bees ("watch") and hear their buzzing ("busy around the hive"). Taste and touch are not directly appealed to, so the other options are incorrect.

30. **(1) The world is filled with miracles.** (Synthesis) The poet establishes this theme by giving many examples of simple things that are all around us. The variety of the examples given as miracles makes options (2) and (3) incorrect. The speaker is not, for the most part, concerned with what other people think, so option (4) is incorrect. The poet mentions people in cars, conversations at dinner tables, and ships, so he does not restrict his idea of miracles to nature; thus, option (5) is incorrect.

UNIT 4: UNDERSTANDING DRAMA
Lesson 25
GED Skill Focus (Page 211)
1. **b.** It is Minnie's birthday.

2. Sophie and Frank

3. **a.** Minnie's birthday present is a piece of land.

GED Practice (Pages 212–213)
1. **(4) Chick will criticize the toy.** (Application) Chick is very critical of the polka-dot dress that Lenny gave to Peekay, so it is likely that she would be critical of any other present, too. The excerpt does not give much information about Peekay, so option (1) is unlikely. Options (2) and (3) are more likely to describe Chick's behavior than Lenny's. There is no evidence that Chick is cruel to Peekay, so option (5) is incorrect.

2. **(1) If you cannot be nice, be polite.** (Application) Although Lenny seems to be hurt by Chick's cruel remarks, she is still polite. She is not honest about her feelings, so option (2) is incorrect. Although she is not thrilled with Chick's gift, option (3) is not relevant to the excerpt; neither are options (4) and (5).

3. **(4) to portray Chick as inconsiderate** (Analysis) Lenny is "crushed" by Chick's remarks, demonstrating that Chick's behavior is inconsiderate. There is no evidence that Peekay is disappointed, so option (1) is incorrect. Chick may be attentive to details, but this is not the reason she discusses the shortcomings of the polka-dot dress, so option (2) is incorrect. If anything, Lenny has bad taste despite her efforts, so option (3) is incorrect. There is no reason that Chick would be particularly interested in showing off her understanding of fabrics, so option (5) is incorrect.

4. **(3) She often says what others want her to say.** (Comprehension) Option (3) is correct since Lenny usually echoes what Chick has already said. Option (1) is the opposite of option (3). Lenny says that candy is a nice gift, not that she prefers it to anything else, ruling out option (2). Options (4) and (5) are not supported by the excerpt.

5. **(4) resourceful and determined** (Comprehension) Nora is not humble and obedient, option (1); hysterical, option (2); nor evil, option (3). Although she may have an impulsive streak, option (5), her determination and resourcefulness are her most obvious qualities.

6. **(2) secretive** (Synthesis) The two are engaged in a conversation about the secrets Nora is keeping from her husband. Mrs. Linde seems uncomfortable and Nora seems worried about her husband, but neither is especially frightened; therefore, option (1) is incorrect. Nora has hope that she can change things, so option (3) is incorrect. Although Nora does seem in good spirits, the seriousness of the situation means that options (4) and (5) are not the best answer.

7. **(5) insist that her friend be straightforward** (Application) Mrs. Linde wants to ensure that Nora makes a reasonable and honest decision. Therefore, she would probably want a friend facing a similar situation to be straightforward as well. Mrs. Linde does not react to the situation in the excerpt by taking offense, so option (1) is incorrect. Neither does Mrs. Linde offer to help, option (2); she just expresses a lack of understanding. There is no evidence to support options (3) or (4).

8. **(2) She wants to do what is best for her husband's health.** (Comprehension) Nora tells Mrs. Linde that this is the way to save her husband's life. Option (1) is one way Nora tries to get him to go South but is not her real reason for wanting to go. Options (3), (4), and (5) are not supported by the excerpt.

GED Mini-Test (Pages 214–215)

1. **(4) reasonable and firm** (Comprehension) Karen does her best to reason with Mary, but she is also firm with her. She is not prim, option (1); harsh, option (2); or easily intimated, option (5). Nor is she overly forgiving toward the girl, option (3).

2. **(5) sneaky and uncooperative** (Comprehension) Mary's tears and tantrums, threats, and refusal to tell the truth tell us that she is hard to control. She may be lonely and misunderstood as well, option (1), but those are not her chief traits. There is no evidence for options (2), (3), and (4).

3. **(1) make excuses for turning in work late** (Application) Mary does not want to take responsibility for her actions, so as a worker she would probably make excuses or try to blame others. There is no evidence that Mary is timid around others, so option (2) is incorrect. She seems unhappy, but she does not say anything about quitting school; therefore, there is not enough evidence to conclude that she would quit a job right away, option (3). She does not seem to be successful or a good communicator; therefore, options (4) and (5) are incorrect.

4. **(3) tense** (Synthesis) The clash of wills between Mary and Karen makes this a scene full of conflict. There is no evidence for options (1), (2), (4), or (5).

5. **(3) Mary is trying to manipulate Karen.** (Analysis) Mary attempts to manipulate Karen by feigning illness and threatening to tell her grandmother if Karen insists on reprimanding her. Karen is straightforward about her thoughts and feelings with Mary, so option (1) is incorrect. Mary is interested in Karen's opinion, if only because Karen has the power to punish her. So, option (2) can be ruled out. Mary and Karen are not involved in trying to gain each other's affection, rather they are working out a conflict; therefore, option (4) is incorrect. Mary may not like what Karen is saying to her, but there is no evidence that she does not trust Karen; therefore, option (5) is incorrect.

6. **(1) Mary feels no shame about lying.** (Analysis) Karen implies that Mary makes a habit of lying; therefore, it is likely that Mary is lying in this excerpt. To be able to look directly at someone while she lies indicates that she is brazen about it. Option (2) is incorrect because Karen does have reason to accuse Mary. Mary is not trying to calm Karen down, option (3); nor is she trying to communicate her ideas more clearly, option (4). There is no evidence to support option (5).

7. **(3) She does not like what Karen said.** (Analysis) Mary is upset that Karen has punished her and so dramatically falls to the floor to express herself. Because Mary seems to be falling in reaction to Karen's words, it seems unlikely that she is really fainting; therefore, option (1) is incorrect. The appearance of Mary's pain, which she points to vaguely, seems too coincidental to be genuine, so option (2) is incorrect. There is no support for options (4) or (5).

8. **(3) assign Mary an extremely harsh punishment** (Application) Mrs. Mortar's comment (lines 54–55) regarding how she would treat Mary indicates that she is less patient with Mary's misbehavior than Karen is, so options (1), (2), and (4) are incorrect. There is no support for option (5).

9. **(1) Karen does not value Mrs. Mortar's opinions.** (Analysis) The stage directions show that Karen ignores Mrs. Mortar. This implies that Karen does not value her opinions. The fact that Karen openly ignores her shows that the two women are not close friends, option (2). It also shows that Karen is not careful to protect Mrs. Mortar's feelings, option (3), nor does she respect her, option (4). There is no evidence for option (5) in the excerpt.

10. **(3) pretend to be ill to get sympathy** (Application) Mary uses the tactic of pretending to be ill in the excerpt; therefore, this is the best choice. Mary does not beg, tell the truth, show affection, or try to bargain; she manipulates and threatens. Therefore, the other options have little or no support.

11. **(4) wait for Mary to decide to get up** (Analysis) Karen does not appear worried when Mary says she feels ill, so options (1), (2), and (5) are unlikely. Option (3) is incorrect because Karen ignores Mrs. Mortar earlier in the excerpt.

Lesson 26
GED Skill Focus (Page 217)

1. Leticia

2. Possible answers include the following:
   She does not believe in shooting deer.
   Alejo is her friend.
   Orlando thinks she is crazy.

She thinks deer are beautiful.
She would stand in the way of the bullets to keep a deer being from being killed by a hunter.

3. He is a lieutenant commander and dresses in an army uniform.

4. **d.** an authoritative, confident man

GED Practice (Pages 218–219)

1. **(2) She is a very shy person.**
(Comprehension) The typing instructor refers to Laura as "terribly shy" (line 41), which is evidence that option (2) is the correct response. There is no evidence to support options (1) or (4). Laura does not make any statements that sound angry; therefore, option (3) is incorrect. Laura continues to try to find out why her mother is upset; she does not try to change the subject, option (5).

2. **(2) She wants to make a dramatic effect.**
(Comprehension) Amanda is acting as if something awful has happened to get Laura's attention. Because she does not state what the problem is, she makes the situation seem more dramatic than it actually is. There is no mention of tuition money, so option (1) is incorrect. Options (3) and (5) are incorrect because she is trying to make Laura feel uncomfortable. Option (4) is incorrect because the incident is not really tragic.

3. **(4) Amanda is pausing while she thinks of what to say next.** (Analysis) Based on the context of the excerpt, the stage directions indicate that Amanda is upset and nearly at a loss for words. The stage directions refer to Amanda's behavior; therefore, option (1) is incorrect. Option (2) is incorrect because Amanda speaks again immediately after the pauses. Options (3) and (5) have no support in the excerpt.

4. **(5) absentminded** (Analysis) Sister Mary Agnes forgets the story she is telling, cannot find her glasses, and calls students by the wrong names. There is no evidence for options (1), (2), or (4). Although she may be hopeful, option (3), this is not the focus of the excerpt.

5. **(3) neat and clean clothing** (Application) Sister Mary Agnes is bothered by Maria Theresa's long bangs that hide her face. She also tells a scary story about someone who did not keep her hair clean. This indicates that she is quite concerned with neatness and cleanliness. There is no support for options (1), (4), or (5). The story she tells shows her lack of concern about fashion; therefore, option (2) is incorrect.

6. **(1) lighthearted** (Synthesis) A humorous, lighthearted mood is created based on Sister Mary Agnes's being pleasantly unaware of the students' sarcasm and impatient attitude.

There is some tension, option (2), but it is not the general mood. There is no evidence for options (3), (4), or (5).

7. **(4) to change classes** (Comprehension) Maria Theresa responds to her teacher with some impatience and disrespect; she wants to get on with the next activity, her next class. Maria Theresa shows no interest in a new hairdo, option (1), or in earning her teacher's affections, option (2). Although she may want to be liked by her classmates, this is not the focus of the excerpt, option (3). There is no evidence to support option (5).

8. **(3) to get Maria Theresa to cut her hair** (Analysis) There is no evidence for option (1). Although the hairdo story might be humorous to the class, this is not the Sister's main intention, option (2). There is no evidence that the Sister is mean-spirited or angry, so option (4) is incorrect. The point of the hairdo story is to persuade Maria Theresa, not just to fill up class time, option (5).

GED Mini-Test (Pages 220–221)

1. **(4) not doing his chores** (Comprehension) Troy believes that football is taking Cory away from his responsibilities. There is no support for options (1) and (3). It is Troy who refuses to speak to the recruiter, so option (2) is incorrect. Option (5) is incorrect because Cory is cutting back his hours at the A&P.

2. **(3) Troy is opposed to Cory's desire to play football.** (Comprehension) Troy makes a number of arguments trying to change Cory's mind; therefore, options (1) and (2) are incorrect. There is no support for option (4). Option (5) is incorrect because Troy doesn't ask Cory to quit school.

3. **(2) to go to college** (Comprehension) Cory states that he wants to play football because he sees it as an opportunity to go to college. Options (1) and (5) are Troy's desires, not Cory's. There is no evidence for option (3). While option (4) may be correct, there is no support for it in the excerpt.

4. **(5) tense and disharmonious** (Synthesis) The conflict between Troy and Cory over football and Cory's job produces an air of tension. No evidence is present for options (1) and (3), so they are incorrect. Although there may be elements of options (2) and (4), each overstates the overall mood.

5. **(5) Cory will try to reason with Troy.** (Application) Throughout the excerpt, Cory tries to reason with his father. There is no evidence in the excerpt that Cory's mother will have any further involvement, option (1). Mr. Stawicki

works with Cory to arrange a new schedule, and there is no indication Mr. Stawicki is unhappy with Cory's work, option (2). Corey has not demonstrated that he wants to spite his father, option (3). Troy shows no evidence of changing his mind, option (4).

6. **(2) Cory** (Comprehension) It is Cory who faces the major dilemma of whether to follow his father's wishes or disregard them. Mr. Stawicki, option (1); Cory's coach, option (3); and Cory's mother, option (4), are secondary characters who do not appear directly in this excerpt. Although Troy, option (5), plays a major part, it is Cory who has to solve the central problem.

7. **(4) Troy has been treated unfairly in the past and is warning Cory.** (Analysis) The reference to "white man" implies a racial concern that suggests Troy is aware of unfair treatment. Troy wants Cory to keep his A&P job, but there is no real indication that he would lie or manipulate in order to get Cory to do this; therefore, option (1) is incorrect. There is no evidence to support options (2), (3), or (5).

8. **(5) Seeking immediate gain can cost you later on.** (Analysis) Troy believes that steady work at the A&P is the right choice and does not seem to believe that his son will achieve anything in football. He is ignoring the fact that football could be his son's ticket to a college education and a bright future; he is looking at short-term economic gain and ignoring the long-term benefits. There is no evidence that Troy's main focus is on trying to avoid spoiling Cory, option (1). Troy does not seem to be leading Cory. Instead, Cory seems to be trying to make his own decisions; therefore, option (2) is incorrect. Troy wants Cory to be obedient, but not necessarily to live the same life as he does; therefore, option (3) is incorrect. There is no support for option (4).

9. **(3) so Cory will have a job that cannot be taken away** (Analysis) Troy says in lines 39–40 that he wants Cory to have a job that can't be taken away. There is no evidence to support options (1) or (5). Troy wants Cory to do his chores whether he works at the A&P or not, so option (2) is incorrect. Troy approves of college but doesn't want Troy to go to college because of football—especially because this means giving up a solid job at the A&P; therefore, option (4) is incorrect.

10. **(5) supportive** (Analysis) Mr. Stawicki agrees to adjust Cory's hours to fit Cory's football schedule. Therefore, options (2) and (4) are incorrect. There is no evidence to support options (1) or (3).

Lesson 27
GED Skill Focus (Page 223)
1. **b.** wants to express doubt about someone else's behavior
   c. is determined to prevent someone from taking a certain action
   a. hopes to persuade someone to share a certain viewpoint

2. **a.** He wants to hide from her exactly how expensive the flamingo was.
   c. He wants to prove to her that the flamingo was worth the price he paid.

GED Practice (Pages 224–225)
1. **(2) She doesn't want Annie to leave.** (Analysis) Kate is trying to get Annie to stay. By pointing out that Helen folded a napkin, she is attempting to prove to Annie that Helen is capable of learning. Kate loves Helen and sees the good in her, so options (1) and (5) are incorrect. Option (3) is incorrect because there is no evidence that Kate takes care of Helen. There is no support for option (4).

2. **(1) uncooperative** (Analysis) The first few lines of the excerpt reveal the difficulty Annie is having with Helen. There is no support for options (2) and (5). Options (3) and (4) describe the opposite of Helen's behavior.

3. **(1) "I think everybody else here does." (line 9)** (Comprehension) This line refers to everybody else's underestimating Helen and her abilities. Option (2) is incorrect because it refers to the negative change since Helen's illness. Options (3), (4), and (5) do not deal with whether Helen is hopeless or not; they are details of the conversation.

4. **(3) They must be taught, not pitied.** (Application) Annie says pity stands in the way of teaching Helen. Option (1) is untrue, or she would not be a teacher of a blind and deaf child. Options (2) and (5) are the opposite of what she has said she believes. Option (4) is obviously something they are all trying to avoid in Helen's case; therefore, Annie would be unlikely to agree with this statement.

5. **(5) to understand his father's absence** (Analysis) This point is made by David's frequent questions on this topic. Option (1) is not supported. Options (2) and (3) may be true, but there is no evidence to support them. Option (4) is true but only supports David's main motivation.

6. **(3) Luke was a great musician.** (Comprehension) After making this statement, David lists two famous musicians, which implies that he is putting his father in the same category. Option (1) is incorrect because David states he

was hurt by his father and felt ashamed of him. There is no mention of where Luke lived; therefore, option (2) is incorrect. David does not say that his mother hid Luke's records, only that she did not allow them to have a phonograph; therefore, option (4) is incorrect. There is no support for option (5).

7. **(5) He wanted to be connected to his father.** (Analysis) Lines 21–28 explain David's desire to be connected to his father and his dreams of playing piano with him. Although David may be talented, option (1), that is not the central reason for his playing piano. There is no evidence to support option (2). Option (3) may be true, but only because his father was a musician. David's mother discourages him by not letting him listen to his father's music, so option (4) is incorrect.

8. **(2) hurt and angry** (Comprehension) The last part of the excerpt reveals David's hurt and anger at Luke for being absent. Option (1) may be true for Luke's musical talent, but not for his role as father. There is no evidence for options (3) or (4). Although option (5) is true, these emotions are not David's strongest feelings about Luke as a father.

9. **(5) emotional and earnest** (Synthesis) This excerpt conveys the sincerity of both father and son as they discuss the painful issue of the father's absence. Option (1) is incorrect because there is no peace for either father or son yet. There is no evidence to support options (2) or (4). Though the son is sad, other emotions such as anger and shame are also important in this excerpt; therefore, option (3) is not the best answer.

GED Mini-Test (Pages 226–227)

1. **(3) having self-respect** (Comprehension) Everything Esperanza says indicates a wish to think well of herself and others. Option (1) is important to her, but it does not mean the same as "dignity." Option (2) is something Esperanza would do to gain self-respect. There is no support for option (4). Based on her words, she does not wish to be more powerful than others, option (5).

2. **(2) to grow without driving others out of business** (Application) Esperanza states that she wants to rise without pushing others down (lines 42–43). Options (1) and (3) are the opposite of what Esperanza would likely believe. There is no evidence to support option (4). Esperanza believes in working together, which is the opposite implied by option (5).

3. **(3) the Anglos treat the Mexicans** (Comprehension) Option (3) is correct because of Esperanza's words in lines 28–34, which

would also rule out option (5). Options (1) and (4) are possible comparisons, but they are not Esperanza's. Because in this case the Anglos are the bosses and the Mexicans the workers, option (2) must also be ruled out.

4. **(3) Men and women cannot be friends.** (Comprehension) Ramón resists Esperanza's wish that he be her friend. Option (1) can be ruled out since he is taking part in the strike. Option (2) also is incorrect because the strike implies that there are differences between the workers and the bosses. Options (4) and (5) must be ruled out because of Ramón's current views of women and of the strike.

5. **(1) Human dignity is worth defending.** (Analysis) In the strike and in her relationship with Ramón, Esperanza is searching for dignity. Option (2) is not supported by the excerpt. Option (3) is too specific to be the theme of this excerpt. Option (4) is a theme statement but is not correct here. Because it refers to specific characters, option (5) is not a theme statement.

6. **(1) Esperanza has been doing work that is not respected.** (Comprehension) In her answer to Ramón, Esperanza discusses the way in which the Anglo bosses look down on her and call her a "dirty Mexican" (lines 28–31). This indicates that she does not receive respect for her work. There is no evidence in the excerpt to support options (2) or (4). Esperanza seems to be a very serious and thoughtful person; therefore, option (3) is incorrect. Although Ramón seems to dislike Charley Vidal, there is no evidence that this friend of Esperanza's is disreputable, option (5).

7. **(4) She will not allow Ramón to hit her again.** (Comprehension) The stage directions indicate that he begins to strike her and then stops. Her lines reinforce that decision. Option (1) is not the case; she wants them to struggle together. Options (2) and (3) are not supported by the excerpt. Option (5) is incorrect because she already is Ramón's friend, although he does not believe it.

8. **(1) Ramón and Esperanza's relationship will change.** (Analysis) Esperanza's determination to change things is apparent at the end of the excerpt; so, option (5) is incorrect. There is no support for option (2). Option (3) may be true; however, the content of the excerpt does not give it support. Option (4) refers to a detail meant to be taken figuratively, not literally.

9. **(2) She firmly supports it and its goals.** (Comprehension) Esperanza expresses her support for the strike in lines 1–8. This makes options (1) and (3) incorrect. She states in lines 2–3 that her side is stronger than ever, so

option (4) is incorrect. Esperanza directly states that Ramón couldn't win without her, so option (5) is incorrect.

10. **(1) heated** (Synthesis) Esperanza and Ramón are upset with each other. Option (2) understates the tone of the excerpt; the pair's shouting indicates that they are more than just annoyed. Although this is a dialogue, the passion of the characters' words is not best described as conversational, option (3). There is no evidence to support options (4) or (5).

11. **(2) an active volcano** (Analysis) The stage directions indicate that he snorts and explodes. Although a pot of coffee is hot and steaming, option (1), this image does not suggest Ramón's short temper as well as option (2) does. Option (3) is incorrect because Ramón does not seem exhausted, but on the contrary is very lively. There is no evidence to support options (4) and (5).

Lesson 28

GED Skill Focus (Page 229)

1. **c.** An incompetent employee can cause unfortunate but humorous situations.

2. The ambassador hires his incompetent son and puts him in charge.
   Magee's own Embassy hung him in effigy.
   Magee was recalled from his posts in Africa and other parts of the world.

3. **b.** inability to perform a job

GED Practice (Pages 230–231)

1. **(5) She is rude and touchy.** (Analysis) Mrs. Dudgeon's actions and statements toward Judith reveal these traits. Options (1), (2), and (3) are incorrect based on her behavior. Though she may be stingy, option (4), there is no evidence of that trait in this excerpt.

2. **(2) smug and self-satisfied** (Analysis) Although her words are sweet, the stage directions suggest that Judith has a very high opinion of herself. If the reader had only the characters' speeches to rely on, option (1) would be correct. There is no support for options (3), (4), or (5).

3. **(2) Judith is an unexpected guest for the reading of a will.** (Comprehension) Mrs. Dudgeon is surprised to see Judith but says, not very nicely, that she can stay. The occasion is stated in lines 5–7. Option (1) has no support. Options (3) and (5) are the opposite of what is suggested. Option (4) might be true, but it is too general to be the main idea and does not best describe the situation.

4. **(2) tense** (Synthesis) These two women can barely manage to be polite to each other.

Option (1) is incorrect because there is no evidence of sadness even though someone has died. Options (3) and (5) both suggest a pleasantness not found in this excerpt. Option (4) has no support.

5. **(4) She thinks Judith was insincere about wanting to clean.** (Analysis) Mrs. Dudgeon is unhappy with her unexpected guest's arrival. In addition, Mrs. Dudgeon has already gotten the house ready so there is no need for Judith to offer to help with this. These facts suggest that Mrs. Dudgeon thinks Judith was offering to help ready the house only to appear polite and was actually insincere. There is no support for option (1). There is no evidence that Mrs. Dudgeon thinks Judith would be especially good at greeting people, option (2). Mrs. Dudgeon may think that Judith is untidy for leaving the door open, but this is not enough evidence to support option (3). Mrs. Dudgeon doesn't express any truly kind feelings towards Judith (in fact, she speaks "half sneering" to her), so option (5) is incorrect.

6. **(2) She is fond of Josephine.** (Comprehension) Evelyn's concern about Josephine's forgetfulness, her willingness to listen to Josephine's stories, and the way she kindly reminds Josephine of what she had been talking about the night before support this conclusion. She may be upset about Josephine's forgetfulness, but there is no evidence that she is upset with Josephine herself; therefore, option (1) is incorrect. There is no support for options (3), (4), or (5).

7. **(4) She is usually an early riser.** (Comprehension) Josephine states that she overslept, which is unusual for her. There is no evidence to support options (1) and (2). Thayer is Josephine's grandson since she talks about her husband as Thayer's grandfather; therefore, option (3) is incorrect. Josephine is forgetful due to her age, but not because she is worried about something, so option (5) is incorrect.

8. **(3) enjoy telling stories about her youth** (Application) Josephine apparently enjoys talking about Grandfather and would likely enjoy telling other stories from the past. In this excerpt, there is no support for options (1), (2), or (5). The opposite of option (4) is true since she remembers the past very well.

9. **(2) one of the problems of aging** (Synthesis) The excerpt centers on Josephine's not remembering what she did the night before, but recalling events of long ago. This is a common condition of old age. Although options (1), (3), (4) and (5) are included in the excerpt, they are not the author's main focus.

10. **(1) with disbelief** (Analysis) The stage directions indicate that Josephine is puzzled. There is no evidence to support options (2), (3), (4), or (5).

GED Mini-Test (Pages 232–233)

1. **(5) He does not live with the family.** (Analysis) There is no mention of Medvedenko's father in the excerpt; additionally, if the father were present, Mevedenko would probably not be completely responsible for supporting his mother and siblings. Therefore, it is a logical inference to conclude that he is not present. There is no support for the other options.

2. **(1) sincere and lonely** (Analysis) Medvedenko's statements to Masha are sincere, and he would like to have a wife. There is no evidence to suggest that Medvedenko is arrogant, option (2); lighthearted, option (3); or uneducated, option (4). Although his character may be somewhat pathetic and victimized, option (5), the focus of this excerpt is on his sincerity and love for Masha.

3. **(2) She appreciates his feelings.** (Analysis) Masha understands that Medvedenko has strong feelings for her, but she does not love him back. This makes option (1) incorrect. She does not express anger at his visiting her, option (3). There is no evidence to support options (4) and (5).

4. **(1) one-sided love** (Comprehension) Medvedenko says that he loves Masha even though she appears to be indifferent towards him. Masha does not indicate that she has a secret love for Medvedenko; therefore, option (2) is incorrect. Although they may have a friendship, there is no evidence that their friendship is deep; therefore, option (3) is incorrect. Because Masha does not seem to respect Medvedenko's view of what it means to be poor, option (4) is incorrect. Medvedenko's love for Masha brings their relationship to a level beyond simple acquaintanceship; therefore, option (5) is also incorrect.

5. **(1) Happiness does not depend on money.** (Synthesis) The central conflict between Masha and Medvedenko is whether the lack of financial wealth is due cause for unhappiness. There is no support for option (2). Options (3) and (4) are the opposite of what is exhibited by the characters in this excerpt. Although Medvedenko may believe that option (5) is true, this is not the author's main point.

6. **(1) restlessness** (Analysis) Masha expresses that she feels stifled and unhappy with Medvedenko's discussion. Her restlessness is mirrored in the weather. She certainly is not at ease; therefore, option (2) is incorrect. There is no evidence to suggest danger, option (3); sudden freedom, option (4); or unearthly power, option (5).

7. **(3) Medvedenko feels compelled by love to visit Masha.** (Analysis) Medvedenko states that he walks four miles to see her even though she is indifferent towards him. Medvedenko has not abandoned his family, option (1). He may feel that he does not deserve Masha, but there is no evidence that he feels he doesn't deserve his home and family; in fact, he feels responsible for supporting them, option (2). The opposite of option (4) is true. Medvedenko is not doing anything wrong; he is a single man who responsibly supports his mother and siblings. Therefore, he has no reason to feel guilty for seeing Masha, option (5).

8. **(5) He contrasts their relationship with his relationship with Masha.** (Analysis) Medvedenko states that there is no common point between himself and Masha, unlike the couple he mentions. Although this statement does give additional meaning to the play, option (1), Medvedenko does not make the statement for that reason. There is no evidence that Medvedenko thinks Masha's feelings will change, so option (2) is incorrect. There is no support for options (3) or (4).

9. **(2) because he is poor** (Analysis) Medvedenko says, "Who wants to marry a man who can't even feed himself?" (lines 42–43). Masha is willing to attend the play with him, so she does not entirely dislike him, option (1). There is no evidence to support options (3) or (5). Although Medvedenko does not understand Masha's sadness, option (4), he does not seem to consider it sufficient reason for her refusal.

10. **(4) He is upset that Masha doesn't love him.** (Comprehension) Masha offers the snuff immediately after saying that she doesn't love Medvedenko. There is no evidence to support option (1). Though the play is about to begin, or may have already begun, there is no evidence that this is the reason he refuses snuff; so, option (2) is incorrect. He may prefer to continue talking, but there is no reason that taking the snuff would stop him from saying what he wants to say; so, option (3) is incorrect. Masha already knows his financial situation, so option (5) is also incorrect.

11. **(1) He would be persistent and try to win over customers.** (Application) Medvedenko continues to visit Masha even though she doesn't return his affections, so it is likely that Medevedenko would approach customers in a similar way. He is not shy because he continues to visit Masha, so option (2) is incorrect. He

complains about his own situation, but not about other people, so option (3) is incorrect. There is no evidence to support option (4). He walks four miles to see Masha, who has lukewarm feelings for him, so option (5) is incorrect.

Unit 4 Cumulative Review (Pages 234–241)

1. **(2) disbelief** (Comprehension) Alceste cannot believe that he is summoned merely because he dislikes the poem. Although he may be angry later in the excerpt, option (1), this is not his initial reaction. There is no evidence to support joy, anxiety, or fear; therefore, options (3), (4), and (5) are incorrect.

2. **(2) Be less indignant about the poem.** (Analysis) Philinte encourages Alceste to express a milder opinion about the poem in order not to create more trouble for himself. Philinte is not referring to Alceste's treatment of others; therefore, option (1) is incorrect. Philinte is more concerned with Alceste than with respecting the Marshals; therefore, option (3) is incorrect. There is no evidence to support option (4). Philinte is not concerned with having Alceste recognize the poem's gentle qualities, he just wants Alceste to stay away from trouble; therefore, option (5) is incorrect.

3. **(3) He would confidently choose the one pie that he was convinced was best.** (Application) Alceste is very clear about what he believes is right. So, he would not have any difficulty making a decision, option (1), nor would he be persuaded by other judges, option (2). There is no evidence to support options (4) and (5).

4. **(5) The violent loss of family causes sadness.** (Synthesis) The point of view expressed about the killings of the husband and son is that the mother cannot forget the tragedy. Although option (1) may be true, it is not the author's main point. Option (2) is only part of the disagreement. There is no evidence to support option (3). Option (4) is true, but not the most important point of this excerpt.

5. **(1) that her second son will also be killed** (Comprehension) The mother says that she will never stop talking about the deaths of her husband and son (lines 38–39). She also does not want her second son to carry a knife with him (lines 34–35). These details indicate that she is worried that her second son will meet the same fate as her husband and first son. She certainly feels that knives and guns are dangerous, option (1), but this does not explain her statements about her husband and first son or the depth of her distress; therefore, it is not the best answer. She feels it is important to remember

the tragedy and is not concerned with trying to forget it, option (2). There is no evidence to support options (3) and (4).

6. **(2) impatience** (Analysis) The son asks his mother if she is through talking about the tragedy; he has heard enough. If the son were indifferent, he would not care enough to ask his mother to stop talking, option (1). The son may have some empathy toward his mother, option (3), but this excerpt emphasizes his desire to move on and have his mother stop talking about the tragedy. Although the son does speak forcefully in the last line of the excerpt, option (4), he does not seem angry throughout most of the excerpt. There is no evidence to support option (5).

7. **(4) anguished** (Synthesis) The mother is sad and upset about the deaths of her husband and son. Option (1) is incorrect because the opposite is true. The mother loves her family, but this is not the dominant mood expressed in the excerpt, option (2). There is no evidence to support option (3). There may be some tension between the mother and son, option (5), but the overriding mood of the piece is connected to the mother's grief.

8. **(1) Opposites attract.** (Analysis) Despite their differences, the two men seem to like each other. The excerpt focuses on the relationship between the two; options (2) and (5) have nothing to do with that idea. Option (3) is not supported in the excerpt. The topic of "home" and its meaning is not discussed; therefore, option (4) is incorrect.

9. **(2) napping in the afternoon** (Application) It is suggested that Felix likes to stay busy. Option (1) is incorrect because he apparently likes to cook. Options (3), (4), and (5) are incorrect because he seems to enjoy having everything clean and orderly.

10. **(4) Felix talks about the money he saves.** (Application) Felix states in the lines immediately preceding that he saves a lot of money by cooking and cleaning (lines 2–4). Later in the excerpt Oscar implies that Felix talks a great deal but that Oscar does not really enjoy it (lines 30–37). Since it is unlikely that Felix is actually counting money, it is logical to infer that Felix keeps Oscar awake by talking about the money he saves. Options (1), (2), and (5) are not supported by the excerpt. Oscar's statement is referring to the money Felix saves, not the cleaning he does; therefore, option (3) is not the best answer.

11. **(4) Oscar is getting used to Felix.** (Comprehension) Based upon Oscar's claim that he is worried that he is beginning to listen to Felix, it can be inferred that he fears he is getting

used to living with Felix. Options (1) and (3) are not supported by the excerpt. Oscar agrees that Felix saves them money, so option (2) is incorrect. Option (5) is incorrect because Oscar does not behave like Felix. Felix cleans while Oscar throws his clothes on the floor; Felix talks while Oscar tries to do other things.

12. **(5) They need to get exercise.**
(Comprehension) Gertrude encourages the group to take a walk after lunch so that they will feel better from the exercise. Option (1) has no support. Gertrude seems interested only in having the group take a walk, not in showing them the beach, option (2), or keeping them entertained, option (3). Although she does believe that the others should follow her wishes, she does not voice this belief aloud; therefore, option (4) is incorrect.

13. **(4) Gertrude's children** (Comprehension) Stage directions indicate that when Vivian has leaped to Gertrude's side, "Molly too has come forward to be with her mother" (lines 25–26). There is no evidence to support options (1), (2), (3), or (5).

14. **(3) insecure and demanding** (Analysis) As the stage directions indicate, Gertrude is apprehensive about her role directing the others; however, she continues to give them commands. There is no evidence that Gertrude is uncaring, option (1); lighthearted, option (2); secretive, option (4); or arrogant, option (5).

15. **(2) uneasy** (Synthesis) Gertrude is uneasy with directing the others, and they are uneasy about following her commands. Though the scene may be serious, option (1), this choice does not address the central theme, which concerns the conflict between Gertrude and the other characters. There is no evidence to support options (3), (4), or (5).

16. **(3) Gertrude would prefer to walk without the children.** (Analysis) Gertrude asks the children to either stay where they are or to walk somewhere else (lines 28–30). She also seems somewhat annoyed and calls Frederica a baby when she wants to come with the adults (lines 33–34). These details indicate that she likely does not want the children to walk with the adults. There is no evidence to support options (1), (4), or (5). The children have just had lunch with the adults; therefore, option (2) is incorrect.

17. **(2) tense** (Synthesis) Walter argues with his wife and disagrees with his mother, creating a disturbed and tense mood. There is no evidence to support options (1), (3), (4), or (5).

18. **(5) strong and caring** (Analysis) Mama's concern for her son and his wife comes through in the strong stand she takes about his behavior. Options (1) and (3) are incorrect because being calm is not the same as being patient or passive, and Mama is not tolerating Walter's behavior. Although Mama does tell Walter to sit down and listen to her, she does so out of concern for him; therefore, option (2) is not the best answer. Option (4) suggests the opposite of her character.

19. **(2) Walter does not want to be with Ruth.** (Comprehension) Ruth states that Walter makes her ill and that she hopes he drinks himself to death; therefore, option (1) is incorrect. Though Ruth leaves the room, she does not openly state a desire to leave Walter, so option (3) is incorrect. There is no evidence for option (4). Option (5) is incorrect because even though Walter is more respectful of his mother, this does not indicate a desire to be with her rather than Ruth.

20. **(3) to accompany Walter and talk with him** (Application) Ruth's desire to speak to Walter and her feelings for him are both evident, even when she leaves the room. In the first part of the excerpt, Ruth states that she needs to talk to Walter; therefore, option (1) is unlikely even though she is angry. Option (2) is a literal interpretation of the figurative meaning of Ruth's words. There is no support for option (4). Although Walter makes reference to nagging, it is with regard to his mother, so option (5) is incorrect.

21. **(1) getting married to Ruth** (Analysis) Walter speaks about his greatest mistake as Ruth slams the door to her room; therefore, his words are referring to her. There is no evidence to support options (2), (4), or (5). Although Ruth does refer to Walter's drinking in the previous lines, Walter's response indicates that he is more interested in attacking Ruth than in examining his own behavior; therefore, option (3) is incorrect.

22. **(2) Bad things can result even when someone means well.** (Analysis) Mr. Brooks may mean well, but his wife is quite unhappy. This is why she brings up her grandmother's saying. The issue of trust is not present in this excerpt, so option (1) is incorrect. There is no evidence suggesting what Mr. Brooks was like earlier in his life, so option (3) is incorrect. There is no evidence to support options (4) and (5).

23. **(1) She has thought for a long time about leaving Mr. Brooks.** (Comprehension) Mrs. Brooks refers to "the last straw," implying that this decision had been building up over time. There is no evidence for options (2), (3), or (5). Although Ruby tries to persuade Mrs. Brooks not

to leave her husband, there is no evidence that Mrs. Brooks will change her mind; therefore, option (4) is incorrect.

24. **(3) Disagreements over money can affect relationships.** (Synthesis) The Brooks' marriage is affected by how they both react to money. Mr. Brooks may feel that his wife complains unnecessarily, option (1), but this is not supported in the excerpt. Option (2) is a generalization that is probably false. Although Ruby may not be as supportive as Mrs. Brooks would like, option (4), this is not the focus of the excerpt. There is no support in this excerpt for option (5).

25. **(5) pretend he did not hear it** (Application) Lane would probably ignore Algernon's comments just as he ignored Algernon's piano playing. He has not argued with Algernon; therefore, option (2) is incorrect. He humors Algernon, but does not take to heart what Algernon says; therefore, options (1) and (3) are incorrect. There is no evidence to support option (4).

26. **(4) Algernon and his dinner guests drank it.** (Analysis) Algernon seems to make assumptions that have little basis in reality, such as the idea that his piano playing, which he admits is inaccurate, is nonetheless wonderful. It seems reasonable to infer that his assumption about the champagne is also inaccurate and that in fact he simply does not realize just how much he and his guests actually drank. There is no evidence to support the other options.

27. **(1) unromantic** (Synthesis) Algernon thinks of marriage as a business contract as well as a potentially unpleasant situation. For instance, he calls it "demoralizing" in line 35. Although he seems uninterested in Lane's marriage, this does not mean he is uninterested in marriage in general, option (3). There is no evidence to support the other options.

POSTTEST (Pages 243–257)

1. **(2) single-minded** (Analysis) Topper's sole interest is in chasing the plump sister, much to the amusement of everyone at the party. There is no direct evidence supporting options (1), (3), (4), or (5).

2. **(3) organize a group of riders that included the plump sister** (Application) Topper's preoccupation with the plump sister would be likely to cause him to include her. Because he seems to be outgoing and fun-loving, option (1) is incorrect. Although Topper is interested in the plump sister and likely would enjoy inviting her to ride, option (2), he seems to be trying to get her attention in a less direct

manner at the party. Therefore, option (2) is not the best choice. He would not want to hurt the plump sister, option (4), and he does not seem very competitive based on his behavior at the party, option (5).

3. **(3) Scrooge has made them laugh by being the object of a game.** (Comprehension) Fred states that Scrooge has "given us plenty of merriment" (line 49) by being the subject of the guessing game. The partygoers do not seem to hold a high opinion of Scrooge; therefore, option (1) is incorrect. There is no evidence to support options (2), (4), or (5).

4. **(1) invisible** (Analysis) The words "unconscious company" (line 57) and "inaudible" (line 58) imply that Scrooge is not visible to the others and that they are not aware of him. Additionally, he is in the company of a ghost or spirit. There is no evidence to support the other options.

5. **(5) joyful and unpleasant** (Synthesis) The last paragraph says that Scrooge became "gay and light of heart" (lines 55–56) and that he wanted to thank the people playing the game; this description indicates that he is joyous. The people playing the game, however, seem to view Scrooge as grumpy and mean. Although Scrooge may normally be a resentful person, he does not exhibit resentful behavior in this excerpt; therefore, option (1) is incorrect. The partygoers do not seem to view Scrooge as happy—they see him as "a disagreeable animal" (line 29); therefore, option (2) is incorrect. The game-players do not mention Scrooge's seriousness, but rather focus on how disagreeable he is; therefore, option (3) is not the best answer. The reason Scrooge does not speak is not due to timidity, but because the Ghost does not allow him to; therefore, option (4) is also incorrect.

6. **(3) wordy but lively** (Synthesis) Although wordy by today's standards, the style is full of life and feeling. It is not simple, option (1); dry and scholarly, option (2); solemn, option (4); or flat and unemotional, option (5).

7. **(1) He is in love with her.** (Analysis) Gabriel's love for the woman can be inferred from the information in the first and the last paragraphs. Although Gabriel is concerned about the woman, he does not seem to question her sanity, option (2). There is no evidence for options (3) and (4). Although option (5) may be true, you cannot make that inference from the information in the excerpt.

8. **(2) She sent him away for his own good.** (Comprehension) The answer can be found in line 41, which states that she "implored of him to go home at once." Though options (1) and (5)

may be true, there is not enough evidence to support them. Options (3) and (4) are the opposite of what happened in the excerpt.

9. **(4) He stayed out in the rain.** (Comprehension) The woman warned him that he might "get his death in the rain" (lines 42–43). Option (1), although true, had been true for some time and was not the immediate cause of his death. There is no evidence to support options (2), (3), or (5).

10. **(3) He did not want to live without the woman he loved.** (Analysis) The excerpt states that Michael Furey was very fond of the woman (lines 15–16) but that she was going to a convent. He then came to see her as she was packing to leave and told her that he did not want to live (line 43). You can infer from these facts that he had lost his desire to live because of the hopelessness of his love for the woman. There is no support for options (1), (2), or (4). Option (5) may be true, but there is not enough evidence in the excerpt to make this the best answer.

11. **(2) to contrast the stormy feelings of the woman with the quiet feelings of the man** (Analysis) The last two sentences describe how the characters' actions reflect their feelings. The woman is choking with sobs, while the man is shy, quiet, and gentle. Options (1), (4), and (5) are not supported by the last two sentences. Although the woman does feel that Michael Furey's death was tragic, option (3), his death is not the focus of the description.

12. **(2) more emotional about the story she tells** (Synthesis) By the end of the excerpt, the woman is sobbing and "overcome by emotion" (line 54). There is no change in the woman's response to the man she is speaking with; therefore, option (1) is incorrect. She shows no signs of anger, so option (3) is incorrect. There is no evidence to support options (4) and (5).

13. **(1) mournful** (Synthesis) The woman tells a touching story of a man who seemed to love her and who died of an unknown ailment. She cared about him but did not have a chance to say goodbye. She seems filled with grief. There is no evidence to support options (2), (3), or (4). Although there is some suspense, that is not the overriding mood of the excerpt; therefore, option (5) is not the best choice.

14. **(1) Commission amounts can vary significantly.** (Comprehension) Most employers do not use commissions alone because they do not provide a secure salary for employees. The other options may be true of some employers but are not supported by evidence from the excerpt.

15. **(1) Employees get bonuses if the company makes money.** (Analysis) When an employee or a company fulfills certain criteria such as sales and profit goals, employees are rewarded with a bonus. Options (2) and (5) may be true, but are not directly tied to meeting sales goals; therefore, they are incorrect. A bonus plan that is dependent on meeting certain criteria is not automatic; therefore, option (3) is not correct. Option (4) is not supported by the excerpt.

16. **(4) Employees must reach a sales goal to earn a base salary.** (Comprehension) The risk of the salary at-risk is that the sales goals must be met for employees to receive a salary. Options (1), (3), and (5) are either not true or do not describe a salary at-risk plan. A salary at-risk plan does not necessarily depend on individual performance; it may depend on the performance of an entire workforce. Therefore, option (2) is not the best answer.

17. **(2) offers a salary at-risk bonus plan** (Application) A high-achiever is most likely to earn more on a salary at-risk bonus plan. Options (1), (3), (4), and (5) are not necessarily targeted to high-achieving salespeople.

18. **(2) to provide information about incentive plans** (Synthesis) Several types of incentives are discussed, along with the advantages and disadvantages of each. The discussion suggests that incentive plans can be effective, so option (1) is incorrect. The discussion does not discourage the use of incentive plans, option (3), or try to convince the reader that profit sharing is the best type of incentive plan, option (4). The document points out both the similarities and differences among incentive plans; therefore, option (5) is incorrect.

19. **(1) would not be missed if she died** (Analysis) The speaker refers to her "doom," or death, which no one would mourn. She is certain that no one would miss her; therefore, option (2) is incorrect. Although options (3) and (5) may be true, the ideas that they express are not included in the first stanza. The speaker directly states the opposite of option (4); therefore, this option is incorrect.

20. **(1) not have any friends to stay with** (Application) Lines 7–8 state that she is "As friendless after eighteen years, / As lone as on my natal day." In other words, she does not have any friends. There is no evidence to support the other options.

21. **(3) She fears that she is corrupt.** (Analysis) The speaker is upset to find that she is as corrupt in character as others when she had thought she was different. The speaker implies that she has trusted herself; therefore, option (1) is incorrect.

Although option (2) may be true, it does not express the main focus of the lines. The speaker does express the opinion given in option (4), but not in lines 23–24. Option (5) is the opposite of what the lines express.

22. **(4) She holds a very low opinion of humanity.** (Analysis) The speaker thinks of humanity as "hollow, servile, insincere" (line 22). Options (1) and (3) may be true, but there is no clear, direct evidence to support them. There is no evidence to support options (2) and (5).

23. **(2) hopeful, then unhappy** (Synthesis) The unhappy speaker says that "First melted off the hope of youth" (line 17); this line indicates that as a young girl she had felt hopeful. Option (1) is the opposite of what is described. There is no direct support in the poem for the speaker being fearful, option (3); hostile, option (4); or manipulative, option (5).

24. **(5) disillusioned** (Synthesis) "I am the only being whose doom" describes a sad, lonely person whose hopes for someone to love her "have died so long ago" (line 15). The title of the second poem also describes someone who feels alone, despite being surrounded by a beautiful summer day. This situation reinforces a mood of loneliness hopelessness. There is no support for the other options.

25. **(1) She charged too much at Connell's.** (Comprehension) Mary's father is upset because he feels she has taken advantage of being able to charge things at Connell's. Mary does not speak disrespectfully, option (2). The scene in the excerpt takes place during Mary's childhood, before she cancelled her wedding to Clifford; therefore, option (3) is incorrect. Mary's father does not indicate that she should not spend her allowance; therefore, option (4) is incorrect. There is no support for option (5).

26. **(3) easily deceived** (Analysis) Mary's father easily believes her lie about giving the money to Queen Esther. He may not be fair to Queen Esther but seems kind to his daughter; therefore, option (1) is not the best answer. Although Mary does say that her father takes a long time getting to the point, this does not necessarily mean that he is indecisive, option (2). He does not seem terribly strict, option (4), or especially grateful, option (5); therefore, these options are incorrect.

27. **(1) from fear to relief** (Synthesis) During the beginning of the excerpt, Mary has a bad feeling in the pit of her stomach and is terrified. By the end, after her father believes what she has to say, she feels a sense of relief. Although Mary is momentarily disturbed by her father's anger, she does not seem to regret her lie; therefore, option (2) is incorrect. Although Mary probably loves her father, her behavior in the excerpt does not demonstrate this emotion; therefore, option (3) is incorrect. Mary is not angry in the excerpt; therefore, options (4) and (5) are incorrect.

28. **(2) Lying sometimes has its benefits.** (Synthesis) Mary "learned that lying pays" (lines 64–65); in other words, her lie helped her avoid getting into trouble. Option (1) is incorrect because the idea of forgiveness is not referred to in the excerpt. Lying did not get Mary more money—it kept her out of trouble; therefore, option (3) is incorrect. Mary's lie does not harm her relationship with her father; therefore, option (4) is incorrect. Mary is lying to help herself, not someone else; therefore, option (5) is incorrect.

29. **(5) Say that you swerved to avoid a child.** (Application) In the excerpt, Mary lies and says she did something bad in order to help someone else; the lie not only gets her out of trouble but also makes her father think highly of her. Therefore, she would likely advise a friend to take a similar course of action. In the excerpt Mary does not say anything about her charges at Connell's until she is confronted; therefore, option (1) is incorrect. Although she does lie, Mary does not say that she did not make the charges; therefore, option (2) is not the best answer. Mary does not tell the truth; therefore, option (3) is incorrect. There is no support in the excerpt for option (4).

30. **(1) Mary's father thinks that Queen Esther is untrustworthy.** (Synthesis) Mary's father believes Mary's lie and blames Queen Esther for Mary's large bill at Connell's. That Queen Esther is later fired indicates that Mary's father finds her too untrustworthy to employ. Although option (5) may be true, there is no direct evidence to support it. There is no support for the other options.

31. **(1) is wasting time** (Analysis) Willy criticizes his son by saying, "it's more than ten years now and he has yet to make thirty-five dollars a week!" (lines 58–60). Although he may believe Biff has many talents, Willy does not express this opinion in the excerpt; so, option (2) is incorrect. Willy asks if his son apologized to him, suggesting that Willy feels mistreated; therefore, option (3) is incorrect. There is no evidence to support options (4) and (5).

32. **(4) even-tempered** (Application) Linda appears to be the steady voice of reason in this family; therefore, she would most likely be even-tempered on the job as well. There is no evidence that Linda would be overeager, option (1); disorganized, option (2); or

exhilarated, option (5). She tries to discourage Willy's apprehension about his job; therefore, option (3) is not the best answer.

33. **(1) dissatisfied** (Analysis) Willy feels overlooked at work and is disappointed with his son. His behavior could be described as the opposite of easy-going, option (2). His attitude toward his son is not generous, option (3). Willy wants what he feels he is owed, but there is no evidence that he wants more than that; therefore, option (4) is incorrect. Although Willy may love his family, the emphasis of this excerpt is on his discontent; therefore, option (5) is incorrect.

34. **(3) Biff is hurt by his comments.**
(Analysis) Speaking of Biff, Linda states, "He was crestfallen, Willy. You know how he admires you" (lines 49–50). There is no evidence in the excerpt to support options (1) and (5). Biff admires his father, so option (2) is incorrect. "Crestfallen" indicates disappointment rather than anger, so option (4) is incorrect.

35. **(4) for his accomplishments to have meaning** (Synthesis) Willy is dissatisfied with his accomplishments at work; he feels unappreciated. In addition, he is unhappy with the way at least one of his sons has turned out. He states "Work a lifetime to pay off a house. You finally own it, and there's nobody to live in it" (lines 28–30); this also indicates that he is unhappy with what he has accomplished in his life. Willy does want to work in New York; he also wants his son Biff to settle on a good career. However, neither of these hopes is broad enough to fit the description of "massive dreams" or "turbulent longings"; therefore, options (1) and (5) are not the best choices. He seems unhappy that his house is somewhat empty but does not indicate that he wants his grown sons to move back in with him; therefore, option (2) is incorrect. There is no support for option (3).

36. **(1) if the patient remains in good health**
(Comprehension) The reviewer states that the healthcare system "is fabulous as long as we are healthy" (lines 67–68). There is no evidence in the excerpt to support options (2) or (5). Although the reviewer may think the system is adequate for illnesses that do not require hospitalization or that are easy to diagnose, he does not express these opinions; therefore, options (3) and (4) are incorrect.

37. **(5) Find a doctor who has a good bedside manner.** (Application) The review emphasizes the importance of a caring physician. There is no evidence to support options (1), (2), (3), or (4).

38. **(2) Doctors need to practice being compassionate.** (Synthesis) The reviewer states that medical schools should offer courses in "humility, sensitivity, and compassion" (line 41). Although the excerpt gives an example in which a doctor should have done more extensive testing, the review does not focus on the need for more testing; therefore, option (1) is not the best choice. The idea expressed in option (3) is contrary to the points made in this review. There is no evidence in the excerpt to support options (4) and (5).

39. **(5) caring and indifference** (Synthesis) Physicians who are caring are contrasted with physicians who are indifferent and lacking empathy. The notion of ignorance is not featured in this review; therefore, option (1) is incorrect. There is no evidence to support options (2) and (4). Although the second story described from the book does feature a medical mistake, the first story does not; therefore, option (3) is not the best answer.

40. **(1) The book makes a good argument about medical care, but not every point made is valid.** (Synthesis) In the excerpt, the reviewer seems to think that the book effectively makes many good points about the dehumanizing and dangerous effects of a lack of compassion on the part of both doctors and the insurance companies. The added information, however, is less positive. The words "too frequent" indicate that the reviewer did not appreciate this particular repeated point. Therefore, this new information shows that the reviewer did not like everything about the book. There is no support for the other options.

SIMULATED TEST (Pages 259–273)

1. **(3) by using jazzy arrangements**
(Comprehension) Options (1) and (2) name aspects of Pura Fe's sound that do not necessarily make it innovative or unique. Options (4) and (5) are not mentioned as characteristics of the group's music.

2. **(2) to give an idea of what Pura Fe's music sounds like** (Analysis) The author says Pura Fe's tunes could be "sandwiched . . . between" the other groups' music; the author does not say Pura Fe is better, option (1), or should imitate them, option (3). The author does not ridicule Pura Fe, option (4). Option (5) is not supported by the excerpt.

3. **(1) "Their lyrics . . . set Pura Fe apart from the mainstream" (lines 19–21)** (Analysis) This statement points out something about Pura Fe that makes it different from, and more interesting than, most other music groups. Option (2) contains a historical fact but does not directly address Pura Fe's music; therefore, it is incorrect. Options (3) and (5) are statements

made by one of Pura Fe's musicians; therefore, they do not indicate the opinion of the reviewer. Option (4) contains details of what Pura Fe is trying to do in its music, but does indicate whether the reviewer thinks the music is interesting; therefore, it is not the best choice.

4. **(2) arrange it in a more modern style** (Application) The excerpt says that Pura Fe takes traditional songs and chants and interprets them in an innovative, progressive manner. Pura Fe does have "an ear tuned to history" (line 21), but the excerpt does not indicate that the group's main intention is to educate; therefore, option (4) is incorrect. The other options are not supported by the excerpt.

5. **(5) to show how Pura Fe is representative of the youngest generation of Native Americans** (Analysis) The reviewer indicates that Pura Fe, like the youngest generation of Native Americans, has managed to connect the past with the present. Options (1) and (2) are not supported by the excerpt. Pura Fe's musical style, option (3), may be influenced by recent Native American history. However, that influence is not the main reason that the reviewer includes the information. Although Pura Fe's music may appeal to Native Americans, there is no support in the excerpt for the idea that the music is primarily for Native Americans, option (4).

6. **(4) A description of the music is followed by historical background and personal stories.** (Synthesis) The opening paragraph describes a Pura Fe concert and the sound of Pura Fe's music; the review then discusses Pura Fe's history and quotes the group's musicians. There is not a list of topics; therefore, option (1) is incorrect. The statements about the music are very specific, so option (2) is incorrect. There is no support for option (3) because the music's faults are not discussed. The focal point of this review is not an analysis of Native American culture in general but only of Pura Fe's music; therefore, option (5) is not the best choice.

7. **(4) youth** (Comprehension) The answer is found in lines 7–8. Options (1), (2), (3), and (5) refer to other images and symbols in the poem.

8. **(1) It emphasizes how precious youth is.** (Analysis) The doll represents a youthful state of mind that must be carefully preserved. The other options are not supported by the poem.

9. **(1) worked for** (Comprehension) The answer is in line 4. According to the speaker, age is not given freely; it must be achieved. Option (2) is not supported by the poem. Options (3), (4), and (5) refer to youth.

10. **(5) enjoy participating in their games** (Application) The speaker is fond of her childhood and youth and would probably enjoy revisiting youthful activities. There is no evidence to support options (1), (2), (3), or (4).

11. **(3) growing old gracefully** (Synthesis) The answer is found in lines 2–3. Options (1) and (4) are the opposite of what is said in the poem; options (2) and (5) are literal interpretations of statements that are figurative.

12. **(3) He is not popular with women.** (Comprehension) Marty's dilemma is that women are not interested in him. The other options are facts about Marty that may contribute to the overall problem but are not themselves the main problem. Therefore, the other options are incorrect.

13. **(2) frustrated** (Analysis) Angie says that Marty is becoming a drag (lines 26–27) and that his mother is making him crazy. Therefore, Angie is not optimistic, option (1), or content, option (4). Option (3) overstates Angie's attitude toward the other characters. Although Angie may be charming, this characteristic is not supported in the excerpt; therefore, option (5) is incorrect.

14. **(3) defeated** (Analysis) Marty does not see a way out of his situation and seems unable to take any action. Although Marty may be angry, anger is not the main emotion he displays; therefore, option (1) is not the best answer. If Marty were resourceful, he might not be in this situation; therefore, option (2) is incorrect. There is no evidence that he is manipulative, option (4), and although he may be humble, option (5), his humility is not the focus of the excerpt.

15. **(3) sitting around his house** (Application) Option (3) can be inferred from Angie's statement in lines 9–10 that he and Marty always end up staying at home. This statement also rules out option (1). Option (2) is incorrect because Marty seems to have given up on marriage even though he says he wants to get married. Options (4) and (5) are not supported by the excerpt.

16. **(5) Lonely people sometimes stop being socially active.** (Synthesis) Even though they are together in this scene, Marty and Angie are clearly lonely and have stopped trying to do much about it. Option (1) is incorrect because the central focus is not on marriage itself. Option (2) is not the main issue in this excerpt. Option (3) refers to a specific person, and option (4) refers to a specific plot line; therefore, these options do not express a theme.

17. **(2) Angie is more comfortable with women than Marty is.** (Synthesis) Marty's

speech in lines 32–34 implies that Angie's sense of humor helps him get along with women. Angie, not Marty, wants to do something besides watch television; therefore, option (1) is incorrect. Both men are annoyed by their mothers, but there is no evidence that one is more annoyed that the other; therefore, option (3) is incorrect. There is no support for option (4). Option (5) is not true: Angie wants to telephone but Marty is unwilling.

18. **(4) emotionless** (Analysis) Raskolnikov was "dumbfounded" (line 3) and "stood like one dead' (line 23). This description indicates that he showed no reaction to his family. There is no evidence in the excerpt for the other options.

19. **(4) They know each other well.** (Analysis) Razumihin seems to be taking care of Raskolnikov through a major illness; he also seems to be emotionally involved judging from the intensity with which he insists that Raskolnikov is doing well. He would not be behaving this way if he did not know Raskolnikov well. Razumihin refers to "the doctor"; therefore, he is not a doctor himself, option (1). There is no support for options (2) or (3). It is unlikely that Razumihin would be so involved in this situation if he were only a recent acquaintance; therefore, option (5) is not the best answer.

20. **(2) They would feel that Razumihin is partially responsible for Raskolnikov's recovery.** (Application) When Razumihin tells the mother and sister that Raskolnikov is getting better and that he "is all right again" (lines 39–41), the mother and sister are grateful and look on him as "their Providence" (line 46). Their response shows that they feel he is helping Raskolnikov. The mother and sister are not angry in the excerpt and so would not likely become angry with either Razumihin or Raskolnikov; therefore, options (1) and (4) are incorrect. There is no evidence that Raskolnikov has followed the doctor's orders; therefore, option (3) is incorrect. The mother and sister do not refer to fate in the excerpt; therefore, option (5) is incorrect.

21. **(5) agitated** (Synthesis) The mother and sister were weeping and anguished while Raskolnikov was out; they then become ecstatic when he returns. After he collapses, they are filled with anxiety, and Razumihin is intense in his attempts to reassure them. All of these details indicate that the mood is intense and agitated. There is no support in the excerpt for options (1), (2), or (3). Even though the scene is not a happy one, option (4) is not the best choice since the excerpt includes hope and gratitude as well as darker emotions.

22. **(1) He has selfish reasons for keeping Raskolnikov's family away from him.** (Synthesis) It is likely that Razumihin is not telling the whole truth because there is no evidence in the excerpt that Raskolnikov might become frenzied. You can conclude that Razumihin might in fact be trying to keep the mother and sister away because he has something to hide. There is no support in the excerpt for options (2) and (3). Razumihin seems not to want Raskolnikov's family around, but there is no evidence that he distrusts them; therefore, option (4) is not the best answer. Although the mother and sister are emotional, there is no direct evidence that they are fragile; therefore, option (5) is not the best answer.

23. **(1) appears to contain more of the product** (Comprehension) The memo indicates that the Quick Wax container seems smaller, even though it holds the same amount of product as Easy Shine. That fact suggests that Easy Shine appears to contain more product. The memo suggests that Easy Shine's label is easier to read because of the coloring of the lettering, not the size of the package; therefore, option (2) is incorrect. There is no evidence to support the other options.

24. **(1) special purchase offers** (Comprehension) The memo directly states that "Our special purchase offers . . . have had the intended effect of keeping customers satisfied . . ." (lines 34–37). Options (2), (3), and (4) are the opposite of what is stated to be true in the excerpt. Although option (5) may be true, the memo does not mention Easy Shine's pursuit of new customers; therefore, option (5) is not the best answer.

25. **(5) ensure that the lettering on the package is easy to read** (Application) The lettering on the packaging of Easy Shine is easy to read and is partially responsible for its success in the market. Therefore, the marketing director would be likely to use similar lettering on another type of product. Based on this memo, experienced sales representatives are important; therefore, option (1) is incorrect. There is no evidence to support option (2). Options (3) and (4) are the opposite of what the excerpt indicates are effective marketing tools.

26. **(3) factual statements supported by evidence** (Synthesis) The memo begins by stating that "Quick Wax has been unsuccessful in Territory 12"; the remainder of the memo provides evidence to support that statement. Discussion of advertising is not the main point of this memo, so option (1) is incorrect. It is not a list of rules but rather an analysis, so option (2) is incorrect. The memo explains the sales of the

products, not advantages of using the products; therefore, option (4) is incorrect. There are no descriptive stories in the excerpt; therefore, option (5) is incorrect.

27. **(2) to examine** (Synthesis) The memo is an analysis or examination of the reasons for the product's success. There is no evidence to support the other options.

28. **(5) They share similar goals.** (Synthesis) They both want to sell as much of their product as they can. Quick Wax does not seem to be much of a threat to Easy Shine. Therefore, option (1) is incorrect. They are competing with each other for sales and so are not working together as partners; therefore, option (2) is incorrect. For that same reason, they are not relying on each other to help with sales; therefore, option (3) is incorrect. There is no direct evidence that the companies are longtime competitors, option (4).

29. **(4) Lance's father** (Comprehension) As Lance's passion for art is discussed, so is the Master's career. Speaking of Lance, Mrs. Mallow states, "Will it be a career to . . . provoke the machinations that have been at times almost too much for his father?" (lines 43–46). This statement indicates that the Master is Lance's father. Peter is not referring to himself when he speaks of the Master; therefore, option (1) is incorrect. Lance is twenty, and Mrs. Mallow is more than forty; it is unlikely that they have the same father, option (2). There is no mention of a brother, option (3). Lance's career potential is being compared to that of someone else; therefore, option (5) is incorrect.

30. **(2) a career as a painter** (Analysis) The excerpt begins with a reference to "brush," as in paintbrush, and refers to his career as an artist in line 17. There is no evidence to support options (1) or (4). The excerpt indicates that Lance's academic career is not working out; therefore, option (3) is incorrect. A brush is more likely to be a symbol of a painter than an architect; therefore, option (5) is not the best answer.

31. **(3) be ahead of his time** (Analysis) This phrase refers to Lance's going further with his ideas and artwork than his countrymen, with their limited and unrefined tastes, are able to appreciate. In other words, Lance's artwork may be of better quality than they are able to understand. There is no reference to traveling in this excerpt; therefore, option (1) is incorrect. There is no evidence to support options (2) or (5). Doing better than expected would not be described as a "misfortune" (line 52); therefore, option (4) is incorrect.

32. **(2) Great art does not always lead to great wealth.** (Synthesis) Great art is portrayed as a "curse of refinement and distinction" (lines 49–50) that can lead to "begging one's bread" (line 51). There is no evidence to support the other options.

33. **(2) gossipy** (Synthesis) The phrase, "broke it to their friend, who shared, to the last delicate morsel, their problems . . ." (lines 4–6), suggests the gossipy tone of the excerpt. Mrs. Mallow and Peter go on to discuss Lance's personal life. There is no evidence to support options (1), (3), or (4). Although there is some suspense about what Lance's future will be, option (5), suspense is not the main focus of this excerpt.

34. **(1) unappreciative of the Master's art** (Synthesis) The Master is considered a great artist; Peter does not understand his ideas. Peter also indicates in the excerpt that he "hoped (Lance's passion for art) would burn out." (lines 28–29). These details indicate that he likely does not appreciate either Lance's or the Master's art. Peter gives no hint that he can recognize artistic talent; therefore, option (2) in incorrect. He also gives no indication of jealousy; therefore, option (3) is incorrect. There is no support in the excerpt for option (4). Peter does not seem to be terribly critical; therefore, option (5) is incorrect.

35. **(1) point of view** (Comprehension) Peggy is explaining her reasons why patrons must be courteous and follow the library rules. She is not explaining how to be a librarian (option 2). She is responding to insults ("they got insulting" line 15), not insulting patrons (option 5). The patrons are not asking Peggy for her location or advice about books (options 3 and 4).

36. **(4) tell the patron not to worry about the book** (Application) Peggy understands that there are times when a patron cannot follow the rules. She thinks, "We honor manners, patience, good deeds, and grave misfortune . . ." (lines 23–25). There is nothing in the excerpt to suggest that she would spend money on a patron (option 1). She would consider the house burning down to be "grave misfortune" and not penalize the patron by charging for the lost book (option 2) or refusing to let the patron check out more books (option 5). There is no evidence to support option 3.

37. **(2) She takes pride in her work.** (Analysis) It is very important to Peggy to serve her patrons well, so she is disappointed in herself for failing to help James find an answer to his question. She says, "He'd asked me a straightforward question and I had not come close to providing an answer" (lines 46–48).

38. **(5) to show why Peggy worried that James might stop coming to the library** (Analysis) In the first half of the excerpt, Peggy explains that if she and a patron have an argument, sometimes the patron stops coming to the library. In the second half, Peggy compares the potential results of her situation with James to the results of having an argument with a patron. She says, "James and I had not argued, but I'd felt I'd done something much worse in so misunderstanding what he'd wanted, . . ." (lines 33–35).

39. **(4) They are rude people who deserve to be embarrassed.** (Synthesis) When a patron demands to see a manager, Peggy takes great pleasure in informing the patron that she is the director of the library, saying, "I *loved* this moment" (line 18). However, Peggy makes it a point to be polite to these patrons—"I'd say, politely, no" (line 14) and "when I politely, smilingly remembered them by name" (lines 30–31). This rules out option 1. But Peggy also does not accept excuses, such as being too busy to return books on time, which makes options 2 and 3 unlikely. There is no evidence to support option 5.

40. **(1) Peggy fears that James will find the book insulting.** (Synthesis) The book, *Medical Curiosities,* contains out-of-date information about physical extremes. Knowing that James is unusually tall for his age lets the reader see that Peggy, beyond being worried that she's let James down by not finding a book that would answer his question, fears she has insulted James.

Glossary

active reading strategy a technique such as summarizing used by a reader to engage with and understand reading material

apply to take information and transfer it to a new situation

applying ideas extending ideas from a reading passage to a new and related situation

atmosphere the mood or emotional setting of a work of literature

autobiography a person's life story told by that person

biography a person's life story told by another person

cause an initial thought, word, or action that makes something else happen

character a person who is a central participant in the events in a work of fiction or drama

climax the moment in the plot in which tensions reach their highest point

compare to show how things are similar

comparison an examination of two or more things in order to discover how they are alike or different; also a technique used in metaphors and similes to create vivid word pictures

complication event that occurs after the exposition and is a hurdle a character(s) must overcome in order to resolve a conflict

conflict increase in the story's tension; a struggle between opposing forces; it may be between characters, between a character and the outside environment, or within a character (internal conflict)

context clues around unfamiliar words or phrases that can help you figure out their meaning

contrast to show how things are different

dialogue conversation between two or more characters in a play

drama a type of literature that is meant to be performed by actors on a stage

drawing conclusions making decisions based on all the facts provided in a given situation

effect the result of an action

essay a short piece of nonfiction usually written from a personal point of view

exposition the beginning of a play, which introduces the characters, setting, and other details and hints at an unstable situation

fiction a story based on the writer's imagination that may refer to real things but is not true

figurative language language in which ordinary words are combined in new ways to create vivid images

image a description that appeals to one or more of the five senses; a mental picture created by words

implied main idea in passages without a clearly stated main idea, the most important idea that is suggested or hinted at without being actually expressed in words

infer to figure out the meaning by using clues

inference an idea the reader figures out based on stated and suggested information

literal factual language that is not exaggerated

main idea the most important idea or point in a piece of writing

making an inference putting together clues or details to reach a logical conclusion when facts are not stated directly

metaphor a comparison that states one thing is another

mood the emotional climate or atmosphere conveyed by the words a writer chooses

moral a lesson that can be applied to your life

motivation the reason a character does or says something

nonfiction writing that is based on facts about real places, real people, or events that actually took place

personification a type of figurative language that gives human qualities to non-human objects

plot the events in a story or play and the order in which they occur

poetry a special form of writing that is more rhythmical and imaginative than ordinary writing and is often characterized by the use of figurative language; poems may be divided into stanzas that may or may not rhyme

...ist the central character who has a ... to solve and is often the hero of the play

...lution the element of drama and fiction that occurs after the conflict is settled and the end of the story is reached

restating ideas showing that you understand something by putting it into your own words

review a type of nonfiction writing that expresses a writer's opinions about the quality of something

rhyme the similarity in the sounds at the ends of words, which ties two or more words together

rhyming pattern the arrangement of rhyming words in poetry; usually repeated in a specific order

rhythm a pattern created by the rise and fall in the sounds of words as well as by the use of punctuation

simile a comparison between two different people, places, or things signaled by the words *like, than, similar to,* or *as*

stage directions the words in parentheses in a play that give information about what a character is doing or how the character is responding

stanza a group of lines in a poem

style the way a writer writes; the words and sentence structure used to convey ideas

summarize to express the main points of a piece of writing in your own words

supporting detail information that supports or explains the main idea

symbol a person, place, or thing that stands for a larger idea

theme the central idea in a piece of literature; in a work of literature, the main idea or a basic comment about life that the writer wants to share

tone the details present in a writer's work that suggest how he or she feels about a subject

topic the general subject of a piece of literature

topic sentence the sentence that contains the main idea

viewpoint a writer's attitude or opinion about a subject

. Excerpted from *Flyin' West and Other Plays* by
[...]ge, copyright © 1999 by the author. Published by
[...] Communications Group, Inc. Used by permission.
[...]1)

Cofer, Judith Ortiz. From "Nada" by Judith Ortiz Cofer, from
The Latin Deli: Prose & Poetry, 1995. Reprinted by permission
of The University of Georgia Press. (p. 162)

Craven, Margaret. From *I Heard the Owl Call My Name* by
Margaret Craven, copyright © 1973 by Margaret Craven. Used
by permission of Doubleday, a division of Random House, Inc.,
and International Creative Management, Inc. (p. 100)

Croce, Arlene. From "Twyla Tharp Looks Ahead and Thinks
Back" by Arlene Croce from the "Talk of the Town" section in
The New Yorker, January 23, 1995. Reprinted by permisson;
© 1995 The New Yorker Magazine, Inc. All rights reserved.
(p. 61)

Cullen, Countee. "From the Dark Tower" Reprinted by
permission of GRM ASSOCIATES, INC., Agents for the Estate
of Ida M. Cullen from the book *Copper Sun* by Countee Cullen.
Copyright © 1927 by Harper & Brothers, copyright renewed
1955 by Ida M. Cullen. (p. 196)

Danticat, Edwidge. From *Krik? Krak!* by Edwidge Danticat. Soho,
N.Y. Reprinted by permission. (p. 114)

Daudelin, Art. From "Keys to Effective Web Searching" by Art
Daudelin from *Physicians Financial News*, 17 (10):s8, 1999.
© 1999 by PFN Publishing, Inc. Reprinted by permission of the
author. (p. 44)

Dickinson, Emily. Reprinted by permission of the publishers
and the Trustees of Amherst College from *The Poems of Emily
Dickinson*, Thomas H. Johnson, ed., Cambridge, Mass.: The
Belknap Press of Harvard University Press, Copyright © 1951,
1955, 1979 by the President and Fellows of Harvard College.
(p. 188)

Diggs, Elizabeth. Excerpt from *Close Ties* by Elizabeth Diggs.
Copyright © 1981 by Elizabeth Diggs. Reprinted by permission
of William Morris Agency, Inc. on behalf of the Author. All
rights reserved. CAUTION: Professionals and amateurs are
hereby warned that *Close Ties* is subject to a royalty. It is fully
protected under the copyright laws of the United States of
America and of all countries covered by the International
Copyright Union (including the Dominion of Canada and the
rest of the British Commonwealth), the Berne Convention, the
Pan-American Copyright Convention and the Universal
Copyright Convention as well as all countries with which the
United States has reciprocal copyright relations. All rights,
including professional/amateur stage rights, motion picture,
recitation, lecturing, public reading, radio broadcasting,
television, video or sound recording, all other forms of
mechanical or electronic reproduction, such as CD-ROM, CD-I,
information storage and retrieval systems and photocopying,
and the rights of translation into foreign languages, are strictly
reserved. Particular emphasis is laid upon the matter of
readings, permission for which must be secured from the
Author's agent in writing. Inquiries concerning rights should be
addressed to: William Morris Agency, Inc., 1325 Avenue of the
Americas, New York, New York 10019, Attn: George Lane.
(p. 231)

Doolittle, H. D. "Oread" by H. D. Doolittle, from *Collected
Poems, 1912–1944*, copyright © 1982 by The Estate of Hilda
Doolittle. Reprinted by permission of New Directions
Publishing Corp. (p. 182)

Dostoesvky, Fyodor. From *Crime and Punishment* by Fyodor
Dostoesvky, translated from the Russian by Constance Garnett.
(p. 266)

Epstein, Daniel Mark. From *The Book of Fortune* by Daniel Mark
Epstein. Copyright © 1982 by Daniel Mark Epstein. Published
by The Overlook Press, Woodstock NY 12498. Used by
permission. (p. 191)

Erdrich, Louise. From "The Red Convertible" by Louise Erdrich
in *Love Medicine, New & Rev. ed.*, by Louise Erdrich, © 1984, 1993
by Louise Erdrich. Reprinted by permission of Henry Holt and
Company, LLC. (p. 112)

Fitzgerald, F. Scott. Reprinted with permission of Scribner, a
Division of Simon & Schuster and Harold Ober Associates,
Incorporated from *The Great Gatsby* (Authorized Text) by F. Scott
Fitzgerald. Copyright 1925 by Charles Scribner's Sons. Copyright
renewed 1953 by Francis Scott Fitzgerald Lanahan. Copyright
© 1991, 1992 by Eleanor Lanahan, Matthew J. Bruccoli and
Samuel J. Lanahan as Trustees under Agreement Dated July 3,
1975, Created by Frances Scott Fitzgerald Smith. (p. 151)

Fornes, Maria Irene. From "The Conduct of Life" from *Maria
Irene Fornes: Plays* by Maria Irene Fornes. © copyright 1986 by
PAJ Publications. Reprinted by permission of PAJ Publications.
(p. 217)

Fowler, H. Ramsey and Jane E. Aaron. Excerpt p. 708 from *The
Little, Brown Handbook, 6th ed.* by H. Ramsey Fowler and Jane E.
Aaron. Copyright © 1995 by HarperCollins College Publishers.
Reprinted by permission of Addison-Wesley Education
Publishers, Inc. (p. 268)

Frost, Robert. From "The Road Not Taken" from *The Poetry of
Robert Frost,* edited by Edward Connery Lathem. Copyright
© 1969 by Henry Holt and Co. Reprinted by permission of
Henry Holt & Co., LLC. (p. 173)

Gardner, Herb. Excerpted from the work *Conversations With My
Father* by Herb Gardner from *Herb Gardner: The Collected Plays*
(Applause Books). Reprinted by permission of Applause Books,
151 West 46th Street, New York, NY 10036. (212) 575–9265. (p.
223)

Gehrig, Lou. From "Farewell to Baseball," a speech by Lou
Gehrig. TM/© 2001 Estate of Eleanor Gehrig under license
authorized by CMG Worldwide Inc., Indianapolis, Indiana,
46256 USA www.lougehrig.com. (p. 67)

Gibson, William. Reprinted with the permission of Scribner, a
Division of Simon & Schuster and Flora Roberts, Inc. from
The Miracle Worker by William Gibson. Copyright © 1956,
1957 William Gibson. Copyright © 1959, 1960 Tamarack
Productions, Ltd. and George S. Klein & Leo Garel as trustees
under three separate deeds of trust. (p. 224)

Golden, Marita. From *Long Distance Life* by Marita Golden,
copyright © 1989 by Marita Golden. Used by permission of
Doubleday, a division of Random House, Inc. (p. 110)

Golding, William Gerald. From *Lord of the Flies* by William
Gerald Golding, copyright 1954 by William Gerald Golding,
renewed 1982. Used by permission of Putnam Berkley, a
division of Penguin Putnam Inc. and Faber and Faber Ltd.
(p. 150)

Goldsborough, Reid. From "We've All Got E-Mail" by Reid
Goldsborough in *The Editorial Eye*, December 1999. Reprinted
by permission of the author. (p. 48)

Gordimer, Nadine. From "A Correspondence Course," from *Something Out There* by Nadine Gordimer, copyright © 1979, 1981, 1982, 1983, 1984 by Nadine Gordimer. Used by permission of Viking Penguin, a division of Penguin Putnam Inc. and Penguin Books Canada Limited. (p. 157)

Griffith, Thomas. From "What's So Special About News Magazines?" by Thomas Griffith from *Newsweek*, June 26, 1989. Reprinted by permission. (p. 39)

Hansberry, Lorraine. From *A Raisin in the Sun* by Lorraine Hansberry, copyright © 1958 by Robert Nemiroff, as an unpublished work. Copyright © 1959, 1966, 1984 by Robert Nemiroff. Used by permission of Random House, Inc. (p. 238)

Harris, Robert R. From "Too Embarrassed Not to Kill" by Robert R. Harris as appeared in *The New York Times Book Review*, March 11, 1990. Copyright © 1990 by The New York Times Co. Reprinted by permission. (p. 20)

Hellman, Lillian. From *The Children's Hour*, by Lillian Hellman, copyright 1934 by Lillian Hellman Kober and renewed 1962 by Lillian Hellman. Used by permission of Random House, Inc. and Lantz Harris Literary Agency. (p. 214)

Hemingway, Ernest. From "A Day's Wait." Excerpted with permission of Scribner, a Division of Simon & Schuster, from *The Short Stories of Ernest Hemingway*. Copyright 1933 by Charles Scribner's Sons. Copyright renewed © 1961 by Mary Hemingway. © Hemingway Foreign Rights Trust. (p. 165) Excerpt from *The Old Man and the Sea*. Reprinted with permission of Scribner, a Division of Simon & Schuster, from *The Old Man and the Sea* by Ernest Hemingway. Copyright 1952 by Ernest Hemingway. Copyright renewed © 1980 by Mary Hemingway. © Hemingway Foreign Rights Trust. (p. 118)

Henley, Beth. From *Crimes of the Heart* by Beth Henley, 1982. All inquiries should be made to Peter Hagan, The Gersh Agency, 130 W. 42nd Street, New York, NY 10036. Reprinted by permission.

Higgins, D. George. "Changing Autumn Weather" by D. George Higgins. Reprinted by permission of the author. (p. 172)

Hughes, Langston. Excerpt from "Thank You, M'am" from *Short Stories* by Langston Hughes. Copyright © 1996 by Ramona Bass and Arnold Rampersad. Introduction copyright © 1996 by Arnold Rampersad. Compilation and editorial contribution copyright © 1996 by Akiba Sullivan Harper. Reprinted by permission of Hill and Wang, a division of Farrar, Straus and Giroux, LLC. (p. 109) "Harlem" from *Collected Poems* by Langston Hughes. Copyright © 1994 by the Estate of Langston Hughes. Reprinted by permission of Alfred A. Knopf, a Division of Random House, Inc. (p. 176)

Ibsen, Henrik. From *A Doll's House* by Henrik Ibsen, translated by James McFarlane. © James McFarlane 1961 from *Henrik Ibsen: Four Major Plays* (Oxford World's Classics, 1998). Reprinted by permission of Oxford University Press. (p. 213)

Institute of Financial Education. From *In Plain Words: A Guide to Financial Services Writing*, © 1984 by The Institute of Financial Education, a division of BAI. Reprinted by permission. (p. 49)

Jacobson, Michael F. From "The Body Politic" by Michael F. Jacobson in *Boston Magazine*, March 2000, pg. 182–183. Reprinted by permission. (p. 256)

Jarrell, Randall. "The Woman at the Washington Zoo" from *The Woman at the Washington Zoo* by Randall Jarrell. Permission granted by Mary Jarrell, Executrix. (p. 186)

Jeffers, Robinson. "Carmel Point" by Robinson Jeffers. Reprinted from *The Collected Poetry of Robinson Jeffers*, edited by Tim Hunt, with the permission of the publishers, Stanford University Press. © 1987 by Jeffers Literary Properties. Copyright transferred 1995 to the Board of Trustees of the Leland Stanford Junior University. (p. 201)

Jellema, Rod. "Migrants" from *The Eighth Day: New and Selected Poems* by Rod Jellema. © Rod Jellema. Published by Dryad Press, 1985. Reprinted by permission of the author. (p. 202)

Jones, Max and John Chilton. Excerpt from *Louis, The Louis Armstrong Story 1900–1971* by Max Jones and John Chilton. Reprinted by permission. (p. 73)

Joyce, James. From "The Dead," from *Dubliners* by James Joyce, copyright 1916 by. B.W. Heubsch. Definitive text Copyright © 1967 by the Estate of James Joyce. Used by permission of Viking Penguin, a division of Penguin Putnam Inc. (p. 246)

Knowles, John. From *A Separate Peace* by John Knowles. Copyright © 1959 by John Knowles. Reprinted by permission of Curtis Brown, Ltd. (p. 158)

Kroeber, Theodora. From *Ishi in Two Worlds: A Biography of the Last Wild Indian in North America* by Theodora Kroeber. Copyright © 1961 Theodora Kroeber. © renewal 1989 John H. Quinn. Reprinted by permission of Jed Riffe and Associates, Ltd. Co-Copyright Holder and Exclusive Agent. (p. 64)

Kurti, Casey. From *Catholic School Girls* by Casey Kurti, Copyright © 1978 by Casey Kurti. CAUTION: Professionals and amateurs are hereby warned that *Catholic School Girls* being fully protected under the copyright laws of the United States of America, the British Commonwealth countries, including Canada, and the other countries of the Copyright Union, is subject to a royalty. All rights, including professional, amateur, motion picture, recitation, public reading, radio, television and cable broadcasting, and the rights of translation into foreign languages, are strictly reserved. Any inquiry regarding the availability of performance rights, or the purchase of individual copies of the authorized acting edition, must be directed to Samuel French Inc., 45 West 25 Street, NY, NY 10010 with other locations in Hollywood and Toronto, Canada. (p. 219)

Landa, Victor. From "My 20-Hour Workweek Never Arrived" by Victor Landa. Reprinted by permission of the author. (p. 60)

Lee, Li-Young. "Eating Together" and "The Gift" copyright © 1986 by Li-Young Lee. Reprinted from *Rose, poems by Li-Young Lee*, with the permission of BOA Editions, Ltd. (pp. 183 and 190)

Lessing, Doris. "A Mild Attack of Locust" from *The Habit of Loving* by Doris Lessing. Copyright © 1957 Doris Lessing. Reprinted by permission of HarperCollins Publishers, Inc., and reprinted by kind permission of Jonathan Clowes Ltd., London, on behalf of Doris Lessing. (p. 120)

Lewis, William and Nancy Schuman. From "Temping: Who, What, and Why" from *The Temp Worker's Handbook, How to Make Temporary Employment Work for You*, by William Lewis and Nancy Schuman. Reprinted by permission. (p. 91)

Lorca, Federico García. *Bandas de Sangre* by Federico García Lorca © Herederos de Federico García Lorca. Translation by Ted Hughes © Ted Hughes and Herederos de Federico García Lorca. Enquiries should be addressed to William Peter Kosmas, Esq., at lorca@artslaw.co.uk or at 8 Franklin Square, London W14 9UU, England. (p. 235)

ule. Reprinted, by permission of The Feminist Press
University of New York, from Paule Marshall, *Brown
wnstones*. Copyright © 1959, 1981 by Paule Marshall.
01)

Martin, James. From "O Pioneers" by James Martin from
America, © 1995 America Press, Inc. All rights reserved. Used
with permission. (p. 94)

Masters, Edgar Lee. "Abel Melveny" from *Spoon River Anthology*
by Edgar Lee Masters. Originally published by Macmillan Co.
Permission by Hilary Masters. (p. 179)

McCaig, Donald. "The Best Four Days in Highland County"
by Donald McCaig, *An American Homeplace*. Reprinted by
permission of the author. (p. 40)

McCullers, Carson. Excerpt from *The Member of the Wedding*.
Copyright © 1946 by Carson McCullers, © renewed 1974 by
Floria V. Lasky. Reprinted by permission of Houghton Mifflin
Co. All rights reserved. (p. 125)

Meisler, Andy. From "The Man Who Keeps 'E.Rs' Heart
Beating," by Andy Meisler from *The New York Times*, February
26, 1995. Copyright © 1995 by the New York Times Co.
Reprinted by permission. (p. 74)

Miles, Josephine. "Moving In" from *Collected Poems, 1930–83*.
Copyright 1983 by Josephine Miles. Used with permission of
the University of Illinois Press. (p. 24)

Millay, Edna St. Vincent. "Recuerdo" by Edna St. Vincent
Millay. From *Collected Poems*, HarperCollins. Copyright 1922,
1950 by Edna St. Vincent Millay. All rights reserved. Reprinted
by permission of Elizabeth Barnett, literary executor. (p. 174)

Miller, Arthur. From *Death of a Salesman* by Arthur Miller,
copyright 1949, renewed © 1977 by Arthur Miller. Used by
permission of Viking Penguin, a division of Penguin Putnam
Inc. (p. 254)

Molière. From *The Misanthrope* by Molière, translated by
Bernard D. N. Grebanier, Copyright © 1959 by Barron's
Educational Series, Inc. Reprinted by arrangement with Barron's
Educational Series, Inc. (p. 234)

Mora, Pat. "Fences" by Pat Mora is reprinted with permission
from the publisher of *Communion* (Houston: Arte Público
Press—University of Houston, 1991). (p. 198)

Moran, Michael. From "Saving downtown's gems" by Michael
Moran in *The Chicago Tribune*, 2/29/00. Reprinted by permission
of the author. (p. 63)

Morgan, Elizabeth. From "Economics" by Elizabeth Morgan
from *Downhome* edited by Susie Mee, Harcourt Brace & Co.,
1995. Reprinted by permission of the author. (p. 252)

Morrison, Toni. From *Sula* by Toni Morrison. Reprinted by
permission of International Creative Management, Inc.
Copyright © 1973 by Toni Morrison. (p. 164)

Mosley, Walter. From *Black Betty* by Walter Mosley. Copyright
© 1994 by Walter Mosley. Used by permission of W.W. Norton
& Company, Inc., Walter Mosley and the Watkins/Loomis
Agency. (p. 116)

Mueller, Lisel. "English as a Second Language" reprinted by
permission of Louisiana State University Press from *Second
Language: Poems*, by Lisel Mueller. Copyright © 1986 by Lisel
Mueller. (p. 189)

Myers, Bernard S. From *Fifty Great Artists* by Bernard S. Myers.
Reprinted by permisson. (p. 77)

Newsweek. From "Living Well" in *Newsweek*, 3/1/99, © 1999
Newsweek, Inc. All rights reserved. Reprinted by permission.
(p. 72)

Norman, Marsha. Excerpt from *'night, Mother* by Marsha
Norman. Copyright © 1983 by Marsha Norman. Reprinted by
permission of Hill and Wang, a division of Farrar, Straus and
Giroux, LLC. (p. 222)

Norris, Kathleen. Excerpt from *Dakota*. Copyright © 1993 by
Kathleen Norris. Reprinted by permission of Houghton Mifflin
Co. All rights reserved. (p. 66)

O'Connor, Flannery. Excerpt from "A Good Man Is Hard to
Find" in *A Good Man Is Hard to Find and Other Stories*, copyright
1953 by Flannery O'Connor and renewed 1981 by Regina
O'Connor, reprinted by permission of Harcourt, Inc. (p. 108)

Ortiz, Simon J. "Earth and Rain, the Planets & Sun" by Simon J.
Ortiz. Permission granted by author. Published in *Woven Stone*,
University of Arizona Press, 1992. (p. 192)

Piercy, Marge. "To Be of Use" from *Circles on the Water* by
Marge Piercy. Copyright © 1982 by Marge Piercy. Reprinted by
permission of Alfred A. Knopf, a Division of Random House,
Inc. (p. 178)

Plath, Sylvia. "Mirror" from *The Collected Poems of Sylvia Plath*
edited by Ted Hughes. Copyright © 1960, 1965, 1971, 1981 by
the Estate of Sylvia Plath. Editorial material copyright © 1981
by Ted Hughes. Reprinted by permission of HarperCollins
Publishers, Inc. and Faber and Faber Ltd. (p. 177)

Porter, Katherine Anne. Excerpt from "The Jilting of Granny
Weatherall" in *Flowering Judas and Other Stories*, copyright 1930
and renewed 1958 by Katherine Anne Porter, reprinted by
permisson of Harcourt Inc. (p. 127)

Pound, Ezra. "The River Merchant's Wife: A Letter" by Ezra
Pound, from *Personae*, copyright © 1926 by Ezra Pound.
Reprinted by permission of New Directions Publishing Corp.
and Faber and Faber Ltd. (p. 204)

Roethke, Theodore. "My Papa's Waltz," from *Collected Poems
of Theodore Roethke* by Theodore Roethke, copyright. Used by
permission of Doubleday, a division of Random House, Inc.
(p. 171)

Rushin, Steve. Reprinted courtesy of Sports Illustrated: "In Pool,
the Shark Still Leaves a Wide Wake" by Steve Rushin, (*Sports
Illustrated*, June 6, 1988), Copyright © 1988, Time, Inc. All rights
reserved. (p. 90)

Russell, Charlie. From *Five on the Black Hand Side* by Charlie
Russell. Reprinted by permission of Samuel French, Inc. (p. 239)

Sagan, Carl. Reprinted with the permission of Simon & Schuster
from *Contact* by Carl Sagan. Copyright © 1985, 1986, 1987 by
Carl Sagan. (p. 104)

Seabrook, John. From "Selling the Weather" by John Seabrook.
Originally published in *The New Yorker*. Reprinted by permission
of the author. (p. 85)

Seiler, Andy. From "'Love and Basketball' misses the net" by
Andy Seiler in *USA Today*, April 21, 2000. Copyright 2000, USA
TODAY. Reprinted with permission. (p. 87)

Shapiro, Karl. "Calling the Child" from *Collected Poems 1940–1978* © Karl Shapiro by permission of Wieser & Wieser Inc. (p. 199)

Shaw, George Bernard. From *The Devil's Disciple* by George Bernard Shaw. Reprinted by permission of The Society of Authors, on behalf of the Bernard Shaw Estate. (p. 230)

Shepard, Sam. From "True West," copyright © 1981 by Sam Shepard, from *Seven Plays* by Sam Shepard. Used by permission of Bantam Books, a division of Random House, Inc. (p. 216)

Silko, Leslie Marmon. "Lullaby" Copyright © 1981 Leslie Marmon Silko, reprinted with permission of The Wylie Agency, Inc. (p. 143)

Simon, Neil. Excerpt from THE ODD COUPLE © 1966 by Neil Simon. Professionals and amateurs are hereby warned that THE ODD COUPLE is fully protected under the Berne Convention and the Universal Copyright Convention and is subject to royalty. All rights, including without limitation professional, amateur, motion picture, television, radio, recitation, lecturing, public reading and foreign translation rights, computer media rights, and the right of reproduction, and electronic storage or retrieval, in whole or in part and in any form are strictly reserved and none of these rights can be exercised or used without written permission from the copyright owner. Inquiries for stock and amateur performances should be addressed to Samuel French, Inc., 45 West 25th Street, New York, NY 10010. All other inquiries should be addressed to Gary N. DaSilva, 111 N. Sepulveda Blvd., Suite 250, Manhattan Beach, CA 90266-6850. (p. 236)

Singer, Isaac Bashevis. Excerpt from "The Spinoza of Market Street" from *The Spinoza of Market Street* by Isaac Bashevis Singer. Copyright © 1961 and copyright renewed © 1989 by Isaac Bashevis Singer. Reprinted by permission of Farrar, Straus and Giroux, LLC. (p. 138)

Sommer, Sally R. From "Superfeet" by Sally R. Sommer from the *Village Voice*. Reprinted by permission of the *Village Voice*, copyright © 1986. (p. 84)

Song, Cathy. "The Wind in the Trees," from *Frameless Windows, Squares of Light: Poems* by Cathy Song. Copyright © 1988 by Cathy Song. Used by permission of W.W. Norton & Company, Inc. (p. 194)

Sontag, Susan. Excerpt from "America, Seen Through Photographs, Darkly" from *On Photography* by Susan Sontag. Copyright © 1977 by Susan Sontag. Reprinted by permission of Farrar, Straus and Giroux, LLC. (p. 81)

Stearns, David Patrick. From "Majestic *Henry V* does justice to the bard" by David Patrick Stearns in *USA Today*, 11/10/89. Copyright 1989, USA TODAY. Reprinted with permission. (p. 86)

Steinbeck, John. From *Cannery Row* by John Steinbeck, copyright 1945 by John Steinbeck. Renewed © 1973 by Elaine Steinbeck, John Steinbeck IV and Thom Steinbeck. Used by permission of Viking Penguin, a division of Penguin Putnam Inc. (p. 18) From *The Grapes of Wrath* by John Steinbeck, copyright 1939, renewed © 1967 by John Steinbeck. Used by permission of Viking Penguin, a division of Penguin Putnam, Inc. (p. 131)

Swenson, May. "How to Be Old" by May Swenson. Used with permission of the Literary Estate of May Swenson. (p. 262)

Tan, Amy. "Two Kinds," from *The Joy Luck Club* by Amy Tan, copyright © 1989 by Amy Tan. Used by permission of G.P. Putnam's Sons, a division of Penguin Putnam Inc. (p. 113)

Taylor, Peter. Excerpts from "Dean of Men" from *The Collected Stories* by Peter Taylor. Copyright © 1968 by Peter Taylor. Reprinted by permission of Farrar, Straus and Giroux, LLC. (p. 160)

Templeton, Brad. From "It's Net Worth It" from "Bill Gates Wealth Index," a website maintained by Brad Templeton. Reprinted by permission of Brad Templeton (www.templetons.com/brad). (p. 50)

Time Magazine. From "A Quarter Century Later, the Myth Endures" in *Time*, 8/25/86. © 1986 Time Inc. Reprinted by permission. (p. 41)

Vásquez, Enedina Cásarez. From "The House of Quilts" by Enedina Cásarez Vásquez. Reprinted by permission of the author. (p. 136)

Wasserstein, Wendy. Excerpt from "The Heidi Chronicles" in *The Heidi Chronicles and Other Plays*, copyright 1990 by Wendy Wasserstein, reprinted by permission of Harcourt Inc. (p. 228)

Weinraub, Bernard. From "In The Eyes of Many, T.V., Not the Movies, is the Higher Calling" (retitled—"Pssst . . . TV Nudging Movies Aside as High Art. Pass it On." by Bernard Weinraub in *The New York Times*, February 14, 1995. Copyright © 1995 by the New York Times Co. Reprinted by permission. (p. 36)

Welch, James. From *Fools Crow* by James Welch, copyright © 1986 by James Welch. Used by permission of Viking Penguin, a division of Penguin Putnam Inc. (p. 121)

Welty, Eudora. Excerpt from "Why I Live at the P.O." from *A Curtain of Green and Other Stories*, copyright 1941 and renewed 1969 by Eudora Welty, reprinted by permisson of Harcourt Inc. (p. 133)

Wetherell, W.D. From "If a Woodchuck Could Chuck Wood" by W.D. Wetherell from *The Virginia Quarterly Review*, 1981. Reprinted by permission. (p. 111)

White, E.B. From "Once More to the Lake" from *One Man's Meat*, text copyright © 1941 by E.B. White. Reprinted by permission of Tilbury House, Publishers, Gardiner, Maine. (p. 70)

Williams, Tennessee. From *The Glass Menagerie* by Tennessee Williams, copyright 1945 by Tennessee Williams and Edwina D. Williams. Copyright renewed 1973 by Tennessee Williams. Used by permission of Random House, Inc. (p. 218)

Williams, William Carlos. "The Poor" by William Carlos Williams, from *Collected Poems: 1909–1939, Volume I*, copyright ©1938 by New Directions Publishing Corp. Reprinted by permission of New Directions Publishing Corp. (p. 197)

Wilson, August. From *Fences* by August Wilson, copyright © 1986 by August Wilson. Used by permission of Dutton Signet, a division of Penguin Putnam Inc. (p. 220)

Wilson, Michael. Reprinted by permission of The Feminist Press at the City University of New York, from *Salt of the Earth*, screenplay by Michael Wilson, commentary by Deborah Rosenfelt. Screenplay Copyright © 1953 by Michael Wilson, Commentary and Compilation Copyright © 1978 by Deborah Rosenfelt. (p. 226)

Wylie, Elinor. "Velvet Shoes" from *Collected Poems* by Elinor Wylie. Copyright 1921 by Alfred A. Knopf, Inc. and renewed 1949 by William Rose Benet. Reprinted by permission of Alfred A. Knopf, a Division of Random House, Inc. (p. 170)

Language Arts, Reading

Name: _____ Class: _____ Date: _____

○ Pretest   ○ Posttest   ○ Simulated Test

1 ①②③④⑤	9 ①②③④⑤	17 ①②③④⑤	25 ①②③④⑤	33 ①②③④⑤
2 ①②③④⑤	10 ①②③④⑤	18 ①②③④⑤	26 ①②③④⑤	34 ①②③④⑤
3 ①②③④⑤	11 ①②③④⑤	19 ①②③④⑤	27 ①②③④⑤	35 ①②③④⑤
4 ①②③④⑤	12 ①②③④⑤	20 ①②③④⑤	28 ①②③④⑤	36 ①②③④⑤
5 ①②③④⑤	13 ①②③④⑤	21 ①②③④⑤	29 ①②③④⑤	37 ①②③④⑤
6 ①②③④⑤	14 ①②③④⑤	22 ①②③④⑤	30 ①②③④⑤	38 ①②③④⑤
7 ①②③④⑤	15 ①②③④⑤	23 ①②③④⑤	31 ①②③④⑤	39 ①②③④⑤
8 ①②③④⑤	16 ①②③④⑤	24 ①②③④⑤	32 ①②③④⑤	40 ①②③④⑤

WASHINGTON IRVING EDUCATIONAL CENTER
ADULT AND CONTINUING EDUCATION
422 MUMFORD STREET
SCHENECTADY, NEW YORK 12307